NATHAN BANGS, D.D.

LIFE AND TIMES

OF

NATHAN BANGS, D.D.

BY ABEL STEVENS, LL.D.,

AUTHOR OF "THE HISTORY OF THE RELIGIOUS MOVEMENT OF THE EIGHTEENTH CENTURY, CALLED METHODISM."

New York:

PUBLISHED BY CARLTON & PORTER,

200 MULBERRY-STREET.

1863.

PREFACE.

Dr. Bangs was repeatedly advised in his latter years, by his official and other associates, that a record of his life would be important for his Church, if not for himself; and that he should not fail to leave, at his death, such notes of the momentous ecclesiastical measures in which he had shared as might aid in their historical illustration. When it was made known to me, soon after his decease, that he had committed to me his papers for a task so important and delicate, I felt no little reluctance to undertake it; for though an author is held responsible for the interest of his book, yet in biography its interest must depend more on its subject than on its writer; and I supposed that the life of my venerated friend had been so absorbed in purely ecclesiastical labors, that however interesting its official events might be in the history of his denomination, it could afford but comparatively few incidents of biographic and popular entertainment. I was agreeably surprised, however, in examining his abundant manuscripts, to find that they abound in personal and characteristic facts; that the early years of his public life were spent amid frontier scenes of extraordinary interest; that his vigorous manhood, for nearly half a century, was identified with the most popular, as well as most momentous measures and events of his Church; and that his declining years, singularly prolonged and serene, presented the picture of an evening of life, enviable alike to the philosopher and the Christian. I have seldom, indeed, met with a biographical study more entertaining or profitable to me personally; presenting a more effective, a more symmetrical, or a more complete life. If the narrative I have drawn from these materials fails to make a similar impression on its readers, I must acknowledge that the failure is chargeable on the author rather than the subject. I feel assured, nevertheless, that no defects of literary execution can essentially impair the rich lessons of spiritual life and consolation which are cited from the original manuscripts.

By the license of the title of the book, as the "Life *and Times*" of my subject, I have introduced into the narrative many of his cotemporaries, who were more or less associated with him in public life; but the volume will still be found very deficient in this respect. Repeated requests, through the public press, for letters and other materials from his old associates or their families, have been but slightly successful. Should there be hereafter an opportunity to repair this defect, I shall be happy to avail myself of it. I would also invite corrections of any errors of facts, especially of dates. No small amount of my facts is historical, and it is important for the history of Methodism that it should be accurate. An erratum has escaped my attention on page 70, where Embury is mentioned as leaving Ireland in 1765. The date should be 1760. The former is the date given by Dr. Bangs and most of our other historians. I have long been convinced that it is wrong. It has been corrected in this volume, but not till after many sheets were printed.

ABEL STEVENS.

MAMARONECK PARSONAGE,
Nov. 2, 1863.

CONTENTS.

CHAPTER X.

FRONTIER MINISTERIAL LIFE.

CHAPTER XI.

FRONTIER MINISTERIAL LIFE.

CHAPTER XII.

MINISTERIAL LIFE IN THE STATES.

CHAPTER XIII.

MINISTERIAL LIFE IN THE STATES.

CHAPTER XIV.

MINISTERIAL LIFE IN THE STATES.

CHAPTER XV.

MINISTERIAL LIFE IN THE STATES.

CHAPTER XVI.

SERVICES IN THE BOOK CONCERN.

CHAPTER XVII.

SERVICES IN THE BOOK CONCERN.

CHAPTER XVIII.

SERVICES IN THE GENERAL CONFERENCE OF 1828.

CHAPTER XIX.

SERVICES FROM 1828 TO 1832.

CHAPTER XX.

SERVICES FROM 1832 TO 1836.

CHAPTER XXI.

MISSIONARY SECRETARY.

CHAPTER XXII.

SERVICES FROM 1836 TO 1844.

CHAPTER XXIII.

MATURE CHRISTIAN LIFE.

CHAPTER XXIV.

MATURE CHRISTIAN LIFE.

CHAPTER XXV.

MATURE CHRISTIAN LIFE.

CHAPTER XXVI.

MATURE CHRISTIAN LIFE.

CHAPTER XXVII.

MATURE CHRISTIAN LIFE.

CHAPTER XXVIII.

LAST DAYS AND DEATH.

LIFE AND TIMES

OF

NATHAN BANGS, D.D.

CHAPTER I.

IMPORTANCE OF HIS SERVICES TO THE CHURCH.

DR. NATHAN BANGS was not only a public but a representative man, in the Methodist Episcopal Church, for more than half a century. During nearly sixty years he appeared almost constantly in its pulpits. He was the founder of its periodical literature, and of its "Conference course" of ministerial study, and one of the founders of its present system of educational institutions. He was the first missionary secretary appointed by its General Conference, the first clerical editor of its General Conference newspaper press, the first editor of its Quarterly Review, and, for many years, the chief editor of its Monthly Magazine and its book publications. He may be pronounced the principal founder of the American literature of Methodism; a literature now remarkable for its extent, and of no inconsiderable intrinsic value. Besides his innumerable miscellaneous writings for its periodicals, he wrote more volumes in defense or illustration of his denomination than any other man. He became its recognized historian. He was one of the founders of its Missionary Society, he wrote the Constitution and first Circular Appeal of that great cause, and through sixteen years, prior to the organization of its secretaryship as a salaried function, he labored indefatigably and gratuitously for the society, as its vice-president, secretary, or treasurer. During more than twenty years he wrote all its Annual Reports. After his appointment as its resident secretary he devoted to it his entire energies, conducting its correspondence, seeking missionaries for it, planning its mission fields, pleading for it in the Churches, and representing it in the Conferences. It will be monumental of his memory in all lands to which its beneficent agency may extend, and if no other public service could be attributed to him, this alone would render him a principal historic character of American Methodism, if not, indeed, of American Protestantism. He was, withal, a man of profound piety, of universal charity, and much and admirable individuality.

GROWTH OF METHODISM DURING HIS PUBLIC LIFE.

When he began his public career, Methodism reported, in all the New World, about eighty-six thousand communicants and three hundred and fifty preachers; at the time of his death they amounted to more than two and a half millions of communicants and thirteen thousand traveling preachers.* Few men, if any, have longer or more successfully labored to promote those great interests of the denomination which have given it consolidation and permanence. If greater men have, especially in his latter years of comparative retirement, more actively represented it, no one, in our day, has embodied in himself more of its history, no one has linked so much of its past with its present. It has been justly said that he ranks next to Asbury in historical importance in his Church. Twice did his brethren offer him the Episcopal chair, which Asbury had so ably occupied, and he would

* Compare "Minutes of Methodist Episcopal Church, 1801," with Schem's "Ecclesiastical Year-Book, 1860." The estimate, in the text, includes the West India Islands and the British North American Provinces.

probably have been elevated to it had not his characteristic self-distrust, and the conviction that he could be more useful in his literary labors, interfered. The services of such a man merit public commemoration. His history is a public property, and can hardly fail to be alike interesting and instructive.

HIS PURITAN ANCESTRY.

He was born in the town of Stratford, Conn., May 2, 1778, and sprang from a good Puritan stock. Edward Bangs, supposed to be the first American ancestor of all who bear the name of Bangs in this country, came from England in the Anne, one of the first three vessels which arrived at Plymouth, Massachusetts. The other two were the Mayflower and the Fortune. The passengers in these three vessels are commonly called the Pilgrims, as they united in forming the Colonial Government, and shared in the division of the colonial lands. The Mayflower arrived in December, 1620; the Fortune in November, 1621; the Anne in July, 1623.

In the year 1623 a division of their lands was made by the Plymouth colonists. Among these is the name of Bangs, (no Christian name being given,) to whom four acres are assigned. The portion of "Bangs" was one of the allotments which are described as lying on the "other side of town, toward the Eel River." In 1627, at a public court, it was agreed to divide the "stock" of the settlement, by lot, among the companies of the three ships, the Mayflower, the Fortune, and the Anne. The settlers were divided into twelve companies, and lots were drawn. Edward Bangs was in the twelfth, with twelve other persons. In 1627 a second division of lands was made, of twenty acres to each family, in addition to the former apportionment; Edward Bangs's name is in the list of the six "layers-out." Such are a few traces of the American progenitor of the family, to be found in "The Old Colony Records." Slight as they appear, to American minds they have a higher significance than any aristocratic heraldry of the Old World.

In 1644 Edward Bangs moved with his family to a new settlement on Cape Cod, at or near the spot where the Pilgrims first set foot on land previous to their final landing at Plymouth. This settlement was afterward named Eastham. The place where the new settlers located themselves is supposed to be that part of Harwich which is now called Brewster, as the descendants of Edward Bangs for several generations were interred in the burial-ground of Brewster, where some of their tombstones still remain, bearing legible inscriptions. Edward Bangs was probably buried there, but no vestige of his grave remains. He died in 1678, aged eighty-six years. His descendants are scattered over the United States. "I believe," writes one of them, "that the Bangses have generally been active and useful men. I know many who have filled important civil, military, and ecclesiastical offices."* The name is still familiar on Cape Cod, in Boston, and other parts of Massachusetts, in New Hampshire, Vermont, and New York. Mementoes of its Pilgrim honor are preserved with reverent care.†

HIS PARENTS.

Lemuel Bangs, the father of Nathan, left a genealogical record, in which he says: "My father's name was Joseph, of the town of Harwich, in the county of Barnstable, on Cape Cod, Massachusetts. He died in Phillips's Patent, in the State of New York, in 1757." Lemuel Bangs, himself, was an honest, intelligent, stalwart blacksmith, and a staunch Churchman withal, notwithstanding the Puritanic traditions of his family. He relieved the toils

* "Genealogical Account of the Family," prepared by T. Dwight Bangs, Esq., of Lima, N. Y. See "Life of Rev. John Bangs," Appendix.

† In Worcester, Mass., the family of Edward D. Bangs, late Secretary of State, preserves the family "coat of arms," of very curious workmanship, and other relics.

of his laborious craft by a habitual devotion to books, and acquired sufficient mathematical knowledge to become a successful surveyor, an art which he taught his son Nathan.

Another son, Rev. Heman Bangs, writes: "My father, Lemuel Bangs, was from Cape Cod, Massachusetts. He was a commissary in the old French war, an adjutant in the war of the Revolution, and fought for the independence of his country. I have sat at his feet, when a little boy, for hours, hearing his war stories; his graphic account of Tories and Cow-boys interested me exceedingly. I conceived a perfect abhorrence for both, and such a love for the Whigs of those days, and the freedom of my country, as has never cooled in my heart to this day. The education of my father was above the mediocrity of his times. He was a great reader during his whole life, and his memory was so tenacious that he retained what he read. One instance I give you. He sat once, in his old age, hearing his son Nathan preach. In his ardor or haste Nathan made an incorrect quotation from an English author. My father noticed it at once, and spoke right out to him before the congregation, making the necessary correction.

"He had taught school and surveyed lands, but his business properly was that of a blacksmith. He married for his first wife a Miss Hall, by whom he had five children, all of whom are dead. His second wife was Rebecca Keeler, of Ridgefield, Conn. They had nine children, seven of whom experienced religion young and joined the Methodist Episcopal Church; four sons becoming preachers. They have all gone home to heaven but one sister and myself. My father was strongly attached to the Protestant Episcopal Church, and all his children were baptized in that Church. When the Methodists first came into his neighborhood he was bitterly opposed to them; and although most of his children joined them, he would not consent to hear them preach.

because they were uneducated. But the old man's prejudices were overthrown when his son Nathan came down from Canada a Methodist preacher. He consented to allow him to preach in his house, because he thought Nathan had some sense and learning. From this time he went frequently to hear them. He was a man of strict integrity and truth; and in the new country to which he moved with his family in 1793, I have known him frequently to call the scattered neighbors together and read prayers and a sermon for them, and when the preacher was absent or sick he would read the liturgy in the church. He found redemption in the blood of Christ when he was about seventy years of age, lived many years afterward, and died in the faith.* He was a candid and shrewd judge of preaching. I remember well what a cross it was, when I first began to preach before him. My mother was a noble woman; with little of this world's goods, she kept her children comfortable in a new and poor country, and lived to see eight of them grow up to man's estate; all, but one, members of the Church, and half of them ministers of the Gospel. In 1809 the family moved into Upper Canada, where she died in the faith, as I have been informed."

HIS CHILDHOOD.

When Nathan was about four years old, the family moved from Stratford to the parish of Poquanock, in the town of Fairfield, near Bridgeport, Connecticut. In an autobiographical sketch he records that his earliest recollection was his passage to this new home. His second remembrance was characteristic of the New England life of that day; it was of his first walk from home to the district school, with a Bible in his hand. He could read it; and it was to be the text-book, not only of his school days, but of his whole life. He had an avidity for knowl-

* He never joined the Methodist Church. The reasons he gave were his age, and the similarity of the doctrines of the two Churches.

edge; but the severity of the village schoolmaster excited in him an aversion to the school. "The boys were flogged most unmercifully for every little fault." He acknowledges, however, that he himself was naturally irritable, and that it was owing to the determination of his mother, "a most sensible, resolute woman," that he endured the discipline of the unrelenting pedagogue; she sometimes drove him to the school, whip in hand. He records with affectionate gratitude and admiration her motherly tenderness in all other respects, her skill in the management of her household, the enjoyments she provided for her numerous circle of children, the competence which her economy secured to their humble home; but also the matronly authority and firmness with which she governed it.

THE VILLAGE "PARSON."

The family papers before me afford but few glimpses of the domestic life at Fairfield: but these all show that it was virtuous and happy; of the genuine type of the New England life of that, and, it may be added, of our day. The father, after the labors of the anvil, spends the long winter evenings in his favorite recreation of reading; he instructs Nathan, apparently his most hopeful child, in matters of learning, especially in the mathematics of surveying; he teaches him the lessons of the Bible, and trains him in the habit of reading it through once a year. He holds the family group spellbound, late into the night, by the story of his adventures in the old French war and the Revolution; and fails not to inspire them with enthusiastic love of Washington and their country, and with detestation of all tories and traitors. The "parson" of the village occasionally appears in the circle. Nathan recites the Church Catechism to him on Sunday afternoons. "I owe," he writes, "much of that religious bias by which my mind was afterward swayed, to this fact." The parson, however, did not come up to his ideal of an apostle. He was very kindly disposed toward the young people of his parish; he approved of their dancing parties, and favored the village fiddler. The latter was sometimes permitted to perform in the parsonage while the youth of the parish "tripped it on the light fantastic toe;" and the few village churchmen often "drank to excess," and were given to card playing. At "pastoral visitations" to the Bangs family, the fiddler and the young men and maidens of the parish would close the evening in the highest spirits under the smiles of the indulgent parson; while the latter, and the equally indulgent blacksmith, would conduct elaborate arguments among the older guests in defense of the happiness and hilarity of the young people. "The young people," concluded the parson, "must have some amusement, and they may as well have this as any other." "Thus was I taught in my youth," wrote Nathan in later years.

THE BAPTIST PASTOR.

The Baptist preacher of the village, a very different character, occasionally sat in the family group at the winter evening hearth. He was "a good, pious man, though of small abilities as a preacher," writes Dr. Bangs. "The impression of his conversation and preaching has never been effaced from my mind. I think I can see him now, very aged, with a long visage, few teeth, strong voice, and quaint wit." His preaching was home-directed and often alarming. He was fond of colloquial theological discussions, and held many a sturdy argument with the blacksmith on the "succession," episcopacy, and baptism; exciting the curiosity and wonder of the school-boy, and usually bringing the debate to such a conclusion as left both preacher and blacksmith claiming the victory.

LEE'S ITINERANT ADVENTURES IN CONNECTICUT.

When Nathan was about eleven years old, rumors became rife of a strange man who had come to the state from the South, and was traveling through its villages on horseback, and in a costume of Quaker-like simplicity; a very "remarkable man," who preached every day and several times a day, and went everywhere, without knowing any person; exceedingly good-humored, witty even; of a most musical voice, making his hearers smile or weep as he pleased, but mostly weep; "holding forth" in the court-houses, the school-houses, sometimes in the more liberal village churches, but oftener under the trees of the highway. He frequently lighted the court-house himself, and then rung the bell to call out the people. The pastors and deacons valiantly resisted him as a heretic, for he was an Arminian. They turned his discourses into interlocutions by their questions and disputations, but he confounded them by his tact if not by his logic. He scattered the village wits or wags by his irresistible repartees; and scores and hundreds of drunkards and other reprobates were reformed, and many a good man, despondent under the old theology, was comforted by the refreshing doctrine of the itinerant evangelist. Many who liked his theology could not approve his preaching, because he acknowledged that he was not an "educated minister." The pastor, and sometimes the village lawyer or doctor, tested him with Latin and Greek phrases; he responded in Dutch, a knowledge of which he had picked up in his childhood. They supposed this to be Hebrew, and retreated, or took sides with him as competent to preach. But above all, he was evidently an earnest and devout man; he prayed mightily and preached overwhelmingly. This evangelist was Jesse Lee, the "Founder of Methodism in New England," the results of whose labors are now seen in almost every city, town, and hamlet in the Eastern States. Lemuel Bangs was not an illiberal man, for he had broken away from the Puritan Church, but he was given to books, and held to the New England traditional reverence for education. He resisted the temptation of his curiosity to hear this wonderful itinerant, because Lee was not educated. Lee came to the town, induced the schoolmaster to send word by the children to their families, that he would preach in the court-house that evening, and he did preach there with good effect; but the blacksmith's family were kept in close quarters at home. They could not fail, however, to hear of the doctrines of the new "sect," which was soon "everywhere spoken against," and the staunch father was to live to see nearly all his children in its communion, and most of his sons in its ministry.

NEW ENGLAND LIFE AND CHARACTER.

Nathan became a robust youth, of athletic habits and active mind. He had succeeded well in the studies of the village school, and his father fondly hoped to be able to afford him a liberal education; but the increasing wants of a large household began to press heavily on the worthy blacksmith's energies. He was compelled, like many of his eastern countrymen, to look westward for a new home. At last, in the thirteenth year of Nathan, the family pulled up its stakes, and "emigrated" to what was then a wilderness region of New York. But the character of the boy and of the whole family had been thoroughly moulded by their Puritan life. It was now next to impossible that they could fail to be intelligent, virtuous, industrious, and successful.

"Diederich Knickerbocker" early drew pictures of New England life, designed as harmless caricatures, which have unfortunately left a false impression of its character on much of the public mind, not only of Europe, but of America beyond the limits of the Eastern States. Soberly and literally may it be said that the mass of the people, in no other community of the globe, have better provisions for education and religious instruction, more social or industrial advancement, more comfortable homes, more of what constitutes the intrinsic improvement and happiness of a people, than the American states formed from the Puritan Pilgrims. The New Englander's peculiar skill in business, in bargains, has been imputed to peculiar avarice rather than to his peculiar intelligence and enterprise; but no people expend so liberally on schools, churches, public roads, and on the comfort of their homes. None prize education more; the statistics of none show better general morals; none carry with them better elements for the formation of new states in the great domains of the West. One third of the population of the nation has sprung from these people; but it owes to them two thirds of its intelligence and enterprise. The severity of their climate and their long winter evenings give a peculiar importance to their home life, and the universal diffusion of intelligence, by an unsurpassed system of common schools, gives to their in-door life the charms of books, of the literary journal, of music, and fireside converse. Happy the children who carry with them into the world the reminiscences of such homes! Young Bangs going, for the first time, to the primary school with the Bible in his hand, presents, we have said, the best type of the New England training of childhood. The primary school and the Bible will reveal their effects in all the remainder of his life.

CHAPTER II.

EARLY EMIGRATION.

THE emigration of a New England family was a much more serious undertaking, in that day, than it is in ours, though the "far West" was then but the interior of New York, or the western regions of Pennsylvania and Virginia. Adventurous spirits—pioneer hunters rather than "settlers"—pushed beyond, and disappeared, with ax and rifle, in the distant wilderness; but most large families were content to pause within the frontiers of civilization. The public conveyances were poor, the roads were bad, and travel slow. The male members of the moving company trudged along on foot, with knapsacks on their backs, while a large wagon conveyed the women and children. The breaking up of the old homestead was often a scene of pathetic interest. There were the adieus of neighbors, the final farewells of the old, the pledges of the young to meet again in the far-off lands; the benedictions of pastors; and the rending of a thousand endeared local ties. But the adventures of the long journey, the romance of the new wilderness life, its very privations and hardships, were captivating to the imaginations of not only the young but of the old. To the latter such a domestic revolution seemed a re-beginning of life, to the former its real beginning.

A HOME IN THE WILDERNESS.

A boy yet, hardly more than a child—thirteen years of age—young Bangs set out with his oldest brother, "the advance guard" of the domestic party, "to prepare the way." "We traveled," he says, "a hundred and fifty miles on foot, with our knapsacks on our backs, and endured no small difficulties on the way, but safely arrived in what is now called Stamford, Delaware County, New York, in the autumn of 1791."

They found themselves in the primeval wilderness; and "went to work, preparing log-cabins for the accommodation of the family during the winter, which was at hand." It was laborious work for boys, and they had hardly got one of their rude structures erected when it was destroyed by fire. "So all our labor," he writes, "was lost; and when we saw that we could do nothing to save it, we sat down and wept." There were a few scattered settlers in the region; "they sympathized with us," he adds, "and turning out, helped us to repair our loss; and soon my father arrived to cheer us with his presence. Still later came my mother, with the rest of the family, and we were all at last safely domiciled in our humble habitation. Being in a new country, hard labor was necessary to make a living. Sometimes my father had to go twenty or thirty miles to obtain bread for us, and we learned thoroughly the hardships and privations incident to a pioneer life." But he describes this life as having also peculiar charms. Every energy was called into play—and that was genuine happiness. Nature around them was clothed with grandeur, even in the midwinter. The scenes of the wilderness; the mountains which stretched away to the east; the romantic streams which have their sources in that country; the deer chased by the hunter over the snows; the wild music of the birds in the spring-time; even the grand storms at night, bending the forest and resounding among the mountains, gave interest to the days and evenings of their solitude.

MOTHER AND CHILD LOST IN THE WOODS.

This solitude was not, however, without its alarms, if not its perils. The few settlers were remote from one another, and the roads, or paths, were slight and often obliterated by the snows of winter. "My mother," he says, "went, with a little daughter, to visit one of our nearest neighbors. On returning, night overtook them, and they were lost in the woods. After wandering a long while, they sat down in despair of finding their way out. We became uneasy and dispatched a messenger for them. We ascertained that they must have lost their way, and all of us turned out in every direction, shouting to our utmost, but could not find them. Early in the morning, however, they made their appearance, and I shall never forget the countenance of my mother at that moment; it was the very expression of grief and anxiety, mixed with grateful joy. She informed us that, failing to find her way home, she sat down in the forest, covered the child as well as she could with her clothes, and by friction kept it and herself from freezing during the long night, for it was cold with the frosts of March, and there was snow on the ground. She had heard our voices, but could not decide which way to go to find her way out, and her replies were too feeble to be heard by us. But though the night had been sad, the morning was joyful in our log-cabin, and we ate our bread with gladness."

STUDIES AND AMUSEMENTS.

The hardy labors of the farm were a good physical education to young Bangs; and his intellectual training was not neglected during the long winter evenings. When about seventeen years old he was judged competent to be a teacher, and was received into the family of a merchant near Schoharie, Ulster County, as domestic tutor. It was in a Dutch neighborhood, and afforded him interesting opportunities of studying new phases of human nature. "The family," he says, "treated me with more respect than I deserved. They observed some of the forms of religion; at least 'grace' was said aloud at every meal, by one of the children, with folded hands. I had sufficient leisure to indulge my ruling passion for acquiring knowledge; but I also indulged my love of frivolous amusements among the neighboring young people, especially dancing, of which I was excessively fond. I suffered, however, much disadvantage in not knowing the Dutch language, for they used it habitually among themselves. After residing with this kind family about four months, I had so far gained the confidence of its head, Esquire Hardenburgh, as to be recommended by him to teach a public school. I took charge of one, on the east branch of the Delaware, near what is now the town of Roxbury: a romantic region, with mountains, rising on either side of the valley, robed in dense forests; the Delaware, a mere streamlet, flowing along the vale from its fountain in one of the mountains, and banked with rich meadows on which already grazed herds and flocks. Altogether it was a most picturesque scene, and filled my imagination with delight. I cannot describe the emotions I felt when I first entered this settlement and gazed upon the grand and beautiful outlines around me. The majority of the settlers were Dutch, but though they spoke their native language among themselves, they could generally converse with me in English, and with few exceptions they treated me not only with respect, but with hearty rustic kindness. I entered upon my duties with delight, and, as far as I could learn, discharged them to the satisfaction of my employers. But had my lot been cast among a different people I might have made considerable literary advancement. I hungered for knowledge, but the general ignorance of the settlers and the want of books deprived me almost entirely of the means of gratifying this taste. An intimacy, however, which I formed with an intelligent young merchant, afforded us some opportunities of profitable and delightful intercourse, in reading and conversation, on subjects which came within our reach.

We met together once a week, and read, and strove hard to understand, Locke's Essay on the Understanding. Having learned the art of surveying, both theoretically and practically, from my father, who was county surveyor while he lived in Fairfield, Connecticut, I taught it to my friend, and we used to amuse ourselves, at least, with mathematical studies."

His knowledge of surveying was a source of some pecuniary advantage to him in the settlement. Much of his leisure time was spent in measuring lands, dividing farms, and in preparing deeds and leases.

"But," he continues, "these advantages were more than counterbalanced by the evils with which I was surrounded. Dancing, card-playing, and gay associations with the young people, and the almost universal custom of drinking ardent spirits (though seldom to excess) drove all serious thoughts from my mind."

THE METHODIST ITINERANTS.

"There was no regular religious worship yet in the settlement; but a Methodist itinerant occasionally reached us and gave us a sermon, and a small Methodist class met in the neigborhood. These people were considered, by those with whom I associated, as fanatics, and were treated with contempt. I would sometimes, however, go to hear their preacher, and I remember one Sabbath morning I was sitting in the little assembly, listening with much sobriety to the sermon, when a witty young man at my side, with whom I had been on a 'frolic' a few evenings before, whispered in my ear a jocose allusion to the gay occasion, whereupon we both burst into an immoderate laugh, an irreverence which I never allowed myself to be guilty of willingly. The preacher stopped, stamped his foot, and said, 'There is no laughing in hell!' I was ashamed of my conduct; but it was only an example of the manners of the time in the treatment of the Methodists."

SATIRIZES THEM—CONSCIENCE AWAKENED.

He had but little scruple, however, in privately joining in the common ridicule of these supposed fanatics. About this time he was attacked by an epidemic disease and suffered seriously; but, when visited by one of his gay comrades, he raised himself in his bed and "made a prayer in mockery of the Methodists!" Yet he records that he was inwardly wretched during this apparent recklessness, "troubled with a secret misgiving that they were right and he wrong." He could not get rid of a certain religious thoughtfulness, the effect, perhaps, partly of his education, partly of his temperament, and which, immediately after this profane scene, overwhelmed him. In a few days he rose from his sick bed, but was so feeble that he returned to his father's house at Stamford for rest and medical treatment. There his mind was smitten with anguish; he refused to eat; he apprehended death as at hand. "My conscience," he writes, "awoke; all the sins of my life seemed vividly brought to my recollection. Such was the weight of my guilt that I felt as if I should sink into perdition. For the first time in my life I began to call upon God; for though I had habitually used the prayers taught me in my childhood, I had never really prayed before. God was graciously pleased to restore me by degrees to health. After my recovery I felt a strong desire to devote myself to his service; but how delusive are the snares of the world! I did not long yield to that desire, although I have no doubt that at the time He gave me a measure of grace and peace, for I felt much sweetness in secret prayer, in reading the Scriptures and other religious books, in meditating devoutly on the works of God so grandly spread out around me; and I could not but praise him for his tender mercy in sparing my life. To seclude myself from company and spend my time in reading and devotion were my principal delight. But the rock upon which I was wrecked was the fact that I did not make known my new condition to any one, nor seek to associate with those who could instruct me, from their own experience, in the ways of godliness. Having failed to confess Christ, I 'grieved the Holy Spirit.' I gradually lapsed into negligence, and began to hanker after my old pleasures. I evaded my conscience even in prayer; as an example, I may state that I was invited to a Christmas-eve ball about this time, and actually, on my knees, asked liberty from God to attend it; saying, with Naaman, 'The Lord pardon thy servant in this thing.' I went, but, alas! what trouble of conscience I felt while leading off the dance!" He attempted to drown his anguish by ardent spirits, and by plunging into the gayest hilarity of the evening, but he could not. "And though I continued," he adds, "for more than four years in this state, I did not lose my convictions, nor did my desire to serve God ever become extinguished."

FRONTIER DANCING.

His scruple against dancing was entirely the suggestion of his awakened conscience. He had been educated to esteem that recreation as quite innocent. It was approved by his father and by the strictest Christians of the settlement, as was also the use of intoxicating liquors. A considerable community of Scotch Seceders had, by this time, settled in the neighborhood; and no more rigid sect was known in the nation; yet the evening ball and the social dram had their fullest practical sanction. Almost every week, in the long leisure of the autumn and winter nights, a dancing assembly for the young people of the settlement was held. Religion itself gave countenance to these occasions. At about 10 o'clock P. M. the father of the house, attended by the aged members of his family, would enter the ball-room with the old family Bible, brought from the fatherland, in his hand. The dancers would pause with reverence, listen to a chapter, join in a long psalm, hear a longer prayer, and then, after a few words of religious counsel, resume the sport with a hearty "Good-night" to the retiring elders; and the hilarity of the company kept pace with the remaining hours till the dawn. The pastor himself would sometimes attend these occasions, and after the prayer would take his leave of the dance-room with the apostolic benediction!

DRAM-DRINKING.

As for dram-drinking, the good repute of a family for hospitality was forfeited if it offered not the bottle to every visitor. Drunkenness, of course, could not but be frequent in such temptations; but, though treated with much lenity, it was discreditable. The most rigid of the Seceders were sometimes overtaken by it; and if they fell into the fault on Saturdays, which was most commonly the case, they were likely to be detected the next day, for their strict consciences would not allow them to shave on Sundays, and their neglected faces would tell the story in the congregation. Their old pastor, a man of mighty authority, would sometimes point them out publicly, and thunder at their self-convicted sins; not so much, however, because they had been drunk, as because they had deferred their self-indulgence till Saturday, and thereby risked the right observance of the Sabbath. He himself had his freaks with the bottle, and was kindly disposed toward such frailties, if they were only not allowed to interfere with his Kirk rights over the people. On town-meeting days and all secular holidays a large liberty was allowed, and many a grave Seceder availed himself of it among his hilarious juniors. The old pastor himself forgot his usual official dignity on one of these occasions. He had indulged himself so freely among his neighbors that a group of youths in the street perceived his condition. They called upon him for a sermon, to be paid for by a glass of brandy, a choicer luxury than whisky, their common dram. Taking his stand in a gateway, and sustaining himself, with outstretched hands, by the gate-posts, he attempted to "hold forth," but ignominiously broke down. As it was, however, a public day, and the disgraceful scene was venial, he was only fined by his Church authorities some twelve dollars, and resumed his usual dignity and severity in the pulpit. It was amid such examples that the conscience of young Bangs was now struggling with him for the life of his soul.

MORAL STRUGGLES.

He had heard of the Methodists while yet in the East; and here, in the wilderness, had he again found them on his track; though they had been but objects of his ridicule, yet he had listened to them, and now could not escape the lessons they had taught him. He was to meet them again, and until that meeting—during all these four years in fine—he was an "awakened" man. "Sometimes," he writes, "such awful apprehensions of God's just displeasure would seize upon my soul as to embitter all the enjoyments of life, and make me wish for annihilation. When I would do good, evil was present with me, and bore me away in its torrent toward the gulf of destruction. No one can tell, but he who has felt the like, the bitter anguish I felt while wandering alone in the forests mourning my hopeless condition; and often, while in the seeming gayeties of life, have I envied the dog his happiness. In short, I went on sinning and repenting, vowing amendment and breaking my vows, until it is a wonder that the long-suffering of God did not consign me over to remediless misery."

There are few men, perhaps none, in Christian lands at least, who do not know more or less of such experiences; for "it is the Spirit that quickeneth," and "the manifestation of the Spirit is given to every man to profit withal." They are epochs in the lives of thoughtful men. They are, indeed, the "awakening" of the soul.

It is then that its illuminated sight pierces through the vail of visible things and sees the spiritual universe—sees the far-off and everlasting realities that give importance to our probationary life, and significance and dignity to death itself: as the astronomer, by telescopic vision, beholds, beyond the range of the visible worlds, the shining of other suns and systems. When in early life they are profound and enduring, as in this case, they cannot fail to impress the whole moral man; the heart becomes more tender, the conscience more scrupulous; there can be no little sins to such a mind; all truth and duty take a diviner hue in the light reflected from the higher worlds; life, suffering, death, receive their clearest, sublimest explanation. It should be no matter of surprise if the mind, suddenly thus awakened, loses somewhat its tranquil self-control, and becomes even morbid; for so purely physical, or rather animal, is our ordinary life, so limited its view to material and passing things, that the sudden apprehension of our relation to the spiritual universe and of our everlasting destination in it, is dazzling and overwhelming as would be the sudden breaking away of the clouds and outshining of the sun at noonday to a man who had always lived in darkness.

Young Bangs seemed now for the first time to understand why he lived, and why he was to die; and the discovery was like the awakening from a dream which had hitherto deluded his whole life. "Though immersed," he writes, "in youthful gayeties, and apparently cheerful, yet inwardly I felt such anguish as made me desire death. I often wished for some secluded spot in the desert, where I might dwell in solitude and bemoan my sad state as a sinful man, beyond the haunts of men. In my occasional meditative walks in the woods I felt the truth which Wordsworth puts into the mouth of the Wanderer:

> "'He who, by willful disesteem of life,
> And proud insensibility to hope,

Affronts the eye of solitude, shall learn
That her wild nature can be terrible;
That neither she nor silence lacks the power
To avenge their own insulted majesty.'"

"To pass over many incidents of this period of my life, I will only remark that after continuing about three years in this state of mind, though well enough off as to the interests of this world, I again returned to my father's house and taught a school in the vicinity."

EMIGRATES FURTHER WESTWARD.

"In the spring of this year my brother-in-law, Seth Smith, and two of his brothers, determined to move still further westward, to Upper Canada. I resolved to accompany them; my parents gave their consent; and on the 9th of May, 1799, having just entered my twenty-first year, we set off. It was no small trial to bid farewell to father and mother, brothers and sisters, for what was then deemed a distant land. My father presented to me his surveying instruments, thinking it probable I might obtain employment with them in the new country. We traveled with an ox team, which carried our goods, clothes, and provisions. Our progress was slow, the roads, after leaving the Mohawk Valley, being bad, as the country was but recently and quite sparsely settled. We enjoyed ourselves, however, very agreeably on the way; the vernal scenery, the passage along the streams and valleys, the night camps in the woods, the open air life with its keen appetite and exhilarating freshness, relieved the tediousness of our slow progress. When we arrived at Buffalo, we found only two or three log-huts, occupied by some half-clad miserable people. We crossed the Niagara River from Buffalo to Fort Erie, at the outlet of Lake Erie; and so we were in a strange land, beyond the limits of our native country. But I believe a good Providence conducted my wayward feet thither for my own good, and, I hope, for the good of others; for here, in the remote wilderness, was I to find the light and peace which I had so long sought, and thence proclaim the same blessings through most of Upper Canada, and in many parts of my own nation."

NIAGARA FALLS IN 1799.

"The day after our arrival in Canada we reached the Falls of Niagara. Here we made a halt, and went down to the river's bank to view the stupendous scene. The water comes rushing and foaming down for two or three miles, before it reaches the chute, where it plunges, in two immense masses, one hundred and seventy feet into the yawning gulf, and then sweeps away, in whirling eddies and billows, about seven miles, into Lake Ontario. We stood in silent awe as we gazed upon this wonder of creation. I lay down upon Table Rock, which shelved over a part of the frightful abyss and shook with the unceasing thunder of the waters; and as I looked down, I became dizzy and appalled. The rock has changed much since that day. No description of this grand scene, that I have seen, approaches the reality as it thus appeared to me at the close of the last century. Its incessant thunder, heard for miles around, its solemn grandeur, its indescribable combination of power, beauty and sublimity, overpowered the mind, and silence was the best expression of the spectator. At that time there was no house near the falls on either side of the river, but they burst upon the view of the visitor in the midst of the aboriginal wildness of nature. I have seen them perhaps a hundred times since; the falls themselves are sacred from the hand of man, but how have their surroundings been changed? Now there are busy villages on both shores, a suspension bridge in sight, a railroad upon it, a ferry across the river almost beneath the cataract, a bridge from the American side to Goat Island. Nearly every thing around has changed; but the grand, the awful falls, thunder on."

CHAPTER III.

LIFE IN CANADA.

He had thus plunged further into the western wilder ness, but more for the diversion and relief of his troubled mind, than from motives of adventure or gain. He could not, however, escape from himself. He was here still surrounded with the native grandeur and solemn solitude of nature. Contemplative minds behold in these vast and tranquil scenes a reflection of the infinite, and experience not only a poetic, but a religious thoughtfulness, often tinged with sadness, if not with melancholy. Reverence for nature rises into awe for its Creator; the contrasted pettiness of the ordinary works and pursuits of man startles the soul, and awakens aspirations for something better. The pioneer populations of the American frontiers have always shown a profound susceptibility to religious impressions, and among the many heroic and saintly men who have illustrated the itinerant ministry of Methodism, none have exhibited more religious sensibility, more eloquent pathos, more saintliness or heroism, than those who have come forth from the grand scenes of the far West. To young Bangs these scenes had an irresistible and pensive fascination, and in many a lonely woodland walk did he prayerfully review those thoughts of good and evil, of the soul and God, which, for nearly four years, had been transforming life, death, and the whole universe to his mind. And here also was he again to meet the persecuted people whom he had ridiculed, who seemed so strangely to beset his path, and who were, at last, to afford his anxious spirit its only genuine relief, and open before him the successful career of his public life.

"Not finding employment as a surveyor," he writes, "I took a school, in a Dutch neighborhood, about ten miles from Newark, at the head of Lake Ontario, six miles from Niagara Falls. The mournful thoughts which passed through my mind while wandering alone in the forests of this strange country I cannot well express. Sometimes I would seat myself in the solitary woods and bewail my condition till my heaving heart found relief in floods of tears. The best satisfaction I could find was in being alone, reading, praying, and meditating. On one thing I resolved: being now separated from my former associates, I determined not to entangle myself again in the vain pleasures of life. When not engaged in my school duties, reading the Bible and other good books, and secret prayer, occupied most of my time."

He discovers among the settlers a family which has a small library. Milton's Poems, Bunyan's Progress, Hervey's Meditations entertain and relieve his melancholy leisure. He is successful as a teacher, commands much respect from the people, accumulates some funds, and is in danger of relapsing into his former moral indifference; but the slightest occurrences recall the subjects of his serious reflections. He is overtaken in the woods by night and must cross a dangerous stream in the dark, upon a narrow branch of a tree; after passing over, he pauses to look back in the dim light at the peril he has escaped; it presents a figure of his moral danger, wandering in darkness through life, through death, to the infinite future; and his spirit trembles within him. He resumes his early habit, enjoined by his father, of reading the Bible "by course." The dealings of God with the Hebrew people, their frequent defections, his mercy and judgments upon them, deeply impress him. "This reading," he says, "gave me more important knowledge than all the books I had ever read. In studying the New Testament light poured into my understanding through the agency of the Holy Spirit, as I now believe, and though the plan of salvation, by grace through faith, was not yet clearly revealed to me, I saw myself a justly condemned sinner, and perceived the necessity of repentance, though I did not fully comprehend its nature. I was led to earnest prayer, in secret, for more light, and for deliverance from the difficulties under which I groaned."

DOCTRINAL SOPHISMS.

A drowning man will catch at straws. He opened his Bible, one Sabbath morning, at the text, "As in Adam all die, so in Christ shall all be made alive;" the sophism that the final salvation of all men, and therefore his own safety, could be inferred from this passage, was eagerly seized by him; he cited it to some of his neighbors; they reminded him that it only declares the resurrection of all men, but that among those who "in the dust of the earth shall awake," there shall rise "some to everlasting life, and some to shame and everlasting contempt." His tender conscience recoiled from the fallacy it had dared to entertain, and again he bowed his head in compunction before his God. He was, in fine, passing through a moral training which was to afford an important preparation for his ministerial life. He was learning by experience the struggles of a soul in the process of its regeneration. He was destined to be, for two generations, the guide and comforter of such souls, and it was necessary that he should know well their needs. Had his inveterate prejudices allowed him to hear the few Methodists who were scattered about him, he would have found in their liberal but evangelical doctrines the guidance and consolation he needed; but he shunned them as dangerous fanatics. The remote region where he now lived was occasionally reached by wandering clergymen or itinerant missionaries. One, who was of the denomination in which he had been trained, arrived there, but could give him no satisfactory instruction. Though in holy orders, he was a card-player and a drunkard, and performed the liturgical service with indecent haste, following it with a brief, rapid, and vapid prelection. A Calvinistic preacher paused some time in the settlement; the young teacher conversed much with him, and sought refuge from his anxious perplexities in the dogmas of election and the final safety of the elect. Were he one of these he could not be lost, whatever his errors, whatever even his sins. He records that he found a momentary, but pernicious relief in this opinion. He became a zealous polemic among his rustic friends, and held many a sturdy dispute in defense of his new creed; more, however, to fortify himself in it than to win them to it, and with self-complaisant fallacies which no good Calvinist would admit. A Methodist came across his path and was immediately attacked on the subject; but the devout Arminian had other and more personal topics to discuss with him, and left him with still greater alarms of conscience. "His words came," he writes, "like a dagger to my heart, and I could make no reply, but turned from him, begging him to pray for me. Soon after, while walking the lonely road, these words of Job came to my mind with power: 'Who is he that hideth counsel without knowledge? Therefore have I uttered that I understood not; things too wonderful for me, which I knew not.' They so strongly arrested my attention that I stood still, in silent amazement and unutterable humiliation. Such a penetrating sense of my utter inability to comprehend the deep subjects upon which I had been disputing entered my soul, that I was prostrated before God confessing my littleness and sinfulness. For a time I dared not to advance; I looked this way and that, I gazed upon the heavens over my head and the earth beneath my feet, and seemed surrounded with God, shut in on every side. I acknowledged my sinfulness, my ignorance, my utter insufficiency; I knew that I had 'uttered things too high for me,' and 'things that I understood not.' I concluded, therefore, that it was more fitting me to cease disputing, to humble myself before God, and to supplicate his mercy as a condemned criminal at his throne, than to contend about the deep things of religion, to which I was a stranger. These reflections humbled me in the dust, and I resolved to trouble myself no more with speculative points of divinity, but rather to seek until I should find his mercy."

THE METHODISTS—JAMES COLEMAN.

"Although I accepted, thus humbly, this pointed rebuke, I could not yet bring myself willingly to receive the Methodist doctrines and usages as rightful expositions of God's word; such influence had early prejudices still over my mind, strengthened as they were by daily reports of the tongue of slander. I supposed that a people of whom so much evil was said must be under a fatal delusion. Thus I went on, stumbling over the truth and warring against my conscience." But this very people seemed, as we have seen, providentially to beset him. He now found himself boarding with a family who, nominally at least, belonged to their communion. "One night," he continues, "I could not rest. I sat up after the family had retired. I opened the Bible, and my eye fell upon those words of Jeremiah, 'But thy life will I give unto thee for a prey in all places whither thou goest.' They seemed addressed to me, and to foretoken my destiny. I knelt in prayer, and, committing myself to God's mercy, found some repose in sleep."

About this time a Methodist itinerant penetrated to the settlement. James Coleman, a man who, with no great talents, achieved great usefulness, not only preached there, but lodged with the very family where the baffled inquirer resided.

James Coleman was a good example of the heroic Methodist itinerant ministry of that day. He was born in New Jersey, settled early beyond the Alleghanies, on the Monongahela, and was there reached and saved, about the time of the Revolution, by the pioneer preachers of Methodism. He entered the ministry, a hardy and zealous evangelist, about 1791, and went to New England to help Lee in founding Methodism in the East. A missionary in spirit, he made his way, in 1794, to Canada, among the first preachers of the denomination in that country. On his route to, and in his travels in the province, he endured the severest privations. While passing up the Mohawk River, he was obliged to go on shore fifteen nights in succession, and kindle a fire to keep off the wild beasts; and his food failing, he was reduced to a single cracker per day. But such was his zeal that no privations or difficulties could arrest him, or even dampen his ardor. Though his abilities were not great, yet such was the peculiar impression that attended his prayers, and so entirely was he a man of one aim and of one business, that great results attended his labors; and, say his brethren, in their Minute obituary, "his crown in heaven is not without many stars, and some, too, of the first magnitude." "I recall him distinctly," wrote Dr. Bangs, after many years, "a man of small stature, piercing black eyes, an intelligent countenance; a good devoted man. I often heard him preach, and was greatly pleased with his fervent manner. He frequently spoke to me about religion, though I did not open my heart to him. In his prayers he would mention me by name, with affectionate simplicity, which so affected me that I would weep like a child, and, when I rose from my knees, would seek some secluded place to hide my emotions. I have indeed great reason to remember, with gratitude to God, the prayers and conversations of James Coleman. He was truly a man of God, and tenderly felt for the salvation of souls. He soon, however, left the country, to return no more. After his departure there were no preachers of the Gospel near us, except the poor drunken card-playing minister of the Church of England, whom I sometimes heard mumble over his form of prayer so fast that I could scarcely understand a word of it, and then read his short manuscript sermon with the same indifference and haste."

MENTAL STRUGGLES.

The words of the good James Coleman had, however, sunk into his heart. Some days after the evangelist had left the settlement, the young teacher walked in the woods, late at night, mourning over the desolation of his soul. He had lost the opportunity of revealing his condition to a man who could have solved his perplexities, and he now endeavored again to find their solution in his own confused and harassed reflections. The moon and stars shone magnificently upon and through the grand natural temple of the primeval forest. Awestruck by the majesty of God, he felt his own insignificance and sinfulness. He tried to pray, but could not; "such a contrast," he says, "appeared between the holy, tremendous God, and my unholy, miserable self, that I dared not open my lips in prayer. I stood in trembling silence and condemnation. I had no view of the Saviour of sinners. Had I beheld him as my atoning High Priest, and relied on his merits, I might have been delivered from my guilt, and have received 'peace in believing;' but this blessed vision was yet hidden from my view, and I only saw God out of Christ, and he was as a consuming fire."

The true light was approaching, however, and the morning was at hand. A day or two later, after dismissing his school, he again walked and meditated in the forest, pondering over the truths he had heard from the Methodist itinerant. He knelt in prayer, and then continued his walk, still looking heavenward for light and comfort. "Suddenly," he says, "I felt my burden removed. Filled with gratitude for God's long forbearance, I stood and silently adored. It was immediately suggested to my mind, 'What is this?' and answered, 'It is the love of God.' 'Are my sins forgiven?' Something seemed to answer, 'No.' I rejoiced, however, in God my Saviour, and a desire to immediately make known to some one my hopes and fears arose in my heart, but it was suggested, 'This will not be wise; you may be deceived; and a profession of religion may be followed with failure and disgrace.' I continued in this state, rejoicing in the goodness of God, about three days, when, in consequence of following the suggestion of my fears, and thereby failing of the sympathies and counsels of experienced Christians, doubt, darkness, and condemnation succeeded to the peace and illumination I had received. Although I was well assured that a great change had taken place in my whole moral being, yet I did not believe that I was fully justified in the sight of God, nor was the plan of salvation by grace, through faith, fully disclosed to my mind; yet I now think that if I had obeyed the voice of the Spirit by making known my condition to the people of God, I should even then have entered into the rest of faith."

A QUARTERLY LOVE-FEAST.

The light was, however, soon to dawn more fully. The Methodists were again at hand. "Not many days after this," he continues, "information came that two Methodist preachers had arrived, and that a Quarterly Meeting was to be held at Christian Warner's house, near St. David's. I rejoiced at this news, as I had prayed long and urgently that God would send some one who could instruct us 'more perfectly' in his ways, and I was now determined to divest myself of all prejudice, and receive with candor the truth, whencesoever it might come to my troubled soul." At this opportune moment he found one of his friends, in the same state of mind as himself, and accompanied him to the love-feast—the *Agape*, derived by Wesley, through the Moravians, from the primitive Church—an occasion which always accompanied the "Quarterly Meeting."

The two inquirers went, praying that they might find light and peace. As they approached the house, they heard singing and prayer from the barn where the assembly was held. "Their hearts were thrilled," and "filled with solemn awe." The Itinerants present were Joseph Sawyer and Joseph Jewell, notable men of that day. At the close of the love-feast, Sawyer stood up to preach; young Bangs placed himself in a corner of the barn, determined to hear as for his life. The evangelist discoursed on the beatitudes of the Sermon on the Mount. "In commenting on the passage, 'Blessed are they that mourn,' etc., he unfolded all the enigmas of my heart more fully than I could myself. I was powerfully affected, and wept much. I was fully persuaded that he was a man of God, and could show me the way of salvation. When the meeting concluded, Mr. Warner invited me to dine at his house with the preachers. Though I was an entire stranger to him and to them, I gladly assented, for I had an eager desire to converse with them. On the way I rode in company with Joseph Sawyer, who commenced a conversation with me on religion. For the first time in my life I fully disclosed the struggles of my mind, acknowledging my doubts, my fears, and my desires. He endeavored in the kindest manner to instruct and comfort me. At his request I accompanied him to his lodgings, and when I was about to depart we kneeled down, and he prayed for me that God would convert my soul, and even commission me to preach the Gospel. 'What does this mean?' said I to myself; for, as to preaching, the thought had never entered my mind."

To save his own soul was his absorbing anxiety; but

the itinerant saw that God had been leading him through a significant moral training, and that there were in him the qualities which make mighty men. He instinctively divined something of the destined career of the young struggling soul before him. He explained the revelation of gracious light which had been given him in his meditative walk on the highway—that the consolation he then received was legitimate, but that his faith had failed. He exhorted him to go forward; a clearer light would dawn upon him, and he would yet receive assurance, "the witness of the Spirit."

A SISTER'S USEFULNESS.

His brother-in-law moved into the settlement about this time, and received him as a lodger. His sister was a devout woman, and had already been instrumental in the salvation of another brother. John Bangs, on taking leave of the parental home at Stamford, to go out into the world, was, he says, "accompanied some distance on the way by a pious and devoted sister; when about to part, she held me by the hand and seemed unwilling to let me go. I looked into her face and beheld the tears coursing down from a countenance impressed with sorrow and anxiety. I could not think what was the matter until she said, 'My dear brother, remember that if you die in your sins, where God and Christ are you never can go!' She turned away from me and passed on." This parting word, he adds, "wounded" his heart; "a thunderbolt" could not have struck him with more effect. He became a laborious and successful preacher of Methodism.* This sister was now in the wilderness of Canada, a guide and comforter of her brother Nathan, before whom the same career was about to open. They communed together, as brother and sister only can, respecting his spiritual struggles and hopes. He records the consolation he received in these conversations: "I resolved," he adds, "to

* Memoir of Rev. John Bangs.

devote myself wholly to the service of God, come what might." He began practically to do so.

PERSECUTION.

He now daily opened his school with prayer; but the innovation raised a storm of opposition. He had been very highly appreciated by the families of his pupils; they now railed against him in the streets. "A robust Dutchman" so far violated the hospitality of his own house as to rush upon him, when he entered its door, with clenched and uplifted fist, exclaiming, "Did you ever see a man mad? if not, look at me!" Others also threatened him with personal violence, and the whole settlement was thrown into agitation. They accused the Methodists of deluding and infatuating him. He remained calm, but resolute. They at last threatened to expel him from the neighborhood, and transport him across the river into the United States. "Finding," he says, "I could have no peace among them, I called a 'School-meeting;' they voted that I might continue the school, but should not pray in it. I finally told them that, as they owed me three months' wages, I would give them three days in which to pay me, and meanwhile teach the school, but continue the prayers. I went around to their houses, collected my bills, heard many regrets, one family blaming another for the trouble, but I quietly left them. God, indeed, stood by me in that hour of trial, and gave me words and arguments which they could not resist; and, so far from feeling any resentment, I felt the tenderest pity for them and their children, and could weep and pray for them."

DOFFS HIS CUE AND RUFFLES AND BECOMES A METHODIST.

This trial was a great blessing; it committed him publicly to religion, and opened the way for his entrance upon the career of his life as a preacher of the Gospel. "I had now," he continues, "taken a stand from which

I could not well recede. I felt much inward peace, and the Holy Scriptures were indescribably precious to me." He conformed himself to the severest customs of the Methodists. He had prided himself on his fine personal appearance, and had dressed in the full fashion of the times, with ruffled shirt, and long hair in a cue. He now ordered his laundress to take off his ruffles; his long hair shared the same fate, not, however, without the remonstrances of his pious sister, who deemed this rigor unnecessary, and admired his young but manly form with a sister's pride. He was received into the Society of the Methodists. He had considered them unworthy of his regard; he now considered himself unworthy of theirs, and took his place among them with deep humility. "When I became acquainted with the 'General Rules,'" he says, "I was struck with their Scriptural character, and could not but remark the truth of Mr. Wesley's saying: 'All these, we know, the Spirit of God writes on truly awakened hearts.' Before I knew these Rules, as in the Methodist Discipline, or any of the rules of that Discipline, the Holy Spirit had written most of them on my heart."

CHRISTIAN EXPERIENCE.

"Having thus united myself with the people of God, it was now my principal concern to make sure work of my salvation. Though I had frequent manifestations of the grace of God, and could occasionally rejoice in him, I had not yet attained to a clear witness of my acceptance with him. The subject of religion engrossed my attention, and I sought every opportunity to converse with devout people on my state and prospects. Some said that they believed me to be already justified, while others exhorted me to be thankful for what I had received, and to persevere until I should find a satisfactory evidence of my acceptance with God. My prayer was for some miraculous, some physical manifestation of divine grace. It pleased the Lord to disappoint me in this respect, as in so many others. After struggling hard, praying much, reading the Holy Scriptures, fasting, and conversing with religious friends for some days, he showed to my mind a scene such as I had never fully seen before. All my past sins seemed pictured upon my memory; and the righteous law of God, so often broken by me, shone in overwhelming splendor before me; I saw and acknowledged the justice of my condemnation. Christ was then exhibited to my mind as having 'fulfilled the law and made it honorable,' 'bearing my sins in his own body on the tree;' so that I, receiving him by faith, need not bear them any longer myself. This view humbled me to the dust. At the same time I felt a gracious power to rely upon his atoning merits by simple faith. Instantly I felt that my sins were canceled for Christ's sake, and the Spirit of God bore witness with mine that I was adopted into the family of His people. My mind was filled with awe and reverence. The wisdom, power, and goodness of God in devising such a scheme for the recovery of fallen man struck me with astonishment. With an ecstasy of holy joy did I lay hold upon the cross of the Lord Jesus as my Saviour. All boasting was excluded, except of the matchless love of God, who sent his Son to die for the world, that 'whosoever believeth in him should not perish, but have everlasting life.' This view of the plan of redemption and salvation was as clear to me at that time as it has been at any time since, though not by any means so comprehensively defined in my mind as in my later experience and studies. It has since been enlarged, and made to appear more and more exact, symmetrical, and beautiful in all its parts. Here let me record my grateful, adoring sense of the loving-kindness of my God in watching so providentially over my infant days, in leading me through the perilous intricacies of youth up to manhood, bearing with my sinfulness, conducting me to a strange land, where he directed my steps among his people, opening the path of life and peace to my troubled soul, and receiving me at last, by adoption, into the household of his saints. I was now, August, 1800, in the twenty-second year of my age, having been twenty-one on the 2d of May preceding."

Thus was the momentous work wrought, the regeneration of this struggling soul. Thus had he at last and forever turned his brow heavenward, whence fell upon it a light which was to "shine brighter and brighter even unto the perfect day." Henceforth, for more than threescore years, he will maintain his unaverted gaze toward that divine height, till at last he is caught up to it, away from our sight, as if sharing in the ascension, as he had shared in the redemption of his Lord.

CHAPTER IV.

NEW SCENES AND STUDIES.

It seemed now that he had to begin life anew. He had been thrust out from his occupation and his home; but this trial, as has been said, was providential; it was to hasten him into the appointed career of his public life. "When my old friends cast me off," he writes, "the Lord raised me up new and better ones." Before he left the settlement he bore a faithful testimony for his God. "The divine love burned in my heart," he adds, "and I felt compelled to warn all around me to flee from the wrath to come. I went from house to house declaring what God had done for my soul, exhorting the people to seek his mercy, and praying with those who would permit me. Some mocked, some wept, and a few received the word with joy. No sooner was I brought from darkness to light, and from the power of Satan unto God, than I was led to embrace the doctrines and usages of Methodism, with all my heart, as far as I understood them. Being about three hundred miles from my father's house, I wrote him an account of the change wrought in my views and life. In answering me he expressed thankfulness that I had given my attention to religion, but thought I had gone too far in assuming a knowledge of my personal salvation, as knowledge supersedes the necessity of faith. I wrote him a reply, in which, though the sentiments were true, I believe my zeal led me to express myself too positively, and not with that respectful deference which befits a child addressing a father. I would also observe that, during the previous struggles of my soul, few things gave me keener sorrow than remembered acts of disobedience to my parents, and I could not rest till I made them a humble acknowledgment and begged their pardon, which they affectionately accorded me."

He obtained another school, in a Methodist neighborhood, where he found congenial society and providential aids in his new life. "Before I became acquainted with the Methodists," he says, "my theological reading had been confined mostly to Calvinistic authors; but now I began to read the writings of John Wesley and John Fletcher. I thereby became acquainted with those eminent men of God, and now truth shone more fully upon my understanding. Some portions of Mr. Wesley's Journals fell into my hands, and gave me a knowledge of the manner in which God had led him on, step by step, in the great work to which his life was devoted. I thanked God for raising up such a man to be a means of light and reformation in the modern Church. Simultaneously with my conversion it was impressed upon my mind that it was my duty to warn sinners of their danger. It seemed as if I had been awakened from a profound sleep, and I thought I could see others in the same dangerous condition. I felt an unappeasable desire to apprise them of their danger, and induce them to escape it by repentance toward God and faith in the Lord Jesus Christ. For such an important task I felt quite inadequate. Sometimes I feared that this impression of what seemed an impossible duty was a temptation of the adversary to induce me to exhibit my weakness, and thereby bring reproach on the cause of God; and such was my natural timidity, that whenever I attempted to pray in public I trembled like a leaf, and I concluded that if I attempted to speak in public I never could succeed. The impression that I must sooner or later preach beset me, however, by night and by day; and frequently, while walking in the forests, texts of Scripture would be presented to my mind, and their meaning unfolded; and

I found myself following out the train of their truth with all my soul, while my heart burned within me with a divine fervor.

JOSEPH SAWYER—CHRISTIAN WARNER.

"Joseph Sawyer, who received me into the Church and who had become as a father to me, frequently urged me to use what he called my 'gift' in public. Although I consented to lead a class, a few miles distant from my home, such was my timidity that the attempt was an entire failure. This induced me to doubt my capacity for any such public labors, and I hastily concluded that I would try no more.

"Soon after this failure I removed my lodgings to another place, and boarded with Christian Warner, my class-leader, a man of sweet spirit, and for whom I shall ever entertain an ardent affection. He was a pattern of religion, always consistent in his conduct, and acted the part of a parent toward me. Such was my diffidence that I gave up my judgment almost entirely to others whom I esteemed on account of their experience and piety. I found Christian Warner worthy of my utmost confidence, and he became my counselor and guide in this critical period of my Christian life."

THE DOCTRINE OF SANCTIFICATION.

The doctrine of sanctification, as taught by Paul and expounded by Wesley and Fletcher, was a favorite theme in the conversations of his new associates, especially of Christian Warner. Wesley attached supreme importance to this doctrine. While yet at Oxford he became convinced that the Mystics, with all their errors, had apprehended in it a great truth of Christianity. The Sketch of a Perfect Christian, by Clemens Alexandrinus, excited his ardent aspirations. Bishop Taylor had irradiated that ideal of religious character by his rare eloquence. William Law had written ably upon it.

Thomas à Kempis and other Catholic saints had taught and exemplified it. Fenelon had been an illustrious example of it, in both his writings and life. Wesley translated the life of Fenelon's friend, Madam Guyon, and gave it to his people as a practical demonstration of the great trnth. He also published in his Christian Library the essay of Dr. Lucas on Religious Perfection,* as presenting generally the Scriptural view of the subject. The Scriptural phrases "sanctification," "perfection," "perfect love," would, independently of these authorities, have suggested to him a pre-eminent standard of spiritual life; but these writers had given a specific and even technical character to the words. Their opinions, glowing with the very sanctity of the Gospel, and aspiring to what most men deemed an altogether preter-human virtue, have been rendered familiar to the Methodist itinerants throughout England, and later throughout the world, in the writings of Law, Fletcher, and Wesley. Every one of them, at his reception into the traveling ministry, avows his belief in the doctrine, and that he is "groaning after," if he has not already attained, this exalted grace. Perhaps no single fact affords a better explanation of the marvelous success of Methodism. Wesley observed and declared that wherever the doctrine was preached revivals usually prevailed. "It is," he said, "the grand depositum which God has given to the people called Methodists; and chiefly to propagate this, it appears, God raised them up. Their mission was not to form a religious party, but to spread holiness over these lands." The doctrine of personal sanctification was, in fine, the great potential idea of Methodism. It not only gave it life and energy, by inspiring its congregations with devout and transforming aspirations, but it was the precise sentiment needed as the basis of its ministry. Nothing short of entire self-sacrifice could

* The third part of "An Inquiry after Happiness," by Dr. Lucas, Prebend of Westminster.

consist with the duties and privations of that ministry; and, according to their doctrine of perfection, entire consecration was the preliminary of entire sanctification. These holy men, then, in making an entire public sacrifice of themselves, did so as a part of an entire consecration to God, for the purpose of their own entire personal sanctification, as well as their usefulness to others. What ideal of ministerial character and devotion could be more sublime or more effective? And this ideal they realized in the exceeding labors and purity of their lives, and the martyr-like triumphs of their deaths.

Wesley defined this Scriptural truth more clearly than any other modern writer. Evangelical theologians cannot deny his definition of the doctrine. They can dissent from him only in respect to the time in which entire sanctification may be practically reached by the believer. All admit it as at least an ideal, yet Scriptural standard of spiritual life, to be habitually aspired to by good men, though attained, with rare exceptions, only at death. Wesley claimed it as, like justification, an attainment of faith, and practicable at any moment.* It is the purification of the believer subsequent to regeneration. It is usually gradual; it may be instantaneous, as, like just-

* Alexander Knox, Esq., the friend and correspondent of Bishop Jebb, says, (Thirty Years' Correspondence with Bishop Jebb, Letter XIX,) "Nay, the very point you aim at in them, I mean their view of Christian Perfection, is in my mind so essentially right and important that it is on this account particularly I value them above other denominations of the sort. I am aware that ignorant individuals expose what is in itself true by their unfounded pretensions and irrational descriptions; but with the sincerest disapproval of every such excess, I do esteem John Wesley's stand for holiness to be that which does immortal honor to his name. . . . In John Wesley's views of Christian Perfection are combined, in substance, all the sublime morality of the Greek fathers, the spirituality of the Mystics, and the divine philosophy of our favorite Platonists. Macarius, Fenelon, Lucas, and all of their respective classes, have been consulted and digested by him, and his ideas are essentially theirs." See also Knox's Essay on Wesley's Character, addressed to Southey. Appendix to Southey's Wesley.

ification, it is received by faith. "When we begin to believe," Wesley said in his Minutes of Conference, "then sanctification begins; and as faith increases holiness increases." But this experience, he taught, should be sought immediately; and as it is obtained by faith, it is the privilege of all believers at any time. He called it "perfection," a name which has incurred no little animadversion, but which he used as Scriptural, and as having been so used by Law, Lucas, Macarius, Fenelon, and other writers, Protestant and Papal.

Wesley's statement of the doctrine, in its right analysis, agrees with the highest standards of the theological world. He differed from them only in his clearer and more urgent promulgation of the great truth; in making it an exoteric rather than an esoteric opinion; in declaring that what other theologians taught as a possibility, the rare enjoyment of some, is the privilege of all. Fletcher has given us a remarkable essay on the doctrine, proving it to be Scriptural, and in accordance with the theological teachings of the best divines.* Wesley wrote an elaborate treatise upon it.† He taught not absolute or Adamic, but Christian Perfection. Perfect Christians "are not," he says, "free from ignorance, no, nor from mistake. We are no more to expect any man to be infallible than to be omniscient. . . . From infirmities none are perfectly freed till their spirits return to God; neither can we expect, till then, to be wholly freed from temptation; for 'the servant is not above his Master.' But neither in this sense is there any absolute perfection on earth. There is no perfection of degrees, none which does not admit of a continual increase."

To one of his correspondents he says, "The proposition which I will hold is this: 'Any person may be cleansed from all sinful tempers, and yet need the aton-

* Last Check to Antinomianism, Works, vol. ii.

† Plain Account of Christian Perfection, Works, vol. vi.

ing blood.' For what? For 'negligences and ignorances;' for both words and actions, (as well as omissions,) which are, in a sense, transgressions of the perfect law. And I believe no one is clear of these till he lays down this corruptible body."* Perfection, as defined by Wesley, is not then perfection according to the absolute moral law; it is what he calls it, *Christian Perfection;* perfection according to the *new moral economy introduced by the atonement*, in which the heart being sanctified, fulfills the law by love, (Rom. xii, 8, 10,) and its involuntary imperfections are provided for, by that economy, without the imputation of guilt, as in the case of infancy and all irresponsible persons. The only question, then, can be, Is it possible for good men so to love God that all their conduct, inward and outward, shall be swayed by love? that even their involuntary defects shall be swayed by it? Is there such a thing as the inspired writer calls the "perfect love" which "casteth out fear?" (1 John iv, 18.) Wesley believed that there is; that it is the privilege of all saints; and that it is to be received by faith.

In a letter to one of his female correspondents he says: "I want you to be *all love.* This is the perfection I believe and teach; and this perfection is consistent with a thousand nervous disorders, which that high strained perfection is not. Indeed, my judgment is, that (in this case particularly) to overdo is to undo; and that to set perfection too high, is the most effectual way of driving it out of the world." When he thus explained his opinion to Bishop Gibson, the prelate replied: "Why, Mr. Wesley, if this is what you mean by perfection, who can be against it?" "Man," he says, "in his present state, can no more attain Adamic than angelic perfection. The perfection of which man is capable, while he dwells in a corruptible body, is the complying with that kind command: 'My son, give me thy heart!' It is the

* Letter 190, Works, vol. vi.

loving the Lord his God, with all his heart, and with all his soul, and with all his mind." Such is his much misrepresented doctrine of Christian Perfection.*

EXPERIENCE OF SANCTIFICATION.

A mind so profoundly imbued with religious earnestness as that of young Bangs, could not fail to seize on a truth like this. "From reading the Holy Scriptures," he writes, "Mr. Wesley's 'Plain Account of Christian Perfection,' and Mr. Fletcher's writings on the subject, I clearly saw the necessity of a deeper piety than I had yet attained; of being sanctified throughout, soul, body, and spirit. As I went on in observance of God's commands, divine light shone more brightly upon my understanding, disclosing to me the remaining impurities of my nature. This gave me a more and more acute sense of my native depravity than I had ever had, so much so, that doubts were sometimes excited in my inexperienced mind whether I had indeed been justified. And yet on mature reflection I could not question the reality of the change which the Spirit of God had wrought in my heart, for I felt no condemnation for past sins, and I was often blessed with great peace and joy in the Holy Ghost. My experience verified St. Paul's description of the justified man: 'Being justified by faith, we have peace with God through our Lord Jesus Christ.' My conscience also was extremely tender, so that I could not neglect any known duty, as fasting, secret prayer, social or public worship in class-meetings or the congregation, or exhorting others to flee the wrath to come, in doing which I enjoyed much inward comfort, and rejoiced in hope of the glory of God. But notwithstanding all this, I felt such an exquisite sense of moral defect that I was led, like Job, to abhor myself as in dust and ashes. There was, however, a great difference between my present distress and my former

* History of the Religious Movement of the Eighteenth Century, called Methodism, etc., vol. i, 405; vol. ii, 411.

sense of condemnation. Formerly I was condemned as a guilty sinner, and hardly dared to look up to God for mercy; now I felt reconciled to him, could pray in faith, and enjoyed peace, while a sweet compunction weighed me down at the footstool of divine mercy. I hated sin with a perfect hatred, and consequently felt an utter aversion to all its pleasures. Such confidence had I in the Christian purity and influence of Mr. Warner, who professed the blessing of sanctification, and, I doubt not, enjoyed it, that I loved his very presence, and in prayer-meetings I wished to kneel close by his side.

"In this temper I went struggling on for some time, until, on the 6th of February, 1801, being that evening on a visit to a pious family with some Christian friends, we conversed till quite late on religious subjects, and then prayed, as was the Methodist custom; for Methodists in that day seldom parted from even their casual interviews without prayer. When we knelt, I felt an unusually earnest spirit of devotion. Mr. Warner first prayed, and, without rising, called upon me to pray. When I commenced, my emotions deepened, my desire for a pure heart became intense, and my faith grew stronger and stronger. My supplications were importunate, so that I know not how long I continued to pray. When I ceased, I sank down into an inexpressible calmness, as lying passive at the feet of God. I felt relieved and comforted, as though I had been 'cleansed from all filthiness of the flesh and spirit.' I had no extraordinary rapture, no more than I had often experienced before, but such a sense of my own littleness that I thought, 'What a wonder is it that God condescends to notice me at all!' All my inward distress was gone. I could look up with a childlike composure and trust, and behold God as my heavenly Father.

"We staid all night, and the next morning in family prayer I seemed surrounded with the divine glory. I certainly was filled at that time with the 'perfect love which casteth out fear,' for I had no fear of death or judgment. I could trust all things to my merciful God, through my infinitely sufficient Redeemer. Such a sense of God's ineffable goodness pervaded my soul, that I seemed to sink, confounded by his very love, into nothingness before him. I felt that I was the least of all saints, but had an evidence bright as the noonday sun that all my sins were taken away, and that without fear I could depart and be with Christ at any moment he should see fit to call me.

"I here simply relate the facts as they occurred. The change in my nature was as evident to me as had been my justification. Whatever name others may attach to this gracious experience, I believe I was then sanctified by the Spirit of God mercifully given unto me.

CALL TO PREACH.

"Having been made a partaker of this great blessing, the thought that I must preach the Gospel recurred to my conscience with increased force; but being more deeply sensible than ever of my deficiency in the qualifications requisite for so responsible a work, I dared not yet to yield to the impression, though it followed me by day and by night. Nor did I open my mind to any one respecting it, lest it might be imputed to vanity or pride. I prayed much that God would show me plainly my duty. One day, as I was walking the road, in deep meditation upon this subject, a sudden ray of divine illumination struck my mind like a flash of lightning, accompanied with the words, 'I have anointed thee to preach the Gospel.' I sank to the ground, and cried out, 'Here am I!'"

Sublime culmination of a heroic soul! a soul overcoming the world, and—still greater achievement—overcoming itself; struggling through years of internal combat; laying hold, in the American desert, upon the highest ideal of moral character taught by the saints of the elder world; and listening for a voice from the higher world to summon him to live and die an apostle of divine truth! To one class of minds this record of moral conflict and triumph will present only the history of a morbid temperament. Another will accept it as an example of the divine regeneration of a human soul. From all candid minds, however predisposed to rationalistic solutions of its problems, its examples of a struggling conscience, of devout aspirations, of self-denial, and of final and life-long consecration, will command not only respect, but reverence.

CHAPTER V.

THE ITINERANT MINISTRY.

He was now to enter the humble ministry of Methodism, that itinerant host of evangelists which Wesley had organized and extended throughout the Anglo-Saxon world, and which, for its heroic character and extraordinary labors, sufferings, and successes, has been called the *legio tonans* of modern Protestantism. He had heard marvelous stories about it from the time that Lee arrived in his native state; had read in the writings of Wesley, and other publications, with admiring wonder, of its almost military discipline, its hardships and triumphs. He had seen it exemplified in the persons of its Canadian pioneers, Coleman, Jewell, and Sawyer, who had penetrated to the remote settlements whither he had wandered.

It presented romantic attractions to his fervid spirit, notwithstanding its extreme privations and toils. He even dreamed about it. John Wesley seemed yet its great apostle, calling him in the night-watches to its invincible ranks. On a mountain height he saw the mighty evangelist "passing with great velocity in a chariot of light, throwing out to him a shining sword and crying, 'Take this and conquer!'" "I awoke," he writes, "and behold it was a dream, but one of thrilling suggestions."

EXPERIMENT IN PREACHING.

Joseph Sawyer returned, again and again, to the settlement in his rapid ministerial tours, and now became his providential guide. Joseph Sawyer was a distinguished preacher of that day, a Boanerges in the desert. He saw in the youthful convert the qualities requisite for the itinerant ministry of the times. He admitted no delay; for there were then no better means of qualification for the Methodist ministry than its practical work, and the moral destitution of the country required immediately all possible labor. The young disciple yielded to his urgency. "Strongly pressed," he says, "by Mr. Sawyer, whose fatherly care for me I shall never forget, I consented to make a trial in a little society about fifteen miles from my home. I went on Saturday; I was up early on Sunday morning and earnestly prayed for divine aid. My mind was sorely oppressed, and in family prayer I was much bound in spirit, and wished I had not undertaken the task. The principal part of the time, after rising from my bed till the hour appointed for the meeting, I spent upon my knees. I felt burdened with an insupportable load, and my mind was shrouded in darkness. I finally besought God that, if he had called me to preach, he would be pleased to open my mouth and bless me and the people with the consolation of his spirit; but, if he had not called me, he would shut my mouth, and I would return home and try no more. After coming to this conclusion I was tranquil, and waited the result with resignation. The people assembled, and, after singing and prayer, I no sooner opened my mouth than the Lord filled it with words and arguments; the Scriptures seemed like a fruitful field before me. The word of God was like fire in my bones, and its utterance was attended with the 'Holy Ghost and with power.' I felt as if I were in the very suburbs of the heavenly Jerusalem, and the people of God were refreshed as with new wine. The Lord indeed answered 'as by fire from heaven.'

ANOTHER EXPERIMENT.

"I then thought I could never again doubt my call to the ministry; but, alas for the unbelief of the human heart! 'except ye see signs and wonders ye will not believe!' Soon after this time I had an appointment in the neighborhood of my sister's residence. I was much perplexed for a text, and could find none that suited me. I finally concluded to abandon the thought of preaching and meet the people, sing, pray, exhort, and send them home. I went to the meeting with this determination. After rising from my knees I took up my little Bible, opened it, and the first words I saw I read, and the first thoughts that came to my mind I spoke, and thus I went on through a sermon. I doubt whether I have ever had greater liberty in preaching from that day to this; I was at no loss for ideas or words. I preached about three quarters of an hour. The text was, 'But when the husbandmen saw him, they reasoned among themselves, saying, This is the heir: come, let us kill him, that the inheritance may be ours.' Luke xx, 14. I have never preached on them since, nor do I remember how I then treated them. They were given to me, I believe, for the occasion, for the people appeared as if thunderstruck, and the effect was remarkable." He does not, however, record this fact as an example for others; thus used it would be abused; he considered it as a gracious and special condescension of God to his peculiar weakness.

SUCCESS AND DEFEAT.

Sawyer now determined to initiate him into the "itinerancy" by taking him around the circuit. "At the first appointment he said I must exhort after he had preached, a customary thing in that day among Methodists. I sat trembling during the sermon, for, in addition to the consciousness of my inadequacy for the ministerial work, my natural timidity was so extreme that it almost unfitted me for any public exercise. When I rose to follow him I shook in every limb, my lips stiffened, and I could hardly speak; but soon they were loosed, and the power of the Spirit descended on the assembly in such a manner that some sobbed aloud, some praised God audibly, and others fell to the floor as if shot dead. I felt unusually comforted and encouraged; but the adversary took advantage of my inexperience by suggesting to my mind, 'See what you have done. You have excelled even the preacher!' I said, 'Get thee behind me, Satan! It is not I that do these things, but the grace of God that dwelleth in me!' The temptation, however, pursued me all the rest of that day and the following, until we reached the next appointment, where the Lord humbled me by showing me my own weakness. There, when I rose to exhort, my mind was barren; I could only stammer out a few words, and at last sat down, utterly confounded and mortified. What a merciful God have we to deal with! This mortification was one of his greatest blessings to me; it taught me a necessary lesson which has never been forgotten.

"On the fifth day of our tour I consented to try to preach. I took for my text the words, 'One thing I know, that whereas I was once blind, now I see.' I went blundering on, as I thought, from beginning to end, though Mr. Sawyer said I preached a good sermon. Among other blunders I made a very palpable miscitation or misapplication of a passage from Milton. I immediately perceived my mistake, but could find no ready way of correcting it. I tried hard, but only made it worse. I sank into the quagmire of my confusion, and sat down, covered with humiliation and shame. No sooner was the meeting concluded than I set off, profoundly chagrined, to get my horse. The preacher, suspecting my purpose, hastened toward me and asked me where I was going. 'For my horse,' I replied, 'and then for home, as I have disgraced the cause of my God and killed the Church here!' The good man comforted me, and persuaded me to relinquish my design. I wept bitterly over my infirmities. We kept on around the circuit. I tried to preach several times, and again had good success. Thus was I trained, experimentally; it was the only ministerial preparation practicable to one under my circumstances." They ended the journey at an "old-fashioned" quarterly meeting at Lyon's Creek." He had been "broken in," rudely enough, so far as his feelings were concerned, but with salutary lessons, which were to be serviceable through all the rest of his life.

BECOMES AN ITINERANT.

In the month of August, 1801, about one year after he had joined the Church, and three months after he had been licensed as an exhorter, he received license to preach, and immediately departed for a circuit. Having earned some money as a surveyor, in addition to his salary as teacher, he was able to purchase an outfit of clothing, and a horse and its furniture, not forgetting the indispensable saddle-bags of the "itinerant." "I sold," he says, "my surveyor's instruments to a friend whom I had taught the art, mounted my horse and rode forth to 'sound the alarm' in the wilderness, taking no further thought 'what I should eat, or drink, or wherewithal I should be clothed.'" He had now learned to trust the divine guidance unfalteringly, for God "had found him in a desert land, and in the waste, howling wilderness; he had led him about; had instructed him; had kept him as the apple of his eye. As an eagle stirreth up her nest, fluttereth over her young, spreadeth abroad her wings, taketh them, beareth them on her wings, so the Lord alone did lead him."

CHAPTER VI.

METHODISM — ITS ORIGIN.

Early in the eighteenth century, Voltaire predicted that in the next generation Christianity would be overthrown throughout the civilized world. At the moment of this audacious prophecy, a band of devout students of Oxford University were laying, in penitence, prayer, and divine studies, the foundations of Methodism, and unconsciously preparing to initiate a new era in ecclesiastical history. The next generation was to witness, not the decadence of Christianity, but its greatest resuscitation since the age of Luther. The press upon which the works of Voltaire were printed, in Geneva, was destined to be used in the multiplication of the Holy Scriptures. John Wesley, the greatest of modern ecclesiastical legislators; Charles Wesley, whose psalmody was to become the liturgy of Methodism, and, in our day, reverberate along the outlines of the world; George Whitefield, perhaps the most eloquent preacher of all the Christian ages, and whose voice was to resound not only through the British isles, but through the Anglican colonies of North America; were living, though unknown, when Voltaire uttered his prediction. They became the chief members of the "Holy Club" of Oxford, the first "Methodists."

CHARACTERISTIC FACTS.

It was a providential fact that Methodism began its march from within the gates of Oxford. It was to gather the common people, by hundreds of thousands, around its standard, and their education was to be one of its chief responsibilities; its University prestige was to counteract vulgar prejudices against learning, and predispose it in favor of educational institutions. Wesley early established schools and academies for his people. At his first "Conference" he proposed a Theological Seminary for the training of his preachers. His followers have provided, in England, the most effective, in America, the most extensive series of learned institutions possessed by any Protestant body in the world, not recognized as a State Church.

The chief distinction, however, of the Methodist founders was that, though students of theological science, and all of them churchmen, they bravely broke away from dogmatic prejudices and ecclesiastical traditions; they discovered as by a divine illumination the paramount, the supreme importance of the spiritual life of Christianity. They went forth to revive this life in the land; to proclaim anew, and almost exclusively, the radical doctrines which are essential to it: the sinfulness of man, repentance, justification, regeneration, sanctification, the indwelling and witness of the Spirit of God in the human soul; and the visible proofs of this divine life, in the communion of saints and in all good words and works. Dogmatic controversies sometimes intervened, but they were transient, and hastily set aside for the one great purpose of "spreading holiness over these lands," as Wesley persistently professed.

This, in fine, is the true historical standpoint of Methodism. Its practical system, or "discipline," was rigorously conformed to this supreme purpose. Wesley did not devise his system; he adopted it, as, from time to time, its principal facts were evolved in the "movement;" that is to say, providentially suggested, as he believed. He long hoped that the Establishment, to which he was loyally attached, would be spiritually reformed, and its clergy become his colaborers. He was disappointed; he was excluded from its pulpits, and had to preach on the highways and in the market-places. His societies, springing up in all the country, and composed mostly of the poor, rescued from gross vice and degradation, needed instructors; he appointed some of his most capable laymen to read to them the Scriptures, and conduct their devotions in his absence, while he, night and day, traversed the land. One of these laymen, Thomas Maxwell, ventured sometimes to explain and apply his Scripture readings; the Countess of Huntingdon heard him, and encouraged him to "preach." Susannah Wesley, a chief counselor of her son for many years, admonished him not to oppose this innovation; to her, it appeared a providential indication of the only means which could meet the necessity of his Societies, now not only neglected by the national clergy, but repelled from their sacramental altars. Wesley had been a rigid churchman; he hesitated, and argued against this startling "irregularity;" but he was at last compelled to yield to the providential necessity, and thus arose that mighty lay ministry of Methodism whose voice has since been heard in most of the ends of the earth. The dignified reticence, the fastidious traditional prejudice, of the national clergy, thus led to the uprising of a ministerial host which has equaled them in pulpit talent, at least; overmatched them in influence among the people; surpassed them in appreciable usefulness, and led the way, the vanguard of Christian propagandism, before them in most of the foreign world.

ITS LAY MINISTRY.

The lay ministry is not only one of the greatest facts of Methodism; it is one of the grandest facts of modern ecclesiastical history. It was specially a provision for the New World. The era of transatlantic emigration was at hand. New states, as large as important European kingdoms, were about to spring up, as by magic, in the vast wildernesses of North America. A population, chiefly Anglo-Saxon, was to commence a sublime march, in a line extending from the Gulf of Mexico to beyond the great northern lakes, at an average westward advancement of fourteen miles a year, felling the primeval forests, opening highways, constructing canals and railroads, founding villages, towns, and cities, erecting schools, colleges, court-houses, and churches. The human race had never witnessed a scene of equal moral or political magnificence. But how could the customary tardy methods of ministerial training provide for the religious wants of this overwhelming population, rolling in upon the desert like billows of the rising tide upon the strand of the ocean? The great domains of the West must have been covered with immorality and barbarism, had no more immediate, no extemporary provision met this moral exigency. Providentially, the Methodistic "movement" began early enough to meet it; and the Methodist itinerant lay ministry actually laid the moral foundations of many of the mightiest states of the continent. Methodism became numerically the dominant faith of the country.

METHODISM IN AMERICA.

Whitefield extended the movement to the New World. Jonathan Edwards had prepared the way for him. Whitefield crossed the Atlantic thirteen times. He traversed the colonies from Georgia to Maine, awakening them as by the trumpet of the resurrection.* Before he descended into his American grave, Wesley's itinerants were on his track.

For more than half a century, John Wesley, in his ministerial travels, seemed ubiquitous throughout the United Kingdom. He crossed the Irish Channel forty-two times, making twenty-one visits to Ireland, and spending there about six years of his indefatigable life. In one of these visits, in 1758, he was surprised by the

* For an account of the extent and results of Whitefield's labors in America, see "The History of the Religious Movement of the Eighteenth Century, called Methodism," vol. i, *passim*, but particularly the last chapter.

discovery, in the midst of the native Celtic population, of a Teutonic settlement at Court Mattress and the neighboring villages of Killiheen, Ballygarrane, and Pallas. Whence came these people? They were descendants of Germans who had been expatriated by a terrible war from the Palatinate, on the Rhine. Having no pastors who could speak their own language, they had been half a century without religious instruction, and had sunk into incredible degradation. Drunkenness, profanity, Sabbath-breaking, had become almost universal among them. Wesley's itinerants had penetrated their settlements, and preached in their streets. They had been reclaimed, had built chapels for their families, and the great evangelist declared that "three such towns as Court Mattress, Killiheen, and Ballygarrane could hardly be found elsewhere in Ireland or England." There was "no profanity, no Sabbath-breaking, no drunkenness, no alehouse, in any of them." Their "diligence had turned all their land into a garden." One of their young men, with whom Wesley became acquainted, was afterward licensed as a local preacher.

In 1760 lay in a harbor of Ireland a ship whose decks were thronged with emigrants for America, one of whom stood at the bulwarks, taking leave in a religious discourse of a crowd of friends and spectators on the wharf. The passengers were "Palatine" Methodists, and the speaker was their young local preacher, Philip Embury. They settled in New York. Philip Embury became the recognized founder of Methodism in the United States. He preached at first in his own house, and formed there the first American Methodist society. Two years later he dedicated the first Methodist chapel on the continent.

ASBURY.

Wesley sent them two preachers from his English Conference of 1769; at the session of 1771 he announced that "the brethren in America still call aloud for help; who is willing to go?" Five responded, and two were sent. One of these was a young man who had formed himself by the severest ministerial regimen of Methodism; a man of vigorous frame, of few words, of quick and accurate insight, and of profound humility, not unmixed with occasional melancholy; a tireless traveler, an incessant preacher, a rigorous disciplinarian, but exemplifying himself all the severity he enjoined upon others. His soul was essentially heroic; he saw in the opening new world a field where he might labor and suffer for the Gospel, in a manner befitting his apostolic aspirations. He was not long in that field before his brethren spontaneously turned toward him as their providential leader. At the formal organization of American Methodism, as an independent Church, in 1784, he was, at the instance of Wesley, elected by his fellow-laborers their bishop. His ordination was the first Protestant consecration to the episcopal office in the new world.* For forty-five years he was now to traverse the country, mostly on horseback, from north to south, from east to west, following the trails of the Indians, convoyed sometimes by armed men, fording rivers, sleeping often on the ground, preaching daily, and leading on the hosts of his people and preachers with the authority and ability of a great captain. At his ordination they comprised less than fifteen thousand communicants, and about eighty preachers; he was to fall at last at the head of two hundred and eleven thousand communicants, and seven hundred traveling preachers. His ministerial travels were to exceed those of Wesley himself, being about six thousand miles a year; equal to the circumference of the globe every four years. During the forty-five years of his American ministry he was to average at least one sermon a day, to preside in two hundred and twenty-four annual conferences, and ordain more than four thousand

* Unless some of the small Moravian communities of America had previously ordained bishops.

preachers. He was to continue to travel and preach till his tottering frame had to be aided up the pulpit stairs; till he could no longer stand, but had to sit while addressing the wondering throngs that hung upon his words. Such was Francis Asbury, bishop of the Methodist Episcopal Church, by the imposition of whose hands Nathan Bangs was to be ordained to the Christian ministry. The authority of no man since the apostolic age could more legitimately consecrate the young preacher to his high office.

GREAT SUCCESS — CANADA.

With such a man at the head of the new denomination, it could not fail of success; it broke out on the right and on the left; scores, hundreds of "itinerants," many of them the "giants of those days," entered its militant ministry. The example of their episcopal leader vindicated the severity of their work and their sufferings, and rendered both heroic. They courageously went wherever he sent them, and the post of most danger or hardship was the post of most honor. By the present period of our narrative, 1801, they were traveling as far south as Georgia, as far north as Canada, as far east as Maine, and as far west as the Mississippi. The "old Western Conference" was already organized, the only conference then beyond the Alleghanies; it was soon to extend from Detroit to Natchez; the great frontier battle-ground of Methodism, where Cartwright, Finley, Young, Blakeman, Winans, Larkin, Quinn, and other giant men, now or soon after, bore forward the cross in the van of emigration, traveling vast circuits, on some parts of which they had to be protected from the savages by armed escorts. The denomination reported now more than seventy thousand communicants and more than three hundred preachers. Canada was already a Methodist district. In 1790 William Losee, a member of the New York Conference, penetrated through the western wilds of the state, enduring great hardships, and crossed Lake Ontario to Kingston.* He is usually supposed to have formed the first Canadian Methodist Society.† He was joined the next year by Darius Dunham, and two circuits were formed, reporting at the ensuing conference one hundred and sixty-five members. Canada reported five circuits in 1801. The following year the name of Nathan Bangs appeared in the brief catalogue of ten self-sacrificing men who were traveling the remote and vast region, he having traveled the preceding year "under the presiding elder." During six years he is still to brave its inclement climate and privations, laboring from its most western settlements down to Montreal and Quebec. There were now about eleven hundred and sixty Methodists scattered through the Province, but without a single place of worship entitled to the name of church

* Bangs's History says 1791. See, however, letter of Rev. Anson Green, March 2, 1860, in the (Canada) Christian Guardian: "Losee formed the first class at Adolphusville in 1790; the second at Earnest-town, on the Bay Shore, (date uncertain;) the third on the 2d of March, 1791, near Napanee."

† In Canada, however, as in many other parts of the globe, Methodism was first introduced by a local preacher. A Mr. Neel, from the United States, preached before Losee's arrival, at Queenstown. Bangs, in the History of the Methodist Episcopal Church, (vol. ii, page 122, note,) says: "He was a holy man of God, and an able minister of the New Testament. His word was blessed to the awakening and conversion of many souls, and he was always spoken of by the people with great affection and veneration as the pioneer of Methodism in that country. Among those who first joined the Society may be mentioned *Christian Warner*, who lived near what is now called St. David's. He became a class-leader, and his house was a home for the preachers and for preaching for many years. He was considered a father in Israel by all who knew him. The first Methodist meeting-house erected in that part of the country was in his neighborhood." Cotemporaneous with, if not before Neel's labors, members of the families of Embury and Heck, the founders of Methodism in New York, introdueed it into Canada. A letter dated Frankford, (Canada,) Feb. 25, 1860, says: "The first period of Methodism in Canada may be assigned to the years from the settling of the Hecks and Embury in Augusta, until the arrival of the first itinerant, thirteen years, or from 1778 to 1791. [See note above.] The second period may be considered from the itinerancy of Losee in 1791 to the beginning of the war in 1812."

or chapel. He was to leave them more than doubled in number, (2,360,) and with that supply of chapels begun which has since dotted most of the country; and he was to live to see Methodism numerically the strongest form of Protestantism in British North America, except the national Church.

EARLY CANADIAN ITINERANTS.

The saintly and chivalric itinerants with whom he was associated in Canada were ever afterward dear to his memory. They formed his character as a Methodist preacher; he delighted to speak of them in his latter years as the champions of the cross in those borean regions, transcending in labors if not in sufferings the early French missionaries, who had preceded them in the same field. He alludes to them often, and with glowing language, in his History of Methodism. We have already met with the name of James Coleman, an itinerant, who, the historian records, bore for some time the scar of a blow on the forehead, struck by a persecutor in whose cabin he was uttering words of comfort to an awakened soul. Of Hezekiah Calvin Wooster he speaks with emphasis. "His name is 'like ointment poured forth' to many in that country, and he used to be spoken of as an extraordinary messenger of God, sent to declare his counsels. After exerting all his powers of body and mind in beseeching sinners to be reconciled to God, he returned home with the fatal consumption fastened upon his lungs. But even while in this feeble state, so reduced as not to be able to speak above a whisper, this whisper, being announced to the congregation by another, was frequently attended by such a divine energy and unction that sinners would tremble and fall under the announcement. It is said indeed that his very countenance exhibited such reflections of the divine glory, that it struck conviction into the hearts of many who beheld it. 'Behold how great a matter a little fire kindleth:' though Hezekiah Calvin Wooster could not be regarded as a man of more than ordinary talents as a preacher, yet such was the holy fervor of his spirit, his deep devotion to God, his burning love for the souls of his fellow-men, that he was the instrument of kindling up such a fire in the hearts of the people, where-ever he went, particularly in Upper Canada, that all the waters of strife and opposition have not been able to quench it. This testimony I consider due to such departed worth. The grace of God wrought mightily in him, and great was his glorying in the cross of Christ; nor did he glory in aught else, for he was as much distinguished for his humility, his deadness to self and to applause, as he was for the fervor of his spirit, the strength of his faith, and the boldness and pointedness of his appeals to the consciences of the people."

In 1796 Wooster volunteered, with Samuel Coate, to join the few Methodist pioneers beyond the Canada line. His history during that expedition would form a romantic and almost incredible narrative. Three weeks were spent on their route, during which they lodged every night under the trees of the forest. He traveled about three years in Canada, preaching almost daily, and with a power seldom equaled in the history of the Christian ministry. There was, indeed, an energy in his words quite irresistible. The dwellers in the wilderness, long destitute of the means of religion, heard with amazement his simple but overwhelming eloquence, and often fell, in their forest congregations, like dead men, under his ministrations. "O what awful sensations," exclaims Dr. Bangs, "ran through the assemblies while Calvin Wooster and others of like spirit were denouncing the just judgments of God against impenitent sinners, in such pointed language as made the 'ear to tingle' and the heart to palpitate!" He was a man of Abrahamic faith, and his prayers seemed directly to enter heaven and prevail with God. He maintained an unceasing spirit of prayer. Often at midnight would he rise to pray, while the inmates of the house where he made his temporary abode were awed by the solemn voice of his supplications ascending amid the silence. Such was the unction of his spirit, and the power of his appeals to the wicked, that few of them could stand before him; they would either rush out of the assembly or fall to the floor.

"Nor was he alone in this respect. The other preachers caught the flame, and were carried forward under its sacred impulses in their Master's work. Many instances of the manifestations of divine power and grace might be narrated, which illustrate the authority by which these men of God preached, one of which I will relate. At a quarterly meeting in the Bay of Quinte circuit, as the preacher began his sermon, a thoughtless young man in the front gallery commenced, in a playful mood, to swear profanely, and otherwise to disturb the congregation. The preacher paid no attention to him until he was in the middle of his sermon, when, feeling strong in the Lord and in the power of his might, suddenly stopping, he fixed his piercing eye upon the profane man, and pointing his finger at him with great energy, cried out, '*My God, smite him!*' He instantly fell, as if shot through the heart with a bullet. At this moment, such a divine afflatus came down upon the congregation that sinners were crying to God for mercy in every direction, while the saints of God burst forth in loud praises to his name. Similar instances of God's gracious presence were not uncommon in those days in that country. Indeed, this great work may be said to have been in some sense the beginning of that revival of religion which soon after spread through various parts of the United States."

William Anson, another of Nathan Bangs's colaborers, was also one of the mighty men of those days. He continued two years beyond the line, and afterward traveled circuits in New York and New England; he returned to Canada, and then served again in the states, as presiding elder. One of his districts extended from Rhinebeck, New York, to New Haven, Connecticut. "He had his full share of hardships," says the obituary of the Minutes, "but never flinched."

Seth Crowell was another of the early Canadian itinerants. He joined the Church in Connecticut, entered the New York Conference in 1801, and offered himself immediately as a volunteer for Canada, where he spent two years. Dr. Bangs says, "He was a young preacher of great zeal, and of the most indefatigable industry, and going into that country, he soon caught the flame of divine love which had been enkindled by the instrumentality of Wooster, Coate, and Dunham. He entered into the work with great energy and perseverance, and God blessed his labors with much success. So greatly had God prospered the labors of his faithful servants in this province, that there were returned, in the Minutes of Conference for the year 1801, 1,159 members of the Church. It had indeed extended into the lower province, on the Ottawa River, an English settlement about fifty miles west of Montreal." He possessed superior talents, "and," say his brethren, in the Conference Minutes, "was often heard to speak in demonstration of the Spirit and power, and was instrumental in the conversion of many souls."

Dr. Bangs thus summarily refers to his colaborers in this distant field, in the year 1801: "In Upper Canada, the glorious revival extended up the shore of Lake Ontario, even to the head of the lake and to Niagara, and thence to Long Point, on the northwestern shore of Lake Erie, including four large four weeks' circuits. The district this year was under the charge of the Rev. Joseph Jewell, who traveled extensively through the newly-settled country, preaching in log-houses, in barns, and sometimes in groves, and everywhere beholding the displays of the power and grace of God in the awakening and conversion of sinners, as well as the sanctification of believers. A great work of God was carried on this year under the preaching of Joseph Sawyer, whose faithful labors on the Niagara circuit will be long and gratefully remembered by the people in that country; and it was during this revival that the present writer, after four or five years of hard struggling under a consciousness of his sinfulness, was brought into the fold of Christ. And here he wishes to record his gratitude to God for his distinguished grace in snatching such a brand from the fire, and to his people for their kindness, and more especially to that servant of God, the Rev. Joseph Sawyer, under whose pastoral oversight he was brought into the Church. Nor should the labors and privations, the prayers and sufferings in the cause of Christ, of that faithful servant of God, the Rev. James Coleman, be forgotten. He preceded Mr. Sawyer in the Niagara circuit, and was beloved by the people of God for his fidelity in the work of the ministry, and for his deep devotion to their spiritual interests, evinced by his faithful attention to the arduous duties of his circuit. He had many seals to his ministry, and the writer of this remembers with gratitude the many prayers which James Coleman offered up to God in his behalf, while a youthful stranger in that land, and while seeking, with his eyes but half opened, to find the way of peace."

"The work also prevailed on the Bay of Quinte and Oswegatchie circuits, under the labors of Sylvanus Keeler, Seth Crowell, and others. Like the new settlements in the western country, Upper Canada was at that time but sparsely populated, so that in riding from one appointment to another the preachers sometimes had to pass through wildernesses from ten to sixty miles, and not unfrequently had either to encamp in the woods or sleep in Indian huts. And sometimes, in visiting the newly settled places, they have carried provender for their horses over night, when they would tie them to a tree to prevent their straying in the woods; while the preachers themselves had to preach, eat, and lodge in the same room, the curling smoke ascending through an opening in the roof of the log-house, which had not yet the convenience of even a chimney."

"But in the midst of these labors and privations, they were abundantly compensated in beholding the blessed effects of their evangelical efforts, and the cordiality and gratification with which they were received, more especially by those whose hearts God had touched by his Spirit. For though these people were in the wilderness, and many of them poor, they seemed to be ripe for the Gospel, and it was no less gratifying to its messengers than to its recipients to behold its blessed effects upon the hearts and lives of such as 'believed with a heart unto righteousness.' While they who resisted the truth often manifested their enmity by persecuting those who proclaimed it, such as did 'receive it in the love of it' evinced their affection and gratitude to its preachers by making them welcome to their habitations and entertaining them in the very best manner they could. For the self-denying labors and sacrifices of these early Methodist preachers, thousands of immortal beings in Canada will doubtless praise God in that day 'when he shall come to make up his jewels.'"

Such was Methodism—such its introduction into the United States and its extension to Canada—such the men and scenes of its early history in the latter country, among which young Bangs entered the "itinerancy." We have seen him setting out, with his horse and saddle-bags; let us now follow him in his route through the wilderness. There are noteworthy adventures, trials, and triumphs awaiting him.

CHAPTER VII.

MINISTERIAL LIFE IN CANADA.

LUTHER includes temptations among the means necessary for the training of a successful preacher. Dr. Bangs had this training thoroughly in the early years of his itinerancy on the Canadian frontier. He was appointed to the Niagara circuit, with William Anson, under the presidency of Joseph Sawyer. It had been a two weeks' circuit, but was now so enlarged as to require six weeks' travel, with daily preaching, to supply its numerous appointments. "It extended," he says, "from the head of Lake Ontario over the Grand River, and comprehended all that part of the country, known as Long Point, which juts into Lake Erie. On the banks of the Grand River the Mohawk Indians were settled. They were in a most degraded state, as the missionary, a clergyman of the Church of England, preached to them only on the Sabbath, and then spent his time in drinking ardent spirits, playing cards, and horse-racing. Our preachers tried to preach to them a few times, but without any success.

"The settlements in this country were new, the roads bad, and the fare very hard; but God was with us in much mercy, awakening and converting sinners, and this was abundant compensation for all our toils. In some places a strong tide of prejudice set in against us, and was extremely difficult to resist. Often while traversing those lonely plains and solitary woods did I call to mind the pleasant hours I had spent among my brethren, with whom I first united in Christian fellowship under better auspices.

"On this circuit I continued until December 1, 1801, when that part of it called Long Point was detached, and I set off to travel this alone. There were but two small societies in all this new field. They were made up chiefly of immigrants from New Jersey. In one of them was a local preacher of considerable talents and piety, who was useful in keeping the societies together. As I was to labor alone, my constant prayer to God was that he would give me seals to my ministry as evidence that he had called me to the work. After passing through several little settlements, in which I stopped and preached, I came to the town of Burford, a settlement on the Grand River, about ten miles north of the Mohawk Indian village. Here seemed to be a frank and generous people, and they received me with affection and respect, and listened to the Word with apparent eagerness. While I was with them I heard of a settlement about twenty-five miles distant, in the town of Oxford, where they were anxious to hear the Gospel. Accordingly I set off to pay them a visit. It being the beginning of winter, the ground partly frozen, the mud deep, and the road, if such it could be called, running through a wilderness, though I made all the speed I could, I traveled only about fourteen miles that day. I put up at a small log-hut with a family that had been educated as Baptists. I was treated with hospitality, but they seemed to have little sense of religion. The next day I reached the settlement and lodged with Major Ingersoll, to whom I had a letter of introduction from Captain Mallory, of Burford. I was received with cordiality, and treated with great respect. I preached three times here, and under the two last sermons many were awakened to a sense of their lost condition, and afterward converted."

A SIGNIFICANT DREAM.

This beginning of success lifted a weight from his diffident spirit. Before it occurred he had given way to despair, under a "temptation of the devil," as he believed. Seeing no immediate effect of his labors, he had begun to doubt his call to the ministry, and had resolved to return home and give up his "license." He had actually mounted his horse and was retracing his course, when, arriving at the Grand River, he found that a "January thaw" had so broken up the ice as to render it impossible for him to cross, whether by a boat or on the ice itself. Thus providentially arrested, he returned despondent and confounded. A significant dream relieved him. He thought he was working with a pickax on the top of a basaltic rock. His muscular arm brought down stroke after stroke for hours; but the rock was hardly indented. He said to himself at last, "It is useless; I will pick no more." Suddenly a stranger of dignified mien stood by his side and spoke to him. "You will pick no more?" "No." "Were you not set to this task?" "Yes." "And why abandon it?" "My work is vain; I make no impression on the rock." Solemnly the stranger replied, "What is that to you? Your duty is to pick, whether the rock yields or not. Your work is in your own hands; the result is not. Work on!" He resumed his task. The first blow was given with almost superhuman force, and the rock flew into a thousand pieces. He awoke, pursued his way back to Burford with fresh zeal and energy, and a great revival followed. From that day he never had even a "temptation" to give up his commission.

A CONVERSION ON HORSEBACK.

"I had been laboring," he says, "without any apparent success for some time. I at length reached Burford, preached on Thursday evening, and appointed a meeting on Sabbath morning at ten o'clock. At that time I addressed the people on the parable of the sower and his seed, and I spoke strong words, thinking meanwhile, This will either 'kill or cure.' A small society had been formed there, but not one of its members professed religion. They had only joined together to maintain preaching in the place. After the sermon Captain Mallory came to me much agitated, and uttered some despondent words about 'giving up.' Alas! thought I, I have killed you all. However, he invited me to dine with him, which I did, and talked with him as encouragingly as possible. I had appointed a meeting for exhortation and prayer in the evening, although there was not a soul among them that dared to pray openly besides myself. They sang a while; I then gave them an exhortation and prayed with them."

He observed, after the prayer, that his friend Captain Mallory sat with his head inclined upon a table, in much agitation, and, accosting him, received the reply, "I am alarmed for my soul; I am afraid that God will never have mercy upon me. Pray, O, pray for me!" "I will," said the preacher, "if you will kneel down." "Down he went, and the whole congregation with him. I prayed for him by name. Soon the meeting closed, the people dispersed, and I went to bed. Early next morning a young man by the name of Matthews came into my room before I was up, and with tears in his eyes began a surprising narrative. He said: 'After we left the meeting, Captain Mallory and I walked and talked together until nearly midnight, and parted fearing we should both be lost forever. I went home and to bed, but could not sleep. Suddenly a voice seemed to say to me, "Arise and pray." I replied, "I cannot." A second time "Arise and pray" sounded in my soul, and a third time. I arose, knelt down, and began to pray. Very soon it appeared as if my room was filled with the glory of the Lord, and my soul was pervaded with peace and joy unspeakable.'

'Go,' said I, 'and tell Captain Mallory what the Lord has done for you; and as soon as I have breakfasted I will go over and see him.' I went to Mallory's home, and found him walking the floor and wringing his hands as in an agony. He said to me, 'Sir, what would become of me were I to die in this situation?' 'You would be lost,' said I; 'but you need not be. If you look to God by faith in Christ he will save you, and he is ready to save you now. Look up.'

"He and Matthews had agreed to accompany me that day to a new appointment about eight or ten miles distant, and I requested him to get ready to go. He replied, 'I cannot; I feel so wretched.' 'You must go,' said I, 'for I am a stranger, and know not the way.' He finally saddled his horse, and we set off, he riding on one side of me and Matthews on the other. We had not gone more than forty rods before he leaned forward upon his horse's neck, and said, 'Pray for me, for I feel as if I should sink.' 'I'll pray for you,' said I; 'look by faith to God, and he will save you.' It seemed, indeed, as if the glory of God was all around me, and his love filling my heart. Not more than five minutes afterward the Lord converted his soul on his horse; he praised God aloud, and we then went on our way rejoicing.

THE ROCK SPLIT.

"In Oxford, Major Ingersoll, to whom I was first introduced, was a Universalist; and he told me, on my first visit, that he was an unbeliever in the doctrine of depravity; that he never had himself a depraved heart. 'This assertion,' said I, 'is a sure sign that you never knew your heart.' On my second visit, I found him sitting in his chair, with his head inclined on his hands. He looked up to me, and said, 'O, what a depraved heart I have!' 'Ay!' said I; 'have you discovered that fact at last?' 'Yes, indeed,' he replied; 'what shall I do to be saved?' 'Surrender it up to God by faith in Christ, and he will give you a new heart, and renew a right spirit within you." He did so, and found the promise verified. He, his wife, who was a very sensible and amiable woman, his two daughters, together with the husband of one of them, were soon converted and joined the Church; and the good work quickly spread through the neighborhood, sweeping all before it.* In this way the revival prevailed in both of these places, so that large and flourishing societies were established, and no less than six preachers were raised up; one of whom, by the name of Reynolds, became a bishop in the Methodist Episcopal Church of Canada.

"Thus the rock was split. The reformation extended through many settlements, particularly Oxford, where large numbers were 'turned from darkness to light.'"

Of course opposition was provoked by this prosperity. Slanderous reports against the Methodists were circulated. In some places violent hostility was attempted against their meetings. The young itinerant needed also still further training by temptation, in accordance with Luther's maxim.

LACKINGTON'S MEMOIRS.

"Behold how great a matter a little fire kindleth!" A small book, written beyond the ocean, by an apostate

* More than thirty years later Dr. Bangs, while traveling through the state of New York, wrote in a private letter, now before me:

"On my way in the canal boat a young preacher introduced himself to me, and asked if I remembered one Hitchcock, who lived in the town of Oxford, in Upper Canada, about thirty-four years ago. I replied, 'Yes, very well.' 'I am,' said he, 'his son.' His father and mother were converted under my ministry on the first circuit I ever traveled, and were soon after married together, and here was their son, a minister! This circumstance brought a thousand pleasant recollections to my mind, and made me thank God and take courage. The grandfather of this youth was a Universalist, a Major Ingersoll, to whom I had a letter of introduction in a new place where I went to preach. Himself, wife, and two of his daughters, were soon converted and joined our Church; and now, here is one of the third generation in the itinerant field! I thought I should pray and preach with greater fervor than ever."

Methodist, became a serious obstruction to this good work in the far-off regions of Canada, and, for a season, threatened to arrest forever the career of this man, destined to become one of the most eminent laborers of American Protestantism. "An enemy," he says, "introduced Lackington's Memoirs among us, and it passed from house to house, from hand to hand, counteracting our labors." Lackington, a poor but enterprising young man, had joined Wesley's Society in London. Wesley established a fund for the aid of Christian young men in the beginning of their business. By its assistance Lackington became a noted bookseller; he grew opulent, and rode in his own carriage. He claimed the distinction of introducing the era of "cheap publishing" in England, though that honor belongs to Wesley himself. Lackington, however, deserves credit as a chief promoter of cheap and popular publications, and he ranks with Dunton and Dodsley among the famous typographers and bibliopoles of English literature. He was a diligent but cursory reader, and, by deistical books, was led to abandon his brethren, and to become an avowed infidel. He published his noted "Memoirs," in which he attributes his early religious impressions, and all Methodist "revivals," to morbid excitement of the imagination. He inserted in it prurient love-letters, said to have been written by Wesley in his eighty-first year. These letters he afterward ascertained and acknowledged to be forgeries. Their author himself at last confessed, over his own signature and in deep remorse, that they were forgeries. Lackington repented, rejoined his Methodist brethren, built them a chapel on his country estate, published his "Confessions," and died in the faith.* The first of these books, however, was alone circulated at

* See History of the Religious Movement, etc., called Methodism. Vol. ii, page 376, *note*. Both books are still classed among the "Curiosities of Literature," and are favorites with bibliomaniacs. The best edition of "The Memoirs" is that of Whitaker and Arnot, London, 1830. It gives in an appendix a large part of the "Confessions."

this time in Canada, and the Methodists knew not the real history of its author. They were stunned at first by its plausible impeachments; their inexperienced preacher was unable to refute them as matters of fact, and sunk into despair under their influence on his own mind.

A SEVERE TRIAL.

To him it was now "the hour and power of darkness." His nervous system had suffered; his labors and excitements had exhausted him; he was "thin and pallid," and in a physical condition for morbid impressions. Nor had he yet learned by experience that excessive excitation on religious, as on any other subjects, must, by a physiological law, be attended with reaction. After reading the Memoir he departed on horseback for his next appointment. Though he had hitherto been able to maintain a vivid sense of religious enjoyment, his heart sank within him on his solitary route. Doubts, as by preternatural agency, crowded around his mind, and enveloped him in utter darkness. He was tempted to believe that he had erred in the excitement which his labors had produced among the people, though he saw that their lives were reformed. He resolved to preach differently, and to conduct his public meetings with more moderation. The resolution, however, soon struck him with dismay; he sank, confounded, deeper and deeper into the abyss of darkness, and began to fear that his own spiritual experience had been a delusion. Stopping for the night in a Christian family, he quite failed in the domestic prayer with which he closed the evening. He retired to his bed in indescribable distress. His sleep was troubled, he says, with "awful alarms;" he dreamed that a throng of demons stared at him. "When I saw them I exclaimed, I will not fear you, I know where to go for help, and began immediately to pray; but my prayers seemed like vapor, or words without meaning. I had no access to God. I ceased praying, and the phantoms drew closer around me. I began again to pray, but with the like effect. When I again ceased, the demons rushed at me with increased violence, and I awoke in intense agony. I could no longer rest in my bed, but instantly arose and fell on my knees, but, alas! the heavens seemed to be brass over my head. I sank into despair. I went down stairs. The woman of the house, who was a most amiable Christian, asked me what was the matter, for she perceived my agitation. Not being willing to trouble her mind with a recital of my distress, I evaded for some time a direct answer, but at last said, 'I believe there is no mercy for me.' I spent the night without sleep, sometimes lying on the floor, at others attempting to pray, but without success or hope of deliverance from my anguish. Such torment I am sure I could not have endured for many days; I thought that the lost could experience no greater misery. Frequently was I tempted to open my mouth in blasphemy against God, and to curse the Saviour of men. Which way to look for relief I knew not, for I thought God had deserted me, and I now believe that he gave me up to the buffetings of the adversary of souls for my trial, but so far restrained his malice as not to permit him to destroy me." On the ensuing Sabbath he had two appointments to preach. He went to them in deep anguish. While addressing the people his heart was "filled with horrors." "No one but God," he says, "or such as have had like trials, can conceive of my wretchedness. I could hardly stand up; I felt that I ought not to preach, being, as I feared, lost forever." After the service he appealed to an old local preacher, who was present, for counsel; but the good man could not comprehend the case, and left him more desolate than ever. The thought occurred to his own mind, however, that God was leaving him temporarily to his own weakness, to test him and teach him profitable lessons. This gave him a dim hope "that he would sooner or later deliver" him. He attempted to preach again the next day, but "stood before the people, trembling with despair." Soon after he met an "old experienced exhorter," who gave him some hopeful counsels, but could give him no effectual relief.

To most godless men this morbid anatomization is repulsive; to many good men of healthful temperament it is a mystery, or mysticism. Like morbid anatomy, however, it has its scientific importance, and I am bound to relate the actual facts of the case. There is much truth in "muscular Christianity," and a great deal of divinity in physiology. The physical constitution of man is an essential condition of his probationary life; and these painful experiences have had, in all ages, an historical, if not an essential connection with the moral development of the human soul. Whether essential or accidental in this instance, they soon passed away; and this tried soul came out of its eclipse brightly and serenely, with vigorous, and even robust powers, for a long life of healthful and manly endeavors.

DELIVERANCE—CURIOUS DREAM.

"On the next day," he says, "I returned to the place where I was first seized with this horror, and having a prayer-meeting appointed, I kneeled down and prayed for deliverance. God appeared in gracious power, dispelling the clouds which hung over my mind, removing my doubts and fears, and shining upon my soul with the brightness of his reconciled countenance. All within me rejoiced in God my Saviour. Never was the 'cooling water brook' more refreshing to a thirsty man than Christ was now to my panting heart." He returned the following day to Burford, where Lackington's Memoir, the proximate occasion of his trouble, was first circulated. He entered the house of a family which had been educated as Baptists, but all of whom had recently joined the Methodist Society. As he took a chair at the hearth, his host began to relate a curious, if not ludicrous dream, which he lately had respecting the welcomed visitor. He dreamed that the latter and a venerated old friend, a Baptist clergyman, sat with him in his cottage conversing, when suddenly the itinerant began to be strangely transformed, taking a spiral shape, and diminishing to so small a size as to occupy a space of but three or four inches; he would have smiled had not the itinerant, meanwhile, appeared to be in excruciating torture. Turning to the aged Baptist, he asked what the singular metamorphosis could mean. "God is trying him," was the reply, "for thus the Lord tries all his special servants." "Is he then, indeed, one of God's special servants?" rejoined the host. "Yes," responded the Baptist, "and if you will keep your eye upon him you will see him rise again to his full stature." Directly the prediction began to be verified; the spiral form rose, and the "special servant of God" stood forth "more erect, more fresh and fair than ever before." On hearing this dream the tried evangelist related to his host, with throbbing heart, the terrible ordeal through which he had passed; "and," he writes, "we rejoiced together for the consolation of our God."

Whatever importance may be given to these incidents, his own reflections upon them, written more than half a century later, will be read with interest. He says: "I have been thus particular in relating this severe conflict, its causes, progress, and results, that if any who may read of it should be exposed to similar temptations, they may know that others have had the same terrible trial; that 'there is no temptation but what is common to man,' and that God will 'with the temptation make a way of escape,' and therefore they need not 'think it strange concerning the fiery trial, as though some strange thing had happened unto them.' Another design is to guard young disciples against reading books which are written to disparage experimental religion, under the pretense that they do not attack religion itself, but only hypocrisy or fanaticism. This was the case with Lackington; his subtle poison was well prepared to pervert the minds of unwary Christians, though his book is full of proofs of his own depraved heart and purpose."

CONSOLATION.

He continues: "This storm having passed over, I went on my way rejoicing, and the Lord continued to work powerfully among the people. In riding through the woods, I had a place where I used to stop for prayer, and my horse became so accustomed to it that whenever he arrived near the spot he would turn toward it and stop, as if he knew it and the reason of my dismounting. This was often a Bethel to my soul. Occasionally my temptations would return upon me with great violence; but God gave me power in prayer and faith to resist and conquer them, for which I praised him with a joyful heart. One cold day, while riding through the woods, I was deeply disturbed with thoughts of my loneliness and destitution, for my pecuniary means were about exhausted; my salary was next to nothing; I could see no means for my future wants; I lived from house to house, from settlement to settlement, and the future seemed dreary and forlorn. Here was another temptation by which my mind was greatly perplexed; when, taking out my hymn book from my pocket, my eyes fell upon those words,

"'Peace, troubled soul, thou needst not fear;
Thy great Provider still is near;
Who fed thee last, will feed thee still:
Be calm, and sink into his will.'

"As I read them, such a sudden glow of joy filled and overflowed my soul that I praised God aloud, and I rode on, triumphing in his goodness to me and to all men."

AN EFFECTIVE REBUKE.

His deliverance from these trials inspired him with confidence, and even with "humble boldness." He preached with increased power. His word was like a trumpet sounding through the wilderness. He rebuked gainsayers courageously, and they often cowered before his appeals. A profane "Universalist" accosted him rudely; "after conversing with him some time, with no effect," he writes, "I rebuked him in the name of the Lord, and admonished him that unless he ceased his profanity and turned to God with repentance, he would sink into perdition when he died. This enraged him, and he shook his fist in my face, saying it was too much for him to bear. I told him that I feared him not, and urged my exhortation that he would repent of his sins, before they might prove his ruin, saying, 'Do you think I am afraid of you, you poor child of the devil? You have no power to strike me, and therefore away with your fist, and humble yourself before God, "if perhaps the thought of thy heart may be forgiven thee."' The enraged man was awe-struck; he became immediately calm, and went away, promising to amend, and to pray to God for forgiveness."

A GAINSAYER CAUGHT.

Like St. Paul, he occasionally attempted to catch some by guile. "On some of my early visits to Oxford," he says, "I preached at a public house, where, among others who annoyed us, was a thoughtless young man by the name of Rogers, who was given to all manner of nonsense, making amusement of everything serious. I talked with him privately, but without effect. One day I was dining in company with a number of gentlemen, and him among the rest. He kept up, as usual, his jests and pleasantries about religion, when suddenly a thought struck me by which I could fix him in 'a tight place.' Accordingly, after dinner, when we arose from the table to return thanks, I said, 'Mr. Rogers, will you have the goodness to return thanks to God for his bounties to us here today?' We all stood in silence for some minutes, when he, with confusion, said, 'Sir, I beg to be excused;' and I returned thanks. This appeared to sober him somewhat, but I saw no material change in him for that season. About three years later, while traveling as a missionary on the River Thames, a messenger came after me to visit a man who was very sick. I mounted my horse, and rode several miles to see him. As I approached the gate before the house the invalid came tottering out, looking extremely emaciated, and with tears streaming down his wan cheeks. He gave me his hand, exclaiming, 'O, sir, how glad I am to see you! God only knows what I have suffered for want of you during my sickness. As soon as I heard of your being in this country I sent for you, that I might ask your forgiveness.' 'Why,' replied I, 'what have you done to me, that you need ask my pardon?' 'O,' said he, 'do you not recollect how I treated you at Oxford, and do you not remember asking me to give thanks at the dinner-table? That rebuke went to my heart, and produced an impression which never left me till God relieved it by his saving grace. Can you forgive me?' 'I have nothing against you,' I replied; 'I knew you were a thoughtless sinner, and hoped you would sooner or later see the error of your ways. Has God forgiven you?' 'Yes,' he responded, 'I believe he has; and now that I have seen you and obtained your pardon, I can die in peace.'" They kneeled together in prayer and praise, and parted hoping to meet again in heaven.

FATE OF AN OPPOSER.

A more serious fate attended some of his opposers. The "Christian Guardian" (Canada) relates the following example: "Dr. Bangs was the first Methodist or Christian minister who entered the new settlement of Colchester with the message of salvation. In the settlement was a man named W., whose house was freely opened for the purposes of public worship, and there the doctor opened his commission. He preached a few times, invariably leaving an appointment for a future time. He bore his testimony against all sin, and doubtless in particular against that of intoxication. Satan could not yield the control of his adherents without a struggle, and he never lacks agents to carry out his unholy designs. W., though he had opened his house for the preaching of the Gospel, was not a pious man; but strong hopes were entertained that he might become such. Several other persons were his companions in sin, and some among them much more determined and scheming in evil than himself. They began to think if the preacher should be permitted to go on as he had begun their jovialty would soon come to an end. What was to be done? Some plan must be devised at once to prevent it. It was determined that they should collect together at the house of W. at the next appointment, and that he, who was to be a party to the scheme, should turn the itinerant out of his house and require him not to return. W. readily concurred in the design. To prepare for this unholy work, they met together some time before the appointed hour, and probably brought themselves up to the required point of courage by sundry potations of whisky. As it had been noised abroad that this was to be the last visit of the minister of God, a much more numerous assemblage than usual had taken place in order to witness the sport. On the arrival of the preacher he expressed his gratification to see so many together, and doubtless deemed it an omen of good. But, alas! he was soon to be undeceived. He was permitted to enter the house, and make various preparations for the worship he anticipated he was about to lead. At this juncture W. arose, and taking him by the shoulders, marched him to the door, and then stated that he was not to preach in his house again, and that it was the determination of the neighborhood that he should visit them no more. The announcement of W. was received with universal approbation and a shout of joy. And no doubt fiends in hell raised a shout of applause. The devil had accomplished his end in using W. in ejecting from the neighborhood the Gospel messenger, and rejecting therewith the offer of salvation.

"This, however, was but the beginning. In the presence of all the people, the rejected minister of Christ, in the most solemn manner, followed the directions of the Saviour. Taking a handkerchief from his pocket, and raising first one foot and then the other, he wiped the dust from the soles of his shoes, which they had collected on the ground of W., declaring at the same time he did it as a testimony against them for refusing the message of salvation. This announcement was received with a shout of derision, and the itinerant took his departure from the dwelling, which was never again to be entered by the messenger of saving mercy. As the settlement was then distant from any other, and could only be reached by great effort, the door also being closed against him, it came not in the order of Providence for Mr. Bangs again to visit that community.

"From the time that W. had been guilty of this outrage, prosperity and comfort seemed to forsake his habitation. One untoward event after another occurred until he was a complete wreck, morally, mentally, socially, physically, as well as in his secular affairs. The demon of discontent was already in his abode. Another demon, as a seducer, induced his wife to forsake her family and the home of her husband, and wander into some part of the United States, from whence she never returned. One misfortune followed another until, in the course of a few years, all his property was squandered, and he, wrecked by disease and suffering, was dependent on charity for his daily support. This was little compared with the mental agony he was subjected to in consequence of the gnawings of a guilty conscience for having rejected the Gospel messenger.

"Some years afterward, W., a decrepit and miserable old man, was laid on a sick-bed, which eventually proved to be the bed of death. Suffering and trial had been his lot, and now he who once had been prosperous, and bid fair for a happy and useful life, was dependent on the bounty of others for a morsel of bread and a grave. The Rev. Horace Dean, then being stationed in that part of the province, was called upon to give him spiritual counsel, and lead his heart in prayer to that God whose servant he had turned from his door. But both mental and moral vision seemed to be beclouded. No impression could be produced on his heart, and he died in a state of stolid indifference. The occasion of his death was improved, as a warning to others, by the minister who gave me the narrative.

"The late Rev. William Case succeeded Dr. Bangs in that extensive field of labor, and was the honored instrument of again introducing Methodism into the same community, and forming the first society, where many became holy, happy, and useful Christians."

To his many other trials was added, about the conclusion of his service on this circuit, a severe attack of intermittent fever; he was confined to his bed for weeks, and about two months elapsed before he could resume his travels. At last, though extremely feeble, and reduced almost to a skeleton, he mounted his horse and departed for another circuit. He had been thoroughly tested; he had triumphed; the rock seen in his dream had been shivered; further trials awaited him, but his course henceforth was irreversibly determined.

CHAPTER VIII.

ANSWERS TO PRAYER.

"It was," he writes, "with no little reluctance that I parted from my friends on this circuit, particularly from those in Burford, with whom I had formed a close intimacy. They were the first-fruits of my ministry, and there had grown up between us a relation of indescribable affection, so that I could say of them as St. Paul said of the Philippians, 'Ye are my crown of rejoicing.' They had treated me with the tenderest kindness, had attended me in my sickness, had sympathized with me in all my afflictions, and had rejoiced with me in my joys in the Lord. But the time was come for my departure according to the rules of our Church Discipline. I went down among my friends on the Niagara circuit for a season. There I was received with much cordiality. My fever returning occasionally, I was not able to labor much. It unnerved my mind at times. On September 2, 1802, rising from my bed, where I had been shaking with an ague, I joined with a few disciples in prayer, when the Lord blessed me in an extraordinary manner, dispelling all my depression and fears, and causing me to rejoice with exceeding joy. It broke the spell of my disease; from this day I gradually recovered my health, and prayed and preached with my usual power and success.

"While looking for fruits of my labors and supplications, I was called to visit a young woman who was supposed to be dying. She was one of seven children, the parents of whom were remarkable for their deep piety, the mother being one of the most holy women I have ever known. All the children, except the youngest, were professors of religion; but the one who was sick had declined much in piety. When I entered the room I found her on her bed extremely ill. She appeared quite stupid, and to any question which I put to her, her answer was, 'I do not know.' Several pious persons were present. After conversing and meditating some time, we all knelt down. When I had prayed, I called on one and then another to pray. Her godly mother was kneeling at her bedside, and I was so situated that whenever I opened my eyes I could observe her intense solicitude for her child. After praying for some time the patient began strangely to revive; soon the tears trickled down her pallid cheeks. Her mother then suddenly exclaimed, 'Glory to God!' clasped her hands, and fell on the floor, overpowered by her emotions. Very soon the daughter began to praise the Lord aloud, and it seemed to us all that the glory of God shone around us. As soon as the ecstasy of the invalid subsided, she arose from the bed, walked the room, and was well from that hour. Her restoration seemed given in answer to prayer, and was almost instantaneous. I care not by what name it may be called, of its reality I can have no doubt, for I was an eye and ear-witness of the facts, as were many others, and I have here recorded them to the glory of God's grace in Christ Jesus.

ITINERANT ADVENTURES.

"On the 7th of October I set off, in company with Joseph Jewell, the presiding elder, for the Bay of Quinte circuit. We had a terrible road to travel from the head of Lake Ontario to Little York, as it was then called, now Toronto, over hills and creeks, through mud and water, but at last arrived in safety. We had an appointment for preaching on Yonge-street in the evening of the next day. After the sermon by Mr. Jewell, I gave an exhortation. The people requested that I might be left for a few days to preach in the neighborhood. I accordingly staid behind, with the understanding that I should go on in a short time. At the time appointed I set off, but was taken sick with influenza on the way. Being tenderly nursed in the house where I stopped, I soon recovered, mounted my horse, and rode some miles, when my faithful animal was taken sick and the next day died. Here, then, I was alone in a strange place, without money, without a horse, and, as far as I knew, without friends. I trusted in God alone, and he provided for me. In about half an hour, during which I hardly knew which way to turn, a gentleman came along and offered to lend me a horse on condition that I would defer my journey to the Bay of Quinte, and agree to remain in those parts preaching for some time. I thankfully accepted his offer, mounted the horse, and went on my way rejoicing up to Little York. The settlements in this part of the country were all new, the roads extremely bad, and the people generally poor and demoralized. Our occasional preachers were exposed to many privations and often to much suffering from poor fare and violent opposition. Seth Crowell, a zealous and godly itinerant, had traveled along the lake shore before me, and had been instrumental in the awakening and conversion of many of the settlers, so that some small societies had been formed; but they were far apart, and I found them in a dwindled condition. On Yonge-street, which was a settlement extending westward from Little York in a direct line for about thirty miles, there were no societies, but all the field was new and uncultivated, with the exception of some Quaker neighborhoods. Among these 'Friends' I formed some pleasant acquaintances." He had met with some of them in the scenes of his earlier ministerial labors. They liked his earnest spirit and his doctrine, though they disapproved the practical system of Methodism, especially its organized ministry. Sometimes, traveling at a distance from their settlement, they would join his log-cabin congregations, and after the sermon rise and bear their favorable "testimonies." One of them, hearing him on his first circuit, was so inspired and delighted by his fervent discourse as to ask "liberty to testify" to it, and then proceeded to say that, while listening, "It was given him to rise to the blessed vision of the Revelator—he saw the angel, bearing the everlasting Gospel, flying through the midst of heaven. This is the everlasting Gospel which they had heard that day," and the good Quaker went on to support his Methodist brother with a home-directed exhortation to the wondering people. The two speakers had an agreeable interview after the service, and comforted each other on their way heavenward. The itinerant always afterward liked the Friends, though he deemed some of their peculiarities unscriptural, and frankly told them so. He resolved now to visit their settlements along the extended "Yonge-street" route.

He set out on a winter's day with the determination to call at as many houses as possible on the way and give a "word of exhortation" to each. At every door he said: "I have come to talk with you about religion, and to pray with you. If you are willing to receive me for this purpose I will stop; if not, I will go on." "Only one repulsed me through the entire day; all others heard my exhortations, and permitted me to pray with them. I entered one house where I found the family at dinner. I talked with them for a while and then proposed prayer. When I arose from my knees the man was in a profuse perspiration, and, looking me in the face with much emotion, said, 'Sir, I believe you pray in the Spirit.' I gave him a word of advice and left him, a thoughtful, perhaps an awakened man." Some, however, held eager disputes with him on theological questions, and most were more inclined to show their rustic skill in polemics than to join in his earnest devotions; but all treated him kindly, except a stout High Churchman, a rude emigrant, who avowed himself to "be of the High Church of England, and a believer in her Articles and prayer book." He became so enraged at the preacher's citation of the Church Catechism on the sacramental sign of "inward spiritual grace—a new birth unto righteousness"—that he vociferously threatened to "pitch him, neck and heels," out of the cabin, and would probably have done so had it not been for the interference of his daughter.

IMPRESSIONS.

He learned at least one valuable lesson on this journey. He had given too much importance to "impressions." "At a certain time," says his friend and successor in Canada, Rev. Dr. Fitch Reed, "when the weather was very cold and the newly-fallen snow quite deep, his mind became more than usually impressed with the value of souls, and his heart burned with desire to do all he could to save them. In the midst of his reflections he came opposite a dwelling that stood quite a distance from the road in the field. Instantly he was impressed to go to the house and talk and pray with its family. He could see no path through the deep snow, and he felt reluctant to wade that distance, expose himself to the cold, and perhaps after all accomplish no good. He resolved not to go. No sooner had he passed the house than the impression became doubly strong, and he was constrained to turn back. He fastened his horse to the fence, waded through the snow to the house, and *not a soul was there!* From that time he resolved never to confide in *mere impressions*."

FRONTIER LIFE—ANECDOTE.

He delayed much on this route, preaching often and with success. "There was quite an awakening among the people," he writes, "and many sought redemption in the blood of Christ, so that several societies were formed. But there was a marked line of distinction between the righteous and the wicked, there being but very few who were indifferent or outwardly moral to interpose between them. All showed openly what they were by their words and actions, and either accepted religion heartily or opposed it violently; the great majority, though most of them would come to hear me preach, were determined opposers." Such is the character of frontier communities. Moral restraints are feeble among them; conventional restraints are few; the freedom of their simple wilderness-life characterizes all their habits; they have their own code of decorum, and sometimes of law itself. They are frank, hospitable, but violent in prejudice and passion; fond of disputation, of excitement, and of hearty, if not reckless amusements. The primitive Methodist preachers knew well how to accommodate themselves to the habits, as also to the fare of such a people, and hence their extraordinary success along the whole American frontier. Their simple and familiar methods of worship in cabins and barns, or under trees, suited the rude settlers. Their meetings were without the stiff order and ceremonious formality of older communities. They were often scenes of free debate, of interpellations and interlocutions; a hearer at the door-post or the window responding to, or questioning, or defying the preacher, who "held forth" from a chair, a bench, or a barrel, at the other end of the building. This popular freedom was not without its advantages; it authorized equal freedom on the part of the preacher; it allowed great plainness of speech and directness of appeal. The early memoranda before me afford not a few glimpses of this primitive life of the frontier—crowded congregations in log-huts or barns—some of the hearers seated, some standing, some filling the unglazed casements, some thronging the overhanging trees—startling interjections thrown into the sermon by eccentric listeners—violent polemics between the preacher and headstrong sectarists, the whole assembly sometimes involved in the earnest debate, some for, some against him, and ending in general confusion. A lively Methodist hymn was usually the best means of restoring order in such cases. Our itinerant was never confounded by these interruptions. He had a natural tact and a certain authoritative presence, an air of command, qualified by a concessive temper, which seldom failed to control the roughest spirits. He was often characteristic, if not directly personal, in his preaching, sometimes with quite naive, if not ludicrous results. On one occasion he was contrasting the characters of the righteous and the wicked, "when an apparently well-meaning man," he writes, "sitting before me, said aloud, 'How do you know that, sir?' I made him no reply, but proceeded with the delineation of the godless character, and then remarked, 'It matters not what your condition or name is, if you do thus wickedly you will be damned!' He arose, bowed very respectfully, and said, 'My name is Benaiah Brown, at your service,' and sat down again. Some of my friends, thinking he wished to make disturbance, went toward him to put him out of the house. I requested them to let him alone, as he had not disturbed me at all, but seemed full of respect. After the meeting he remained, and, in conversation with him, I asked him how he came to address me in the manner he did. He replied, 'You described my character so accurately that I thought you knew all about me, and that I might as well give you my name and have done with it.' I gave him some good advice, and we parted on the best terms. He was a stranger in the place; the Word had evidently taken hold upon his heart, and I may hope its effects were lasting."

A FRONTIER FIDDLER.

A more direct case occurred in a settlement about ten miles from Toronto. "There was," he says, "a great awakening among the people, but an inveterate fiddler seemed set on by the great adversary to contest the victory with me, inch by inch. He had earned considerable money as the musician of the winter-night dancing parties of the settlers; but he was now willing to fiddle for nothing, if they would meet to dance and frolic rather than to pray. He contrived every possible method to keep the young people from our meetings. For some time he carried his purpose with a high hand, and the war was at last fully opened between us. One Sabbath morning, however, I fairly caught him. I was preaching on Gal. v, 19–21, and when I came to the word 'revelings,' I applied it to his tactics, and said, 'I do not know that the devil's musician is here to-night; I do not see him anywhere.' But he was sitting in a corner out of my sight, and he now put out his head and cried out, 'Here I am, ha! ha! ha!' making the place ring with his laughter. 'Ay,' said I, 'you are there, are you!' and, turning toward him, looked him full in the face, and addressed myself to him in language of rebuke and warning. I finally told him that if he did not cease alluring the young people into sinful amusements I would pray God either to convert him or take him out of the way, and I had no doubt that God would answer my prayer. The power of God evidently fell upon the assembly; a divine awe seemed to overpower them. The guilty man began to tremble all over like a leaf and turned deathly pale. He finally got up and rushed out of the house. He went home, burned his fiddle, and we were thenceforth rid of his interference with our meetings and his opposition in the community."

A PROVIDENTIAL ESCAPE.

He sometimes had ruder encounters. "I had," he says, "an appointment to preach in a small cabin, the family of which was too poor to entertain me conveniently over night. I therefore intended to return, as had been my custom, about six miles, after the sermon, for lodgings. I was overtaken on my way to the place by a sleigh, with three men in it. I turned my horse out of the road and let them pass me, but they no sooner did so than they stopped and began vociferating blasphemies and blackguard language at me, and if I attempted to pass them they would drive on, obstruct the way, and thus prevent my going forward. In this manner they continued to annoy me about half an hour, keeping up an unceasing stream of Billingsgate. I made them no reply. They at length drove on, and left me to pursue my way in peace. In the evening, as I rose up to preach, these three men stood looking in at the door, and as I was standing at the door-post they closed the entrance, and were close to my right hand. I requested them to take seats; two of them did so, but the other kept his place. I gave out for my text Dan. v, 27: 'Thou art weighed in the balances and art found wanting.' In the introduction to the discourse I made some remarks about Belshazzar's impious feast; I enlarged on the prevalent drinking habits of the settlers, and observed that there were people who were not contented to drink in taverns and in their own houses, but carried bottles of rum in their pockets. The man who still stood at my right hand had a bottle in his pocket; he drew it forth, shook it in my face with an oath, exclaiming, 'You are driving that at me,' and kept up a continual threat. The owner of the house, who was a warm friend of mine, instantly arose, with two or three others, all trembling with indignation, and came toward the offender to seize him and thrust him away. Perceiving their design, I feared there would be bloodshed, and requested them to desist and take their seats, for I was not afraid of my opposer. They sat down, but this only seemed to enrage the man still more. He kept on swearing, with his clenched fist directed at me; but I continued my discourse unmoved by his threats, until I finally called on the God of Daniel, who delivered him from the lions, to deliver me from this lion-like sinner, when suddenly he escaped out of the door and fled; his two companions followed him, and we ended the meeting in peace. My friends, fearing I might meet with some peril should I attempt to return that night, as it was supposed that these ruffians knew that I intended to do so, persuaded me to stay all night. It was well I did so, for these men lay in ambush for me, and seeing a traveler approach on horseback, one of them said with an oath 'There he is, let's have him,' and off they went pursuing him, blaspheming and cursing him as the Methodist preacher. They caught him, and were preparing to wreak their vengeance upon him, but soon discovered that they had committed an egregious and dangerous blunder. The assailed traveler, seeing his peril, turned upon them boldly, and showing a hearty disposition to fight, notwithstanding the odds against him, and using a style of language surprisingly like their own, they became convinced that he could be no Methodist preacher, and took to their heels.* Thus God saved me from these ravening wolves. I blessed his name, and learned to trust more than ever his protecting providence. No little good resulted from this incident; it raised me up many friends; opposers even became ashamed of the malicious rowdies, and were ready now to defend me. In the midst of all these strange scenes I enjoyed great peace with God, I had constant access to him in prayer, and went on my route rejoicing that I was counted worthy to suffer for his name's sake. I passed on from settlement to settlement, preaching and praying with the people; the Divine Spirit was poured out upon them, and many were converted. Some of the neighborhoods were

* This gentleman was a Mr. Hall, who himself related the incident to Rev. Dr. Fitch Reed. (See Reminiscences of Itinerant Life, No. 2, in Northern Christian Advocate, January 1, 1863.) Dr. Reed's narrative differs, in slight particulars, from Dr. Bangs's. I follow the manuscript of the latter.

extremely poor; in some the people had not yet a single stable for the accommodation of my horse. I carried with me oats for him, and, tying him to a tree, left him to eat at night, and ate and slept myself in the same room in which I preached. This I had to do frequently; but God was with me, blessing my own soul and the people."

AMONG THE QUAKERS.

He at last found himself among the Quakers, and was hospitably received by most of them, though some looked askance at him; their chief objection to him being the alleged fact that, though evidently a good, self-sacrificing man, yet, as a Methodist preacher, he was a "hireling." At best the charge could be said to be but theoretically true of the Methodist preachers of that early day. He received only about fifty dollars in the first year of his ministry; in the present year only about twelve; and he was now actually using a borrowed horse, not having funds enough to buy one. The "Discipline" of the Church allowed but eighty dollars a year to an unmarried itinerant, and but double that amount to a married one; and he remarks that "even these pittances were seldom paid." The Methodist ministry have never, either in that day or in ours, made any contract for salaries, and have no legal claim for any deficiency in their "allowance." But these "Friends" revolted from the slightest semblance of pecuniary remuneration for preaching. They entertained their visitor cordially, however, and he read with much interest their standard books, the writings of Fox, Penn, Barclay, and others. They had a few humble but neat places of worship in this new country. He took his seat among them, and for the first time witnessed their simple devotions. A woman rose and said, "Friend, if thee has anything to say, we are willing to hear thee." He wished to learn more fully their public customs, and replied, "I have nothing at present to say." At two other times single texts of Scripture were uttered. At last, according to their universal custom, they shook hands as the conclusion of the meeting, when he rose, and saying "Where the Spirit of the Lord is, there is liberty," asked permission to address them. They gladly resumed their seats, and listened to a warm exhortation on "the Witness of the Spirit," a doctrine which seemed peculiarly to please them. "Take thy horse and ride to my house; thee shall be welcome," said a good man to him when he closed. As it was practically the motto of Methodist preachers to "be instant, in season and out of season," and to become "all things to all men, that they might by all means save some," he continued to visit them in their various settlements, enjoying their hospitality, conversing with and exhorting them from house to house, not, however, without encountering some unyielding prejudices, and some persistent though good-tempered controversies. He felt deeply interested for them, and perceiving that they were losing their spiritual life in this distant region, he endeavored to recall them to the best teachings of their own founders, as well as to the better teachings of Holy Scripture.

His visits produced no small excitement in their settlements. He met them again in their house of worship, and it was now crowded, for they expected his presence. The assembly sat some time in silence. A woman arose, and, quoting a single text, sat down. After a few moments of silence the itinerant stood up among them, and addressed them on the words, "Thus saith the Lord, Stand ye in the ways, and see, and ask for the old paths, where is the good way, and walk therein, and ye shall find rest for your souls." The text, he says, seemed suddenly suggested to his mind, as by a divine inspiration. He spoke from the "fullness of his heart," reminding them that, according to the journals of their early preachers, they very seldom then had "silent meetings," but "found something to say for God;" that here, in the ends of the world, hardly anything like a testimony for the truth was given in their assemblies; that the population around them was perishing; that their fathers taught the duty of family worship, and usually spent half an hour daily in it, but that it seemed generally neglected here, where it was most needed. He concluded by "exhorting them to walk in the good old paths of the Friends; then should they find rest to their souls." The word took effect; they "wept all over the house." Kneeling down, he prayed for them with Methodistic fervor, and was afterward taken to one of their homes, where many of them came together in the evening to converse with him. Long discussions occupied the hours. The "hireling" question especially was canvassed, for these good people seemed to consider that fundamental; but when the itinerant explained to them fully the financial economy of Methodism—that it provided barely for the support of the laborer; that this support enabled him to go out into the world calling sinners to repentance; that the Quakers, so far as they sent abroad preachers, did so on substantially the same plan; and that all Christians should liberally contribute to send them out till the whole world should hear the Gospel—"they all seemed to assent, and one elderly woman lifted up her hands and then brought them down with emphasis, exclaiming, 'That is God's truth; I know it.' The conversation having ended," he continues, "I said, 'I feel it my duty to pray with you.' 'Thee can pray if thee wishes,' said my host. I accordingly kneeled down and prayed with much liberty, and then retired to bed, happy in the love of God, praising him for all his mercies, and slept sweetly under the smiles of his reconciled countenance." He soon after left their settlements, and never saw them again; but he had reason to hope that his brief mission had proved a blessing to them.

AT A NEW YEAR'S DANCE.

On the 1st of January, 1802, he set off to attend some preaching appointments which he had made along the lake shore. The journey was to afford him some farther examples of frontier life. "The roads," he says, "were bad, most of the country being new and in some places a continuous forest of from ten to fifteen miles extent. About sunset I came to a creek, the bridge of which was so broken that my horse would not cross upon it, neither could I lead or drive him over the ice as the middle of the creek was not frozen, but the current ran rapidly, making a noise with the broken ice that frightened him. I went up and down the stream for a considerable distance in the snow and ice to find a place on which I might cross. I was more than an hour in making this useless effort. Being compelled either to stay in the woods all night or to return, of the two evils I chose the last. I found on my way back an Indian trader's house, where a number of people were assembled to celebrate the New Year. They were singing, dancing, and drinking at a high rate. I offered money if any two of the men would go with me and help me over the creek; but no one would consent, for the night had fallen and it was cold. The man of the house assured me that if I would stay with him over night I should be well-treated. I accordingly put up my horse and entered the house. I declined the whisky which was offered me, but told the woman of the house I should be thankful for something to eat, as I had eaten nothing since early in the morning. She kindly prepared me a good supper."

And now a remarkable but characteristic scene ensued. "Seating myself," he continues, "by the fire, I commenced a conversation with a woman on the subject of religion. I found that she was a backslidden Baptist. While talking with her one and another drew near and formed quite a group of listeners, until finally so many assembled around me that the dance could not go on. A large, athletic man now stepped up to me and said, 'Sir, if you will remain here you must be civil; you must not preach.' I replied, 'I am not preaching; but as Providence has cast my lot among you, I think it my duty to talk with those who are willing to hear me on the things that make for their eternal peace. You will not deprive me of this privilege, will you?' 'No,' said he, 'but we must dance,' and he seized the women and dragged them out upon the floor, and resumed the dance with increased hilarity. This they continued until nearly midnight. I then said to the chief trader, who had become very friendly with me, 'With your permission I will address a few words to the people.' He assented, and requested them to give attention. I arose and addressed them in substance as follows: 'It is now midnight, and the holy Sabbath has begun. You have amused yourselves with dancing, I think, long enough to satisfy you, if not to fatigue you, and if you continue it longer you will not only transgress the law of God, but likewise the law of your country. I advise you, therefore, to desist and retire to your rest.' They complied so far as to cease dancing. But the Indian trader came to me and said, 'The Indians are encamped a short distance from us, and they expect a dance here as I have promised them one.' He asked my permission to let them have it. I replied that I had no control over his house or the Indians, but if he would dispense with the revel he would highly gratify me, and, I doubted not, would please God. He rejoined that as 'he had promised them the dance they would expect it, and would be greatly incensed if they were denied it.' He then went to the door and gave the Indian 'whoop,' and down came the savages and began an Indian dance, which, with their drumming upon an old pan, their frequent yells, their stamping and bodily distortions, presented a spectacle fit for pandemonium."

There could be small hope of a serious impression by anything he could say amid such scenes; but it was his rule to lose no opportunity however desperate; he had been faithful to the white dancers; he tried now the Indians. "I requested the trader to assist me in conversing with them. To this he assented, when the chief of the Indians presented himself before me with great dignity and gravity. I asked him if he knew whence they had descended. He replied, 'Yes; the Great Spirit at first made one man and one woman, placed them on an island about an acre in size; thence they were driven for an act of disobedience to the continent, and from them they had all descended.' I then gave him an account of the creation of the world, of man in particular, of his fall and its consequences. I asked him if he had ever heard of Jesus Christ. He replied, 'No.' I then gave him an account of our Lord's birth, his life, miracles, and teachings, his sufferings and death. While describing the death of Christ, the chief pointed to his heart and lifted his eyes and hands toward heaven apparently filled with amazement. When I had concluded he clasped me in his arms, kissed me and called me father, and entreated me to come and live with him and be the teacher of his people. After assuring him of my affection for them and the deep interest I felt for their eternal welfare, I told him that I could not comply with his request, but hoped the time was not distant when a Christian teacher should be sent to them. They then retired to their encampment.

"But the worst of this strange night was yet to come. There were two traders present, one of whom, the head man, had become intoxicated and still wanted more liquor; the other refused to let him have it. The dispute ran high, and the drunken trader raised his fist to strike the other, when I stepped in between them and averted the blow. He then swore that if he was not allowed more whisky he would call the Indians and fall upon and murder us all. He accordingly went to the door, gave the horrible 'whoop!' and the Indians came rushing to the house. Meantime, those within armed themselves as well as they could with sticks and clubs, determined to defend themselves to the utmost. I shuddered for the consequences. The enraged man then said, 'Here are my guards at the door. If you will give me more whisky, well; if you will not, they shall fall upon you, and we will murder you all.' 'Will you?' the other exclaimed, and lifted his arm to strike him down. I again stepped between them, and placing my hand upon the drunken man's shoulder said, 'Come, my friend, let us go to sleep. If you will be my friend, I will be yours!' He consented. We laid down upon a bed, and in a few minutes he was asleep. I then arose; the Indians had retired to their camp, and at dawn of day I started on my way, persuading two men to accompany me to the creek and help me over by laying logs on the broken bridge. I passed on, praising God for delivering me from the perils of this dismal night and for enabling me to prevent the shedding of blood, as well as for the pleasing interview I had with the Indian chief.

DISCORD HEALED.

"I reached my appointment in time to preach that day, and then went down the lake shore, preaching every day, and the Lord was with me and kept me in my way through those wild and dangerous scenes. There was one society on the circuit in quite a disturbed state. It was divided by two parties, and many attempts had in vain been made to unite them both by myself and the presiding elder. One evening I had an appointment among them, and, while preaching, the Spirit of God descended upon me and upon them; his love seemed to fill and overflow every heart. They were all melted into tenderness. Now, I thought, is a good time to bring about a reconciliation, and accordingly I said to them,

'If you are now willing to settle your difficulties, and forgive and forget what is past, rise up, meet one another in the middle of the floor, shake hands, and thus manifest your love one to another.' They instantly rose, seized each other by the hand, some weeping, some praising God aloud, the women kissing one another, the men falling on one another's necks and sobbing. Thus their old difficulties were ended by the healing influence of the Holy Spirit, and they were bound together as the heart of one man. I believe that most of the discords which occur among Christians originate in the absence of the divine love, from which alone the true love of the brethren can spring. The best cure of public troubles in the Church is, therefore, a revival of the personal piety of its members."

Such are some of the "lights and shadows" of frontier life, and of the frontier itinerant ministry of Methodism at the beginning of our century. The inhabitants of this now rich and flourishing region, with a commodious Methodist chapel in almost every city, town, and village, can hardly deem them credible, for the frontier, the "far West," has since passed to the Mississippi River and even beyond it. Besides their interest as remarkable or curious facts, they are not without historical significance as illustrations of conditions in both social and religious life which are fast receding, and in a few generations will be seen no more on our continent.

The faithful evangelist continued to brave the hardships of this field of labor until the next Conference, when he was appointed to the Bay of Quinte, one of the earliest circuits of Canada, and the scene of recent and extraordinary religious interest. He records as an instance of the kindness of his brethren on the Niagara circuit, his "spiritual birthplace," that at the suggestion of Joseph Jewell, his presiding elder, they contributed money enough to purchase a horse for him, on which he rode off to the adventures of his new field. "I received him," he thankfully writes, "as a gift from the Lord, for I had been riding a borrowed one from the time at which mine had died. He was the best I have ever owned, and carried me safely thousands of miles, sharing my sufferings in the heats of summers and the terrible blasts of those northern winters."

He left the circuit in general prosperity. One year before it reported three hundred and twenty members; it now reported six hundred and twenty, and Long Point, the chief field of his labors, was recognized at the conference of 1802 as a distinct circuit. About a hundred souls had been converted in Burford and Oxford through his instrumentality, and in our day his name is still a household word in the Methodist families of that region. Few who knew him remain; yet the descendants of his old hearers, living no longer in log-cabins, but in comfortable if not opulent homes, worshiping no longer under trees or in barns, but in convenient temples, have learned from their pious and departed fathers to revere him as the pioneer champion of the cross among their early settlements.

CHAPTER IX.

BAY OF QUINTE CIRCUIT.

It was not usual at that early day for the young preachers to attend the Annual Conferences. The journey from remote circuits to the place of the session was long and expensive, and the scattered societies needed the continuous attention of some of the laborers. Jewell, the presiding elder of the whole Canadian field, bore, therefore, its reports to the Conference; while most, if not all, the circuit preachers remained at their posts till his return with their new appointments.

The session was held in New York city in the first week of June, 1802. Nathan Bangs was there designated, with Joseph Sawyer and Peter Vannest, to the Bay of Quinte circuit. Of his new field he says, "I found myself agreeably situated among a people deeply experienced in religion, remarkably kind and attentive to all my wants; and, in addition to all my other comforts, I had the satisfaction of being under the oversight of my spiritual father, Joseph Sawyer, whom I loved and venerated as one of the best of men. This region had also been the scene of the labors of some of the most holy men the world ever saw.

A POWERFUL PREACHER.

"Among others, Hezekiah Calvin Wooster had sounded the alarm through these forests, and many were the anecdotes that I heard of him among the people, who delighted to talk of him. He was indefatigable in his labors, 'full of faith and of the Holy Ghost,' and preached with the 'demonstration of the Spirit and of power.'

He professed and enjoyed the blessing of sanctification, and was, therefore, a man of mighty faith and prayer. The people never tired of telling of the power of his word—how that sinners could not stand before him, but would either rush out of the house or fall smitten to the floor. I never found so many persons, in proportion to their number, who professed and exemplified the 'perfect love' of God, as he had left on this circuit."

The name of this powerful preacher has already occurred in these pages; it appears frequently in the early Methodist publications, but only in passing allusions. The extreme winters of the Canadian climate were too severe for his delicate frame; but he would not desert the field till advanced pulmonary disease compelled him to cease preaching. Hopeless of any further health, he returned to his parental home to die amid his kindred. I have discovered a single glimpse of him, on his route homeward, in the journal of Lorenzo Dow. That eccentric man had been laboring sturdily on extensive circuits in New England. Through all his wandering course he carried with him a profound religious solicitude, not unmixed, perhaps, with the infirmities of partial insanity; and amid apparent ebullitions of humor his spirit hungered and thirsted after God. He writes in his own unpolished but explicit style as follows: "When I was on the Orange circuit I fell in with T. Dewey, on Cambridge circuit. He told me about Calvin Wooster in Upper Canada—that he enjoyed the blessing of sanctification. I felt a great desire arise in my heart to see the man, if it might be consistent with the divine will; and not long after I heard he was passing through the circuit and going home to die. I immediately rode five miles to the house, but found he was gone another five miles further. I went into the room where he was asleep; he appeared to me more like one from the eternal world than like one of my fellow-mortals. I told him when he awoke who I was and what I had come for. Said he, 'God has convicted you for the blessing of sanctification, and that blessing is to be obtained by the simple act of faith in the same manner as the blessing of justification.' I persuaded him to tarry in the neighborhood a few days; and two evenings later, after I had done preaching, he spoke, or rather whispered out an exhortation, as his voice was so broken in consequence of praying in the air in Upper Canada, where from twenty to thirty were frequently blessed at a meeting. He told me that if he could get sinners under conviction, crying for mercy, they would kneel down, a dozen of them, and not rise till they found peace; 'for,' said he, 'we did believe God would bless them, and it was according to our faith.' At this time he was in a consumption, and a few weeks after expired. While whispering out the above exhortation, the power which attended it reached the hearts of the people, and some who were standing and sitting fell like men shot on the field of battle; and I felt it like a tremor running through my soul and every vein, so that it took away my limb power and I fell to the floor, and by faith saw a greater blessing than I had hitherto experienced; or, in other words, felt a divine conviction of the need of a deeper work of grace in my soul—feeling some of the remains of the evil nature, the effect of Adam's fall, still remaining, and my privilege to have it eradicated or done away. My soul was in an agony—I could but groan out my desires to God. Wooster came to me and said, 'Believe the blessing is now.' No sooner had the words dropped from his lips than I strove to believe the blessing mine now with all the powers of my soul; then the burden dropped from my mind, and a solid joy and a gentle running peace filled my soul. From that time to this I have not had the ecstasy of joy or a downcast spirit as formerly, but more of an inward, simple, sweet running peace from day to day, so that prosperity or adversity doth not produce the ups and downs as formerly; but my soul is more like the ocean, while its surface is uneven by reason of the boisterous wind, the bottom is still calm; so that a man may be in the midst of outward difficulties, and yet the center of the soul may be calmly stayed on God."

Such was the influence of Wooster on this wayward but energetic man—such the power of his eloquence whispered from lips blanched with mortal disease. He passed on to his home and lay down to die; but before his spirit left the body it seemed already in heaven. He was asked when his power of utterance was almost gone if his confidence in God was still strong. "Strong! strong!" was his whispered but exulting reply. When he was fast declining, and death was almost in view, he exclaimed that "the nearer he drew to eternity, the brighter heaven shined upon him."

OTHER ITINERANTS.

"Here," continues Dr. Bangs, "I became acquainted with Darius Dunham, the first presiding elder of the district, and of whom I had heard much in connection with the labors of Wooster. On this circuit, at a quarterly conference, Dunham received, under a prayer of Wooster, the 'baptism of fire.' This was a most happy event, for while Wooster was spreading the flame on Oswegatchie circuit, and afterward on that of the Bay of Quinte, Dunham, being presiding elder, extended it from circuit to circuit through the district, and great multitudes were awakened and converted. It spread not only through Upper Canada, but ran in its course into the United States. Many preachers caught the sacred inspiration. Among others Elijah Woolsey, a man of sweet spirit, who was at that time itinerating in Canada, and who was greatly blessed in his labors, as may be seen from his 'Lights and Shadows of the Itinerancy.' Indeed, it became a proverbial saying among the people along the way from Canada to the seat of the New York Conference, that the northern 'preachers brought the Canada fire with them.' This Canada fire was none other than the flame of sanctifying grace, which then spread like a conflagration over the Canada circuits."

SEVERE ILLNESS.

He pursued his labors on this circuit with much success till the autumn, when the typhus fever broke out and raged as an epidemic through most of the settlements. In some of them it prevailed so generally that there remained not persons enough in health to take care of the sick. Many perished, but the preacher held on his course, ministering to the diseased and dying, till he himself was seized with the pestilence. About the middle of December he was compelled to give up his labors and take to his bed. He was thoroughly medicated, but the medical skill of the country was yet very imperfect, and it was still the day in which, contrary to the imperative and instinctive dictate of nature, cold water, the best relief in febrile disease, was scrupulously denied to the languishing patient. In three days after his attack he became delirious. His paroxysms were sometimes so violent that it required three men to hold him in his bed. He demanded water, but it was denied him. The intensity of the disease not only deranged his reason, but beclouded his religious feelings. At times he was in spiritual ecstasy, but his raptures were followed by the deepest dejection, in which he says, "Any duty I had neglected, or any cross I had shunned, came vividly to my recollection. I mourned, prayed, and expressed my doubts and fears to the friends who attended me. They endeavored to comfort me by reminding me of the goodness of God in blessing me so often, but these considerations afforded me no relief. I pleaded for consolation in the name of Christ, and help came at last. To record all the wild experiences of a mind bewildered by a burning fever would afford no satisfaction, but there is an important lesson to be learned from this example of the effect of disease on religious feeling; suffering saints should understand it well, and so should also their ministering friends, who often suffer keenly by sympathy in such cases. The clouds which obscure the sun do not extinguish him. Many things that occurred in this trial I should have never known had I not been informed of them by my attendants, who tenderly watched over me in my anguish; but some things I remember as distinctly as any events of my life. This I know, that after being delivered from my mental distress, I was extremely happy in God, and desired to depart and be with Christ. So low was I that the people were called in twice or thrice to see me die."

COLD WATER.

Nature at last prevailed over the fallacies of his physicians and attendants. He demanded cold water incessantly, and threatened to rise up and leave the house if it were longer withheld from him. "I accordingly arose from the bed," he writes, "dressed myself, put on my overcoat, hat, and mittens, and tottered to the door, which they had so fastened that I could not open it. Seeing a pail of water standing upon a bench in the room, I seized hold of it, but, alas! I had not strength to lift it, and dare not stoop down to drink, for I was so weak I should have fallen prostrate. Seeing me so eager, one of the attendants approached and lifted the pail to my mouth, and I drank as long as I had strength to swallow. This is the last that I can remember of the scene. The family told me afterward that I sat down in a chair and continued calling for water, which was now freely given me, as they deemed my life hopeless. I at last told them to lay me on the bed. I there prayed mightily to God for his blessing. The room was now full of people, for they had been called in to see me die. The next thing that I remember is that the heavens seemed to be opened above me, and the glory of God, like a sudden blaze of lightning, illuminated the apartment. I uttered aloud the praises of the Lord until my strength was exhausted, the people adoring him with me. How long I lay senseless after this ecstasy I know not. When I came to myself it seemed like an awakening from a pleasant dream. My soul was exceedingly happy, but my physical strength was so exhausted that I could not raise my hand to my head, nor could I utter a loud word, and when I became able to articulate my voice was like that of an infant. My fever, however, was gone, and returned no more, except in some slight symptoms at intervals. I recovered my strength very slowly, having taken a very violent cold, which was accompanied with a distressing cough, and the expectoration of abundance of blood. Most of those who saw me supposed that I could not live long, but God in mercy raised me up from the gates of death. O the goodness of God! the preciousness of the Lord Jesus! I saw in my extremity that there is 'no other name given among men' by which I could be saved 'but the name of Jesus Christ.' Nothing that I had ever said or done, not even my best works, though ever so sincere, nor even my faith or prayers, preaching, traveling, privations or sufferings, could justify me in the sight of God without Christ. But in that time of extremity I could say in true faith:

"'Jesus, thy blood and righteousness
My beauty are, my glorious dress;
'Midst flaming worlds, in these arrayed,
With joy shall I lift up my head!'

"My soul is indeed overwhelmed even while I now, fifty years after the event, write this account of the merciful dealings of God to me in that hour of deep affliction of body and mind—both, indeed, indescribable."

HIS "DOUBLE VOICE."

He had been confined to his bed seven weeks and three days; three months passed before he could attempt to preach, and even then his voice was so feeble that he could hardly be heard. His friends believed he could never recover strength enough to resume his labors, and his physician concurred in this opinion. The cough and expectoration of blood, which followed the fever, so affected his lungs that his first attempts to ride were attended with acute pains; but he persisted, and horseback riding was probably itself the remedy that at last saved him. The feebleness of his voice, however, occasioned an unnatural effort to speak loud enough to be heard, and to this fact he ascribes "that double sort of voice" which continued through his long life. Many of his hearers have noticed it as a singularity, and perhaps condemned it as a faulty mannerism—little supposing that, like the scarred and mutilated confessors at the Council of Nice, he thus, in our happier times, and before our opulent Churches, "bore in his body the marks of the Lord Jesus,"—a memento of the heroic days of our ministry. This deep, tremulous undertone of his voice, though usually not agreeable, took at times a peculiar pathos. How much more affecting would it have been had his hearers, in his latter years, known that it was caused by his attempts to preach the everlasting Gospel through the frontier wilderness when he was apparently a dying man. Sickness in the family of his colleague rendered it necessary that he should thus prematurely resume his labors on the circuit. "I went to work," he writes, "in the name of the Lord, and as well as I could. I was received as one risen from the dead; the Lord was with me in much mercy, and blessed me in soul and body, and I believe also made me a blessing to the people. I continued my labors until the last quarterly meeting, when I left, in company with another young preacher, Thomas Madden, for the New York Conference."

EARLY MINISTERIAL SUFFERINGS.

He bore with him from this circuit many precious memories. More than a hundred members had been added to the societies, notwithstanding the epidemic pestilence and the disablement of the preachers. He records with gratitude the faithful attentions of the people to him; their liberality in paying for his physician and medicines, and what was rare in that day, not only on the frontier, but everywhere, their full payment of his "Quarterage" at the end of the year—twenty dollars for the quarter, eighty dollars for the year! He alludes to the sufferings of his brethren of those times, occasioned by deficits in such payments, and to the great loss which the Church had to endure by their necessary "location" or their premature deaths, caused both by their excessive labor and deficient support. The growth of their families, or the prostration of their health by labor and privation, compelled many of them to "locate," or "desist from traveling." Of two hundred and eighteen, classed, by a historian of Methodism, as the "first race of Methodist preachers" in England, more than half (one hundred and thirteen) retired from the itinerancy, nearly all of them for such reasons. The itinerants in America suffered still more. Of six hundred and fifty who had been recorded in the Minutes in the United States by the end of the last century, about five hundred died "located," and many of the remainder were a longer or a shorter interval in the "local" ranks, but were able to resume their travels. The early American Conference records show a host of martyrs; nearly half of those whose deaths are recorded fell before they were thirty years old; about two thirds died after twelve years' service, and a majority of the "first race of Methodist preachers" in England, who died in the itinerancy, fell prematurely, victims to their hard work. In America they suffered not only from excessive labors, but by the exposures incident to a new country, and the severities of a variable climate; wilting under the heats of the south or the wintry storms of the north, swimming streams, braving snows, sleeping but partially sheltered in frontier cabins or under the trees of the forest. We have had sufficient proofs of these sufferings already in the life of Nathan Bangs, but more remain.

REVISITS HIS HOME.

He had never yet met in a Methodist annual conference, and departed with eager expectation to see an assembly of his fellow-laborers, and especially their great leader, the model and representative man of them all—Asbury. He had some money in his pocket, and a staunch war-horse, the gift of his brethren on Niagara circuit; and though still feeble in health, yet ardent with the characteristic chivalry of the itinerancy, he went with the determination to offer himself as a missionary for the still remoter region of the River Thames. His route was across the whole state of New York, but he pressed forward cheerfully. His filial affection turned him aside to visit his family, for he had not seen his parents during five years. "I prayed much," he writes, "that the Lord would make my visit a blessing to my friends. They all received me joyfully. As my father was in the field, I went out to find him, and met him on the way, but was so overcome that I could not speak for some time. After recovering myself, I spoke a few words, and then asked him if I might preach in his house that evening. He gave his consent. Word being sent around, the house was filled at an early hour, and my father, who was much prejudiced against the Methodists, occupied an adjoining room. I gave out the following words: 'Come and hear all ye that pass by, and I will declare what he hath done for my soul.' After a brief introduction, I related my Christian experience, and God abundantly blessed my soul, and enlarged my heart, and gave me liberty of utterance. When I concluded my sermon, I asked if any one was present who would close the meeting, and who should arise but my eldest brother Joseph, who had been made a partaker of divine grace in my absence, and who was now a licensed exhorter. We had a 'time of refreshing from the presence of the Lord,' and my soul truly exulted in God my Saviour. I preached a number of times in the neighborhood and the adjacent settlements, and my honored father had his prejudices so far removed that he followed me; and many of my former acquaintances, who never before heard a Methodist preacher, came to hear me. I went also to the East Branch of the Delaware River, where I had formerly resided about three years. Information having been given of my coming, many of my old companions in sin came to hear, and, I suppose, to see 'if any good thing could come out of Nazareth.' After preaching, I related my experience, and pointed to many old facts with which they were well acquainted. They seemed to be much affected, and while the people of God rejoiced, and my own soul was much refreshed, solemnity seemed to rest on all present."

THE GARRETTSON HOMESTEAD.

Taking reluctant leave of his family and old friends, he resumed his course toward the Conference. He paused for a brief rest at the mansion of Freeborn Garrettson, on the Hudson, near Rhinebeck, and records his delight at the beautiful scenery of the vicinity, and the sanctified comforts and hospitality of the family. He had read, and received inspiration from the published journals of the patriarchal itinerant, and now listened with deep interest to his conversation, sharing its rich lessons and romantic incidents with a number of preachers, who, like himself, had found there a brief resting-place on their way to the Conference. He alludes with admiration to the wife of Garrettson, that "elect lady," the personal friend of Washington, Hamilton, and Jay, and correspondent of Lady Washington. The daughter of an opulent and distinguished family, and endowed with rare accomplishments, with wealth and every youthful hope of fashionable life, this noble woman had discovered in Methodism the sterling doctrines of the Gospel, and embraced them courageously, notwithstanding any apparent incompatibility of the social character of the new sect with her own social position. She died in 1849, after a pilgrimage of more than ninety-six years, which had been distinguished by one of the most beautiful developments of character and most useful lives known in the records of female piety. Their residence on the eastern shore of the Hudson still remains, amid one of the most charming pictures of that beautiful scenery. It continues to be as it was in Garrettson's day, a temple for the neighborhood, and an asylum of hospitality, especially to Methodist preachers, who are ever welcomed at its door with the benediction, "Come in, thou blessed of the Lord." While Garrettson sheltered his family in this rural retreat, it was but his headquarters, whither he resorted for occasional repose—not to escape from his duties. His stations were sometimes as remote from it as Philadelphia; and he retired permanently to it only when age compelled him to give up his ministerial labors. Some thirteen or fourteen years before this visit, when Methodism had reached beyond New York city, only as far as Westchester, Garrettson was commissioned by Asbury to explore the extended region of the Hudson, and twelve young preachers were assigned to him. He knew little or nothing of the vast field, but in a dream it seemed to open before him—a magnificent vision—"the whole north country as far as Lake Champlain." He designated his band of laborers to various posts, and traveled himself over the whole region. Now his own home was in one of its most attractive localities, the headquarters of flourishing circuits, and in our day the shores of the noble river are studded with Methodist societies and chapels. The intimacy which young Bangs thus formed with the Garrettson household lasted through his life. He often returned to it as to a social sanctuary, and became the biographer of its patriarch—a man who was one of the chief founders of Methodism from Virginia to Nova Scotia.

BISHOP ASBURY.

They arrived at New York in time for the Conference, which was held in June, 1804. "I was gratified," he writes, "at seeing so many of the preachers, especially Bishop Asbury, whose venerable aspect and dignified manners filled me with admiration. I noticed, however, that his preaching was quite discursive, if not disconnected, a fact attributed to his many cares and unintermitted travels, which admitted of little or no study; but his manner was singularly imposing; he was grave and commanding, his voice sonorous, and his delivery attended with peculiar force and majesty. He seemed like a great military commander who had been crowned by many victories. He slid from one subject to another without system. He abounded in illustrations and anecdotes. I got a very exalted opinion of him, though I was somewhat disappointed in his preaching. My reverence for him was profound; he represented the whole Church, for he was its chief minister and its chief laborer. In the Conference he presided with great wisdom, dispatch, and dignity, and treated the young preachers as a father." Asbury was now but about fifty-seven years old, but had lived the lives of half a score of ordinary men; his brow was indented, his face weather-worn, his locks gray, and his aspect was that of a septuagenarian; no man in the ecclesiastical history of the New World had labored and suffered as he had, and none had achieved greater results. The growing host of itinerant preachers beheld him with admiration and wonder, as he hastily passed over his long routes—meeting them ever and anon for a few days, and then disappearing on the frontier or in the distant north or south—night and day sounding the trumpet of the Gospel, and hastening forward as if the final judgment were about to break upon the world.

ORDINATION.

Nathan Bangs had now passed through the two years of probation in the ministry required by the Discipline of the Church. He was, therefore, received into full membership and ordained a deacon, and two days later he was ordained a presbyter, contrary to the customary course of the Church, which requires a further candidacy of two years for the latter function. This exceptional proceeding was highly complimentary to him; it was justified not only by his faithful services in Canada, but by the fact that he appeared before the Conference as a volunteer missionary to the settlements on the River Thames, where he might need authority for the consecration of the sacraments. He was deeply affected by the solemnity of the ordination service. "It was," he says, "a precious season to myself, and, I believe, to others also. When my name was called in the Conference I was reclining on a seat in the back part of the church. After my presiding elder had favorably represented me, Bishop Asbury remarked, with his ringing, military voice, 'He preached in this [John-street] church yesterday; he was too systematic.' This I thought a curious objection. It was not meant, however, as a serious charge, and I was cordially elected." He had probably been embarrassed in appearing for the first time in the pulpit before the Conference, and had detailed the "skeleton" of his discourse too minutely, without clothing it with sufficient nerve and muscle. "I felt," he continues, "indeed unworthy of being united to such a wise and holy body of men. At my ordination I was impressed with an awful solemnity, as the bishop's hands were laid on my head, and he lifted up his strong and sonorous voice, saying, 'From the ends of the earth we call upon thee, O Lord God, to pour upon this thy servant the Holy Ghost for the office and work of a deacon in the Church of God.' These were the words he used instead of the prescribed form, and as he uttered them such a sense of the divine presence overwhelmed me that my knees trembled, and I feared that I should fall to the floor!"

He thus stepped into the ranks of a host of evangelical heroes; for the New York Conference at that time included such men as Garrettson, Thatcher, Snethen, Ezekiel Cooper, Merwin, Hibbard, Ruter, Ostrander, Clark, Crawford, and many others who were the "giants of those days." It was still an immense field, including most of the state of New York, large western portions of Connecticut, Massachusetts, and Vermont, and all the circuits of Canada. At the close of the session he mounted his horse and set off for the River Thames,* a region still unpenetrated by the Methodist itinerants. Thither let us now follow him.

* I have followed his manuscript mostly, in names and dates, rather than the printed "Annual Minutes;" the latter are often defective. The River Thames does not appear at all in the early lists of appointments; in 1804 the "River la French" is given for it by mistake.

CHAPTER X.

ITINERANT LIFE IN CANADA.

His first travels on the Niagara circuit had extended from the Niagara River westward to beyond Oxford, more than half the distance between Lakes Ontario and Huron; a region then but sparsely settled. They deviated also southward to Long Point, which reaches into Lake Erie, and eastward to Little York or Toronto, on the northern shore of Lake Ontario. His second circuit, the Bay of Quinte, was an immense range on the north-east of Lake Ontario. He had thus gone over most of the region immediately north of the two great lakes, or rather inland seas, of Ontario and Erie. We have witnessed the severity of his trials in these new countries; he had endured them "as a good soldier of the Lord Jesus;" and he would have appeared justified had he, in retracing his steps to his paternal home, and to the Conference in New York city, asked for an appointment nearer his kindred and in a more genial climate, especially as he went to the session almost wrecked in health. But he went thither for the express purpose of soliciting permission to throw himself into a still more westward and more desolate region, a region noted, at that time, for pestilential disease and religious destitution—the recent settlements on the River Thames, a stream which enters the St. Clair, opposite Detroit, beyond the north-western shore of Lake Erie.

A MACEDONIAN CALL.

While he was struggling and triumphing through the first year of his itinerancy, he received a letter at Oxford, from a German Baptist who lived on the River Thames, about sixty miles from Detroit, urging him to come over and proclaim his message in that country, then almost totally without religious provision. He knew nothing of the writer, but the call seemed like that of the Macedonian vision to Paul, and it followed him continually. He repeatedly offered his services for the new field to his presiding elder; but the latter deemed the wants of the nearer fields too urgent, and his health too feeble, to justify the mission. He was sent in the opposite direction, to the Bay of Quinte circuit; but while he there lay, languishing, as we have seen, with fever, and his brethren were gathering around his bed to see him die, he still saw the beckoning vision in the further West, and, expecting to rise no more, actually made his will, bequeathing his horse and watch—all the property he had except his thoroughly worn raiment—to any preacher who would go to that suffering people. He had prayed for them incessantly in secret, ever since the receipt of the letter which called him to them.

After his ordination as a deacon at the conference, he requested an interview with Bishop Asbury, and made known to him his impression of a providential call to this mission. The keen eye of the veteran leader lighted up as he gazed on the young evangelist. "He unhesitatingly replied," writes the latter, "as if catching the inspiration with which my own heart was kindled, 'You shall go, my son.'" The bishop presented the case before the Conference, and ordained him a presbyter, that he might go with full powers to administer the sacraments.

ADVENTURES IN THE WILDERNESS.

"No sooner," he writes, "was my way thus opened, than a host of difficulties rallied to prevent my going; suggestions about my youth, my want of health, want of money, the distance—it being, by the route I must go, about six hundred miles—and a thousand other obstacles; but I resolved, by the help of God, to press through them all and fulfill my mission. With but fifteen dollars in my pocket I set off, in company with William Anson and Daniel Pickett, the former being appointed to Yonge-street, the latter to Niagara. We entered Canada by way of Kingston, then went up the shore of Lake Ontario, passing through the settlements where I had before labored; stopping on the way and preaching to the people, until we finally arrived at the head of the lake, on the Niagara circuit, near the place where I had preached my first sermon. Here I was to part from my traveling companions, and proceed alone. My money was all expended, and I had about eighty miles still to travel before I should reach my destined field. New difficulties presented themselves, and I knew not how I could advance any further. I went into the woods, kneeled down before God, and wept and prayed. Finally the words came forcibly to my mind, 'The earth is the Lord's, and the fullness thereof.' I arose with renewed courage, saying 'I will go in the name of the Lord; for he has the hearts of all men, and he can turn them which way soever he will.' Before I left these parts, one friend and another put into my hands money amounting to eleven dollars, enough for my journey.*

"Before proceeding further I visited my sister, with whom I boarded when I experienced religion. She was a pious, humble follower of the Lord Jesus. Having heard that I had died in my severe sickness at the Bay of Quinte, and having received word of my recovery only about a week before my arrival, she was no less surprised than delighted to see me. This beloved sister was often a comfort to me in that distant land, and I loved her tenderly. After spending a day or two with her, I resumed

* "I deem it my duty to say that the first who gave me anything was Reuben Harris, a poor preacher; and I suppose he induced the others to help me. I trust he has received his reward."

my journey. Unexpectedly, a young man offered to accompany me, and we set off together. August 4th and 5th we attended a quarterly meeting at Oxford, where I was refreshed among my old friends, the first-fruits of my ministry, with whom I now took sweet counsel about the labors and trials before me. Departing with their prayers, we journeyed about thirty miles to Delaware-town, where I preached and lodged in the last house of the settlement. My bed was a bundle of straw, my supper, 'mush and milk.'

"August 10th we arose at break of day, took a little food, and started for a ride through the wilderness, forty-five miles long, with no roads, and only 'blazed,' or marked, trees to guide us. There being not even a beaten path, we were often at a loss to know whether we were right or wrong; but we got safely through at last. The flies and musketoes were so troublesome that our horses could not stand to eat, though we stopped in a shady meadow for that purpose; we therefore rode through the woods without any other refreshment for them than what they nibbled as we passed along. As for ourselves, we had a little Indian bread and dried beef in our pockets, of which we partook; but the water we occasionally met looked so black that we dare not drink it. Our horses seemed as eager to get through as ourselves, for whenever practicable, they would trot on with all their speed. We arrived about sunset, weary, hungry, and thirsty, at a small log-hut, inhabited by a Frenchman. My tired horse lay down as soon as the saddle and bridle were taken off. I asked the woman of the cabin if she could give me a drink of tea, but she had none. Being almost famished, I requested the man to procure us some water, which we sipped a little at a time, as if it were nectar; we then ate some Indian pudding and milk, the best food we could obtain. After praying with the family, we lay down on a bundle of straw, slept sweetly, and rose in the morning much refreshed and invigorated in body and mind. The poor woman was so kind as to send early to a distant neighbor, to beg some tea for us; but she had neither tea-kettle, tea-pot, nor tea-cup, she therefore boiled it in a "dish kettle" and then poured it into a tin cup, from which we drank it with more relish than ever a king drank wine from a golden goblet. I thought it the most refreshing beverage I had ever drunk. We allowed our horses to rest till about ten o'clock, and then rode about seven miles to a Moravian mission, a small Indian village on the River Thames. We dined with one of the missionaries, two of whom were stationed here. I had considerable conversation with him respecting their doctrines and usages, as well as their labors among the Indians. He was very sociable, and seemed to possess much of the simplicity of the Gospel. These good men had much trouble in their work, from the corrupting influence of the neighboring white settlers upon the Indians, and it was hoped by them that our labors among the former would help their mission.

"While here, the Indians were called together for worship, which was performed in a very simple manner, by reading a short discourse in their own language, and singing a few verses of a hymn. The missionaries and Indians treated us with great respect, and seemed to rejoice in the prospect of having the Gospel preached to the white settlements on the banks of the river below."

FIRST RECEPTION.

After this interview with the Moravian missionaries, the itinerant and his companion resumed their route, and, early in the afternoon, reached the first house in the white settlement. "Turning my horse," he says, "toward the fence, before the door, I saw a man in the yard, and after the customary salutations I said, 'Do you want the Gospel preached here?' After looking at me with curious earnestness, he replied, 'Yes, that we do: do you preach the Gospel?' 'Yes,' I answered. 'Well then,' said he, 'get down and come in.' I replied, 'I have ridden a great distance to preach in this region; it is now Saturday afternoon; to-morrow being the Sabbath, I must have a place to preach in before I alight from my horse.' He deliberated a few moments, and then said, 'I have a house for you to preach in, victuals and lodging for yourself, and provender for your horse, and you shall be welcome to them all if you will come in.' I remarked, 'I have one more request to make. There is a young man a little behind me, who has accompanied me through the woods: will you entertain him too?' 'By all means,' he answered. This first interview in my new sphere of labor pleased me much. 'God has made my way plain thus far,' I said to myself, 'and therefore I will praise him.'

A FRONTIER MEETING.

"This man took his horse and rode through the settlement for ten miles, notifying the people that there would be preaching at his house on Sunday morning, at ten o'clock. At the appointed hour the house was crowded. I commenced the service by remarking that 'When a stranger appears in these new countries the people are usually curious to know his name, whence he comes, whither he is bound, and what is his errand. I will try to satisfy you in brief. My name is Nathan Bangs. I was born in Connecticut May 2, 1778. I was born again in this province, May, 1800. I commenced itinerating as a preacher of the Gospel in the month of September, 1801. On the 18th of June, the present year, I left New York for the purpose of visiting you, of whom I heard about two years ago, and after a long and tedious journey I am here. I am bound for the heavenly city, and my errand among you is to persuade as many as I can to go with me. I am a Methodist preacher; and my manner of worship is, to stand while singing, kneel while praying, and then I stand while I preach, the people meanwhile sitting. As many of you as see fit to join me in this way can do so, and others may choose their own method.' I then read a chapter in the Bible, after which I gave out a hymn. When the young man who accompanied me stood up to sing, they all rose, men, women, and children. When I kneeled in prayer, they all kneeled down; such a sight I never saw before. I then read for my text, 'Repent ye therefore, and be converted, that your sins may be blotted out when the times of refreshing shall come from the presence of the Lord.' In explaining and enforcing these words, I felt that my divine Master was with me in truth and power; every cloud was dispelled from my mind, and my heart overflowed with love for these people. I believe I preached with 'the Holy Ghost sent down from heaven.' When I had concluded, I informed them of our manner of preaching, the amount of quarterage we received, and the way in which it was collected. I then said, 'All of you who wish to hear any more such preaching, rise up.' They all rose, every man, woman, and child. I then notified them that in two weeks, God willing, they might expect preaching again, and closed the meeting. Thus was my circuit begun.

SALUTATIONS.

"After seating myself, an elderly man approached, and offering his hand with much affection, asked me if I knew Bishop Asbury. I said 'Yes,' and then asked him if he knew him, to which he replied in the affirmative. He was from the state of New Jersey, had been there a member of our Church, had frequently entertained the preachers, and among others, the bishop; but he had been in this country about seven years, totally destitute of the ordinances of the Gospel, for there was no minister of any order in all this region. I asked him how far he lived from that place. He replied, 'Ten miles, down the river.' 'Will you allow me to preach in your house?' He joyfully replied in the affirmative. 'Have you any sons here with you?' 'I have one,' said he. 'Let him mount his horse, ride immediately home, and notify the people that I will preach at your house at three o'clock this afternoon; you stay and dine with me, and then we will ride on together.' He did so, and when we arrived the house and yard were full of people, to whom I preached with lively satisfaction. Among others present, I observed a veteran man with a long beard. At the close of the meeting he was introduced as *Mr. Messmore*, a German Baptist. He was the person who had written to me the letter about two years before, inviting me to come into this neglected country. The next day I preached at his house, about twenty-one miles distant. Thus did God help me, and open my way. I felt that I was in the order of his providence. Such a sweetness of soul I enjoyed, such a liberty and unction in preaching, as plainly indicated that I was under his guidance, and his smile seemed to light up the wilderness before me. The next day, in company with Mr. Messmore, I rode ten miles and preached in the house of an Indian woman, the widow of a French Canadian, who had left her considerable property. She was a good, simple-hearted, earnest creature, and reminded me of the Shunamite, for she prepared for me, in an upper room, a bed, a table, a chair, and a candlestick. In this room I preached, and ate, and slept, and no one was allowed to enter it in my absence, except to keep it in order. She never asked me to sit at the table with her, deeming herself unworthy, but prepared my food and put it on the table in my room. She considered herself highly honored by having the Gospel preached in her house, and she treated me in this way during all my stay in that country. When I parted with her the next day after my first visit, in shaking hands she left a dollar in my palm. It was much needed, for I was nearly out of money. The next day we traveled, partly through a scattered French settlement and partly through a prairie, fifty miles, to Sandwich, a small village opposite Detroit, where I preached in the evening."

He found there a rude jail, and in it, among other prisoners, a young man, under sentence of death for horse-stealing. He preached to them all, but most of them being French, could not understand him. The young criminal was, however, led to repentance; he confessed his crime with tears, and died with hope of the mercy of God. The sudden appearance of the itinerant thus brought comfort and hope to him in his extremity. He clung to the preacher with a breaking heart as his last, his only friend. "I could not but reflect," says the latter, "upon the severity of that criminal code which condemned a man to death for stealing a horse. Such undue severity, in my opinion, instead of preventing crime, tends to harden the heart and promote crime."

DETROIT IN 1804.

He crossed the river to Detroit, and having a letter of introduction to a Presbyterian minister, called on him, but found him in a "backslidden state, apparently destitute of the fear of God, neither preaching nor praying. He had become a magistrate, and had married a French Roman Catholic wife. He received me, however, with a friendly spirit, and assisted me in procuring the Council House for preaching. I preached that evening to a large congregation. The people here were principally French Papists; the rest were a mixture of English, Irish, and Americans, all as wicked apparently as they could well be. I left another appointment for two weeks from that evening. At the appointed time I appeared among them again, and while preaching there arose a terrible thunder-storm. The lightning flashed vividly, the peals of thunder rattled through the heavens like discharges of artillery. I kept on preaching, and admonished the hearers that this was but a faint resemblance of that day when the heavens shall pass away with a great noise, and the elements melt with fervent heat. Two young men, as they afterward related, sat trembling, fearing that the house would be struck and they killed for their wickedness. They had put powder into the candlesticks, hoping that it would be reached by the lights and explode during the worship; but the meeting closed too early for their design. They said that after the sermon was ended, and I took up the candle to read the hymn, they feared the powder would explode in my eyes. Here again God was with me and delivered me. The next time I visited Detroit a Presbyterian missionary invited me to dine with him, which I thankfully did. I found him a rigid Hopkinsian, and he endeavored in vain to convince me of what he called my errors. He treated me, however, with Christian courtesy. He told me that he had preached until none but children came to hear him, and that he had given up the place in despair, but hoped I would have better success. The people turned out so well in the evening that I made arrangements to give them a Sabbath appointment, but, alas! when the time came only a few children made their appearance, and 'I shook off the dust of my feet as a testimony against them,' and left them. In about four weeks the whole town was destroyed by fire."

In his History of the Church he speaks of Detroit as at that time a most abandoned place. Soon after the fire it was rebuilt. It has become one of the most important cities of the nation, and Methodism is now strongly intrenched there.

REMARKABLE SCENES.

From Detroit he went to Fort Malden, and down the shore of Lake Erie, among settlements of Americans, English, Scotch, Irish, and Dutch emigrants. He thus completed his circuit, and continued to travel it about three months. A more morally destitute region, he says, he had never seen. Young people had arrived at the age of sixteen who had never heard preaching; and he found a Methodist family, as we have seen, who had lived in the country seven years without hearing a sermon. "But," he adds, "although the people generally were extremely ignorant of spiritual things, and very loose in their morals, they seemed ripe for the Gospel, and received and treated God's messenger with great attention and kindness. They treated me as an angel of God; and as St. Paul said, respecting the Galatians, it seemed as if they would willingly have plucked out their own eyes and given them to me if it could have added anything to my comfort. Among those whose hearts the Lord touched were the parents of a German family, who had so disagreed with their children that they had all forsaken their father's house, and there appeared an irreconcilable enmity between them. The parents, when converted, made known to me, with many tears, their unhappy condition, and earnestly entreated me to attempt a reconciliation. After deliberating for a while, I advised them to send an invitation to all their children, some of whom were married and had large families, to come home on a particular day, also to invite a few of their neighbors to come in; to have the table spread in the middle of the room, and a good dinner, all cooked beforehand, ready to be put upon it; and to have their children all seated on one side of the room and they themselves on the other. I proposed then to preach a sermon to them. At the appointed time they all came, and I preached on the parable of the Prodigal Son. At the conclusion I remarked that the Prodigal is represented as saying first, 'I will arise and go to my father;' but I said to the children, 'your parents first sent for you;' and then to the parents, 'your children have complied, at your request; they have come at your call. Here you are all together in the presence of God, and here are some of your neighbors to witness what is done. If you are all willing to forgive what is past, be reconciled, and live hereafter as parents and children should, rise up, meet each other before us, and shake hands together as a token of your reconciliation.' They all instantly arose, met, embraced and kissed each other, and wept over one another most profusely. It was indeed an affecting scene to all present. When their emotions had somewhat subsided I said, 'Now set the food upon the table and let us eat and drink together in token of friendship.' This was done; we all drew around the table, I asked a blessing, and we sat down, ate and drank together. Thus had the Gospel restored harmony to this broken circle. They were truly grateful to God for the reconciliation brought to the household. While I remained in those parts that house was my home, and the family treated me as the messenger of God to them.

"Perhaps no part of our country was more subject to fever and ague, or 'Lake Fever,' as it was called, than that along the River Thames. It was occasioned by the stagnant swamps which lie a little distance from the river on each side, and the unwholesomeness of the water which the people are obliged to use. The fever began to rage in September, and, during its progress, in almost every family less or more were sick; and in some instances every member of the family was prostrated at the same time. When I first visited a house I was usually presented with a whisky bottle, and urged to partake of it as a preservative against the fever; but I declined the beverage, and told them I would drink water and tea, and we would see who should have the better health. Though the fever raged so that I could scarcely visit a family without seeing more or less sick, I constantly traveled the country in health until about the close of the sickly season, when I, too, was seized with the disease, but by timely remedies I escaped with but two or three paroxysms. This is mentioned to show the mistaken notion of many people, who suppose the use of ardent spirits is a preventive of epidemic diseases. It is believed that it induces them in nine cases out of ten instead of preventing them."

His attack, though brief, was severe; he was delirious some of the time, but he found shelter in the cabin of the good Dutchman, whose family he had reconciled, and to their assiduous attentions he owed his quick recovery. He immediately went forth again, preaching and praying among the suffering people. The fever still raged everywhere. He passed over to Detroit, and found all the taverns crowded with the sick. He could obtain no public lodging, but a Christian friend took him in for a night. He returned, wended his way up the Thames, and found the settlers despondent and perishing. He met a large company of Scotchmen fleeing with their families from the pestilent region; no less than twenty-one of their number had died within a few days. Notwithstanding their affliction, they were drunk and uproarious. He gave them a brief tract on drunkenness; it rapidly passed from one to another, and produced such an impression that their clamors ceased, and he was asked to preach and pray with them, and parted from them the next day with their hearty blessings. He was thus ever ready for his work "in season and out of season." His activity and boldness made even the rude and hardened quail, and they sometimes fled before him. One of his stopping-places was a tavern. As he now approached it on horseback a boisterous crowd, who were gambling and drinking around a large table, caught a glimpse of him, sprung up in terror from their seats, and escaped, some by the windows, some by the back door, and so expeditiously that not one remained when he reached the room. "Thus," he writes, "the wicked flee when no man pursueth." One of them, however, carried away a salutary impression of the scene. "I am fleeing from man," he exclaimed, "but what shall I do when God calls me! I will gamble no more."

PERILS BY WATER.

As he pursued his route he met not only sickness and desolation, but perils to himself and especially to his horse, his indispensable companion. The river was high, and overflowed its banks. In some instances, when he got over it himself with safety, but much difficulty, the noble animal, which he says he loved nearly as much as himself, was carried down the current, and escaped only by his uncommon strength. After relating several examples of this kind, he continues: "At another time, having traveled about forty miles across the plains from Sandwich, and arriving in the night, I made a mistake by putting my horse down the stream. We had no sooner entered the current than the canoe swung upon his back, so that it was carried along by him in this manner. I immediately requested the oarsman to cease paddling and let the horse take us over, for I knew the courage and strength of the animal. I gave him the full length of the bridle, and he landed us safely on the other side, though below the usual landing-place. I blessed the noble brute and thanked God for this deliverance.

"I will relate one more example of a narrow escape in crossing this river. After heavy rains it rises very rapidly. At the time of one of these freshets my horse was on one side and I on the other. I wished very much to cross, and went to the ferry for the purpose. The ferryman was not at home, but his wife said that her daughter, a girl about fourteen years old, could paddle me over. We accordingly started, and, as the river was much swollen and very rapid in the center, and the flats overflowed to a considerable distance, I requested the girl to take me above the usual landing-place before she launched out into the current. I stood on the stern of the canoe and she in the middle. We finally turned into the rapid stream, which was filled with floating logs and fragments of timber. We paddled with all our might, but in spite of our efforts we floated some distance below the landing-place, and finally came into the top of a tree which stood on the flat above the lower bank. I cried to the girl to seize hold of a branch and keep her feet steady on the canoe; I did the same and we held fast. This gave us some time to look around, and see how we might escape. I soon perceived that beyond the tree, shoreward, the water backed and formed an eddy, and if we could manage to get the canoe on the side of the tree next to the land we should be safe. I accordingly directed the girl to pull from branch to branch, and doing the same myself, we succeeded in moving around the tree until we were between it and the land, when we sprung to our paddles and behold we were safe at the land. We then went up to the house, the man of which was a friend of mine, and I got him to take the girl back, after paying her well for her courageous efforts. Such are some of the examples of itinerant ministerial life in that country at that early day."

A NIGHT IN THE WOODS.

As the winter approached he saw that it would be impossible to continue his travels effectively in this new region, for the roads were becoming impracticable and the people were widely dispersed. Some of the settlements were ten, twenty, and even forty miles apart, with intervening forests, which the snows would render impassable. What should he do? "I had," he writes, "many struggles of mind, and earnestly prayed for divine guidance." He finally determined to return eastward to the Niagara circuit, and induce some local preachers to emigrate with their families to the River Thames, thereby supplying its principal settlements with men who could sustain among them the ordinances of religion, intending to return himself in the spring. Accordingly, about the middle of November, he set out for the east. He paused at the Moravian Mission, and had a day of profitable communion with its laborers. Resuming his route, he reached the last house—a log hut—beyond which his way stretched forty miles through the primeval forest to Delaware-town. Providentially, he found in this cabin a traveler, bound on the same course. Mounting their horses early in the morning they entered the woods. There was snow two inches deep on the ground; the streams were high and still open; the mud was often up to the knees of their horses; they frequently had to strip them of saddle and bridle and drive them over the creeks, and then pass over themselves on logs. The route was somber in its winter desolation. Night overtook them on the banks of a stream, and it was impossible to continue their course after dark. They resigned themselves, therefore, to sleep in the woods. They had "carried with them some food for themselves and their horses, and flint, steel, and an Indian tomahawk for use as they might have need. We constructed," he says, "a small wigwam of branches of trees and shrubs. My companion attempted to strike fire for us, but his hands were so stiffened with the cold that he failed. I succeeded with the flint, steel, and a piece of 'punk,' and we kindled a rousing flame, heaping on brush and logs. It melted the snow, and soon dried the surface of the ground some distance around. We tied our horses to trees, gave them some oats, ate some food ourselves, went to the creek and drank, and then, having prayed, lay down to sleep in our booth, the stars shining brightly above us, and the winds moaning through the solemn woods. After three hours I awoke, and found my fellow-traveler up and shivering over the fire, which had nearly burned out. 'Come,' said I, 'let us get more fuel and rouse it up again.' We did so, and soon were comfortable. We then sat down by it and spent the remainder of the night in conversation. It was a wild, picturesque scene, and the hours passed agreeably as well as profitably. At the break of day we mounted our horses and went onward. We arrived at the first house about three o'clock in the afternoon, hungry, thirsty, and exhausted. I had no sooner warmed myself by the fire than I fell asleep. After supper I prayed with the family and went to bed, truly thankful that the Lord had preserved my life and health through all these fatigues and dangers. I slept sweetly that night, and the next morning went on my way to Oxford. The snow had fallen in the night, and was so deep that the traveling was difficult; but my horse, who seemed as glad as myself to get safely through the woods and swamps, trotted on with a brave heart, so that I arrived at Oxford before night, and took 'sweet counsel' with my old friends and spiritual children. I remained there a few days to rest and preach, and then passed on twenty-five miles further, to Burford, where I was received as one risen from the dead, for the man who accompanied me through the wilderness had gone on before me and had magnified our sufferings so much that my friends had almost given me up for lost. We praised God together for his loving-kindness and tender mercies. Not being able to persuade any local preachers to move to the Thames, the people there were left without preaching till the next year, when they were visited by William Case, whose faithful labors were greatly blessed, so that he was able to form societies, and that region has been a regular circuit ever since, and hosts of the people have been gathered into the Church. It was indeed affecting to see with what eagerness they received the 'word of reconciliation.' Many had grown to manhood who had never heard a sermon till I went among them; while others, who had professed religion before they moved thither, I found in a backslidden state, but they were glad to hear again the joyful sound of salvation."

A STARTLING INCIDENT.

The remainder of the year he was retained on the Niagara circuit, among his old friends. His colleague was the Rev. Daniel Pickett. They labored with their might, and great reformations followed them around the circuit. "My own soul," he says, "enjoyed uninterrupted communion with God." In some places the population was still extremely rude, and scenes occurred which could hardly happen in maturer communities. He was often opposed, and sometimes interrupted in his public services, but knew how to turn such trials to account. At one appointment, "a very hardened place," a young woman amused herself and a circle of hearers around her by laughing audibly. He spoke to her, but she persisted, when he paused again and addressed a solemn warning to her. She rose, rushed out of the assembly, was immediately seized with disease, and in a few days died "in a most alarming manner." "When I heard of her death," he writes, "I was shocked. It produced a great sensation among the people; some said one thing, some another; and one man declared he would shoot me, did he not fear that I was a prophet of the Lord, and therefore he dare not." The next time he visited them he preached from the words, "For all this have ye not returned unto me, saith the Lord!" He reminded them of the recent solemn event, and admonished them immediately to repent. His word was in power; the whole settlement was startled, "and from this time a great reformation prevailed, and in about three months an effective Methodist society was organized there." Among its members was a young lady who afterward became his wife—the sharer of the sufferings and sucecsses of his long life.

FIRST CANADA CAMP-MEETING.

It was in this year that the first "camp-meeting" in Canada was held in Adolphustown, where the first Methodist class of the province was organized, in 1790, by its first Methodist preacher, William Losee, and its first Methodist chapel erected in 1792.* Camp-meetings had been

* Letters of Rev. Anson Green, in the Christian Guardian, (Canada,) dated February 25 and March 9, 1860.

extensively held in the Western United States for about five years. They originated among the Presbyterians. They seemed justified by the religious necessities of the frontier, where there were but few chapels, and where, after the harvests, the settlers could conveniently travel considerable distances from home, and avail themselves of a week of camp life for religious instruction and social intercourse. They immediately became favorite occasions; the scattered population from twenty, fifty, or a hundred miles around, traveled to them in wagons, on horseback, or on foot. Some brought tents, some erected booths of trees and shrubs. The scene, circled with these temporary but picturesque shelters, in the midst of a primeval forest, illuminated at night by pine torches, thronged by thousands of people, varied by a daily succession of sermons, of prayer-meetings, of hymns, which sometimes resounded for miles through the wooded solitudes, presented a poetic and indescribable interest, and could not fail to give a profound impression to the powerful, though rude eloquence, of the frontier preachers.

THE "JERKS."

Remarkable demonstrations of religious feeling attended these great assemblies. It is not surprising that anomalous religious "phenomena" should also attend them. The memoirs of the early western Methodist preachers abundantly record these yet insoluble marvels. Hearers, hundreds of hearers would fall as dead men to the earth under a single sermon. The extraordinary scenes called the "jerks" began at one of these meetings. They were rapid, jerking contortions, which seemed to be always the effect, direct or indirect, of religious causes, yet affected not only the religious, but often the most irreligious minds. Violent opposers were sometimes seized by them; men with imprecations upon their lips were suddenly smitten with them. Drunkards, attempting to drown the effect by liquors, could not hold the bottle to their lips; their convulsed arms would drop it, or shiver it against the surrounding trees. Horsemen, charging in upon the meetings to disperse them, were arrested by the strange affection at the very boundaries of the worshiping circles, and were the more violently shaken the more they endeavored to resist the inexplicable power. "If they would not strive against it, but pray in good earnest, the jerking would usually abate," says a witness who has seen more than five hundred persons "jerking" at one time in his large congregations.* The nervous infection spread from one denomination to another, and prevailed as an epidemic through much of the valley of the Mississippi.

Prior to the introduction of camp-meetings infidelity prevailed generally in the new states of the West, the effect, to a great extent, of the writings of Thomas Paine, and of his great personal influence in America during the recent revolutionary struggle. Many wise, as well as devout men, who witnessed the results of these meetings, believed that they were a providential provision for the counteraction of the deism and corruption which seemed to threaten with utter demoralization that vast country—the seat of future and gigantic states—and that the astonishing physical phenomena which attended them were a necessary means of arresting the popular attention. The "great revival" which followed, and which swept over the whole valley of the Mississippi, unquestionably broke down the prevalent deism, and opened the way for the most rapid religious development recorded in the history of any modern people.

This first camp-meeting in Canada appeared to Dr. Bangs a salient fact in the history of Canadian Methodism. He therefore made particular notes respecting it. They show that the confusion incidental, if not inevitable to such occasions, occurred, but also that "it was

* Autobiography of Peter Cartwright, page 48.

attended by extraordinary displays of the favor and power of God."

SCENES IN THE CAMP.

Its announcement beforehand excited great interest far and near. Whole families prepared for a pilgrimage to the ground. Processions of wagons and of foot passengers wended along the highways. With two of his fellow-evangelists, our itinerant had to take his course from a remote appointment through a range of forest thirty miles in extent. They hastened forward, conversing on religious themes, praying or singing, and eager with expectation of the moral battle-scene about to open. They arrived in time to commence the meeting on the 27th of September, though only about two hundred and fifty people had yet reached the ground. "The exercises began with singing, prayer, and a short sermon on the text 'Brethren, pray.' Several exhortations followed, and after an intermission of about twenty minutes another sermon was delivered on 'Christ, our wisdom, righteousness, sanctification, and redemption.' Some lively exhortations again followed, and the Spirit of the Lord seemed to move among the people. After an interruption of an hour and a half a prayer-meeting was held, and toward its close the power of God descended on the assembly, and songs of victory and praise resounded through the forest. The battle thus opened, the exercises continued with preaching, exhorting, and singing, until midnight, when the people retired to their booths. The night was clear and serene, and the scene being new to us, a peculiar solemnity rested upon all minds. The lights glowing among the trees and above the tents, and the voice of prayer and praise mingling and ascending into the star-lit night, altogether inspired the heart with emotions better felt than described. During this day six persons passed from death to life.

"At five o'clock Saturday morning a prayer-meeting was held, and at ten o'clock a sermon was preached on the words, 'My people are destroyed for lack of knowledge.' At this time the congregation had increased to perhaps twenty-five hundred, and the people of God were seated together on logs near the stand, while a crowd were standing in a semicircle around them. During the sermon I felt an unusual sense of the divine presence, and thought I could see a cloud of divine glory resting upon the congregation. The circle of spectators unconsciously fell back, step by step, until quite a space was opened between them and those who were seated. At length I sprung from my seat to my feet. The preacher stopped and said, 'Take it and go on.' 'No,' I replied, 'I rise not to preach.' I immediately descended from the stand among the hearers; the rest of the preachers all spontaneously followed me, and we went among the people, exhorting the impenitent and comforting the distressed; for while Christians were filled with 'joy unspeakable and full of glory,' many a sinner was weeping and praying in the surrounding crowd. These we collected together in little groups, and exhorted God's people to join in prayer for them, and not to leave them until he should save their souls. O what a scene of tears and prayer was this! I suppose that not less than a dozen little praying circles were thus formed in the course of a few minutes. It was truly affecting to see parents weeping over their children, neighbors exhorting their unconverted neighbors to repent, while all, old and young, were awe-struck. The wicked looked on with silent amazement while they beheld some of their companions struck down by the mighty power of God, and heard his people pray for them. The mingled voices of prayer and praise were heard afar off, and produced a solemn awe apparently upon all minds. As the sun was setting, struck by the grandeur of the spectacle and the religious interest of the crowd, a preacher mounted the stand and proclaimed for his text, 'Behold, He cometh with clouds, and every eye shall see Him.' The meeting continued all night, and few, I think, slept that night. During this time some forty persons were converted or sanctified.

"On Sabbath morning, as the natural sun arose in splendor, darting its rays through the forest, we presented ourselves before its Maker, and poured out our songs of thanksgiving to the Lord of the universe. We felt that our early sacrifice was accepted, for the 'Sun of righteousness' shone upon our souls and made all within us rejoice. We could sing with faith:

"'None is like Jeshurun's God,
  So great, so strong, so high!
Lo! he spreads his wings abroad,
  He rides upon the sky!
Israel is his first-born son:
  God, the Almighty God, is thine:
See him to thy help come down,
  The excellence divine.'

"After breakfast, a host being now on the ground, we held a love-feast. The interest and excitement were so great and the crowd so large that while some assembled around the stand, a preacher mounted a wagon at a distance and addressed a separate congregation. The impression of the Word was universal, the power of the Spirit was manifest throughout the whole encampment, and almost every tent was a scene of prayer. At noon the Lord's supper was administered to multitudes, while other multitudes looked on with astonishment and tears. After the sacrament, a young woman, of fashionable and high position in society, was smitten down, and with sobs entreated the prayers of the people. Her sister forced her away; a preacher went forth without the camp and led them both back, followed by quite a procession of their friends; a circle gathered about them and sang and prayed. The unawakened sister was soon upon her knees praying in agony, and was first converted; the other quickly after received the peace of God, and they wept and rejoiced together. A backslider, who had become a maniac, and was in despair, was brought to the camp. His symptoms were like those of the New Testament demoniacs. It required the strength of several men to hold him, especially while prayer was offered for him. We first besought God for Christ's sake to restore his faculties, which was done. He then earnestly prayed for himself, and before the meeting closed he was not only delivered from despair, but filled with joy and peace in believing.

"The time was at hand at last for the conclusion of the meeting. The last night was the most awfully impressive and yet delightful scene my eyes ever beheld. There was not a cloud on the sky. The stars studded the firmament, and the glory of God filled the camp. All the neighboring forest seemed vocal with the echoes of hymns. Turn our attention whichever way we could, we heard the voice of prayer or praise. As it was the last night, every moment seemed precious; parents were praying for their children or children for their parents, brothers and sisters for one another, neighbors for neighbors, all anxious that before they left the consecrated ground they should be 'sealed' as the 'heirs of salvation.' I will not attempt to describe the parting scene, for it was indescribable. The preachers, about to disperse to their distant and hard fields of labor, hung upon each other's necks weeping and yet rejoicing. Christians from remote settlements, who had here formed holy friendships which they expected would survive in heaven, parted probably to meet no more on earth, but in joyful hope of reunion above. They wept, prayed, sang, shouted aloud, and had at last to break away from one another as by force. As the hosts marched off in different directions the songs of victory rolled along the highways. Great was the good that followed. A general revival of religion spread around the circuits, especially that of the Bay of Quinte, on which this meeting was held. I returned to Augusta circuit and renewed my labors, somewhat worn, but full of faith and the Holy Ghost."

The hardy inhabitants of the frontier could well enough endure such a week of excitement, of broken rest, and incessant preaching and praying; but the camp-meeting, as now conducted in most of the country, has been reduced to rigid method. It has its own code and police, and proceeds with the order of the Jewish Feast of Tabernacles. The present occasion, though one of intense excitement, and scarcely intermitted exercises, seems not to have been attended with many of those physical phenomena to which we have alluded, as accompanying such meetings in the Mississippi Valley. Our evangelist, however, relates, with some reluctance, that he had a partial example of them in his own person. At midnight, on the last night, while an indescribable sense of the divine presence prevailed throughout the encampment, he stood on a log and exhorted the people with overwhelming effect, his powerful voice reverberating over the ground and through the surrounding woods. While stretching out his arms, as if to bless the weeping multitude, they stiffened and remained extended, and for some time he stood thus addressing the hearers, weeping with them that wept. He was at last led to a tent, but with still extended arms. The strange effect continued there, but did not disturb his religious joy. "I was continually uttering praise; the tent was soon crowded, and at a single utterance the whole group fell to the ground.

"'O'erwhelmed with His stupendous grace
They did not in His presence move:
But breathed unutterable praise
In rapturous awe and silent love.'"

His arms were now immediately released. His first sensation he describes as not painful though uncomfortable, "a prickling sensation over the whole body, like that felt when a limb is said to be asleep; but this was followed by a soft, soothing feeling, as if I were anointed with oil, and such a consciousness of the presence and peace of God pervaded me as I cannot describe."

Such phenomena are worth recording for the study of both theologians and physiologists.

During the remainder of this ecclesiastical year he pursued his circuit labors with unabated energy and success. On the 27th of April, 1806, he "married Mary Bolton, of the town of Edwardsburgh, Upper Canada." During the remainder of his long career, this day was one of the most grateful reminiscences of his Canada life.

CHAPTER XI.

MINISTERIAL LIFE IN CANADA.

Soon after his marriage he departed for the Conference, which began its session in New York city, on the 16th of May, 1806. He was greeted again by Garrettson, Cooper, Ostrander, Clark, and other chief members as worthy of their ranks: a pioneer hero of their frontier fields. He had now traveled over most, if not all, the settled regions of Upper Canada; he had continued in that hard field longer than most of his fellow-laborers; and, as a married man, was entitled by usage to return to the states and take a more convenient appointment. But his fervid spirit longed for more usefulness in the wilderness. Lower Canada remained yet unexplored by him, and he offered himself to Asbury as a missionary to any accessible part of it. He was designated, in the Minutes, to Quebec; but the nominal appointments of that day, especially on the frontiers, were more a convenience of the Minutes than a restriction on the itinerant. Even in the older portions of the Church, the term of service was not rigorously measured by the interval between the conference sessions, but preachers, sent to Baltimore, Philadelphia, New York, often, after six months' service in one city, passed to another by exchanges which continued the remainder of the year. He knew the uncertainties of his new field; he had but eighty dollars in his pocket, had a wife, and could make no calculations of support from the people to whom he was going. Asbury, however, was then the general almoner of the denomination; he collected funds in his long routes, and distributed them at the conferences to the most necessitous laborers. Many of the early preachers of New England were thus relieved, and the Canada itinerants could expect similar assistance. If not successful in Quebec, he could pass to Montreal or any other eligible point of the country. In fine, he proposed to spend one year more at least in the British possessions, braving, with its little corps of pioneers, the trials of their new work.

EN ROUTE.

"Before I left New York city," he writes, "I was attacked by the fever and ague, but, as the Conference had closed, I concluded to go on. I went in a sloop to Tarrytown, in the neighborhood of which I had left my horse. I had not been long on the dock when a man came and inquired for a sick Methodist preacher. He had doubtless heard of me. I found him to be John B. Matthias, then a local preacher, afterward an eminent traveling minister. He took me to his home, and he and his wife treated me with all the tenderness of a father and mother. My fever soon left me, and on the next evening I preached with much liberty and consolation. After the services, who should present himself but my beloved friend and spiritual father, Joseph Sawyer, with his wife. They gladdened my heart, and we rejoiced together in the fellowship of the Gospel. We had been together in many a severe but successful battle for the truth in Canada, and it was pleasant for us to meet at this distance, and talk over our trials and triumphs. The following day I started on my way, visiting my parents, brothers, and sisters, with whom I staid a few days and preached several times. My father had now surmounted his old prejudices, and heard me gladly. Taking my leave again of them, I hastened on toward Canada, designing to attend a camp-meeting on the Augusta circuit, which was to begin on the first of June. I arrived there on the evening of its commencement, and was soon surrounded by my old friends, who received me with great cordiality, and we had a blessed meeting. After remaining with my wife's father about two weeks, she and I departed in a boat for Montreal. The voyage down the St. Lawrence presented many picturesque and some grand scenes, the mighty river, the dashing cataracts, the 'Thousand Isles,' all illuminated with the brightness of spring, refreshed our minds, burdened with anxiety respecting the untried scenes we were about to encounter. We reached Montreal, a distance of a hundred and forty miles, in twenty-six hours. I remained there preaching till the 26th of August, when, leaving my wife behind, I left for Quebec on board of a sloop.

QUEBEC.

"After a voyage of four days, I arrived at this old city early in the morning. I was struck with its magnificent site and its strong fortifications, the latter dominating over the great river and the habitations of the people, which clung to the sides of the eminence. It looked hoary with age, a fact rare yet in America. As I entered it I felt lost, as in a desert. I was totally a stranger, not having seen a solitary being that belonged there, nor was there any Methodist society or class to welcome me. Samuel Merwin, one of our most eloquent preachers, had visited it two years before, but left it, despairing of success. I had a few names of persons, on whom I called and made known the object of my visit; they received me kindly, and assisted me to obtain a place for preaching, though I had to do much of this preliminary work myself. As I arrived on Saturday morning, I was desirous to begin my mission on Sabbath; I bestirred myself, therefore, and on the next morning had a tolerable congregation, and preached with considerable liberty. I took lodgings with a friendly man by the name of Gibson, who treated me with much kindness. After preaching a few times, such were the encouraging signs that I hired a more eligible room for our meetings, and another to live in, and in about four weeks sent for my wife, who soon arrived in safety. At this time the prospect was quite flattering, the congregation was large, and several persons appeared remarkably friendly; but little did I anticipate what was before me."

TRIALS AT QUEBEC.

His congregation soon dwindled away to half a dozen persons. Curiosity alone had prompted the first numerous attendance. His eighty dollars were at last expended. "It seemed impossible," he says, "for me to bear up under my trials. I could endure opposition, and had been tested in this respect; but to see no result of my labors, to be simply let alone by the great population around me, was insupportable. My mind at times sunk into the deepest despondence. My only relief was in prayer and preaching, for then I forgot my desolation. My money expended, my congregation almost annihilated, among strangers, and fearing the cause I represented would be disgraced by my failure, I could only hide myself in God. But the trial did me good. I learned lessons from it which I have never forgotten. The keenest suffering of my forlorn condition was that my wife had to endure it with me; but I thank God that she bore it better than I did, and became my comforter."

Having learned the French language from her mother, she now taught it to him, and thereby enabled him to converse on religious subjects with the French inhabitants, who after gratifying their curiosity had deserted his congregation. He found some relief also in other studies, having access to the library of a Scotch missionary, which afforded him a few standard books. It was no unimportant blessing to the Church as well as to himself that this season of trial strengthened those habits of self-improvement which afterward raised him to a prominent literary position in his denomination, and fitted him to be, for years, the chief defender of its doctrines and other interests. He had abundance of leisure, and his mental sufferings drove him to books.

Though his discouragements continually increased, he was not willing to give up his post till he could hold it no longer. Even when seemingly at this extremity, he still held on. "I was at last embarrassed," he says, "to meet my smallest expenses. Having engaged a man to saw some wood that I had procured for winter, now setting in with great severity, he came one day to complete the job which he had begun before. Having no money to pay him, and fearing that if I did not I should bring reproach upon my profession, I requested my wife, who could speak French better than myself, to inform him that he need not finish his work that day. He replied that he must, as he could not come again. 'What shall I do?' I said to myself. After praying for a while I went to an acquaintance, and told him I had a favor to ask and he must not deny me; he must lend me one dollar and fifty cents, and if ever I should be able I would return it, but if not, he must wait till the resurrection of the just and the unjust. Without hesitation he granted my request, and I paid the laborer. At another time I was under the necessity of borrowing a shilling to pay the woman who brought me milk. The weekly collection in the congregation amounted to about one dollar, and this was all I had to depend upon for support, after expending all my own money. But behold the goodness of God! When he had sufficiently humbled me to depend entirely on himself, he sent me help in a way I little expected. I suppose that by some means information of my reduced condition was given to some benevolent individuals, who now ministered to my necessities, and that too in a manner which kept their liberality from all ostentation, and this made their gifts the more welcome. A servant would arrive with the kind respects of unknown persons, with valuable presents of food, sugar, or tea, and sometimes money, and these from strangers with whom I never became acquainted. These instances of kindness so overcame me that I could not refrain from tears, and I would retire in secret and pour out my thanksgivings to God, and pray for my benefactors."

AT MONTREAL.

He remained in Quebec, struggling with these difficulties about three months, when, in accordance with the itinerant usage of the times, and by the advice of his ministerial brethren, he passed up the river to Montreal, exchanging for the remainder of the year with Samuel Coate, who had been laboring there since the last Conference. Besides the moral lessons he had learned, and the studies which his leisure had allowed him to prosecute, he had, at least, opened the way for his successor. He had secured an humble place of worship, and left a few Methodists, honest mechanics, to welcome Coate. The latter, by his advice, "advertised" his arrival and the place of his preaching; the dwindled congregation soon began to increase, and Methodism was effectively founded in Quebec, and will maintain its stand there, it may be hoped, till the end of time.

In Montreal he labored under somewhat more cheering auspices. During the remainder of the ecclesiastical year he had incessant work and gratifying success.

He records that upon a calculation of his receipts and expenditures for the year, he found his expenses had been about forty dollars over all he had received. "I did not attend the next Conference, but sent my accounts, and the preachers remitted to me about two hundred and forty dollars, which put me upon my legs again, as I was not in debt. This year I was appointed to the Niagara circuit, about three hundred and fifty miles from home. I purchased a horse and started for my new appointment, but had not gone over ten miles when I met the presiding elder of the Lower Canada District, who requested me to return to Montreal, as Bishop Asbury had said, when he read off the appointments, that the presiding elders might arrange it as they saw best. After deliberating a while I consented to go, and leaving my wife at her father's house, I embarked, in company with William Snyder, a French missionary and most excellent man, on a scow, loaded with boards and flour, and sailed down the St. Lawrence again. We had several hairbreadth escapes among the falls, and were saved only by all hands, preachers and other passengers, working with our might. I hired a room in Montreal and sent for my wife, and we both pursued, with some success but many difficulties, our pastoral labors. The society was small and poor, and I had to grapple with many embarrassments; but God supported me through them all, and now, half a century later, I still praise him for his goodness to me then."

He had now been about seven years in Canada as a traveling preacher, and "had visited," he says, "every city, town, and village, and almost every settlement in it." It was thought, both by himself and his ministerial advisers, that the time had come for his return to the States. He had done faithfully the work of a missionary evangelist; he had endured his full share of the hardships of the frontier ministry, and had achieved no small success. He had traversed Upper Canada thundering, a Boanerges, through its forests and along its scattered settlements. He was the founder of Methodism in many of its localities where it has continued to flourish, and where, before his death, it had become the dominant form of religion, and had intrenched itself in commodious, in some instances, in stately chapels. He may be called its founder in Quebec; for Merwin had preceded him in that city only as a casual visitor, and after a few sermons, had left it without success. The first appearance of its name in the printed Minutes was in connection with his own name, as its first appointed Methodist preacher, and it never ceased to appear in the list of appointments till transferred to the Minutes of the "Wesleyan Connection." Canadian Methodism must ever recognize Nathan Bangs as among its chief founders, and the flourishing Methodist communities of Quebec and Montreal, as they catch the glimpses of their incipient history, from the record of his sufferings and struggles, may well exclaim, "What hath God wrought!"

Methodism has achieved marvels of success in Canada. "The different bodies of Methodists make, in Upper Canada, nearly one third of the Protestant population, and very nearly one fourth of the entire population; in United Canada the Methodists are considerably more than one fourth of the whole number of Protestants, and more than one seventh of the total population of Canada, East and West, Protestant and Catholic. The Canada connection supports a relatively greater number of ministers than do the British Wesleyan societies, and it pays over fifty thousand dollars a year for the support of its missions."*

* **Christian Guardian**, (Canada.)

CHAPTER XII.

HOME AGAIN.

In the latter part of January, 1808, he visited with his wife her father's house in Edwardstown, Canada. Purchasing there a sleigh for the long journey, they soon afterward departed for the states. "We crossed," he writes, "the St. Lawrence at Ogdensburgh, then an inconsiderable village, and arrived at my brother Joseph's on the fourth of March. I rejoiced to find my father and mother, brothers and sisters, well, and some of them happy on their way to heaven. I spent several weeks in visiting my friends and preaching in the vicinity. It was refreshing to me again to address my old associates, and I was received by them with increased courtesy and cordiality. In no instance was I badly treated, except once on the west branch of the Delaware, where, after attending a quarterly meeting in Delhi, I came to the Protestant Episcopal Church, a few miles above, at which an appointment had been given out for me; but on my arrival I found the church closed against me. As, however, the people had assembled, I stood in a wagon and delivered my message; some opposers attempting meanwhile to drown my voice by ringing the bell, a useless attempt against any itinerant whose voice had been toned amid the storms of Canada.

APPOINTED IN THE STATES.

"April 6, the New York Conference met in the town of Amenia, Dutchess county, New York. I was present, and was appointed to the Delaware circuit, among my old acquaintances; my father and mother, and most of my brothers and sisters, were still residing there. ' This appointment," he adds, "was most agreeable to me." It seemed, indeed, like a grateful rest after, if not a happy conclusion of, his itinerant adventures and sufferings. But work was the true rest of a man of his active nature. He felt now more than ever inspired with the energetic spirit which was pervading the great cause to which he had consecrated his young manhood. Methodism was breaking out like a flood all over the country. It was everywhere forming new circuits, erecting chapels, rallying preachers, and gathering adherents. Its hosts of communicants had grown since the year in which he began to preach, from eighty-six thousand to more than a hundred and fifty thousand. Asbury, and most of its original preachers, still remained, leading on the conquering army. Many of the mightiest men then in the American pulpit were among them: William M'Kendree, Jesse Lee, Peter Cartwright, Jacob Young, Isaac Quin, Lovick Pierce, Philip Bruce, John Early, Nelson Reed, Alfred Griffith, Stephen G. Roszel, Joshua Wells, Thomas F. Sargent, Enoch George, Jacob Gruber, Thornton Fleming, Asa Shinn, Thomas Ware, Henry Boehm, Solomon Sharp, Ezekiel Cooper, Phineas Rice, Daniel Ostrander, Freeborn Garrettson, Laban Clark, Joseph Sawyer, William Case, John Broadhead, Daniel Webb, Martin Ruter, Epaphras Kibby, Samuel Merwin, George Pickering, Elijah Hedding, Joshua Soule—but pages could not contain all the names of similar rank. American Protestantism had never seen a mightier ministerial corps: it may perhaps be said that American Methodism has never since seen a mightier one. It was, however, the legitimate product of that singular ecclesiastical system, which, conducted so energetically by Asbury, had providentially arisen to match the moral exigencies of the New World at this critical period in our national history. Five of the men here named became bishops, and it may be soberly affirmed that very few of them were incompetent to fill with dignity and effectiveness that high function. Nathan Bangs, destined to take equal rank with them, intellectually and morally, if not officially, felt as by a moral instinct that they were his befitting companions, that their work should be his work, their sufferings his sufferings, their God his God. They seemed to challenge him forward; and in going to his new circuit, among his relations, he had no thought of rest or ease, much less of a permanent home. He was ready to go anywhere; but the paternal indulgence of Asbury, who loved him with peculiar affection, induced the veteran bishop to give him and his young wife a year's comfort among his relations, now flourishing farmers in that romantic region. Asbury had rallied him, humorously, before the whole conference, for his comparatively early marriage, then a rare event among Methodist itinerants; but excused him on account of his fine appearance and fine character. "I knew," said the bishop, shaking his gray locks, "I knew that the young maidens would be all after him; but as he has conducted the matter very well let his character pass."

GENERAL CONFERENCE.

He wished to know more of these good and great men, from most of whom he had been shut out by his long sojourn in the wilderness. An occasion was at hand on which he could see them in their most important assembly, the General Conference, which was about to meet in Baltimore, and was to be memorable by the adoption of a virtual constitution of the Church, and the organization of a delegated General Conference, as its supreme judicatory. "Four of us," he says, "united, and, hiring a two-horse wagon, traveled together as far as Dover, Delaware, where we left our horses in the care of ex-Governor Bassett, one of the early converts to Methodism in that state. He and his lady entertained us with truly Christian hospitality, both being deeply pious. We held meetings in their neighborhood; and I was particularly interested in the worship of the negroes, which I here witnessed for the first time. These poor people seemed ecstatic in their gratitude for the Gospel and their hope of a better life. They shouted and 'leaped for joy;' they heard the word with intense eagerness, and their prayers and singing were full of animation."

He found Baltimore to be a sort of metropolis of Methodism. In no other American city had it met with equal success; it prevailed among all classes, high and low, and seemed to retain all its primeval life. But he was struck especially by the imposing aspect of the Conference. A hundred and twenty-nine preachers composed it, most of them men of note from all parts of the country. From the east were Hedding, Soule, Pickering, Ruter, and others; from New York Conference, Garrettson, Cooper, Crawford, Thatcher, Clark, Ostrander; from Philadelphia Conference, Hare, Everett, Chandler, M'Claskey, Boehm, Bishop, Budd, Bartine; from Baltimore Conference, Reed, Hitt, Sargent, Roszel, Smith, George, Wells, Gruber, Ryland, Shinn, Roberts; from Virginia Conference, Bruce, Lee, Mead; from South Carolina, Randall, Phœbus, Mills; and from the "Old Western Conference," M'Kendree, Lakin, Blackman. He had never before attended a General Conference, nor seen so many representative men of Methodism together. He gazed upon them with veneration. "It was refreshing," he says, "to become acquainted with so many veteran preachers, who had sounded the alarm through all the land. I had read much and heard much of their pioneer labors, but here they were before me. I looked upon them with emotions which I cannot describe. Bishop Asbury especially impressed me, in this new scene, with a sense of his real but simple greatness. He presided with perfect dignity, and diffused among the preachers a genuine spirit of piety."

WESTERN DELEGATES.

The western preachers especially excited his admiration; they had come to the session from the hardest field of the Methodist world, except the borean region in which he himself had been toiling, and he felt a fellow-sympathy with them. They belonged to the "Old Western Conference," which now comprehended the whole western country, from the lakes to Natchez, and which had lately been the theater of extraordinary religious triumphs, of immense camp-meetings, quarterly meetings, revivals. Every one of its districts comprehends, in our day, several conferences. One of its circuits, at that date, bears the significant title of "Illinois," with a solitary preacher, John Clingan; another the name of "Missouri," where John Walker was founding the denomination. One of its "districts," traveled by John Sale, is entitled "Ohio;" another, under William Burke, bears the name of "Kentucky;" another, under Jacob Young, is called "Mississippi." It was a field for giants; and "there were giants in those days" among its Methodist itinerants. Its representatives appeared in the conference like war-worn heroes. They were distinguished also by their poor attire, made of rude homespun cloth. William M'Kendree was their leader. After extraordiary labors and successes in Virginia and Baltimore Conferences, he had been selected by Bishops Asbury and Whatcoat to superintend the "Western District," which then comprised the whole of what was afterward the "Western Conference." He traversed this vast district at the rate of fifteen hundred miles quarterly, six thousand miles annually, preaching almost daily, and conducting camp-meetings and quarterly meetings which, attended by thousands, sometimes tens of thousands, of settlers, were like battle-fields. He was now known throughout the West as its Methodistic champion, but was still unknown to Nathan Bangs, and but slightly known in the North generally.

M'KENDREE PREACHING.

The Conference began on Friday. Sunday was a great day, and the old "Light-street Chapel" was the center of its interest—the cathedral of the occasion and of the denomination. "It was filled," says the manuscript before me, "to overflowing; the second gallery, at one end of the chapel, was crowded with colored people. I saw the preacher of the morning enter the pulpit, sunburnt, and dressed in very ordinary clothes, with a red flannel shirt, which showed a large space between his vest and small clothes. He appeared more like a poor backwoodsman than a preacher of the Gospel. I felt mortified that such a looking man should have been appointed to preach on such an imposing occasion. In his prayer he seemed to lack words, and even stammered. I became uneasy for the honor of the Conference and the Church. He gave out his text: "For the hurt of the daughter of my people am I hurt; I am black; astonishment hath taken hold on me. Is there no balm in Gilead? is there no physician there? why then is not the health of the daughter of my people recovered?" As the preacher advanced in his discourse a mysterious magnetism seemed to emanate from him to all parts of the house; he was absorbed in the interest of his subject; his voice rose gradually till it sounded like a trumpet; at a climactic passage the effect was overwhelming. "It thrilled," says the manuscript, "through the assembly like an electric shock;" the house rang with irrepressible responses; "many hearers fell prostrate to the floor. An athletic man, sitting by my side, fell as if shot by a cannon ball. I felt my own heart melting, and feared that I should also fall from my seat. Such an astonishing effect—so sudden and overpowering—I seldom or never saw before."

This "backwoodsman" was William M'Kendree. Nathan Bangs now knew him, and saw, as he says, in his History of the Church, "a halo of glory" around his head. It had been determined that a bishop should be elected at the Conference to fill the vacancy occasioned by the death of Whatcoat. The piety, wisdom, and successful labors of M'Kendree had already directed attention to him as the man for the place. "That sermon," said Asbury, "on Sunday morning, will decide his election." On the next Thursday he was declared a bishop by ninety-five votes, the other ballots being divided between Jesse Lee, the founder of Methodism in New England, and Ezekiel Cooper, who was considered the best trained intellect in the Conference.

DELEGATED GENERAL CONFERENCE.

Hitherto all traveling elders of the ministry had a right to attend the General Conference, and the body was unrestricted in its power to enact new rules of discipline and even new tenets of faith. The rapid growth of the Church rendered it necessary that it should be reorganized on a representative basis. Asbury had advocated such an arrangement for some time. The New York Conference brought the proposition before this session by a long memorial which had been approved by the New England, the Western, and the South Carolina Conferences. "When the plan was first presented," says our manuscript, "it encountered great opposition, and was rejected by a majority vote. I suppose some voted against it from a fear that, if adopted, they could never attend another General Conference, and others were jealous of their rights, fearing to intrust the affairs of the Church to so few hands; while some opposed it from opposition to Bishop Asbury, with whom it was a favorite measure, for, notwithstanding his great merits, he had his enemies. Toward the close of the Conference, however, it was reported by a committee in a somewhat modified form, and adopted almost unanimously, and it has remained ever since the Constitution of the Church.

That it has been a means of preserving our doctrines and fundamental system I have no doubt, for had it not been adopted, with its Restrictive Rules, our doctrine, 'General Rules,' and episcopal government, together with the itinerancy, would have been liable to modifications which might have been fatal." The "Restrictive Rules," which form the basis of this reorganization, are virtually the constitution of the denomination. They render impossible any change of the Articles of Religion; and allow no change of the General Rules, and no act doing away the episcopal government of the Church or its itinerant ministry, except by a majority of two thirds of the General Conference, with a concurrent majority of three fourths of the members of the annual conferences. A measure often suggested in later times was proposed at this session by John M'Claskey and Ezekiel Cooper—the election of a bishop for each Annual Conference as a substitute for the presiding eldership, with Bishop Asbury as general superintendent. "It was largely and ably discussed," says Dr. Bangs, "by some of the leading members of the Conference, on each side." There must have been a considerable party in favor of it at first, for when M'Claskey and Cooper proposed to withdraw their motion for it a majority refused their request. But after much discussion it was defeated.

ON HIS CIRCUIT.

It was ever afterward a grateful recollection to Dr. Bangs that he had been a member of this session of the General Conference, second only in importance to the memorable Christmas Conference, at which the Church was organized. "It concluded," he says, "'in peace,' and its members dispersed to the east, the north, the west, and the south, with renewed confidence in the destiny of their growing cause." He returned to Stamford, N. Y., "where," he says, "I had left, at my brother Joseph's, my wife, and which was included in the Delaware circuit, to which I had been appointed this year. When I left Canada my health was much impaired by my sufferings from various hardships and sickness. Having now to travel among the mountains in this rough part of the country, in a bracing atmosphere, with good water and plenty of wholesome food, and among the friends of my youth, my health began to improve, and I felt the vigor of manhood return. My circuit was large, being upward of a hundred miles around, and having more than thirty appointments in four weeks. I deem it a duty to bear testimony to the kindness of my brother Joseph, who treated me and my wife with great hospitality. The people, however, were slack in providing for their preachers, and yet exacting in their demands upon our labors. I planned the circuit so as to save three days in four weeks to be at home; but even this brief leisure was opposed, and occasioned me some disparagement.

"Nothing out of the common routine of the labors of a four weeks' circuit happened this year except a camp-meeting in the town of Kortright, at which the Lord was eminently present, and another in Benham, where I preached twice with lively satisfaction. At the latter, among others who were present from a distance were the Rev. Freeborn Garrettson, his wife and daughter, with whom I again held sweet counsel. On the Delaware circuit I remained one year, and the Lord gave us some refreshing seasons of grace."

CHARACTER AS A PREACHER.

His brother, Rev. Heman Bangs, writes to me: "I joined the Church when he was on our (the Delaware) circuit, in 1808; he was esteemed a powerful preacher. I remember that at a quarterly meeting, after the presiding elder had preached, he rose and began to exhort; in a few minutes the power of his word was like an electrical shock, and the whole assembly rose simultaneously to their feet. He had a notion that it was my duty to preach, and wrote me a long letter about it, especially cautioning me not to marry, as that would interfere with the itinerant work. I was fearful myself that I should have to preach, but determined not to do so if I could avoid it and yet save my soul. I was willing to be a local preacher, but not an itinerant. I drew the inference from his letter, that a wife would be a sure barrier to the traveling ministry; so I determined to marry as soon as I could, and did take a wife three months after I was twenty-one years old. His letter so vexed me that I would not read it a second time for a long while, and yet I thought so much of it that I kept it for fifty years; but it is now mislaid; I cannot put my hand upon it. Nathan and myself have ever lived in sweet fellowship; independent in our own opinions, we often differed, but never quarreled; he afforded me many profitable reflections by judicious criticisms when I was young in the ministry." His life-long friend, Rev. Dr. Samuel Luckey, became acquainted with him on this circuit, and describes him as then a man of mark among his brethren—not an elocutionist, not equal to others in rhetorical or oratorical attractions in the pulpit, but pre-eminent for the vigor and breadth of his mind and the intellectual power of his preaching. "It showed, to the more discriminating portion of his hearers, a peculiarity in the character of the preacher's mind, by which he was distinguished from all others about him, and indicated eminence in his work as a minister. His mind was evidently accustomed to elaborate thought. His mode of preaching was scarcely known among Methodist preachers before his day, and was, in the estimation of his best hearers, an indication of that originality and independence of mind, which, in a young man, promises distinction. And there was a something about him—a moral and mental superiority—which impressed all observers that he was to be a prince and a great man in Israel."

CHAPTER XIII.

ITINERANT LIFE IN THE UNITED STATES.

He attended the Conference of 1809, held in the city of New York early in May. The year had been one of success in most of its territory. The returns of communicants showed a gain of nearly five thousand. The ministry had also been effectively recruited. It now admitted "on trial" ten laborers, among whom were Coles Carpenter, Marvin Richardson, Isaac Puffer, Bela Smith, and other well-known itinerants; while Phineas Rice, Lewis Pease, and ten other candidates, many of whom became veterans, were admitted to "full membership." Nathan Bangs was appointed to the Albany circuit. "I feel it a duty," he writes, "to bear testimony to the kindness of the people on this circuit to me and mine. I labored among them with much satisfaction, and left them with much regret." He was now in the vigor of his early manhood; he had found some leisure for study amid his abundant labors, and his intelligence and native intellectual force gave him rank among the foremost men of his Conference. Many are the recollections of his powerful preaching among the aged members of the Church who still linger within the limits of the old Albany circuit.

CONTROVERSY.

His congregations were large; but the effect of his labors did not correspond at first with their diligence and energy. He consulted with his colleague, Isaac B. Smith, respecting the causes of their comparative failure. They both attributed it chiefly to the prevalent influence of Calvinistic doctrines. Whether legitimately or not, the popular inference from the tenet of predestination was that the final fate of souls is a fixed fact, unalterable by human volition; that only when an "effectual call" is given from heaven can the sinner repent; that it is useless to try to anticipate this call; it will come to the elect in "God's good time;" it will never come to the reprobate: that summarily the man who is predestined to be saved shall be saved, whether heedful or heedless of passing warnings, and he that is predestined to be lost can by no endeavors avert his doom. The most powerful preaching seemed neutralized, to a great extent, by these opinions. The two itinerants concluded that they "should have no revival of religion unless they could break up these pernicious prejudices." "We immediately began," he adds, "to state and enforce our distinctive doctrines—general redemption, the conditionality of salvation—both in respect to its present experience and its final retention; the witness of the Spirit, sanctification, or holiness of heart and life; and we exposed, meanwhile, the error and danger of the contrary tenets." Though opposition was provoked by this course, it tended to "awaken and excite attention; many began to search the Scriptures to see if these things were so. The spell of lethargy was broken, and the result was a general revival, particularly in the town of Durham, where my family lived." Even his opponents reaped advantage from his measures. The Presbyterians of that town shared largely in the fruits of the new interest. Nearly all evangelical Churches were recruited. Liberal Calvinists might indeed gratefully admit that if he had not refuted their creed, he had refuted perilous perversions of it, and prepared the people for better influences from their ministrations.

Toward the end of the Conference year, however, he found himself beset by clerical opposition, and the Calvinists of Durham challenged him to a public controversy, their pastor opening his own church for the purpose. "It might perhaps be supposed," writes the itinerant, "that I took delight in disputation. Far from it; I was led into this controversy against my inclinations; but in those times we were peculiarly situated; the Calvinistic doctrines held yet an unloosened and almost universal hold on the popular mind in many parts of the country. We were compelled to be polemics at times, however we might prefer to go on our usual course of preaching the common truths of religion. We found a great difficulty in exciting the people who were under the influence of these errors to 'seek the Lord while he may be found.' I could not, therefore, as I thought, and still think, avoid this public debate without a dereliction of duty. That God's blessing might accompany it I appointed a day of fasting and prayer in all the Societies of the circuit, and I believe that very good effects followed the discussion."

His early friend, Rev. Samuel Luckey, D.D., who witnessed the debate, thus writes to me respecting it: "The force of circumstances, on the Albany circuit, brought him into public notice in the character (as a controversialist and an author) for which he was afterward so eminently distinguished. His active mind, trained by habits of study and reflection, prompted him to commence the use of his pen as a means of becoming more useful to the Church and the world. When he traveled Albany circuit he carried with him his portfolio and writing apparatus, and wherever he could get a retired room employed his leisure hours in writing. He commenced a work on Christian Theology, and had, it is believed, made considerable progress in it when he came to this circuit. These facts are mentioned to show that he gave early indications of an aspiring and vigorous intellect, which foretokened his future eminence. But circumstances on this circuit called him out as a champion for the faith he professed, and gave a direction to the exercise of his talents, as a preacher and writer, which marked his course through all his subsequent life. Durham, where his family resided, was settled principally by emigrants from New England, as was that entire section of the circuit, embracing Granville and extending to Catskill. The people inhabiting this section had been trained up in the faith and practice of the New England Churches, and had Churches and ministers among them of the same faith and order. Out of this class were raised the Methodist societies in these localities. Many of those who connected themselves with the Methodists were men of talents and education, who had separated themselves from their former religious associations on the ground of doctrine, purely. They rejected Calvinism, as taught in the Confession of Faith adopted by the Congregational Churches, with an opposition bordering on abhorrence; and on this issue the parties were in habitual array against each other. There was no end to the controversies and disputations among them. The preachers would belabor each other's doctrines, and vindicate their own, in their sermons; and the people suffered no opportunity to pass of disputing and contending with each other on the points of difference between them. It was, in fact, an age of religious contention; and the matter was complicated by the modification of Calvinism by Hopkinsianism, which, it was claimed by the advocates of Calvinism, sufficiently explained the most objectionable points in their creed, while those who dissented from them could not see it in that light.

"In this state of things Mr. Bangs disappointed the expectation of his friends in not following the usual course of the preachers on both sides, of making the controversy on doctrine the principal subject of his preaching among them. In the pulpit he preached the Gospel as he understood it, in a style and manner calculated to hold the minds of his hearers to the great fundamental principles of evangelical religion. But the controversy to which the minds of all were alive he seldom introduced or alluded to. No one expected to hear the doctrinal controversy which so much agitated the minds of the people in that section particularly discussed when they went to hear him preach. But, though not dealing with it in this way, he was not indifferent to the subject of the controversy, nor unwilling to enter the arena, in a manner suited to his views, in vindication of the doctrines and usages of Methodism against all opposition. He accordingly consented, at the solicitation of zealous partisans, to hold a public debate with such a person as might be chosen for that purpose, on the points of difference between the Calvinists and Methodists. A Rev. Mr. Benedict, an eminent Congregational minister from New England, who had been educated a lawyer, and had the reputation of being a strong man and able debater, was selected for the opposite side. The debate was held in the Congregational Church in Durham, which was within a few rods of the Methodist Church and of Mr. Bangs's residence. The preliminaries provided that the debate should cover the whole ground of controversy, contained in what are usually called 'The Five Points,' each to be discussed separately, in order, giving a certain time to either disputant, in turn, to state his points and his argument. Rev. Henry Stead, presiding elder of the district, and a Dr. Hotchkiss, pastor of the Congregational Church in Granville, (if my recollection serves me,) were appointed to preside over the meeting; and the Rev. Hugh Armstrong, of the Methodist Church, and another young gentleman, whose name is forgotten, were employed to take notes, to which appeal might be made, in case of dispute or misunderstanding, as to the arguments or expressions of either of the parties. The debate was conducted with great ability, and in a spirit of candor and kindly feeling, which left all parties wiser in many things that they thought they understood perfectly before, and better disposed in their feelings toward each other. Such at least is the impression of the writer respecting Dr. Bangs at the time of his traveling Albany circuit, and of the noted debate he had with the Rev. Mr. Benedict, at which he was present. These incidents in the early history of Dr. Bangs's ministry are chiefly important as having given direction to the future employment of his talents in the cause of truth and righteousness, which has procured for him a name and reputation that will live in the annals of Methodism and the history of the Church in all coming time."

FIRST APPEARANCE AS AUTHOR.

This year was also memorable to him as that in which he first appeared before the public as an author. A preacher of the sect of "Christians" * published a small book denying the divinity of Christ and other fundamental truths of Christianity. It was a publication of no literary or theological ability, but, being circulated among the common people, was doing mischief that the itinerant, in his rapid travels and brief presence, in any one place could not correct. He therefore issued a pamphlet in reply to it. "This," he says, "being my first effort through the press, it was made with fear and trembling; but I have reason to believe that it did good, as the heterodox pamphlet and its author soon disappeared. From being a doubter he afterward became a fanatic. He even believed at last that he could raise the dead, and actually attempted to do so in one instance; but not succeeding, he explained his failure by assuming that the subject of any such miracle must be one who has not died of organic disease. What infatuation!"

* A New England sect, which, while denying some of the most fundamental truths of Christianity, appropriated the title as its denominational style—"Christians with a long i," as George Pickering, a New England Methodist patriarch, sarcastically characterized them.

NEW YORK CONFERENCE, 1810.

The New York Conference for 1810 began on the 20th of May in Pittsfield, Mass., for it still included much of the west of that state, as of Connecticut and Vermont, and also all the Canadas, though at the present session Upper Canada was detached from it and assigned to the Genesee Conference, which now for the first time appeared in the Minutes. A large portion of the territory of the Conference within the state of New York was also incorporated with this new Conference, so that the returns of members were materially reduced; but the denomination was rapidly advancing in all this territory. It received on trial fourteen young preachers, among whom were Tobias Spicer, Arnold Scolefield, Noah Bigelow, Abner Chase, and others who were afterward well known in the Church. It now comprised at least eighty itinerants. It was divided into five districts, some of which include in our day several large and flourishing Conferences. Joseph Crawford superintended the New York district, with such men as Peter P. Sandford, B. Hibbard, Ezekiel Canfield, Coles Carpenter, and William Thatcher under him. Aaron Hunt led on a powerful corps of laborers on the Rhinebeck district, among whom were Elijah Woolsey, Peter Moriarty, Seth Crowell, Phineas Cook, Marvin Richardson, Laban Clark, Lewis Pease, and William Phœbus. William Anson conducted another band on the Ashgrove district, among whom were Samuel Draper, Tobias Spicer, Phineas Peck, and John Finegan. Henry Stead, on the Hudson River district, had command of some mighty laborers, among whom were Daniel Ostrander, Samuel Merwin, Thomas Woolsey, Phineas Rice; while Joseph Lawson led a corps of pioneers beyond the Canada line, who were scattered on the St. Francis River, at Ottawa, Montreal, Three Rivers, and Quebec. The veteran Garrettson was missionary at large in the great field. This mere list of names is pregnant with meaning to all who remember the ministry of the Conference during the first half of our century.

IN NEW YORK CITY.

Nathan Bangs was now placed in the first of these corps under Joseph Crawford, and at the head of the Methodist pastorate of New York city—the "preacher in charge." Eben Smith, John Robertson, James M. Smith, and Peter P. Sandford were his colleagues. With but few intermissions the city was thenceforward to be the headquarters of his labors and influence. Methodism there was still in its youthful struggles. It had but one circuit, with five preachers, and, including its vicinity, but little more than two thousand communicants. The city population comprised but about ninety-six thousand souls. What changes was he to witness there! What struggles and successes of his denomination! What expansion of the city population—from its less than a hundred thousand to more than eight hundred and fourteen thousand—what additions of miles of streets and of stately houses! What almost immeasurable increase of business and opulence! What growth and transpositions of Methodist Churches! By the year of his death, the city and its environs were to comprise about twice as many Methodist preachers as the whole Conference then reported, though, as we have seen, it swept over much of New England, and up the Hudson into Canada, to Montreal and Quebec on the east, and the River Thames, opposite Detroit, on the west. He was to see the five Methodist preaching places of the city (but two or three of them churches) multiplied to about sixty, including Brooklyn, nearly all of them commodious structures, some of them ranking among the best ecclesiastical edifices of the nation. Its two thousand two hundred Methodists he was to see increased to more than seventeen thousand, and it may be said that he was to fall at last in death at the head of this host, the best known, the most venerated, and most beloved of its representative men. A marvelous history for one life.

HE ATTEMPTS REFORMS.

He records that he entered upon his new appointment as preacher in charge of the city Churches with much diffidence, as he was almost an entire stranger among them. He was, however, already a paramount man in the ministry, with a ripe judgment, an amount of intelligence rare at that period among his brethren, a reputation for logical skill and theological thoroughness and soundness, and a commanding person and voice; a staunch disciplinarian, an uncommonly instructive and powerful preacher. It was quickly perceived that he mastered his new position. He soon gave an improved tone to the Methodism of the city. For several years revivals had prevailed in its Churches, but for lack of discipline they had degenerated into extravagant excitements. The oldest members, trained by the first preachers, and peculiarly exemplary by the depth and steadiness of their piety, deplored these errors; but by many, if not most, of the later converts, they were deemed unavoidable, if not, indeed, desirable accompaniments of the spiritual life of the Church. He determined to reform them. "I witnessed," he says, "a spirit of pride, presumption, and bigotry, impatience of scriptural restraint and moderation, clapping of the hands, screaming, and even jumping, which marred and disgraced the work of God. After much consultation with my colleagues, and some of the most judicious members of the societies, and also much prayer for Divine direction, I called a general society meeting, in which I read the 'General Rules' of the Church, and some other particular parts of the Discipline, making such remarks upon them as were suggested to my mind, and likewise gave my views fully and frankly as to the unseemly practices which I considered derogatory to the character of the Church. My mind seemed wonderfully assisted in this delicate business, and I felt the approval of my heavenly Father to rest upon my own soul, and I believe his power and presence were felt throughout the assembly. This course, however, gave great offense to many who thought themselves implicated, and some seemed grieved because they altogether misconceived my meaning. All the preachers, and there happened to be several in from the country at the time, and all the oldest, most experienced, judicious part of the society, not only cordially approved of my attempts and the sentiments I had advanced, but they rejoiced exceedingly at the stand I had taken, believing that the occasion called for a firm hand. We therefore determined to pursue a steady course in correcting these disorders, trusting in God for success. After having the subject brought forward and considerably discussed in the Leaders' meeting, in which several hard things were said, some wishing me to retract what I had advanced, I told the brethren that whatever deference I might have to their judgment, as I was conscious of the Divine approbation in what I had said and done, I was so far from retreating that I would suffer my head to be severed from my body before I would recede from the ground I had taken. This silenced debate, and I believe in a very short time all were fully satisfied of the purity of my motives and the correctness of my course.

SINGULAR DREAM.

"About this time I had a very singular dream. In my sleep I thought a friend came to see me, to whom I showed my garden, which I had taken great pains to put in order. The weeds were all plucked up, and everything was thriving. As we were admiring its beauty and promise my friend said to me, 'Do you see that snake?' I looked, and saw that a green snake, exactly resembling the vegetation in color, had stretched himself around the entire garden. I replied that I saw him and would kill him. My friend rejoined, 'If you attempt to kill him he will kill you, for you can see neither his head nor tail, he is so completely wound round the garden like a hoop.' I then found in my hand one of the most curious whips I ever saw. 'Now,' said I, 'with this will I kill him.' Although I could not see his head I touched him very softly, when I found he squirmed a little. I struck him harder and harder, till at length he started up his head with great fury. When I saw his crest, with one blow of my whip I severed his head. 'There,' said I to my friend, who was looking on with amazement, 'he is dead.' On this I awoke, and behold it was a dream, but 'the interpretation thereof' seemed plain. The garden was the Church, of which I had the oversight, the snake was an enemy with whom I had to contend in the discharge of my duties, and the instrument in my hand was the Discipline. I had to contend with a man who might justly be supposed to have been represented by the snake, but whose power I was determined to break; he soon showed himself in his opposition to the exercise of the Discipline; but he could do nothing, as his personal influence was quickly broken."

His venerable friend, Francis Hall, Esq., of the Commercial Advertiser, one of the few members of the Church who remain from that day, was a witness of these scenes, and writes as follows respecting them: "Dr. Bangs was a man of order in all things, and especially so in the house of God. It is within the remembrance of some old members in this city, when a good deal of disorder took place at our social meetings. There were those who made it a practice to go from one place of worship to another, whose conduct was boisterous; not content with loud outbreakings, some would even go so far that they would jump up and down in the pews, thereby disturbing the quiet of others, and destroying all seeming propriety of behavior. Mr. Bangs saw that the cause of God suffered by such conduct, and he determined to put a stop to it. At this period 'old John-street Church' was the place where special society meetings were held, and here Mr. Bangs called the society together (there being only one charge in the city at that time) for the purpose of exhorting the members to be more orderly in their social meetings. He stated, in the most affectionate manner, his views in regard to the management of those meetings. He told the members that no one was more desirous for lively meetings than himself; that he always encouraged such meetings; yet a lively and good meeting could be had without the disorders so much complained of. The result of this meeting was of the most pleasing character. A change took place, which was followed by a glorious revival. One incident of this meeting I well remember. As we were passing out from the church a good woman remarked that 'Mr. Bangs had done more injury that evening to the cause of God than he could ever be able to make amends for.' This lady had been a warm friend of Mr. Bangs, and she declared she never desired to speak to him again. It was not long before she regretted what she had said, and became a more devoted friend to him than she had ever been before."

INCIDENTS—ASBURY.

The temporary disturbance produced by these measures could not fail to be erroneously reported at a distance. Letters were sent to Bishop Asbury about them. The representations of the opposite parties afforded him but a confused impression of the case. He suspected that both parties had erred, and that personal resentments were mixed with their proceedings. In a letter to Dr. Bangs he alluded to this suspicion, but without personal invidiousness. Dr. Bangs felt, however, that he deserved episcopal support, and not ambiguity in such a case, and replied to the bishop requesting explanations. The latter answered him in a characteristic letter—characteristic of the humility and affectionateness of his own great heart. "My dear brother and son," he said, "it is impossible for me to enter into explanations. Unhappy suspicions have taken place (I said, I think) among us, and something like guile; including myself. I confess I had better not have said anything; I did not mean it for any but those that were charged with it. I did not mean a charge against you or any innocent person. There may be the appearance without reality. I am sorry I am not more prudent, but when I am called upon so often to speak and write I am not sufficiently on my guard. I hope you will bear with me. I am persuaded of your uprightness. Brother Hitt has spoken in the highest terms of you to me, in word and letter. You will pardon me, and pray that I may say, do, preach, and write better. I remain thine in Jesus." Asbury loved him with the tenderness of a parent; he usually addressed him as "My dear son." "God be gracious to you," he writes on another occasion, "and remember you, like David, in all his troubles. I am sorry, seriously sorry, I have not written to you, if I have not written. I am almost sure I had your name upon the docket; but I run, I flee, I forget. I feel for you, my dear, in a tumultuous city, a numerous society, and strange mixtures of people. And we have our work; I suppose I have at least near a thousand letters and papers put into my hand a year, all calling for some responsibility. From the first day I saw and read you I loved you with peculiar affection. I love Brother C.; I love you all; you have been my good, obedient, suffering children." In the paucity of documentary remains of this great and good man every such trace of his magnanimous soul is precious. He was sinking under infirmities, and was to die in about four years. As life dwindled he clung more tenaciously to his old affections and friendships. An increasingly pathetic tenderness marks his occasional writings as the final shadows deepen over his wonderful career.

SUNDAY-SCHOOLS—CATECHISING.

Mr. Hall gives another example of Dr. Bangs's disciplinary firmness in New York. "He was the friend of Sunday-schools; yet he was opposed to the schools being kept open during the time of public worship. A number of meetings were held in which the subject was fully discussed by both clergy and laity. I believe the matter was never brought to a vote, but finally Dr. Bangs, who was then in charge, issued instructions that the schools should not be kept open during divine service. He did so in a very precise and decided manner by the following brief notification: 'You are hereby requested to desist from the disorderly practice of teaching your school during divine service.' At that time it was the custom, in all our churches, to have preaching at three o'clock. The order to close the schools in time for divine service caused some little unpleasantness, but this soon gave way, and the course pursued by Dr. Bangs was generally approved. I believe that no school is now kept open while the public services are going on."

"Not long," continues his own manuscript, "after taking charge of the Church in the city, I proposed to my colleagues the propriety of catechising the children—a practice which, as far as I know, had never been attempted here—and likewise that we should devote two afternoons in the week to visiting from house to house, for our time had been mostly absorbed in preaching. Accordingly I gave notice that on a given afternoon I would meet all the children who would attend, furnish them with our 'Scriptural Catechism,' and give them lessons to learn. At the time appointed there were not less than three hundred children assembled in the Forsyth-street Church, to whom I gave the Catechism, and pointed out the method by which they should study it. I continued this practice during the two years I remained in the city, and some of my colleagues followed my example. I have since found many of those children, now grown to maturity, members of the Church, and eminent for piety, living witnesses for our highest doctrines of holiness. In visiting the families, talking and praying with them, I received a great blessing. Some said that they never had a Methodist preacher in their houses before."

STUDIES—M'KNIGHT—ADAM CLARKE.

While thus employed in "disciplining" the Church, visiting from house to house, and preaching incessantly, he so economized his time as to find opportunity for considerable study. He applied himself to the Greek language, and was ever afterward grateful that he had been able to acquire sufficient knowledge of it to enable him to use it in the study of the sacred text. "This study," he says, "disposed me to less confidence in myself; it made me more diffident and cautious in uttering opinions on subjects which require accurate investigation and profound critical research." M'Knight opened to him the scope of the Pauline Epistles, notwithstanding many heterodox teachings. The commentator's General Preface especially delighted him by its bearings on the Calvinistic controversy. "He is entitled to the more credit, and may be considered as acting from the honest convictions of his own well-informed mind, not only because of his critical acumen, his depth of learning and extensive research, but also because he belonged to the Calvinistic school, and was a minister in that Church. His Critical Notes are a monument of his learning, his industry, and of his fidelity to the interests of the truth."

About this time Adam Clarke's Commentary appeared in America. "Seldom," he writes, "had the announcement of a publication excited so much interest among all classes of the religious community, especially the clergy. A contest immediately commenced between some booksellers respecting the right of precedence in its republication. It was an enormous undertaking for that day, requiring large expenditure. After much vituperation on both sides a compromise was effected, and the work was commenced by Mr. Eastman, of New York, a personal friend of Dr. Clarke, and formerly a member of the Wesleyan Connection. It was issued in numbers, and was read with avidity." Defective as this gigantic work now appears, as compared with later critical commentaries, it was a great production for the times. Its very defects gave it a certain value. Its superabundant and often irrelevant erudition afforded, not only to the Methodist itinerants, but to the American ministry generally, an amount of knowledge which was then not only rare, but comparatively inaccessible to many of them in any other form. Its singularities, not to say whimsicalities, of opinion, served to excite the curiosity and attract the attention of hundreds of readers who would otherwise hardly have cared to trouble themselves with any critical study of the Holy Scriptures. Its value to the Methodist ministry was immeasurably great. It may be said to have initiated critical biblical studies among them. It was an armory of scriptural learning to them, and its vast amount of collateral information prompted their studies in general knowledge. It was a godsend to Nathan Bangs, and, in connection with his study of the Greek language, opened a boundless range of biblical research before him. He devotes a crowded page of his manuscript to the expression of his gratitude for so important a help, and to the end of his life he was a strenuous "Clarkeite," believing that no other commentary approached it in all essential points of adaptation to the mass of Methodist preachers, though he frankly admitted its obvious defects.

SUCCESS IN THE CITY.

The revival which followed his decided disciplinary regulation of the New York Societies was powerful and profound. It resulted in a gain of more than two hundred and fifty members during the first year. In his second year an additional preacher was needed to supply the enlarged work. He was still preacher in charge. His associates were William Phœbus, Laban Clark, William Blagburne, James M. Smith, and Peter P. Sandford. Notwithstanding the usual reaction of revivals, they reported a gain of nearly a hundred and fifty members at the close of the year. Nearly one sixth of the Methodists of the city at that period, about forty-six years after the organization of its first society, had been gathered into the Church in the two years of his pastoral charge. The improved character which he had impressed upon the Methodism of the metropolis was perhaps more important than these numerical gains. His studious habits, and his predilection for theological preaching, had enabled him thoroughly to indoctrinate the Societies. His pastoral diligence, extending, as we have seen, to the catechetical training of their children, gave him a salutary influence in their families, and his firm, but merciful administration of discipline, established order, method, and efficiency in all the operations of the Church.

FIRST DELEGATED GENERAL CONFERENCE.

On the first of May, 1812, about a month before the close of his term of service in the city, the first delegated General Conference began there its session. He had been elected a delegate by the New York Conference, which he had represented in the preceding session of 1808; an honorable testimony of the consideration of his brethren, repeated every four years (with but one exception) for nearly half a century, till, in fine, his advanced years justified his release from such responsibilities.

He has left ample notes of this General Conference, interspersed with remarkably frank animadversions on what he deemed defects in the ecclesiastical system of Methodism. It was an imposing assembly, comprising ninety members. Like the annual Conferences, it met with closed doors; but traveling preachers were admitted to the galleries. Among the New York Conference representatives were, besides himself, such men as Merwin, Garrettson, Ostrander, Clark; from New England were Hedding, Soule, Pickering, Webb; from the great Western Conference, Blackman, Larkin, Quinn, Collins, Young; from Virginia, Lee, Early, Bruce, Hines; from Philadelphia, Cooper, M'Claskey, Sargent, Roszel; from Baltimore, Reed, Wells, Snethen, George, Shinn, Roberts, Brush, Smith; from South Carolina, Pierce, Myers, Kennedy, Dunwody. Never had Methodism gathered a body of mightier men. Five of them were destined to be bishops. Asbury was still the predominant figure in the assembly, especially to the eyes of Nathan Bangs. He had but a few months before returned from a survey of the first battle-fields of the latter, in Canada, and brought good reports of their prospects. "Surely," he said, "this is a land that God the Lord has blessed. I find it like all other stations in the extremities; there are difficulties to be overcome, and prospects to cheer us." There were now nearly three thousand Methodists in its young Societies; Quebec had yet but twenty-six, Montreal but fifty-two; but the early circuits of Nathan Bangs were prosperous; the Bay of Quinte reported more than six hundred, Niagara more than five hundred, Long Point nearly six hundred. About a score of itinerants were traversing the extensive field. Asbury was now venerated by his younger brethren as a scarred veteran. He was about sixty-six years old; infirmities were fast breaking him down; he "limped about," he says, "sung, talked, prayed." "My consolations exceedingly abound, though my sufferings are great. Dr. Coke says fifteen hundred miles in nine weeks—I may say sixteen hundred miles in sixty days." "Such," adds Dr. Bangs, "were episcopal labors in those days;" and these, it must be remembered, were not the days of steamboats and railroads, for the former were yet but locally used, and the latter unknown.

Bishop M'Kendree took the lead in the episcopal presidency of the session. He read a formal address or message before it, on the condition of the Church, the first example of the kind in a Methodist General Conference. Asbury followed in an oral communication. The delegates were cheered by the encouraging representation of their cause made by M'Kendree. "Upon examination," he said, "you will find the work of the Lord is prospering in our hands. Our important charge has greatly increased since the last General Conference; we have had an increase of nearly forty thousand members. At present we have about one hundred and ninety thousand members, upward of two thousand local, and about seven hundred traveling preachers, and these widely scattered over seventeen states, besides the Canadas, and several of the territorial settlements."

Their first bishop, Coke, sent them a congratulatory letter. He had been flying, like the apocalyptic angel, "having the everlasting Gospel to preach," over the West Indies, England, and Ireland, and was now projecting his last great mission to the East Indies.

THE PRESIDING ELDERSHIP.

The two principal questions before the body related to the election of presiding elders and the ordination of local preachers. Dr. Bangs took an active part in the debates on both subjects. The presiding elders had been, as they still are, appointed by the bishops. Many of the leading preachers advocated their appointment by ballot in the annual conferences. At the session of 1808 a motion was introduced to make the office elective; but it was defeated, though fifty-two voted for it. At the present session it was renewed, and lost by a majority of but three votes. All the delegates of the New York, Genesee, and Philadelphia Conferences voted for it; they had been elected by their respective Conferences for the express purpose of promoting it. It may not be irrelevant here to anticipate the result of this question. It continued to be agitated with extraordinary interest down to 1828, "since which time," says Dr. Bangs, "it has been allowed to sleep in peace." At the session of 1816 it was debated with great zeal and ability. He says that "perhaps a greater amount of talent was never brought to bear on any question ever brought before the General Conference than was elicited from both sides of the house in this discussion." But sixty votes were cast against it, and but thirty-eight for it. In 1820 Dr. Bangs was again its staunch advocate; he was associated with Ezekiel Cooper, Stephen G. Roszel, Joshua Wells, John Emory, and William Capers, (two of them afterward bishops,) in a committee, which reported a bill for the election of the presiding elders, reserving as a compromise the right of nomination to the bishops. The proposed change was adopted by a majority of thirty-six, and it was now supposed to be secure; but Joshua Soule, elected bishop at this session, tendered his resignation, declaring to the Conference that he could not, in his episcopal administration, conscientiously conform to the new measure, as he deemed it a contravention of the Restrictive Rules adopted in 1808. Bishop M'Kendree also remonstrated against it for the same reason. Evidently serious disturbance would follow the measure. An attempt was therefore made to reconsider it, but such was the importance which its advocates attached to it that the attempt failed, and Bishop Soule's resignation was accepted. At this critical moment a temporary compromise was proposed and adopted; it was resolved to suspend the measure till the next General Conference. In 1824 it was still further discussed; two bishops, Soule and Hedding, were elected, (the former re-elected;) they were representatives of the two parties; the measure was, however, again suspended, as the only practicable compromise. In 1828 it was rescinded, and the agitation ceased. In his History of the Church, Dr. Bangs has given an important summary of the argument on either side of the question.* I find in his manuscript account of this session, written many years later, the following remarks: "For Bishop Asbury all felt a high respect; and he was opposed to any alteration in the mode of appointing the presiding elders. The motion in favor of their election was supported by some of the oldest and most influential preachers in the Conference, such as Jesse Lee, Ezekiel Cooper, Freeborn Garrettson, Thomas Ware, William Phœbus, Aaron Hunt, etc.; but it was opposed by all the Southern and Western preachers, and by the delegates of the New England Conferences. Whether it would have been better for the interests of the Church to have had this alteration effected or not, I cannot say; but I cannot but think that it is committing too much power into the hands of any one man, however wise and holy he may be, to have the destinies of so many men at his own disposal, as our bishops have. Not only are there more than twelve hundred ministers, whose stations every year are subject to the control of the bishops, but their wives and children, and the people whom these ministers serve, so far as respects the men to whom their spiritual interests are committed. Who will say that this is not a tremendous power? It is, in my humble opinion, a power which not one of our bishops can safely use." He modified his opinion, however, on this subject. In a note to these remarks, written on the 16th of September, 1852, he says

* Vol. ii, anno 1812.

that he is "inclined to think," from later observation of the working of the present plan, the increase of the bishops, and virtual concessions from them in the making of the appointments, that "however faulty our theory may be, its practice is unexceptionable, and justifiable on grounds of expediency."

ORDINATION OF LOCAL PREACHERS.

On the other great question before this Conference he was, if possible, still more decided, and remained so to the last. He opposed the ordination of local preachers, because he could not approve the ordination of any man who would not give himself professionally and entirely to the work of the ministry. He says in the manuscript before me, "I think that, as a Church, we have erred in some things, and been deficient in others. In the first place, in order to secure an experienced, well-informed ministry, such a provision should have been made for its support as to have left no reasonable excuse for 'locations.' Having done this, and it might have been done, those who chose to leave the Word of God to serve tables should have been stripped of their ministerial functions, and left as they were before they entered the itinerancy. This would have prevented locations, on the one hand, and secured an experienced ministry on the other. As it now is, many of our most popular preachers have either located, becoming merchants, doctors, farmers, or mechanics, or have joined other denominations, chiefly the Protestant Episcopal Church. This has thinned our ranks and greatly weakened our force."

These are sharp sayings; they were written, however, in the last generation, when they were more relevant than at present. I find in a note, dated June 14, 1829, this brave addendum: "If this should survive me, and ever be published, I charge those to whom it may be committed not to suppress these remarks respecting our ministry. N. Bangs." In fine, while no man loved Methodism more devotedly than Nathan Bangs, his clear head and robust heart clearly discerned and courageously asserted its faults as well as its excellencies. From the beginning of his official prominence in the Church he was above any petty prejudices or whimsicalities to which it may have, directly or indirectly, given sanction, whether in its popular modes of worship, its social habits, or its disciplinary system. Staunchly conservative of its essential characteristics, he was always "progressive" in matters of expediency. He had, however, his own honest prejudices. Though he never changed his opinion respecting the ordination of local preachers, and never voted for the ordination of one in his own Conference, it may well be doubted whether his judgment was not erroneous in this respect. In most of the country Methodism was yet a missionary system; much of it is still such, and must be for generations. Ordained traveling preachers on long circuits need the assistance of local preachers in the administration of the sacraments, and, aside from this consideration, it may well be questioned whether any tendency to popularize the Christian ministry, to divest it of hierarchical peculiarities, and exalt the lay life of the Church to the religious offices and dignity with which Holy Scripture seems to exalt it, as "a royal priesthood," is not conformable to the original model of the Church, and to the original and sublime design of Christianity; at least it cannot be denied that the local ministry of Methodism holds a most important historical position in its great mission. It has been instrumental in founding the denomination in the United States, the North American British Provinces, the West Indies, Australia, and Africa, and, without pecuniary remuneration, it has always and everywhere done laborious service for the common cause. Throughout the Methodist world it is numerically twice or thrice as strong as the itinerant ministry. It is probable that if the Church has failed at all in respect to it, the failure has been in its encouragement and training rather than in any undue concessions to it.

HIS SERVICES IN THE CONFERENCE.

Though Dr. Bangs had modestly declined to take any active part in the proceedings of the General Conference of 1808, except to vote, in the present session he assumed his due position. He was prominent in its debates. He was one of the chief supporters of his life-long friend, Laban Clark, who introduced the motion in favor of an elective presiding eldership. He initiated the Committee on the Book Concern, a measure which has never been abandoned; he already saw the great capacity of that institution by which, in his own day and mostly through his own exertions, it was to become the greatest publishing agency of the religious world. He was appointed with Cooper, Snethen, Roszel, Bruce, and others, on the Committee on the Episcopacy—the first example of that important committee. He was a member of a committee on the collection and publication of historical documents relating to the Church, and also of a committee to incorporate into the Discipline the new enactments of the Conference.

CHAPTER XIV.

ITINERANT LIFE IN THE UNITED STATES.

THE General Conference of 1812 adjourned on the 22d of May; the New York Conference commenced its session, at Albany, on the 5th of June.* The war with Great Britain was at hand, and the political agitation of the nation had already disturbed its religious tranquillity and prosperity. The returns of members showed, not only no increase, but a loss in the New York Conference.

Asbury's visit to Canada had convinced him of the importance of that country as a promising field for Methodism. Nathan Bangs was the man, in his estimation, to take charge of the part of its territory which appertained to the Lower Province, though it was not now within the jurisdiction of his own Conference, but belonged to that of Genesee. The bishop had seen the results of his labors there, and now solicited him with much urgency to return to it,† taking a station at Montreal, but having, at the same time, charge of all the circuits in the province on the north-western side of the St. Lawrence. "This," he says, "was a great cross to

* In the Minutes it was appointed for the 4th of June; Dr. Bangs's manuscript says it began on the 5th of June.

† Notwithstanding the absolute prerogative of the bishops to appoint preachers in that day, no itinerant was sent beyond the limits of the United States without his own consent. Canada was considered a missionary field—a historical fact by which the General Conference, acknowledging that it had no constitutional power to divide the Church, deemed itself at liberty to allow the separation of the Canadian Conference from the Methodist Episcopal Church in 1828—a precedent of no little importance in judging of the division of the Methodist Episcopal Church in 1844.

me. Indeed, so many difficulties presented themselves in my way that I declined going till after the appointments were read off, at the close of the Conference, and I was announced for the city of Troy. Knowing the state of things in Canada, and feeling much for the people, and perceiving at the same time that the men appointed for it were entirely inadequate to its wants, I at last told Bishop M'Kendree, that if he would allow me to return to the States at the end of four years I would consent to go. He accepted me, and the appointment was made. Soon after the adjournment, news of the declaration of war against Great Britain reached the city of New York, where I then was with my family. This, of course, cut off all friendly intercourse between the Canadas and the United States. For some time I hesitated what to do, but by the advice of friends I finally concluded to pursue my journey, and, after taking an affectionate leave of my people in New York, who had been remarkably kind to me and mine during all my residence among them, I set off and went as far as Lansingburg. Here I halted until Bishops Asbury and M'Kendree returned from the New England Conference. They both decided that it was not expedient for me to proceed further. My mission was therefore abandoned. I took part of a house which Rev. Peter P. Sandford occupied in Troy. I felt somewhat embarrassed, not having any particular station, and, of course, no resources for a livelihood for my wife and two children, except a little money of my own, and these uncertainties in a time of war and great public agitation. There were indeed calls enough for preaching as long as I could preach gratuitously, to which I had no objection were I not dependent upon my labors for my support. The Lord, however, provided for me. I found some relief to my anxieties in occupying my leisure with the composition of an essay on the Reasonableness of Christianity. I had long meditated it, but though I have since nearly completed it, I have not felt at liberty to submit it to the public. If it may never have any other use, the writing of it has at least tended to quicken and enlarge my own mind.

"While in Troy I had various solicitations from my friends in New York, particularly from the venerable Mr. Garrettson, who then presided over the New York district, to remove southward. Accordingly, about the middle of September I left Troy, took a boat at Albany, and conveyed my family to Tarrytown. The day after my arrival I was seized with dysentery, but we were received into the house of a friend, and during the whole of my sickness, which lasted about five weeks, were treated with all the kindness and hospitality I could have expected in my own father's house. For about one week I suffered excruciating pain, but it pleased God to restore me. When sufficiently strong I removed my family to the town of Bedford, on the Croton circuit, which I traveled the remainder of the year. There I found a very affectionate people. They did not merely say, 'Go and be thou warmed, and be thou clothed,' but they gave such things as I needed, and I labored among them with peculiar satisfaction. We had not been long settled in Bedford when my wife was taken sick with every symptom of fatal consumption. She was under the doctor's care about four months, but finally recovered her health. On the whole this was a year of severe affliction, mixed indeed with many mercies. Besides our sickness, we moved no less than three times, and over considerable distances. God, however, was gracious, and sent us 'help from his holy hill.'"

His friend and colaborer, Rev. Dr. Luckey, refers to these events as follows: "Mr. Asbury found it difficult to get men to supply the work in Canada, in consequence of the threatened rupture between the United States and England. Rev. J. Scull, preacher at Quebec, and Rev. J. Mitchell, at Montreal, declined returning to Canada.

Mr. Sampson, the presiding elder, had left his work and never returned to it. Considering Canada as missionary ground, Mr. Asbury would not appoint any but volunteers to it; and under the circumstances he found it difficult to get any to volunteer. Rev. T. Burch, who was a British subject, consented to go to Quebec. Seeing the reluctance of others, Dr. Bangs, after having declined the offer of the appointment, magnanimously volunteered to fill the other vacancy at Montreal. This was a noble example to men of inferior claims. He had reached a position which would secure to him any one of the best appointments in the states. But with this justly merited position, he surrendered all claim to a privileged appointment in order to meet the call of the work where others refused to go. He was accordingly appointed to Montreal, with the charge of the Lower Canada district. The preachers appointed to that field were, at Montreal, Nathan Bangs; Quebec, Thomas Burch; Ottawa, Robert Hibbard; St. Francis River, Samuel Luckey and J. F. Chamberlain. But none of these were able to reach their appointments except Hibbard and Burch. The former was drowned soon after in attempting to cross the St. Lawrence, and the latter took charge of the Church in Montreal, being protected as a subject of the British government. Luckey and Chamberlain, being unable to cross the line in safety, found employment in the regular work in Vermont, within the New England Conference. Dr. Bangs, from the same impediment, found himself far separated from his associates, and without a definite field of labor. He did not remain idle, however. He was employed by the presiding elder on Croton circuit, where he did effective service."*

OLD RHINEBECK DISTRICT.

In this desultory way he passed through the ecclesiastical year and returned to the Conference, which began

* Letter of Rev. Dr. Luckey to the author.

its session at Amenia, N. Y., May 5, 1813, where he was honored by his brethren with one of its most important appointments, the presiding eldership of the Rhinebeck district. It was a grand field for his energies, extending from Rhinebeck through Dutchess county, and through western Massachusetts to Pittsfield, and thence through Connecticut to Long Island Sound. The territory of this old district includes, in our day, some half dozen presiding elders' jurisdictions. It reported, at that time, but three or four chapels and no parsonage whatever. Dr. Bangs was then in the maturity of his manhood. His preaching was powerful: his quarterly meetings and camp-meetings were jubilatic occasions, crowded by multitudes from many miles around. He traversed his great field with tireless energy, and before he left it, was begun that liberal provision of chapels and parsonages which has dotted the whole region with Methodist edifices—a chapel and a preacher's home in almost every village. The old Rhinebeck district may now, in fine, be called the garden of Methodism. He had under his command nearly a score of powerful evangelists, who caught inspiration from his own unflagging zeal. Among them were James M. Smith, Coles Carpenter, Samuel Luckey, B. Hibbard, Aaron Hunt, Elijah Woolsey, Marvin Richardson, Ebenezer Washburn, and James Coleman. Some of them had been trained, like himself, in the heroic itinerancy of Canada. He not only labored with his might for the spiritual advancement of the societies, but incessantly endeavored to promote their financial support, the improvement of their places of worship, and the better arrangement of their circuit appointments. In these respects he was a model presiding elder. Especially did he remonstrate against the penurious maintenance of the itinerants. "When I went upon this district," he writes, "I told the preachers that if they would second me in my plans I would guarantee their full 'allowance.' I submitted my plan to the Quarterly Conferences and it was very generally approved. At the first Quarterly Meeting after the annual Conference we ascertained the amount necessary to meet the demands for the year. This we divided among the several classes, in proportion to their numbers and ability, as nearly as could be ascertained, and then the classes apportioned it among their members. I believe there was very little if any deficiency through the whole four years; and I am persuaded that, if suitable measures were pursued, the full amount of all demands might be collected every year, and thus the hearts of our hard working preachers and of their widows and orphans, who now receive only about one third of their allowance, would be made to rejoice."

He also succeeded in ameliorating the condition of the Church by modifying the plan of circuit ministrations through most of the district. We may indeed claim for him the honor of initiating that change, in this respect, which has since extended its beneficent influences through most of the Atlantic Conferences. "Though Methodism," he continues, "had been planted in this part of the country for a number of years, yet the societies were generally small, the meeting-houses few and located in out of the way places, remote from the centers of population, and most of them but half finished. The itinerants on their four weeks' circuits were in the habit of preaching at each appointment once in two weeks, (there being two preachers usually to each circuit,) mostly in private or school-houses, and after the sermon they were quickly away to the next appointment. As a consequence, though their labors were blessed in the conversion of souls, most of their converts were gathered into other Churches, the pastors of these being on the spot, and usually alert for them. Seeing this state of things, I said to the preachers, 'You might as well go home and go to sleep, so far as Methodism is concerned, as to preach in the manner you do; for though your labors may be blessed, other sects will reap their results, and thus, so far as our own Church is concerned, you lose the fruit of your toils and sufferings.' 'What shall we do?' it was asked. 'We must,' I replied, 'go to work and build churches in all the cities and populous villages, and have preachers stationed in them, that they may perform the duties of pastors, watching over the flock and building them up in holiness.' The necessity of this course was generally conceded, but how to accomplish it was the question. Our people were generally poor and the societies small, and therefore unable to build churches and support pastors. But it manifestly must be done. These views I endeavored to press upon the people and preachers, and we went to work as well as we could; a beginning opened the way for further success, and this policy has ever since been followed on the district with continual advancement. Its results fully justify the views expressed. Through all that region we now have convenient houses, flourishing societies, preachers stationed and comfortably supported. To God be all the glory!" It may indeed be affirmed that throughout the territory of this old district—western Connecticut, western Massachusetts, and the upper Hudson—Methodism presents to-day the bright and indelible impression of the wise and energetic plans of Nathan Bangs. Nowhere else in the world has it better chapels and parsonages, more vigorous societies, or more intelligent and enterprising people.

HIS SUCCESS.

Meanwhile he neglected not his own culture as a man and a theologian. His habits of study were hardly relaxed, though he was constantly in motion on horseback. He now felt, indeed, more than ever the necessity of thorough ability in his professional studies, for he was surrounded by theological difficulties which required the best possible mastery. The rigid Calvinism of New England had yielded to some modifications in the further east, but in Connecticut and western Massachusetts he found it in unabated strength. He deemed it a chief obstacle to the "revivals," which were characteristic of Methodistic preaching. Partially awakened minds were waiting for the "effectual call;" awakened minds felt little or no responsibility for their moral condition, as they had been taught that it was the result of predestination; backslidden converts, believing in their final safety, defended themselves by a theological shield from the warnings of the evangelists. It is unnecessary to argue whether these evils were legitimate consequences of the prevalent creed; they were at least its popular consequences, and Dr. Bangs and his colleagues saw that they must be dispelled before their message to the people could have full sway. They had reluctantly to become polemics as well as evangelists. In doing so they may have sometimes erred by an excess of controversy, but this could be but an occasional fault; their ministerial methods and zeal kept them generally faithful to their main work, the conversion and sanctification of the people, and they were successful. "The Lord," he writes, "blessed our endeavors; we had the happiness to witness several gracious revivals of religion." They led the way in that amelioration of theological opinions which has ever since been advancing throughout this section of New England, and by the end of his four years' superintendence of the district its nine circuits, or stations, had increased to thirteen, its nineteen preachers to twenty-five, and it had gained nearly a thousand Church-members. Besides this numerical success, nearly all its economical interests had improved; chapels and parsonages were springing up all over its territory. Methodism had, in fine, secured in this extensive region not only a lodgment, but a strength which no subsequent adversities have been able to shake.

HIS PREACHING.

His ability in the pulpit attracted the people in crowds at his numerous appointments, for his word was in "demonstration of the Spirit and of power." The clergy of other denominations delighted to hear him, while dreading his supposed heresies. His surviving friend, Francis Hall, who knew him well about this time, describes him as "a master of theology and logic, and better known among other sects than almost any Methodist preacher, except Asbury." "I remember," writes Mr. Hall, "that soon after the war, which commenced in 1812, I was traveling to the north, and had put up for the night at Jaques Hotel, in Rhinebeck. There I found the Rev. Dr. Romeyn and the Rev. Dr. Westbrook—eminent clergymen of that day. The conversation turned to Methodist preaching, when Dr. Romeyn remarked that one of the best sermons he ever heard was from Nathan Bangs, in the Rhinebeck church."* If not intellectually polished, he was intellectually powerful; a certain mightiness of thought and feeling bore down at times all before him, especially when he preached to large assemblies at quarterly and camp-meetings. At one of the latter it was estimated that two hundred hearers were awakened under a single sermon; they fell, like wounded men, on the right and on the left; he preached on for two hours; and it is said that an earthquake, shaking the camp throughout those awful hours, could hardly have produced a more irresistible excitement. The Rev. Dr. Fitch Reed, who began his ministry on this district in 1815, writes of him: "I hardly dare speak in such terms as would fully express my estimate of his character, lest to others I might seem extravagant in eulogy. Very intimate acquaintance was necessary in order really to know him; and the better he was known, the brighter appeared the excellent qualities of his heart. To a stranger

* Letter of Francis Hall, Esq., to the author.

he might seem stern, haughty, and unapproachable; yet really no one could well be less so. In the intimacy and freedom of intercourse with his friends, he was remarkable for his childlike simplicity and gentleness, his entire freedom from guile, and the strength and fervor of his attachments. In his promptness and frankness to recall any hasty words inconsiderately uttered against others, I think I never knew his superior, if indeed his equal. In all that region of country no one stood higher in public esteem. Quarterly Meetings were great occasions, calling out vast multitudes, many of them from a distance of thirty or forty miles. No church edifice would begin to accommodate the crowds of people; and in the summer season an orchard or grove frequently served as our temple of worship, and mighty displays of awakening and saving power were often witnessed under the fervid and heart-searching preaching of our presiding elder."

THE CALVINISTIC CONTROVERSY.

He used his pen in the necessary controversies of these times. The Rev. Mr. Williston, in whose church he had held the debate, at Durham, N. Y., published, as has been stated, a volume on the subjects of the controversy, with severe reflections on the Methodist ministry. Dr. Bangs believed it his duty to answer this publication, in a work entitled "Errors of Hopkinsianism: Letters to Rev. Mr. Williston," etc., issued in 1815. He says, in the manuscript before me, "Whatever imperfections there may be in this book, and there are doubtless many, I enjoy the consciousness of having acted in the fear of God and from a sense of duty. I soberly believe that those features of Calvinism that distinguish it from Arminianism are contrary to the Holy Scriptures and reason, and have a most pernicious influence. While, however, I say this, I fully accredit the good and able men who have been, and are still, conscientiously engaged in their defense. But Calvinism had lately been improved by Hopkinsianism, and in addition to the points of difference alluded to, the peculiarities of Hopkinsianism entered into the present controversy, and rendered it still more intricate and perplexing. The latter system approximates, in some respects, nearer to Methodism; but while it holds that Christ died for all men, and that all may be saved if they will, it holds fast the doctrines of predestination, eternal and individual election, the necessary continuance of indwelling sin, and the final perseverance of the saints, and these make it inconsistent with itself. Notwithstanding these belligerent troubles, during the third and fourth years of my travels on the district we had increasing revivals. The pure doctrines of the Gospel ran and were glorified. New places for preaching were opened in many towns, and we had large and attentive congregations. And though we felt it to be our duty to preach against the peculiarities of Hopkinsianism and Calvinism, many Calvinistic churches were opened to us, and prejudices against us were much weakened, our doctrines being better understood and more favorably received. Though I printed an edition of three thousand of the 'Errors of Hopkinsianism Detected and Refuted,' they were all sold in about six months, and I had orders on hand for considerably more than I could supply. The circulation of this book gave me access to many places which otherwise, I believe, I could never have reached."

While writing the "Letters," he reviewed in his studies the whole Calvinistic controversy. He grappled the gigantic work of Edwards on the Will, admiring its profound ability, but detecting in it the central fallacy which its later critics have imputed to it. Hopkins, Emmons, Williams, and other representative theologians of the time, were assiduously studied by him; he became a master of the controversy, and, in his subsequent editorial life these early inquiries were available for the defense of his Church. For many years he was the most competent polemic in this particular department of theological metaphysics that the denomination could boast of on this side of the Atlantic.

CHURCH AND STATE.

His labors in Connecticut aided much in promoting another great public advantage. The connection of Church and State still existed there. The Calvinistic "standing order" still imposed some grievous disabilities on other religious parties. The state constitution in spirit contravened the federal Constitution regarding religious liberty. The rapid growth of Methodism and the declension of the traditional theology tended much to render this state of things intolerable. "A favorable opportunity," he writes, "occurred for the suffering sects to relieve themselves, and they so far improved it as to effect a revolution. A convention was called, and a constitution adopted which secures to all religious denominations equal rights and privileges." The favorable opportunity here alluded to was the payment, by the Federal government, of the expenses of the state militia, incurred in the late war with Great Britain. The state legislature appropriated the funds thus obtained to the different Christian denominations, for the promotion of religion and morals in the commonwealth; but the disproportionate amount given to the "standing order" dissatisfied the Methodists, Baptists, Protestant Episcopalians, and others, who were really a majority. The dissidents united in a protest against the inequitable apportionment; the result was a convention, the abrogation of the Colonial Charter, the adoption of a Bill of Rights and a Constitution, the Abolition of Church Taxes, and the enfranchisement of all sects. This example led to a similar reform in Massachusetts, and thus completed the separation of Church and State in the United States.

REVISITS THE SCENES OF HIS CHILDHOOD.

The Rhinebeck district included the localities of his childhood, and he visited them with affecting interest. "I had," he says, "been absent from them twenty years; it gave me much joy, therefore, to return to these places of my early remembrances.' At the first house to which I came, and where I used to be known, I found the head of the family old and decrepid. After exchanging a few words with him I inquired for Captain Summers and his brother's family, with whom I had been intimate. The two brothers were dead, and their families dispersed. Many others for whom I inquired were also dead; some of them had perished at sea, some in the far West. Almost all the old people whom I could remember were 'gone the way of all the earth.' My reflections became sad; I seemed in a strange land. My young associates had so changed that I could not recognize them. I turned mournfully away toward the burial-ground to converse with the dead. There I found on the tombstones the names of, alas! how many whom I could recollect. I wandered among their graves a long time; I reflected, not unprofitably nor unpleasantly, upon the transitory nature of all earthly things, and endeavored to lift my heart to the abiding heavens, the final home. I devoutly thanked God for his many mercies to me, a poor wanderer on the earth, who had so strangely found my way back to these first scenes of my pilgrimage. I could not well break away from the spot. My mind seemed fascinated by its many associations." The place where he used to attend school; the public "green," where the village parades were held and his boyish sports were played; the old inn, once a notable place of the parish, now converted into a preaching-house; the fields where he wandered in his boyhood; the church in which he was baptized, and whither his parents used to lead his young feet to the ordinances of God, were all in sight. "How many recollections," he continues, "crowded upon my mind! In my meditations I made a rapid history of the first thirteen years of my life. It was mostly beautiful with the simple poetry of childhood; but what changes had occurred in the twenty years of my absence! The house in which I had lived was demolished; the school-house was gone; the church, though standing, seemed smitten with the general change, for it had been forsaken for another, and was going to decay; the old innkeeper was dead, and many of his aged neighbors and jovial customers lay by his side in the dust; his widow survived; she had become a Methodist, and her house was now the occasional temple of my own brethren. I looked this way and that, but was riveted to the spot by an irresistible yet pleasant melancholy. I did not wish to see a living being, nor to be diverted from my saddening meditations. Whether the friend who was with me perceived my emotions or not I cannot say, but he appeared willing to leave me to my musings. O this was a most profitable hour! I thought it would compensate for whatever I might suffer during my travels on the district.

"Leaving the place consecrated to the dust of my friends, I visited a half sister, who was married and the mother of a family; and here again the fountain of old memories was broken up. In the evening I preached in the old inn. A large assembly, most of whom formerly knew me, were present, and I addressed them with deep and pensive satisfaction. The appearance of so many bowed and gray-headed men, whom I knew in their prime of life, when I was but a boy, reminded me again of the swift flight of the years, and made me think for the first time that I was growing old, though yet but thirty-six years of age. Before I left the village I visited many families, former acquaintances of my father, who remembered me as the 'little white-headed boy' of other years. Some of them told me they used to predict that

I would become a preacher of the Gospel, and seemed to delight in rehearsing incidents of my boyhood."

GENERAL CONFERENCE OF 1816.

While superintending this district he was elected a delegate to the General Conference of 1816, which assembled in Baltimore on the first of May. One hundred and three delegates were present, representing all parts of the nation. Besides himself, New York Conference sent Garrettson, Phœbus, Washburn, Merwin, Sandford, Clark, Ostrander, and others of its chief men; Soule, Hedding, Ruter, Pickering, and similar men were there from New England; Puffer, Gary, Mattison, Case, from Genesee; Quinn, Holliday, Young, Lakin, Sale, from Ohio; Cartwright, Sellers, Axley, and Walker from Tennessee; Myers, Kennedy, Dunwody, Tally, from South Carolina; Bruce, Hines, Drake, Thrift, from Virginia; Wells, George, Smith, Roszel, Griffith, Burch, Shinn, Gruber, Waugh, from Baltimore; Roberts, M'Combs, Sharp, Martindale, Boehm, Emory, and Bishop from Philadelphia. Six of these delegates afterward became bishops in the denomination, and the body as a whole presented an extraordinary example of intellectual and moral strength.

Peace was now restored to the country, but the moral effect of the war was still generally visible. The increase of communicants reported this year was but little more than three thousand; the increase since the preceding General Conference less than nineteen thousand. The aggregate strength of the Church was, however, mighty; it amounted to about two hundred and fourteen thousand members, and seven hundred traveling preachers. Methodism had especially prevailed in the great West; its "old Western Conference," now comprising two Conferences, reported more than one fifth of the whole membership of the Church.

HIS SERVICES IN THE CONFERENCE.

The Journal of the General Conference shows that few delegates were more active or more influential in the proceedings of this session than Nathan Bangs. He was the first named on the committee to whom were referred the Episcopal Address of M'Kendree, and the posthumous address of Asbury; and in the report of the committee defined, to a considerable extent, the course of business which has ever since been pursued in the Conference, by proposing committees on the Episcopacy, the Book Concern, Ways and Means, Review and Revision, Safety and Temporal Economy. Some of these committees had been anticipated at the previous session, but they were now definitively, and it may be said permanently established. He was appointed chairman of the Committee of Ways and Means. He proposed a Committee on Local Preachers, and was appointed a member of it, and also chairman of the Committee to prepare an Address to the English Wesleyan Missionary Society, and a member of the Committee to revise the Discipline. In his manuscript account of the session he says: "At this Conference there were some important changes made in our temporal economy. The 'allowance' of the preachers and their wives was raised from eighty to one hundred dollars each, and the Quarterly Conference was authorized to make provision, by appointment of a committee for that purpose, for the family expenses of the preachers stationed among them. Being a member of the committee on this part of our economy, I drew up the rules of the Discipline on these subjects, and, of course, was an advocate for them. The same committee reported the rule, which was this year incorporated into the Discipline, requiring a course of study for candidates for the ministry. I was the author of this rule. These measures encountered great opposition from many delegates, and were debated through three or four days.

They were amended in such various ways that we could make nothing of them. I finally proposed to a brother delegate, Stephen G. Roszel, that if he would second my motion I would move to lay all the amendments on the table, and take up the original report of the committee and adopt it. To this he assented, and the resolutions, as seen in the Discipline, were adopted. That these regulations have had a salutary influence on the Church I have no doubt, and therefore I reflect with much pleasure on the agency I had in drafting the report and in its adoption."

Both these measures were, indeed, inestimably important as forward movements—the beginning of those advancements in the support and literary improvement of the ministry which have ever since continued. It required a man who was in advance of the times to initiate such changes, slight as they were, compared with their later progress, and it required no small amount of moral courage to withstand the hostile debate they provoked in the Conference, and persistently to press them to a successful issue.

To the Book Concern he gave special attention in the proceedings of this session, for he saw clearly its future importance as an engine of moral and literary power in the Church and the nation. He offered a resolution instructing its agents to publish a monthly magazine. The motion was promptly defeated, but was subsequently reproduced in the Report of the Committee on the Book Concern and adopted, not, however, without a severe contest. He had advocated this measure in the session of 1812; of that session he says: "The importance of publishing a periodical work was strongly urged by some of the leading members, and strenuously opposed by others. The subject was referred to the consideration of the Book Concern Committee, and they finally recommended, and the Conference concurred, 'That the book agents be directed to resume the publication of the

Methodist Magazine, two volumes having been published, (namely, in 1789 and 1790,) to commence publishing the third volume, at furthest, by January next.' The mandate of the Conference was, however, never obeyed, and, unhappily for the literature and character of the Methodist Episcopal Church, we had no magazine, nor scarcely any publication of American growth until 1818, when the Methodist Magazine was recommenced. During a number of years it appears that education of all sorts, as well as writing for the public eye, was laid aside as useless, and we seem to have come to the strange conclusion that we had naught else to do than simply preach the Gospel, and attend to those other duties which are connected with the pastoral office, in order to insure the blessing of God on our labors; hence, the Magazine had been discontinued for more than twenty years, and scarcely anything issued from our press, except what was imported from Europe, and much of this was brought before the public through other mediums. Here and there a small pamphlet made its appearance, but only to disappear, generally before it had time to breathe the breath of life; for it seemed to be taken for granted that American Methodists were doomed to a state of nonage, which unfitted them to instruct one another through the medium of the press. It is true that a few sighed over this state of things, and sometimes vented their feelings to one another in accents of sorrow and regret, but they almost despaired of obtaining redress. When assailed by our adversaries we had no adequate means of defense, and hence the reading public were left to draw their own inferences respecting Methodist doctrines and economy from the distorted representations of those who felt it their duty to caricature us. From these humiliating facts it became proverbial that the 'Methodists were enemies to learning.' It must be confessed that there was too much reason for the taunting remark, and it was not without much labor that the reproach has been, in some measure at least, rolled away from us."

He may thus be said to have been the chief founder of the periodical literature of American Methodism; and he is but the more entitled to this honor by the fact that the experiment made nearly a quarter of a century before had been a complete failure.

DEATHS OF COKE AND ASBURY.

This General Conference was solemnized and saddened by the death, since the preceding session, of its first two bishops—men who, in our times, are constantly rising in historical importance by the results of their extraordinary services. Bishop Coke had died on the 3d of May, 1814, on his voyage to the East, and was buried in the Indian Ocean. Neither Wesley nor Whitefield exceeded him in ministerial travels. It is probable that no Methodist of his day, it is doubtful whether any Protestant of his day, contributed more from his own property for the promotion of religion. He spent nearly forty years in scarcely intermitted travels for the Gospel; he crossed the Atlantic eighteen times; he was the founder of the Wesleyan Missions in the West Indies, Africa, Asia, in England, Wales, and Ireland; he was the official director of the Wesleyan missionary operations from their origin till about the year of his death; he was the first who suggested to Wesley the constitutional organization of English Methodism as provided in the "Deed of Declaration;" and he was the founder, under Wesley, of the episcopal government of American Methodism. He was the first Protestant bishop of the Western Hemisphere. By both the extent and the still greater results of his services he must be pronounced one of the chief representative men of modern religious history, if not indeed, as Asbury declared, "the greatest man of the last century in labors and services as a minister of Christ."

Asbury died in Virginia, about two months before the session of the General Conference, aged more than seventy years, and after preaching more than half a century. He had labored, as a founder of Methodism in America, about forty-five years. His last sermon was delivered in Richmond, Va., on the 24th of March, 1816; he had to be assisted into the pulpit, and to sit while preaching. He was buried in Spottsylvania, but his remains were disinterred and taken to Baltimore, where the Conference entombed them, with solemn ceremonies, beneath the pulpit of Light-street Church. Dr. Bangs, to whom he had been as a father, has recorded his best eulogy: "His attitude in the pulpit was graceful, dignified, and solemn; his voice full and commanding; his enunciation clear and distinct; and sometimes a sudden burst of eloquence would break forth in a manner which spoke a soul full of God, and, like a mountain torrent, swept all before it. During the forty-five years of his ministry in America, allowing that he preached on an average one sermon a day—and he often preached three times on a Sabbath—he delivered not less than sixteen thousand four hundred and twenty-five sermons, besides lectures to the societies, and meeting classes. Allowing him six thousand miles a year, which it is believed he generally exceeded, he must have traveled, during the same time, about two hundred and seventy thousand miles, much of it on the very worst roads. From the time of the organization of the Church, in 1784, to the period of his death, thirty-two years, allowing an average of seven Conferences a year, he sat in no less than two hundred and twenty-four Annual Conferences, and in their infancy their business devolved chiefly upon himself; and he probably consecrated, including traveling and local preachers, more than four thousand persons to the sacred office! Here then is a missionary bishop worthy of the name, whose example may be held up for the imitation of all who engage in this sacred work. His deadness to the world, to human applause, to riches and honors, and his deep devotion to God, made an impression upon all who witnessed his spirit and conduct that he was actuated by the purest and most elevated motives. This pervading impression wrought that confidence in the uprightness of his intentions and the wisdom of his plans, which gave him such a control, over both preachers and people, as enabled him to discharge the high trusts confided to him with so much facility and to such general satisfaction. Hence the apparent ease with which he managed the complicated machinery of Methodism, guided the councils of the Conferences, fixed the stations of the preachers, and otherwise exercised his authority for the general good of the entire body."*

In his manuscript notes of this Conference I find equally emphatic words in praise of this great man, but qualified by frank though tender animadversions on his administration. "There are," he says, "two particulars in which I always thought Bishop Asbury erred. I speak indeed with great deference when I presume to differ from such a man, for I cannot but feel a profound veneration for his character. I think, however, that he showed not enough interest for the intellectual improvement of the preachers and too great a solicitude to keep them poor. If he had encouraged measures to provide a competency for men of heavy and expensive families, and promoted human learning as a subordinate help to the ministry, I think he would have thus rendered essential service to the Church. Having no family of his own to provide for, he did not sympathize with parental affections and anxieties as he otherwise would have done; and hence I am inclined to think that he was not sufficiently attentive to the sufferings of many of the preachers and their families in the frequent and distant removals to which they were subjected. That there were

* History of the Methodist Episcopal Church, vol. ii, book v, chap. 2.

faults in his administration I think all who witnessed it must allow. He knew well the history of the early Church; he knew that wealth and 'science, falsely so called,' had corrupted it, and he feared their influence on Methodism. But whatever defects there might have been in these particulars of his policy, his inextinguishable zeal for the salvation of men, his large views of God's immense love for our lost world, his thorough knowledge of theology, his deep experience of the grace of God, his manly as well as his Christian virtues, his unparalleled labors, his patient sufferings for so long a time, unequaled by those of any of his preachers, his masterly ability in directing the operations of the Church over much of the continent, justly secured to him the confidence of his brethren and the veneration and wonder of all who knew him."

VIEWS OF THE MINISTERIAL "CALL."

These animadversions, even should they be deemed not altogether relevant to Asbury, are nevertheless relevant here, as illustrations of the advanced views of ministerial qualification and support which Dr. Bangs took at this early period, and which he promoted throughout the remainder of his life, more effectually perhaps than any other man of his denomination. He insisted on the effective support of the preachers, not merely for their comfort, but for their moral safety. An incredibly large proportion of them "located" in that day after a few years of travel. The itinerant ministry lost, in this way, many of its most effective men. Believing the holy office to be a "vocation," not merely a "profession," he could not admit the right of a preacher to retire from it unless providentially permitted by extreme disability of health or other insuperable necessity. No man divinely called to the office could leave it without a Divine revocation of the "call." One of the few surviving Methodists of the Rhinebeck district, of this period, writes me: "I lived in Winsted, Conn. While at our Quarterly Meeting there, Dr. Bangs stayed at my home. After love-feast, on Sunday morning, he stepped into the house before preaching to take some refreshment. While seated at the table an aged brother came in, and seating himself said, 'Elder, I wish to ask you a question!' 'Very well,' said Dr. Bangs, 'I will answer you if I can.' He then asked, 'If a man in his youthful days is brought to the knowledge of the truth, and feels "woe is me if I preach not the Gospel," and the impression continues for years, but he refuses to obey it and it finally leaves him, but he still strives to live a good life and dies thus, is it possible for him to get to heaven?' The doctor inclined his head a few minutes, apparently in deep thought, and then replied, 'Brother, there may be a possibility of his getting to heaven, but another will take his crown.' The expression conveyed very much meaning to my mind, and has never left me."*

With such an opinion, he trembled for his brethren who, after making good proof of their ministry, retreated from the field, in the prime of life, to secular occupations; and he demanded that the Church should relieve itself from any share in the responsibility of their failure, for with it was that responsibility more than with them.

* Letter of Reuben Hall to the author.

CHAPTER XV.

NEW YORK CONFERENCE, 1817.

DR. BANGS's four years' term of service on the Rhinebeck district expired June 3, 1817. On that day the New York Conference began its session in Middlebury, Vt.—a singular collocation of names to our eyes—the New York Conference sitting in an interior town of Vermont. But, as we have seen, "there were giants in those days," and most of their plans present gigantic proportions. The New York Conference still comprised more than half of Connecticut, a large part of Western Massachusetts, all Vermont west of the Green Mountains, and Eastern New York, from the mouth of the Hudson to the Canada line. Though it had given the Canadas to Genesee Conference, it still reported more than twenty-one thousand communicants.

Among the recruits whom he welcomed on probation before the Conference, at this time, were his faithful friends, Fitch Reed, John M. Smith, and J. J. Matthias; and among the candidates received into full membership was his own brother, Heman Bangs, who still survives, an effective laborer, after so many years of itinerant service.

Nathan Bangs was appointed by this Conference to New York city, where he was welcomed by his former hearers with the warmest cordiality. His presiding elder was Samuel Merwin, a great man of that day; his colleagues were Daniel Ostrander, Seth Crowell, and Samuel Howe. His old friends of the city could not fail to notice his rapid improvement as a preacher, and, though he was not in charge of the station, he was foremost among his colleagues, in the public recognition, as a man of intellect and of pulpit power.

STUDIES—WRITINGS.

He gave himself diligently to study, especially in theology and mental philosophy. In the latter department of inquiry he had long since mastered Locke, the favorite metaphysical author of his youth; he now mastered Berkeley, Beattie, Hume; and the "Scotch Metaphysicians"—who were the great authorities of the science—Reid, Stewart, and Brown. He has left notes of these studies, which prove his vivid interest in them and his aptitude for them. Reid's "Essays on the Intellectual Faculties and Active Powers" were especially his delight; he made an ample synopsis of them in his commonplace-book, and considered them the best solution of the chief problems of the science which had yet been given to the world.

He found it necessary again to appear in the lists as a polemic. His letters on Hopkinsianism were severely treated in a published sermon by Rev. Mr. Haskil, of Burlington, Vt. The Methodist preachers of that state urged him to reply to it, alleging that the discourse was having injurious influence upon their communities. He answered it in a small volume entitled "Predestination Examined." "Soon after," he says, "Mr. Williston sent out a second volume, in reply to the 'Errors of Hopkinsianism,' called 'A Vindication of some of the Essential Doctrines of the Reformation.' This attempt to identify the peculiarities of Hopkinsianism with the essential doctrines of the Reformation called forth my 'Reformer Reformed,' the title being suggested by the conviction that if the Reformation carried with it errors of such a pernicious consequence as it was believed must flow from the doctrine of an efficient operation of universal and immutable decrees the Reformation itself needed reforming—a sentiment not retracted on more mature consideration. It by no means becomes me to express an opinion of the character or results of this protracted discussion, though I may be allowed to indulge a hope that it had its use in bringing our doctrines more prominently before the public, in rectifying some erroneous impressions respecting our ministry and usages, and in awakening public attention to the precise points of difference between us and our Calvinistic opponents. We were called upon to sustain an arduous conflict with our brethren of other denominations, as well as with some of our own household, who, for various reasons, 'went out from us,' in order to rescue our ministry from reproach, and our doctrines, government, and usages from the numerous objections which were preferred against them."

He esteemed his book "Predestination Examined" "the best" of his "writings, in point of argumentation." "Mr. Haskil," he adds, "was an able writer, and an ingenious though, I cannot but think, somewhat unfair antagonist. I printed an edition of three thousand of this work, and it passed through a second edition. I found it necessary to guard against the influence of so much controversy on my own peace of mind; but as I acted from a consciousness of duty, and in the fear of God, I felt consoled and strengthened in the performance of this labor. As I had not the charge of the Church in the city this year, I had the more leisure to pursue my studies and attend to my other duties. At the Conference at Middlebury, Vt., I moved for a committee to revise our hymn book, and, as I was a member of the committee, a portion of my time was spent in this laborious task. The manner in which it was performed may be seen in the preface to the book, as published in 1820." He thus provided the hymn book, the virtual liturgy of American Methodism, as it was used for about thirty years throughout the continent, except the British Provinces.

LABORS—STUDIES—OLD JOHN-STREET.

"Among other things," he continues, "I revived the catechetical instruction in the Duane-street Church, near which I lived. It had been discontinued from the time I had left the city. Among others who attended my class, Mrs. Palmer, and her sister, Mrs. Langford, who have since been among the most devoted and useful of our Church-members, may be mentioned. I cannot but look back with grateful satisfaction upon these efforts to impart religious instruction to the young."

While pursuing these studies, controversies, and pastoral labors, he appeared habitually in the pulpit, armed with the power of the Divine Word. Preaching was, indeed, his mightiest instrument; his congregations were thronged, and the Societies flourished. At the end of his first year they reported an increase of more than three hundred members, and their aggregate membership was more than three thousand. This success was marred, however, by serious internal troubles. "As these difficulties," he writes, "resulted at last in the secession of a considerable number of our members, headed by a preacher, it may not be amiss to allude to some of the circumstances which caused the rupture. A party spirit had prevailed for some time between the 'down-town' and 'up-town' members, but it did not amount to anything very serious until the trustees commenced rebuilding John-street Church. As it was resolved that the new edifice should be an improvement on the architectural style of the old one, some discontented spirits made this a pretext for discord, and, unhappily for the peace of the Church, the preacher in charge, being displeased because he was not invited to dedicate the church, lent the weight of his influence to the disaffected party, while the great majority of the preachers and people were in favor of the measures of the trustees. He went so far as to say, in a love-feast, that he wished the new building were cast into the ocean. This, of course, increased the irritation, and tended to make the dispute more irremediable. Several ineffectual attempts were made to restore harmony, but it seemed impossible."

The measure however proceeded, and on the 13th of March, 1817, the walls of the old structure were demolished, after an address by Rev. Daniel Ostrander to a large assembly of spectators. On the 4th of January, 1818, the new church was dedicated by Dr. Bangs, in a discourse on the text, "The Lord hath done great things for us, whereof we are glad." Sermons were delivered in it the same day by Samuel Merwin and Joshua Soule. It is described as "one of the most commodious and beautiful chapels in the city" at that time, and a model for many later structures in the country. Engravings, however, represent it so extremely plain as to excite our wonder that it could have been the occasion of any scruple, much less of violent discord. The dispute, nevertheless, continued. "In this unhappy state," says Dr. Bangs, "I came into the charge of the city circuit in 1818. What rendered my position much more embarrassing was, that one of my colleagues threw himself into the ranks of the disaffected party, and did what he could to frustrate my plans for peace. Truth requires me to say that he acted in a most discreditable manner, impugning my motives and misrepresenting my conduct, while I was endeavoring, in every possible way, to save the Church from division. While the storm raged around me, threatening to sweep everything overboard, I trembled for our cause, wept and prayed, and the Lord strengthened my heart and kept my head above the waters."

ORIGIN OF THE MISSIONARY SOCIETY.

The issue was delayed a short time. Meanwhile, amid these strifes, occurred one of the most important events in the history of Methodism: the "Missionary Society" of the Methodist Episcopal Church arose, spanning the local storm, and throwing out its vision of beauty and blessing to distant eyes, a bow of gladdening and sublime promise. One of its original managers says: "Dr. Bangs may justly be called the father of the Missionary Society. He was at its organization in the Second-street (now Forsyth-street) Church, and for many years was its main pillar. Indeed, we may well say that his whole public life was spent in the missionary cause. His ministerial travels in the wilds of Canada, before the ordinary roads were made, were a genuine missionary service, and he then zealously befriended the Indian. The red men to this day speak of him as the great missionary from the states. I remember meeting Captain Beaver, one of the tribe at Grape Island; he wished to ask some questions regarding Dr. Bangs, and, not recalling his name, immediately described him as the 'big missionary from New York, with his head on one shoulder.'" *

He "had long," says his manuscript, "felt the necessity of this measure for the extension of our work among the poor, the colored people, the Indians, and as a relief to many of our suffering preachers." As it was designed to aid domestic as well as foreign missions, an adaptation which it still retains, he considered it not only a promising means of foreign propagandism, but as particularly favoring his views of ministerial support in the destitute portions of the domestic field of the denomination. He made it, therefore, the theme of much preliminary conversation with his colleagues and the principal Methodist laymen of the city. His still surviving friend, Rev. Dr. Laban Clark, introduced it by a resolu-

* Letter of Francis Hall, Esq., to the author. All who knew Dr. Bangs will understand the allusion. His head habitually inclined to his right shoulder. It is reported, as an amusing fact, that the young preachers from his district could be readily distinguished in the Annual Conference by their unconscious imitation of their admired Elder's bearing in this respect. If the imitation extended to most of his other peculiarities it was quite pardonable.

tion to the attention of the metropolitan preachers at their weekly meeting, "consisting," says Dr. Bangs's manuscript, "of Freeborn Garrettson, Samuel Merwin, Laban Clark, Samuel Howe, Seth Crowell, Thomas Thorp, Joshua Soule, Thomas Mason, and myself. After an interchange of thoughts the resolution was adopted, and Garrettson, Clark, and myself were appointed a committee to draft a constitution. When this committee met we agreed to write, each, a constitution, then come together, compare them, and adopt the one which should be considered the most suitable. The one prepared by myself was adopted, submitted to the Preachers' Meeting, and, after some slight verbal alterations, was finally approved. We then agreed to call a public meeting in the Forsyth-street Church on the evening of the 5th of April, 1819, which was accordingly done. I was called to the chair, and after the reading of the constitution Joshua Soule moved its adoption, and supported his motion by a powerful speech, concluding by an appeal to the people to come forward and subscribe it. He was seconded by Freeborn Garrettson, who also plead in favor of the scheme, from his own experience in the itinerant field from Virginia to Nova Scotia. The constitution was unanimously adopted, and the following officers were chosen: Bishop M'Kendree, President; Bishops George and Roberts, and Nathan Bangs, Vice-Presidents; Thomas Mason, Corresponding Secretary; Joshua Soule, Treasurer; Francis Hall, Clerk; Daniel Ayres, Recording Secretary.*

* The following managers were also chosen: Joseph Smith, Robert Mathison, Joseph Sandford, George Suckley, Samuel L. Waldo, Stephen Dando, Samuel B. Harper, Lancaster S. Burling, William Duval, Paul Hick, John Westfield, Thomas Roby, Benjamin Disbrow, James B. Gascoigne, William A. Mercein, Philip J. Arcularius, James B. Oakley, George Caines, Dr. Seaman, Dr. Gregory, John Boyd, M. H. Smith, Nathaniel Jarvis, Robert Snow, Andrew Mercein, Joseph Moses, John Paradise, William Myers, William B. Skidmore, Nicholas Schureman, James Woods, Abraham Paul.

He was not only chairman of the Preachers' Meeting at which this great scheme was initiated, the author of its constitution, and president of the first public meeting for its adoption, but, as its only resident vice-president, he became its first actually presiding officer. As such he was chairman of its Board of Managers, and at their request prepared its first "Address," and its first "Circular" to the Annual Conferences. The historian of the society says: "It is obvious that almost the entire business of the Society was conducted by him for many years. In addition to writing the constitution, the address and circular, he was the author of every Annual Report, with but one exception, from the organization of the society down to the year 1841, a period of twenty-two years. He filled the offices of Corresponding Secretary and Treasurer for sixteen years, without a salary or compensation of any kind, until his appointment to the first named office by the General Conference of 1836. That he has contributed more than any other man living to give character to our missionary operations, by the productions of his pen and his laborious personal efforts, is a well authenticated fact, which the history of the Church fully attests."*

"There is no act," wrote Dr. Bangs years afterward, "there is no act of my life upon which I reflect with greater pleasure than my agency in the formation of this Society, as it has been instrumental in extending the work of God in many directions at home and abroad." In this single instance of his manifold public life he was to be identified with a grand religious history. He was to see the annual receipts of the Society enlarged from the $823 of its first year to $250,374, (including its offspring of the Methodist Episcopal Church, South, to half a million,) and its total receipts, down to the last year of his life, more than four

* Strickland's History of the Missions of the Methodist Episcopal Church, etc., chap. i.

and a half millions, not including the southern Society. He was to witness the rise (chiefly under the auspices of this Society) of American German Methodism, an epochal fact in the history of his Church, next in importance to the founding of the Church by Embury and Strawbridge. Without a missionary for some time after its origin, the Society was to present to his dying gaze a list of nearly four hundred missionaries and more than thirty-three thousand mission communicants, representing the denomination in many parts of the United States, in Norway, Sweden, Germany, Switzerland, Bulgaria, Africa, India, China, South America, and the Sandwich Islands. Assisting in this great work, and rejoicing in its triumphs, he was to outlive all its original officers but three, Joshua Soule, Francis Hall, and Daniel Ayres; and all its original managers save three, Dr. Seaman, James B. Oakley, and William B. Skidmore.

In the course of a year or two after the organization of the Society he succeeded Joshua Soule as its treasurer. In April, 1836, he was elected the fourth Vice-president and Corresponding Secretary; in 1838 the resident Corresponding Secretary; and thenceforward, as we shall see, devoted his whole energy to it down to 1841. All its Annual Reports to this date save one are attributed to his pen. "It is supposed," said his associates of the Board at his death, "that he never missed a meeting, when in the city, from the very first, except on account of sickness. Everything with him gave place to the missionary meeting, being, with his early associate, Rev. Joshua Soule, of opinion 'that the time would come when every man who assisted in the organization of the Society, and persevered in the undertaking, would consider it one of the most honorable periods of his life.'"

METHODIST EDUCATION.

While this important measure was being introduced, the party discord, occasioned by the rebuilding of John-street Church, continued, and was an oppressive grievance to him. It did not deter him, however, from attempting another momentous step forward; the establishment of the "Wesleyan Seminary" of New York city. Methodism, like the Reformation in Germany and Switzerland, was cradled in a University; a providental fact, as has been said, for the cause of learning. Its most distinguished founders had secured to it a prestige in favor of education, for the Wesleys, Whitefield, Coke, Fletcher, were all collegiately educated men. As early as 1784, the year of the formal organization of the Methodist Episcopal Church, its two bishops,. Coke and Asbury, projected a college; its foundation was laid the next year at Abingdon, twenty-five miles from Baltimore, and in 1787 it was opened with public ceremonies by Asbury. In 1795 it was destroyed by fire. A second edifice was soon after erected in the city of Baltimore, but it shared the fate of its predecessor. Absorbed in other labors, the denomination gave little or no attention to academic education till, in 1818, Dr. Samuel K. Jennings and other Methodists attempted a college in that city, but failed. Dr. Bangs deplores, in his History of the Church, the inference which Asbury and the other American leaders of Methodism drew from these early failures. They considered them "an indication of Divine Providence that it was no part of the duty of the Methodist Episcopal Church to engage in founding and raising up colleges. On the same principle of reasoning we should refuse to build a church, or a dwelling-house, or even to embark in any business which might be injured by the elements. Job's repeated losses were permitted to try his patience, and this might have been permitted for a similar effect on the Church."

He himself never lost sight of this great interest, and now urged its claims on the attention of the laymen of New York, who had been consulting for some time on the subject. They were encouraged by the example of their New England brethren, who, about this time, had, chiefly through the agency of Dr. Martin Ruter, formed a seminary at New Market, N. H., which was afterward transferred to Wilbraham, Mass., where it has been an incalculable blessing to the denomination. Dr. Bangs brought the project before the city Quarterly Conference, "where," he says, "it met with violent opposition from the same man who had opposed the new John-street Church. The majority, however, approved of the plan, and I was appointed to draft a constitution, which was adopted, but not without encountering much hostility, chiefly from preachers. This was the beginning of our exertions in favor of education. From the opposition I met in this feeble endeavor in behalf of so important a cause I often felt much discouraged; but Martin Ruter, coming into the city about this time, strengthened my hands, and said that he could not doubt that God had sent me hither for this very purpose. I therefore persevered, and finally succeeded, by the help of God and those generous brethren whose liberality enabled me to get the seminary into operation. We thought ourselves fortunate in the selection of teachers, but, alas! how short-sighted is man. The good work was to be severely tested. The male teacher apostatized, and the preceptress, Matilda Thayer, who was at that time a literary notability by the success of some of her publications, turned Swedenborgian and left us.*

* He adds in a note: "The apostasy of the principal was of the grossest kind, and he was expelled from the Church. He soon became a poor, heart-broken man, and died a premature death. On his deathbed I visited him frequently, and a more sincere penitent I never saw. Believing in his repentance, and perceiving satisfactory signs of his having obtained the pardon of his sins, I called on the preacher in charge, Mr. Washburn, who again took him into the Church and gave

The seminary, however, struggled on for several years, and was finally removed to White Plains, N. Y.

This seminary was, with that of New Hampshire, a pioneer of Methodist education in the New World—the beginning of that series of educational provisions in the denomination, north and south, which was to number before the death of Dr. Bangs not less than a hundred and twenty institutions, comprising boarding academies, colleges, and theological schools. Nathan Bangs was not only one of the earliest, but one of the most active and persistent promoters of education in the denomination. Down to the last year of his life, his zeal for this great interest never abated. His early New England training had left an indelible impression of the importance of sound learning upon his liberal mind. He believed that the success of Methodism rendered it more responsible than any other American Christian body for the education of the common people, immense masses of whom had been gathered under its guardianship. Nor did he fear the influence of learning on its more intimately religious or ecclesiastical interests. As far as these might be risked by education he was willing to risk them, assured that the result could not fail to be favorable to genuine religion.

"On the whole," he writes, "the two years I spent in the city Churches were a period of incessant labor, of no little anxiety and trial, and of much spiritual consolation."

PRESIDING ELDER—THE STILLWELLITES.

He was elevated at the Conference of 1819 to the presiding eldership of the district, which included the metropolis. It extended into the state of New York as far as Cortland, into Connecticut as far as Stamford,

him the sacrament of the Lord's supper. He died in peace. How great the mercy of our God in Christ Jesus!" Mrs. Thayer rejoined the Church in the South-west, and, I believe, died in its communion.

and over the whole of Long Island. It included more than a score of itinerants, among whom were some of the strongest men of that day: Freeborn Garrettson, William Phœbus, Samuel Merwin, Laban Clark, Alexander M'Caine, Marvin Richardson, Elijah Woolsey, J. B. Matthias, and Phineas Rice. "This," writes Dr. Bangs, "was a year of sore trial to me on several accounts. My family was now large, my children needed my attention, and the provision for my support was quite inadequate. I endeavored, however, to discharge my duties as well as I could, and enjoyed much of the Divine presence and consolation. But as nothing occurred out of the ordinary course of things, except the secession, in 1820, of a preacher, William M. Stillwell, and many members of the Church, the result of the old quarrel about John-street Church, it is not necessary to make an extended record of the events of the year. The split in the Church was marked by that violence of spirit which usually accompanies such occurrences, and deeply depressed my mind. I had to take officially an active part in the measures which were used in vain to prevent it, and of course I had to share in their responsibility and in the reproach of those who stood faithfully by the Church. Two trustees and several class-leaders, with the members of their classes, amounting in all to three hundred, withdrew and organized an independent sect. They seemed formidable indeed, but did not long continue to prosper; most of them, sooner or later, became sensible of their error and returned to the Church. As I continued in the city, as Book Agent, after my charge of the district, I was well acquainted with most of them, and they generally came to me to make known their dissatisfaction with their new position. At one time a brother, who was a trustee and class-leader before he left us, and was a leader still among the seceders, came to me and said that there were three class-leaders, with their classes, about seventy persons, who wished to return; but the class-members wished to come in a body and to retain their leaders. He desired to know if there was any way by which this could be done. I replied that I knew of none except the usual probation. 'Indeed,' said he, 'I would rather stand on probation six years than remain any longer where I am.' I went to Samuel Merwin, who then had charge of the city stations, and related to him their proposition, advising him to receive them en masse, and let them remain under their present leaders. After further consultations with them I had the happiness to see them all restored to their former fellowship and well cured of their discontent. I believe that nine tenths of those who withdrew came back. They thus escaped final shipwreck. How dangerous to make a breach in the Church of God for such trifling reasons! For the part I took in this unhappy affair I suffered much. The tongue of slander was active, and some of my old friends became so prejudiced against me that they would not hear me preach."

The "Stillwellite Methodists" remained for some time an anomalous sect, but at last disappeared from public notice, and they have now almost disappeared from the memory of the New York Methodists.

CHAPTER XVI.

SERVICES IN THE GENERAL CONFERENCE OF 1820.

Dr. Bangs had hardly been on his district one year when he was again sent by his Conference as one of its delegates to the General Conference, which began its session in Baltimore, May 1, 1820. Eleven annual Conferences were represented by delegates who were mostly leaders of their respective sections of the Church. The old Western Conference had already been divided into four Conferences extending over most of the Mississippi valley. Mississippi Conference was represented by two delegates, Thomas Griffin and John Lane; Missouri had also its small delegation of Jesse Walker and two others; Tennessee was more strongly represented by Cartwright, Axley, Holliday, and two others; Ohio by Finley, Collins, Stamper, Quinn, and four more. The chief men of the cis-Alleghany Conferences were also there: Hedding, Merritt, Ruter, Pickering, from New England; Garrettson, Bangs, Merwin, Soule, Rice, Sandford, Richardson, from New York; Chamberlain and Case from Genesee; Cooper, M'Combs, Ware, Lybrand, Wells, Sharp, from Philadelphia; Griffith, Waugh, Burch, Roszel, Emory, from Baltimore; Hall, Cannon, Drake, from Virginia; Capers, Andrews, Myers, Kennedy, Dunwody, from the Carolinas. Seldom or never had greater interests of the Church come under the consideration of the body than those which occupied its attention at this session—missions, education, literature, the hymn book, the "presiding eldership question," and vital disciplinary matters; and few if any delegates took a more important part in these deliberations than Nathan

Bangs. In the twenty-seven days' proceedings of the session there are but four or five on which he does not appear in the record of the Journal as introducing important resolutions, advocating improvements, or appointed on committees. Evidently he now stood out before the Conference and the denomination as one of its foremost men. He is associated in these proceedings with nearly all those great measures which were destined to give elevation and permanent importance to the Church. He was chairman of a committee, consisting of such men as Soule and Merritt, on the interests of his earliest field of labor, Canada; and also chairman of a committee to prepare a plan for the institution of denominational seminaries, a subject which he brought before the body by a memorial from his own Conference, written by himself. He thus initiated the great interest of education in the General Conference, having anticipated it by his efforts for the Wesleyan Seminary in New York; and in his report, as chairman of the General Conference Committee, he obtained its recommendation that all the "annual Conferences establish, as soon as practicable, literary institutions under their own care," and its order that "it be the special duty of the episcopacy to use their influence to carry" this "resolution into effect by recommending the subject to each annual Conference." He brought before it also the Missionary Society, in the organization of which he had been, as we have seen, the principal actor. He moved the appointment of a committee to revise and harmonize the book of Discipline, and was a member of this committee, with Soule, Ostrander, and the bishops. With Cooper, Roszel, Capers, Emory, and Wells, he procured the passage of a resolution by which the presiding elders became an "advisory council," or cabinet of the bishops, in the appointment of the preachers. He advocated the election of the presiding elders by the annual Conferences, and introduced the resolution by which was appointed the compromise committee that reported in favor of this measure, modified by giving to the episcopacy the right of nomination. He was appointed a member of this committee. He was nominated for the office of bishop, though against his will, and failed of an election to that dignity by but seven votes. Finally he was elected the Editor and Publishing Agent of the Book Concern by fifty votes, the late Bishop Emory having thirty-six.

EDUCATION—MISSIONS.

Referring to these initial efforts in the Conference for education, he says: "That opposition should be manifested to endeavors to raise the standard of education by any of the disciples of the illustrious Wesley, whose profound learning added so much to his character as an évangelical minister, may seem strange to some. This, however, was the fact, and their unreasonable opposition, exemplified in a variety of ways, tended not a little to paralyze, for a season, the efforts of those who had enlisted in the cause; while the apathy of others retarded its progress, and made its final success somewhat uncertain. And it has not been without much labor and persevering industry that this opposition has been measurably overcome, and the dormant energies of the Church awakened and excited to action in favor of this noble enterprise. Its onward march, however, has been hailed with no less delight by its friends than deprecated by its enemies, while its success thus far has added greatly to the character which Methodism was acquiring in the public estimation. All we now want, to place our literary institutions on a permanent foundation, and make them eminently useful, is the simultaneous and general effort of the members and friends of the Church to contribute liberally for their support and endowment."

In his advocacy of the new missionary cause before

the Conference he was effectively seconded by Dr. Emory, who had now become a leading man in the body. Emory submitted an elaborate report on the subject. After reasoning at length upon it, he asked, "Can *we*, then, be listless to the cause of missions? We cannot. Methodism itself is a missionary system. Yield the missionary spirit, and you yield the very life-blood of the cause. In missionary efforts our British brethren are before us. We congratulate them on their zeal and their success. But your committee beg leave to entreat this Conference to emulate their example."

The Conference adopted, with some emendations, the constitution prepared for the Society by Dr. Bangs. He thus saw his great favorite measure incorporated, it may be hoped forever, into the organic structure of the Church. He writes: "These doings of the Conference in relation to the Missionary Society exerted a most favorable influence upon the cause, and tended mightily to remove the unfounded objections which existed in some minds against this organization."

HISTORY OF THE BOOK CONCERN.

At the adjournment of the Conference there was no one of its delegates who returned to his home a happier man than Nathan Bangs. He had witnessed the success of his fondest schemes—schemes which his large mind saw would strengthen the very foundations of the Church, and extend its walls and battlements over the land, if not indeed over the world. He had escaped the onerous responsibilities of the episcopate—always when urged upon him by his brethren, as it repeatedly was, a profound dread to him, for he was constitutionally diffident of high and burdensome trusts. Its interference with domestic life, by its incessant travels, was repugnant to his feelings, and he believed that he could serve the Church more effectively, and even with more real distinction, by the pen and the powerful agency of the denominational press. He says in his manuscript that his "appointment was, on many accounts, a very agreeable one, more especially as my wife was in feeble health, and my children were young and needed my care."

The Methodist "Book Concern" is now the largest religious publishing house in the world. Nathan Bangs may be pronounced the founder of its present effective organization. Before his appointment it had no premises of its own, no printing-press, no bindery, no newspaper. Under his administration it was provided with them all. As early as 1789, John Dickens, then the only Methodist preacher in Philadelphia, was appointed "Book Steward" of the denomination. The first volume issued by him was the "Christian Pattern," Wesley's translation of à Kempis's celebrated "Imitation;" the "Methodist Discipline;" the "Hymn Book;" "Wesley's Primitive Physic;" and reprints of the first volume of Wesley's "Arminian Magazine," and Baxter's "Saints Rest," followed. The only capital of the Concern was about six hundred dollars, lent to it by Dickens himself. In 1790 portions of Fletcher's "Checks" were reprinted. In 1797 a "Book Committee" was appointed, to whom all books were to be submitted before their publication —a guardianship of its press which has ever since been maintained by the Church. In 1799 Ezekiel Cooper became Book Steward. "The Concern," says Dr. Bangs, "is greatly indebted to his skillful management for its increasing usefulness, as at the end of his term, in 1808, its capital stock had increased, from almost nothing in the beginning, to about forty-five thousand dollars." In 1804 the Concern was removed from Philadelphia to the city of New York, where Ezekiel Cooper continued its superintendence, being assisted by John Wilson for the last four years. At the General Conference of 1808 Mr. Cooper resigned his office, and was succeeded by John Wilson as principal, and Daniel Hitt as assistant editor and book steward.

At this General Conference, on the recommendation of Mr. Cooper, the term of service in the agency was limited to eight years, a regulation which was afterward found to be attended with many inconveniences, so much so that in 1836 the rule was abrogated. The agents had thus far received pastoral appointments like other preachers, and were held responsible for the double duties of agents of the Concern and of stationed ministers, though they were relieved from much of their pastoral labors by their colleagues in the ministry. In 1808 they were entirely released from pastoral labors. In 1812 Daniel Hitt was elected the principal, and Thomas Ware the assistant, editor and book steward; and the General Conference, chiefly at the instance of Dr. Bangs, ordered the resumption of the Magazine in monthly numbers; but neither this order was obeyed, nor were the hopes of the friends of the establishment at all realized by any increasing prosperity of the Concern from 1812 to 1816. He gives a list of its publications in 1813, and adds: "In this list, the whole of which—that is, a copy of each volume—independently of Coke's Commentary—which was imported—might be purchased for $29 75—there are but three American publications, namely, Abbott's and Watters's Lives, and the Scriptural Catechism. Nor was it possible under the circumstances—for, to our certain knowledge, several attempts were made—to increase the variety; such was the low feeling in the heads of the department, and the apathy in general, on the subject of literature in our Church at that period. And be it remembered that the above books had been issued so repeatedly, without adding anything to the variety, that it is believed if the Concern had gone on at this rate much longer it would have run down for want of pecuniary support." In 1816 Joshua Soule and Thomas Mason entered upon the agency. They found the Concern much embarrassed with debt, with but scanty means to liquidate it, the number and variety of publications small, and its general prospects quite discouraging. They, however, applied themselves to their work with prudence and diligence, and succeeded in keeping it from sinking under its own weight, and in infusing new energy into some of its departments, by increasing the variety of its publications, and lessening the amount of its debts. In 1818 the order for resuming the publication of the Magazine, which had been made again in the General Conference of 1816, by the urgency of Dr. Bangs, was carried into effect, "agreeably," he says, "to the desire and to the joy of thousands. Indeed, the appearance of this periodical, filled as it was with useful matter, was generally hailed with delight by the members of our Church as the harbinger of brighter days, especially in regard to the spread of literature and sound knowledge among us as a people; though it must be confessed that there were some then who would even sneer at this most laudable attempt to diffuse useful knowledge and scriptural piety by means of the press. I could relate many anecdotes in confirmation of this statement, as dishonorable to their authors as they were mortifying to the more enlightened friends of the Church. But as that day is past, let these 'times of ignorance' be 'winked at' and forgotten, from the joy that a more bright and vigorous state of things has so happily succeeded."

The appointment of Dr. Bangs, with Thomas Mason as assistant, in 1820, led to a renovation of the whole establishment. His friend, Rev. Dr. M'Clintock, himself long and honorably connected with it, says: "When Dr. Bangs was made book agent, in 1820, the entire business was carried on in a small store in John-street. The Concern was deeply in debt, and yet its scale of operations was very small. The new agent went to work with his accustomed promptitude and energy. He boldly resolved 'to increase the debt' in order to pay it. New and costly works, such as Benson's Commentary, etc., were undertaken; a system of exchanges with other publishers was arranged; old stock was sold off at low prices, and new life was given to the movement of the business in all its branches. A bindery was added in 1822, and a printing office in 1824. In that year, too, the premises of the old Wesleyan Seminary, in Crosby-street, were purchased, and fitted up for the uses of the Concern at large expense. In 1824 Dr. Emory was associated with Dr. Bangs, and zealously seconded the energetic movements of the principal agent. A characteristic illustration of Dr. Bangs's fearless enterprise in carrying out plans approved by his judgment, is furnished by the purchase in Crosby-street. There were croakers in abundance to predict evil; the proposed purchase was 'rash, reckless, unconstitutional,' and everything else but prudent and right. The agents used but one argument in reply—a practical one. They offered to make the purchase on their personal responsibility, agreeing, in case the General Conference should not sanction it, to take the entire establishment as their own. The result justified the sagacity of the agents. Had they waited for a previous authority from the General Conference, we should probably have had no printing-house till now. In 1823 the 'Youth's Instructor,' a monthly work, was begun. The same spirit of enterprise led to the publication of the Christian Advocate and Journal, which appeared, for the first time, on the 9th of September, 1826. The paper was at first nominally edited by B. Badger; but the editorial matter, from 1826 to 1828, was chiefly furnished by Dr. Bangs, though he was still discharging the arduous duties of senior book agent. During the whole period of his agency, 1820–1828, he was also editor of the Methodist Magazine. Such an amount of labor would have worn out any man not endowed with great intellectual and bodily vigor—qualities which, in Dr. Bangs, were supplemented by indomitable industry and perseverance."

The success of the Advocate was remarkable. "In a very short time," writes Dr. Bangs, "its number of subscribers far exceeded every other paper published in the United States, being about twenty-five thousand; and it soon increased to thirty thousand, and was probably read by more than one hundred and twenty thousand persons, young and old." The continual enlargement of the establishment, while it secured energy in its operations and mightily extended the sphere of its usefulness among the reading community, increased also its debt; but it also increased the means of payment, and must ultimately both tend to its entire emancipation from its pecuniary embarrassment, and enlarge its sphere of usefulness in respect to the number, variety, and character of its publications. It should be noticed, also, that, at the earnest request of brethren west of the mountains, the General Conference of 1820 authorized the establishment of a branch of the Book Concern in Cincinnati, and Martin Ruter, of the New England Conference, was appointed to its charge, to act under the direction of the agents in New York.

The debts of the Concern were thus very considerably increased; but they were increased by the procurement of an office for printing and binding, presses, stereotype plates, and all sorts of tools for each department, such means as must, if properly managed, finally lead to the liquidation of the debt, and thus place the Concern on a permanent foundation, beyond the reach of danger by the fluctuations of the times, so often occasioned by the frequent pressures of the money market. Its credit was good, its liabilities were always promptly met, its working hands paid, and all its parts were in vigorous operation.

In his manuscript he says his new position "was attended with numerous fears and labors, for which I felt myself quite inadequate. When I went into the Concern

I found it deeply in debt, with but slender means of its liquidation, the number of books published few and of dull sale, so that I greatly doubted the success of the establishment. My colleague, who kept the accounts, was a very energetic man, of good business habits, but not of enlarged views in respect to the manner of conducting the affairs of the Concern. We went to work as well as we could, though often much embarrassed for want of means to meet the demands against us, being forced to discount largely at the banks and borrow from other sources to enable us to carry forward the business. At this time stereotype plates were not in use among us, and therefore we had to reset the types for every new edition of a book, and we were in the habit of reading the proofs of every reprint, as well as the first edition of each new book. This, together with editing the Magazine, gave me work enough, and even more than one man ought to do. Besides this, I was in the habit of preaching twice every Sabbath, and frequently on week evenings, in which I often found great enlargement of heart. I never would have submitted to such drudgery in the Book Concern but from the belief that I was subserving the cause of Christ in editing and sending forth books upon religious subjects which thousands might read, and thereby be instructed more fully in the truth of God."

No labor of his life, except in the cause of missions, has been attended with grander results. He has sketched the history of the ".Concern" down to 1841. At the General Conference of 1828, when he was appointed editor of the Advocate, John Emory and Beverly Waugh (both afterward bishops) were elected agents. On the broad foundations he had laid the new agents went to work in good earnest, and soon succeeded in paying off the debts of the establishment, and in widening the sphere of their operations greatly. Wesley's and Fletcher's Works were published, the Methodist Magazine was improved by commencing a new series under the title of the "Methodist Magazine and Quarterly Review," the number of Sunday-school books and tracts was multiplied, these being still under the charge of Dr. Bangs. The rapid increase of the business very soon led to the necessity of enlarging its buildings. Accordingly all the vacant ground in Crosby-street was occupied. But even these additions were found insufficient to accommodate the several departments of labor, so as to furnish the needful supply of books, now in constantly increasing demand. To supply this deficiency, five lots were purchased in Mulberry-street, between Broome and Spring streets, and one building erected in the rear for a printing office and bindery, and another of larger dimensions projected. At the General Conference of 1832, Dr. Emory being elected bishop, Beverly Waugh was appointed to fill his place, and Thomas Mason assistant. Acting on the principles which had been laid down by their predecessors, they carried out the plans which had been proposed with great energy and success. At the same Conference, in consequence of the increased labors in the editorial department, Dr. Bangs was removed from the editorship of the Christian Advocate and Journal to the editorial charge of the Methodist Magazine and Quarterly Review and the general books, John P. Durbin was elected editor of the Christian Advocate and Journal and Sunday-school books and tracts, and Timothy Merritt his assistant. Dr. Durbin introduced one very important improvement into the Sunday-school department, the commencement of a Sunday-school and Youth's Library, which has grown to seven hundred and thirty-two volumes. This division of labor had a most beneficial tendency. "What an alteration in this respect!" exclaims Dr. Bangs. "In the infancy of the Concern the agent did all the work of editing, packing up the books, and keeping the accounts, besides doing the work of a stationed preacher. In 1804 he was allowed an assistant; but no clerk was employed until 1818, when, on resuming the publication of the Magazine, the agents, by the advice of the Book Committee, employed a young man to assist in packing the books and shipping them off. From 1820 to 1828 the writer had the entire responsibility of the establishment on his shoulders, both of editing and publishing the Magazine and books, and overseeing its pecuniary and mercantile department. It is due, however, to his assistants to say, that they labored faithfully and indefatigably to promote the interests of the Concern, and the labor of keeping the books and attending to the pecuniary business devolved chiefly on them, under his advisement. In 1825 a clerk was first employed to keep the books; and after the Christian Advocate and Journal was commenced, and the Sunday-school books and tracts began to multiply, it became necessary to employ several clerks to keep the accounts, and to pack up and send off the periodicals. In taking charge of the Methodist Magazine and Quarterly Review, the editor found himself exceedingly cramped, as he was not at liberty to offer any remuneration to contributors, but must take such as he could get, chiefly by selections from other books or furnishing matter from his own pen. This defect was as mortifying to him as it was a disappointment to its readers and patrons; and he rejoices that his advice, long urged without effect, was at last adopted, and that hence a brighter day has dawned upon this department of our literature."

Soon after the General Conference of 1832, the new agents began the erection of the front building on Mulberry-street; and in the month of September, 1833, the entire establishment was removed into the new buildings. In these commodious rooms, with efficient agents and editors at work, everything seemed to be going on prosperously, when suddenly the entire property was consumed by fire! The Church thus lost not less than two hundred and fifty thousand dollars. The buildings, all the printing and binding materials, a vast quantity of books, bound and in sheets, a valuable library which the editor had been collecting for years, were in a few hours destroyed. There will be occasion hereafter to allude to this disastrous event. Fortunately the "Concern" was not in debt. By hiring an office temporarily, and employing outside printers, the agents soon resumed their business, the smaller works were put to press, and "the Church's herald of the news, the Christian Advocate and Journal, soon took its flight again (though the first number after the fire had its wings much shortened) through the symbolical heavens, carrying the tidings of our loss, and of the liberal and steady efforts which were making to reinvigorate the paralyzed Concern."

At the General Conference of 1836, Beverly Waugh being elected a bishop, Thomas Mason was put in his place, and George Lane was elected his assistant. To this Conference the plan of a new building was submitted and approved, and the new agents entered upon their work with energy and perseverance. Samuel Luckey, D.D., was elected general editor, and John A. Collins his assistant. The new buildings went up with all convenient dispatch, in a much better style, more durable, better adapted to their use, and safer against fire than the former. The front edifice is one hundred and twenty-one feet in length and thirty in breadth, four stories high above the basement, with offices for the agents and clerks, a bookstore, committee rooms, etc. The building in the rear is sixty-five feet in length, thirty in breadth, and four stories high, and is used for printing, binding, etc.

In our day the Methodist Book Concern, aside from that of the Methodist Episcopal Church, South, which was founded by a division of its funds, comprises two branches, eastern and western, and five depositories, with an aggregate capital of more than $760,000. Four "Book Agents," appointed by the General Conference, manage its business. It has twelve editors of its periodicals, four hundred and sixty clerks and operatives, and between twenty and thirty cylinder and power presses constantly in operation. It publishes above five hundred "General Catalogue" bound books, besides many in the German and other languages, and about fourteen hundred Sunday-school volumes. Its Tract publications number about nine hundred in various tongues. Its periodicals are a mighty agency, including one Quarterly Review, four monthlies, one semi-monthly, and eight weeklies, with an aggregate circulation of over one million of copies per month. Its quarterly and some of its weeklies have a larger circulation than any other periodicals, of the same class, in the nation, probably in the world.

The influence of this great institution, in the diffusion of popular literature and the creation of a taste for reading among the great masses of the denomination, has been incalculable. It has scattered periodicals and books all over the valley of the Mississippi. Its sales in that great domain, in the quadrennial period ending with January 31, 1860, amounted to nearly $1,128,000. If Methodism has made no other contribution to the progress of knowledge and civilization in the New World than that of this powerful institution, this alone would suffice to vindicate its claim to the respect of the enlightened world. Its ministry has often been falsely disparaged as unfavorable to intelligence; but it should be borne in mind that its ministry founded, has conducted, and actually owns this stupendous means of popular intelligence. They have been, as we have seen, its salesmen; they have scattered its publications over their "circuits." Wesley enjoined this service upon them in their Discipline. "Carry books with you on every round," he said; "leave no stone unturned in this work;" and thus have they spread knowledge in their courses over the whole land, and built up their unparallelled "Book Concern." There has never been an instance of defalcation on the part of its "Agents;" it has never failed in any of the financial revulsions of the country; and it is now able, by its large capital, to meet any new literary necessity of the denomination.

Before Dr. Bangs's appointment to the Book Concern he had written a work, which he now published, entitled "A Vindication of the Methodist Episcopacy." It was appropriate to the times, for already had the "Radical Controversy," so called, begun in the Church, involving grave questions respecting its episcopal powers, the appointment of the preachers, and lay representation. On some of these topics he had no little sympathy with the "Reformers," for, as we have seen, he was always "progressive," and had become distinguished as an advocate of the election of presiding elders, being the candidate of his party on that question for the office of bishop at the last General Conference; but he doubted the expediency of many of the measures of the "Reformers." He deprecated the tendency of their violent discussions and proceedings; he foresaw the schism which at last ensued; and believing that graver evils than any alleged defects of the Church would result from the party organization which was rapidly forming, he deemed it his duty to waive, for the present, his predilections of opinion, and stand on the defense for the Church against the menacing peril. With Hedding and other leaders of the original party of reform in the General Conference, he was led at last by these dangers to modify, as I have shown, his views of the "presiding elder" question. He did not believe it befitting the Church of God to follow, even in a genuine reform, the example of wrangling and party combat which political communities consider necessary for their progress. The Church, the kingdom of God, the *civitas Dei*, he believed to be founded on principles which require a different policy, a policy of peace and charity—discussion and labor, but not passion and discord; and however much its history betrays the working of human infirmity, even more, perhaps, than that of civil states, good men should, and for that very reason, the more resolutely guard against tendencies toward violent measures. In a comparatively pure and successful Church, as he deemed his own to be, did he especially doubt the expediency of discordant party organizations, for any merely economical or governmental change, however desirable it might appear. If it could not immediately be effected without such a degree of agitation and internal disturbance as must divert the attention of the Church from its higher works of piety and charity, it was his opinion that the reform should be left to the more gradual progress of opinion; that where there is already essential purity peace is the essential policy, fulfilling the apostolic rule, "first pure, then peaceable." With perhaps a natural aptitude for controversy—an energetic temperament and quick sympathies—disposing him to take a decided stand on any and every question, yet, so thoroughly was he swayed by these convictions, and so complete an accordance had they with his warm and generous piety, that if fight he must, it was, in almost every case, a fight against fighters. With good Bishop Hall, his habitual prayer was, "O God, who art at once the 'Lord of Hosts' and the 'Prince of Peace,' give us war with spiritual wickedness, and peace with our brethren." And with Gurnall, he believed that "we stand at better advantage to find truth, and keep it also, when praying for it, than fiercely wrangling and contending about it. Disputes soil the soul, and raise the dust of passion; prayer sweetly composeth the mind, and lays the passions which disputes draw forth; and I am sure that a man may see further in a clear, still day than in a windy and cloudy." This, in brief, is the true explanation of his public life, so far as it was connected with the agitated questions of his Church—the just characterization of the man. Always in sympathy with progressive measures, always seen staunch and erect, on advanced ground, yet was he always resisting heedless ultraists. Reform in the Church, but loyalty to the Church—this was his summary maxim.

It is not necessary, nor would it be interesting, to trace here in detail the progress of the "reform" movement which about this time shook the very foundations of American Methodism, and at last rent it with schism. The record of those lamentable events belongs to the history of the denomination rather than a personal history like this, and they will hereafter receive due notice. Dr. Bangs has fully recorded them in the former, and they are well known; in the manuscript which he has left for my guidance in the preparation of this narrative he only alludes to them, and with evident reluctance. The controversy was to him a sad reminiscence, as involving some most important principles, but marred, and rendered disastrous by human infirmities.

CHAPTER XVII.

GENERAL CONFERENCE OF 1824.

DR. BANGS represented the New York Conference, as a delegate, in the General Conference of 1824, which assembled on the 1st of May in the city of Baltimore. Most of the leading delegates in the sessions already noticed were again there; others destined to become leaders now appeared in the body for the first time: Fisk, of New England; Luckey, of New York; Peck and Paddock, of Genesee; Elliott and Morris, of Ohio; Paine, of Tennessee; Winans, of Mississippi; Bear, of Baltimore; Pitman, of Philadelphia. Three of these were, in later years, elected to the episcopal office,* and there were present no less than seven delegates who attained to that honor in either the northern or southern sections of the denomination.

The last four years had been prosperous, and the Church had steadily advanced. Twelve Conferences were now represented, comprehending the whole settled territory of the nation, and all Upper Canada; more than three hundred and twelve thousand communicants were reported, and more than twelve hundred traveling preachers. The increase for the quadrennial period was more than seventy-one thousand members, and more than four hundred preachers.

The interest of the session was greatly enhanced by the presence of the first official representatives of the English Conference, Reece and Hannah. Dr. Bangs, as usual, took a prominent part in the proceedings. He was chairman of its most important committee, the one

* Fisk was elected but did not accept the office.

to which was referred the great question of the day, on lay representation, and with him were associated Morris, Capers, Paddock, Beauchamp, Pitman, and six others.* He was also chairman of a committee, including Sandford and Fisk, on the Rules of the Discipline for the Admission and Trial of Church-Members, and of another, including Ostrander and Sandford, on Revisal of the Discipline. He was a member of the Committee on African Colonization, with Soule and Myers. He represented particularly the interests of missions, education, and literature as connected with the publishing agency of the Church. Since his efforts for the second of these interests, in the preceding General Conference, seminaries had been springing up in various parts of the denomination. He and his friend, Laban Clark, now proposed a General Conference College, or University; but they were unfortunately defeated. Had they been successful the measure might have secured for us a commanding central collegiate institution, and prevented the waste of double the amount of money requisite for its endowment, and the dishonor of numerous failures of experimental institutions, which have defeated one another. The report of the Book Concern showed the effect of his energetic devotion to that great interest. Its whole property was now valued at more than $270,000. Deducting its debts, (about $48,500,) its balance of stock was estimated at more than $221,000. Instead of the small store on John-street, it had now its "Book Rooms" on Fulton-street, and a bindery on Crosby-street. It was about to establish a printing department and to provide premises of its own. Its catalogue of books had been enlarged by the addition of important works. Dr. Bangs was re-elected "Editor and General Book Steward" by ninety-four votes, Beauchamp receiving

* He did not, however, write its Report, and had left the session before that document was presented. It is supposed that Dr. Capers wrote it. Letter of Bishop Morris to the author.

twenty-one, Emory eight, and Fisk one. Emory was afterward elected his assistant by seventy-two votes.

Dr. Bangs writes: "This election I could not otherwise consider than as a special providence in my favor, particularly on account of my domestic circumstances. My brethren, who were acquainted with these, I suppose, believing that I had filled my station with fidelity, sympathized with me, and used their influence for my reappointment. Had it not been done I know not how I could have continued in the itinerant ministry, for my wife's health was so feeble that she could not be removed, and my children were growing up around me and needed my care; but God provided for me, for which I desire to record my gratitude."

SERVICES IN THE BOOK CONCERN.

He now prosecuted, more vigorously than ever, his enlarged plans respecting the Book Concern, finding in Emory a congenial spirit of enterprise and a rare capacity for business. They established a printing office in the month of September, 1824, in the second story of the academic edifice on Crosby-street, and before the year closed purchased the whole property from the trustees of the "Wesleyan Seminary," and projected additional buildings. They printed costly standard works, among others the whole of Adam Clarke's Commentaries. On the 9th of September, 1826, they issued the first number of the "Christian Advocate," a courageous experiment, but one of signal success, as we have seen. In a short time it had a greater circulation than any other religious newspaper of not only the New World, but of the whole world; and its proceeds afforded annually a large increment to the capital of the Concern, and annual appropriations of thousands of dollars for the relief of superannuated preachers and the widows and orphans of the itinerant ministry. On the 5th of July, 1827, the corner-stone of an additional building was laid, and in the ensuing year twelve printing-presses were in operation. When Bishop Soule, the immediate predecessor of Dr. Bangs, retired from the agency, the report of the Concern to the General Conference represented that, until about a year previous, the agents had "in addition to the editorial labor, and the various branches of clerkship, to perform with their own hands all the laborious work of the Concern, such as packing, hooping, and shipping boxes. Now there were in the book department three clerks assisting the two agents; in the printing department fifty employés; thirty-four in the bindery, and seven clerks in the periodical department. The assets of the establishment advanced from about $270,000 in 1824, to nearly $457,000 in 1828; its liabilities being in 1824 about $48,500, and in 1828 about $101,200. He had reason indeed to rejoice over these grand successes; but they imposed upon him extraordinary labors, for in addition to the chief responsibility of the publishing agency he was practically the editor of the Magazine, the Youth's Instructor, and the Christian Advocate. Work was to him, however, recreation, and to these severe tasks he added habitual preaching, two sermons on the Sabbath, and often many on week nights.

Successful as his present public service was, and inestimably important by diffusing useful literature through nearly the whole length and breadth of the nation, it could afford no incidents of popular interest for our narrative. I find, however, among his manuscripts the record of some episodes in his present term of laborious business life.

HE VISITS CANADA.

The last war with Great Britain had profoundly disturbed the relations of the Church to its vast Canadian field. By an arrangement between the General Conference and the English Conference, Lower Canada had been set off to the jurisdiction of the latter; Upper Canada still, however, appertained to the Methodist Episcopal Church as a part of the territory of the Genesee Conference. At the last General Conference some of its preachers applied, by memorials, to be made an independent Conference, with power to elect a bishop, who should reside within the province. The General Conference was not prepared to concede so much; it organized a Canada Conference, but retained it under the jurisdiction of the Methodist Episcopal Church. No little disturbance ensued in the Canadian Societies, and before the new Conference could meet a convention assembled, an independent Conference was organized, and a declaration of grievances and rights published. Dr. Bangs, as one of the founders of Canadian Methodism, was requested by the bishops to visit the province and endeavor to allay the agitation. Bishops George and Hedding also hastened thither, and, for a time, the menacing peril was abated.

GENESEE CONFERENCE—HIS FATHER'S GRAVE.

"I set off," writes Dr. Bangs, "on the 22d of July, 1824, and arrived at the seat of the Genesee Conference on the 25th. This is a very growing Conference, including a most fertile and highly cultivated country. Its populous villages, rich farms, neat and even elegant houses, the intelligence of its people, and the lately constructed canal by which its produce is conveyed to the eastern markets, all conspire to render it one of the most splendid parts of the nation. It is a delight to the eye of the traveler. The name of Clinton will be handed down to posterity as a chief promoter of the agricultural and commercial interests of his country. Among the things which tend to enhance the value of this region is the zeal with which religion is maintained and spread. Houses for divine worship everywhere adorn the beautiful scenery, and their existence shows the devoutness with which the early emigrants (mostly from New England) began their settlements, or the eagerness with which they afterward received the Gospel. From Lansing, which is on the east side of the beautiful lake of Cayuga, I passed on through the delightful villages and the charming intervening landscapes of Ithaca, Geneva, Canandaigua, Geneseo, Moscow, to Perry, whence I went up the Genesee River, about two miles above the falls, to visit my sister, Sarah Smith, whom I had not seen for eight years. Here my father died, in the peace of the Gospel, on the 9th of May last, aged more than eighty-four years. Two years since I was within about seventy miles of him. He then expected to see me, and was so disappointed that he shed tears, a thing very unusual with him. I was much affected on hearing of this fact, and blamed myself for not going, as I might have done by a little extra exertion; but, alas! I postponed the meeting for my present journey! About three weeks before I was to set off I received the mournful tidings of his death. I suffered very poignant feelings of regret, and could not forgive myself. I determined, however, to visit his grave. While standing by it I wept bitter tears. I left, with my brother-in-law, some money for a plain head-stone; all I could do, besides my tears, to relieve my agonized feelings.

"Having discharged this filial duty—for the privilege of doing which I feel truly thankful to God—and preaching in the house of my sister, I passed on to Batavia, and thence to Buffalo. About twenty-six years ago I went through the wilderness from Genesee River to Buffalo; then there was not a solitary house in all that distance. The roads, if such they could be called, were rude. We had an ox team, and lay five nights in the woods. Now this is one of the most delightful countries I ever beheld. What beautiful villages and thriving towns have sprung up, as by magic, since that adventurous journey!

SCENES IN CANADA.

"I arrived in Canada with emotions which I cannot describe. Here was the place to which I wandered in my youth; here God revealed himself to my soul; here I began my ministry twenty-four years ago. I had the unspeakable pleasure of meeting with some who were converted under my early preaching, and with many with whom I had often been refreshed in the worship of God.

"From Niagara we traveled by land, around the head of the lake, by York down to Hallowell, a distance of about three hundred miles, holding meetings nearly every day and sometimes twice a day. The country has greatly improved, and many of the people have become wealthy since my old travels. At Hallowell we met the preachers who had assembled for the first Canada Conference. There was great anxiety and searchings of heart on account of a division which had taken place, headed principally by local preachers. Two of the messengers who had been sent to the last General Conference by the brethren with their petition for an independent Conference—H. R. and D. B.—the latter a local elder, were much disappointed by the result, and bearing back some wrong impressions about the manner in which their affairs were treated, a spirit of disaffection was infused into many minds, particularly among the local preachers. A Conference was held by the latter on the Bay of Quinte District, where H. R. presided; they formed themselves into an independent body and invited their brethren generally to join them. Many of the people had also declared in their favor. This was the state of affairs when we reached the province. In order to correct the wrong impressions which prevailed, Bishop George and William Case crossed into Canada at Ogdensburg, visiting the preachers and people in the lower part of the province; while Bishop Hedding and myself, crossing at Buffalo, visited all we could, made explanations, held meetings, and satisfied the greater proportion of the people; so that, by the time we reached the Conference, the power of the adverse party was very much broken, and they themselves seemed generally satisfied with what had been done by the General Conference. Indeed, when the local preachers were rightly informed they behaved like men of God, and were willing to relinquish the ground they had taken and stand on the old platform.

"The plea they made for a separate organization was that, as the Methodists in Canada acknowledged an ecclesiastical head in the United States, they could not expect the favor of their own civil government nor the protection of the laws, for the government looked upon them with a suspicious eye. The Methodist preachers were not allowed to consecrate marriage, and it was said that forasmuch as their Church property was deeded to the Methodist Episcopal Church they could not legally hold it. The people still seemed very generally to wish a separate organization. On these accounts the bishops pledged themselves to use their influence to effect such an arrangement at the next General Conference. On this pledge peace was restored.

"Having finished our mission in Canada, I took my leave, feeling great peace in my own soul and deep affection for my old and afflicted brethren, for there is no people on earth who seem so near to me as they, and the present visit has tended to endear them to me more than ever. Such kindness and brotherly affection they evinced in all places, on all occasions, that I could not but love them."

The agitation in Canada was checked, but not extinguished. In August, 1827, Dr. Bangs was again sent to his old friends to consult with and advise them. He writes: "The Conference was held in Hamilton, district of Gore. As this was the last session before our General Conference, it became necessary for them to come to a determination respecting the propriety of asking for an independent organization. The Conference almost unanimously resolved to petition for such an arrangement. Though my own mind was not perfectly satisfied of the expediency of the measure, I did not feel at liberty to oppose it. On this visit I had an opportunity of renewing my acquaintance with many of my old associates, and many a sacred friendship was revived. These old ties are my most precious ones—old wine is better than new."

SUNDAY-SCHOOLS.

About a year before the close of his present appointment he assisted in founding another of the great interests of his denomination: the "Sunday-School Union of the Methodist Episcopal Church," which was destined to become a mighty auxiliary to the Book Concern by the publication of juvenile volumes and periodicals. Sunday-schools had already been generally introduced into the Methodist Societies. A Methodist young woman, afterward the wife of Samuel Bradburn, (one of Wesley's most eloquent preachers,) first suggested their institution to Robert Raikes, assisted him in organizing the first school, and accompanied him, with its ragged procession, through the streets of Gloucester to the parish church. John Wesley gave the plan and labors of Robert Raikes their first public recognition in his Arminian Magazine of 1785. The Methodist Societies of England were the first to incorporate the institution into the Church as one of its permanent agencies, and Bishop Asbury formed the first Sunday-school in the United States.* Hitherto, however, American Methodism had made no provision for the general organization or affiliation of its Sunday-schools. Its Book Concern

* History of the Religious Movement, etc., called Methodism, vol. ii, page 483.

had issued some volumes suitable for their libraries, but no adequate, no systematic attention was given to this sort of literature. It was obvious, on a moment's reflection, that an almost illimitable field for the enlargement of the business of the Concern and the diffusion of useful knowledge was at its command in this direction. Accordingly the "Union" was organized on the 2d of April, 1827. Dr. Bangs says: "The measure indeed was very generally approved, and hailed with grateful delight by our friends and brethren throughout the country. It received the sanction of the several annual Conferences, which recommended the people of their charge to form auxiliaries in every circuit and station, and send to the general depository in New York for their books; and such were the zeal and unanimity with which they entered into this work that at the first annual meeting of the society there were reported 251 auxiliaries, 1,025 schools, 2,048 superintendents, 10,290 teachers, and 63,240 scholars, besides about 2,000 managers and visitors. Never, therefore, did an institution go into operation under more favorable circumstances, or was hailed with a more universal joy, than the Sunday-School Union of the Methodist Episcopal Church." This great success, however, could not save it from the misfortunes of bad management. Under "an injudicious attempt," writes Dr. Bangs many years later, "to amalgamate the Bible, Tract, and Sunday-school Societies together, by which the business of these several societies might be transacted by one board of management," and by other causes, it declined, if indeed it did not fail, until resuscitated by the zeal of some New York brethren and by an act of the General Conference of 1840. It passed through modifications till it assumed its present effective form of organization. He lived to see it grow into colossal proportions. Before his death it reported (aside from its offspring in the Methodist Episcopal Church, South) 13,600 schools, nearly 150,000 teachers and officers, and more than 826,000 scholars, more than 17,000 of whom were reported as converted during the year. There were in the libraries of these schools more than 2,400,000 volumes. They were supported at an annual expense of nearly $140,000, besides nearly $12,000 given to the Union for the assistance of poor schools. There were circulated among them semi-monthly nearly 200,000 "Sunday-School Advocates," the juvenile periodical of the Union. The number of conversions among pupils of the schools, as reported for the preceding fifteen years, amounted to more than 233,000, showing that much of the extraordinary growth of the Church is attributable to this mighty agency. The increase of scholars during this same period was more than half a million. The Union has four periodicals for teachers and scholars, two in English and two in German, and their aggregate circulation was, the year before the death of Dr. Bangs, more than 260,000 per number; the Teachers' Journal being a monthly, the scholars' a bi-monthly issue. Its catalogue of Sunday-school books comprises more than 1,300 different works, of which nearly a million of copies were issued in the last year of his life. Including other issues, it has nearly two thousand five hundred different publications adapted to the use of Sunday-schools. In fine, few if any institutions of American Methodism wield a mightier power than its Sunday-School Union.

GREAT SERVICES.

Thus concluded his eight years of labors as "Book Agent," a period scanty in incidents of popular interest, but crowded with signal services for missions, education, and literature, besides continual preaching, and zealous attention to every interest of the Church that came within his reach. Considering both the character and multiplicity of these services, it may be soberly doubted whether any other one man of the denomination achieved for it during this time more important labors. The denomination was now feeling the power of these great measures in all its length and breadth; its Book Concern had become a gigantic institution; its volumes and periodicals were flying like the leaves of autumn over all its territories; seminaries and colleges were rapidly multiplying, and threatening even to encumber it by their excess; its missionary enterprise had extended in auxiliary branches from Conference to Conference, and was fast extending from Church to Church; its Sunday-School Union had sprung into life, and was reaching one arm around the children while circling with the other a new and immense department of its publishing agency. To assert that the Church owes these great permanent powers exclusively to Nathan Bangs, would of course be extravagant; but to say that he had a chief agency in them, an initial agency in most of them, and thus far a more direct and continuous agency in them than any other one man, is to state but an historical fact. They would doubtless have arisen in the development of the denomination without him; but this is a truism which may be affirmed of almost any great advancements, and of their ostensible agents in any communities, civil or religious. "Circumstances make great men" doubtless, though the maxim needs some qualification. It takes a great man usually to make great use of "circumstances," whatever they may be. Nathan Bangs was providentially placed in positions in the Church which gave him the command of auspicious circumstances for the promotion of its interests in some of the most momentous respects; he used them without abusing them. Other men might have done as well in his circumstances; but he being in them availed himself of them, and the record of his success is gratefully and forever in the history of the Church.

CHAPTER XVIII.

GENERAL CONFERENCE OF 1828.

Dr. Bangs was elected a delegate of the New York Conference to the General Conference of 1828. Such was the prominence of his position in the Church that it seemed now a matter of course that he should be in its supreme body. He headed the list of eighteen representatives of his Conference,* among whom were Emory, Clark, Sandford, Rice, Ostrander, Luckey, Heman Bangs, and Burch. Excepting the first two days, devoted mostly to preliminary business, there is but one of the Journals in which his name is not recorded in connection with some important appointment, motion, or discussion. He was chairman of the committees on Missions, on Canada Affairs, on Appeals, and on the preparation of the Address to the British Conference. As heretofore, he gave his attention particularly to education, missions, and the publishing or literary agency of the Church. He procured the appointment of a committee on the first of these important interests, consisting of such men as Fisk, Bascom, Akers, and Capers. He represented before the Conference the new Sunday-School Union, advocating it in a speech; and presented the affairs and documents of the Book Concern and the Missionary Society. At a former session he had procured a modification of the rule requiring the biennial change of the appointments of preachers, in favor of such as might be employed in educational institutions; he now obtained the same relief for chaplains to seamen, etc. He was a

* Garrettson was elected, but, as he died before the session, his name is not given in the list of delegates.

staunch advocate of the "itinerancy," but believed in no Procrustean rule for it.

PROTESTANT METHODISM.

He took an active part in the discussion of the questions introduced into the Conference by the petitions of the "Reformers." The agitation of these questions had been conducted with disastrous violence. As early as 1820 the "Reformers" started a journal—the "Wesleyan Repository"—in Trenton, N. J., which had assumed a tone of unjustifiable belligerence against the institutions and authorities of the Church. A "Union Society" was formed in Baltimore to promote their designs. In 1824 they began a periodical, "The Mutual Rights," in the latter city, and the war now raged with perilous severity. Nicholas Snethen and Alexander M'Cain, men of distinction in the ministry, became champions of the movement. Henry B. Bascom wrote in defense of it. Disorders ensued which led to ecclesiastical trials and expulsions. Dr. Thomas E. Bond appeared in "An Appeal to the Methodists" as the defender of the Church. Compromises were attempted, but personal passions had become so commingled with the questions in debate that pacificatory counsels could not be heeded. Emory answered M'Cain in a memorable pamphlet, "The Defense of our Fathers." A new society, "The Associated Methodist Reformers," was organized in Baltimore, and about six months before the Session of the General Conference—November, 1827—a convention assembled which prepared a memorial to the Conference, which, together with similar petitions from various parts of the country, brought the whole controversy before that body. Emory presented from the Committee on Petitions an elaborate review of the subject—a report written by Dr. Bond—and the demands of the petitioners were declined. The "Protestant Methodist Church" soon after arose from this unfortunate dispute, and, through many struggles, has continued to our day. The insurmountable difficulty of the controversy was the acrimony, the reckless spirit with which it was conducted. Dr. Bangs hesitates not to blame both sides, though he does not admit the principal charge of the "Reformers." He says, "Whoever will consult the writings of those days will find complaints, on the part of the 'Reformers,' that an attempt was made by the advocates of the present order of things to suppress inquiry, to abridge the freedom of speech and of the press, and that trials were instituted, in part, at least, as a punishment for exercising this freedom on the subjects that were then litigated. This was a great mistake. It was for an *abuse* of this freedom, for indulging in criminations injurious to individual character, that the delinquents were tried and finally condemned. This will appear manifest to every person who will impartially inspect the charges, the specifications, and the testimony selected from 'The Mutual Rights' to support the accusations, and also from the Report of the General Conference on petitions and memorials. It was indeed expressly disavowed at the time by the prosecutors, and by all who had written on the subject, that they wished to suppress freedom of inquiry, either in writing or speaking, provided only that the debaters would confine their discussions to an investigation of facts and arguments, without impeaching the character and motives of those from whom they dissented."

As conductor of the Magazine, and afterward of the Advocate, he did not judge it proper to plunge those publications—family periodicals—into the controversy. The "Itinerant" was established by the Church party in Baltimore as an independent organ of its defense. "At last," he says, "the spirit of contention, which had long been impatient of control, became wearied, and the combatants gradually retired from the field of controversy, the Itinerant was discontinued, and the Christian Advocate and Journal, which had, indeed, said but little on the subject, proposed a truce, which seemed to be gladly accepted by the dissentient brethren, and they were left to try the strength of their newly-formed system without further molestation from their old brethren."

SEPARATION OF CANADA.

He took an active part at this session in the question of an independent organization of the Upper Canada Conference, being chairman of the committee to which that subject was referred. In his manuscript notes I find the following remarks upon it: "The prayer of the petitioners was granted; that is to say, it was left for the Canada Conference, if they saw fit, at their next session, or at any time previously to the next General Conference, to form themselves into an independent Methodist Episcopal Church, with liberty to elect, either from among themselves or from the United States, a bishop, one or more of our bishops having liberty to consecrate him to that office. Knowing that the Canada brethren had their eye on me as their bishop, and feeling a great reluctance to comply with their wishes, and at the same time fearing that the new organization itself was premature, if not, indeed, wrong, I felt it to be my duty at first to oppose the adoption of this measure, so very important itself, and involving so many interests in its consequences. In the first place, I doubted the constitutional power of the General Conference to divide the Church by declaring an Annual Conference separate and independent. They might declare it themselves, and the General Conference might acknowledge their independence, if it saw fit. Secondly, I doubted the expediency of the measure. The Canada Conference was composed of but few preachers, young in experience, and much shaken by faction. The end also proposed to be attained—important privileges from government—I thought very problematical. On these accounts, and others which might be mentioned, I could not consent to give my voice in favor of such a resolution. But when the subject was presented on a reconsideration in a modified shape, so as to leave it optional with the Canadian Conference to declare itself independent on its own responsibility, though I still had fears as to the final result, my mind was relieved, and I gave it my feeble support.

"No one can tell, but such as have had similar experience, what were my anxieties on this trying occasion. I sometimes feared that I had allowed my repugnance to triumph over my judgment, and had resisted the dictates of my conscience, and perhaps grieved the spirit of God, to gratify my own inclination, for I felt an unconquerable aversion to accept the call of my brethren to go to Canada as their superintendent. I finally, after the discussions of the Conference were over, and the Canada delegates had made known their wishes as to my appointment as their bishop, suspended any definite answer, telling them that they should hear from me in sufficient time not to embarrass their plans. Accordingly, a little before their next session, I wrote to them that I definitively declined, and they elected Dr. Wilbur Fisk, a man every way qualified for the office. He, however, declined also. Besides the reasons for my declining, already alluded to, serious objections arose from the state of my family. My wife, children, almost all my relations whom I could consult, were decidedly against my going to Canada. Still, I must confess that these objections do not entirely satisfy my mind. There is a secret something which intimates that it may have been my duty to have gone. He that loveth father or mother, wife or children, brother or sister, houses or lands, (of these last I have, thank God! none,) is not worthy of me, sounds in my ears, and sometimes makes me tremble for myself. I must leave the event to my merciful God, praying him, as my heavenly Father, to pardon me if I were wrong." These remarks were written soon after the events alluded to. The history of the Canada Church in later years could hardly fail to confirm his apprehensions.

PROSPERITY OF THE CHURCH.

Notwithstanding the internal commotions of the Church during the last four years, its attitude at the time of this General Conference was one of commanding strength. The ratio of representation had, by the growth of the ministry, increased greatly the magnitude of the Conference. There were present one hundred and seventy delegates from seventeen Annual Conferences. The New York and Genesee Conferences had each eighteen, Philadelphia fifteen, New England seventeen. The aggregate of communicants was nearly three hundred and eighty-two thousand; the aggregate of traveling preachers, sixteen hundred. The increase for the quadrennial period was nearly seventy thousand members, and three hundred and fifty preachers.* The great agencies and permanent interests of the Church, its Educational institutions, its Sunday-School Union, its Missionary enterprise, its literature and Book Concern, had grown vigorously. The Book Concern now required a further division of labor. Dr. Bangs's constitutional term of office, as agent, having expired, Dr. Emory and Beverly Waugh (both afterward bishops) were elected agents; but the editorship of the Christian Advocate was made a distinct office, and Dr. Bangs appointed to it. He was thus again returned to the virtual headquarters of the Church, which he had so long and so ably occupied at New York.

* My estimates are made from the last General Minutes preceding the sessions of 1824 and 1828, respectively.

CHAPTER XIX.

EDITORIAL LABORS.

Of his reappointment to New York in 1828 Dr. Bangs wrote: "I considered it as another providential opening, for which I felt deeply thankful, as my family circumstances rendered it extremely difficult, if not entirely impossible, for me to move from one place to another. Were it not for these domestic embarrassments I should much prefer to be exclusively devoted to the work of the ministry. I write under a grateful sense of the loving-kindness of my heavenly Father, who has so mercifully provided for me and mine." His new office imposed upon him excessive tasks. Besides the editorial labors of the weekly journal, he was editor and publisher of the "Child's Magazine," of Sunday-school Books and Tracts, and *ex officio* a member of the New York Book Committee, and, what must seem odd enough in our day, he had charge of all the clerks and "all business connected with the Advocate department"—so prescribed the law, as enacted at this session of the General Conference. Meanwhile he was the chief agent in the operations of the Missionary Society, its representative before the general Church, the commanding man in all the meetings of its managers, the writer of all its Annual Reports.

DOMESTIC BLESSINGS AND TRIALS.

On the 10th of January, 1829, he was cheered with the information that one of his sons was converted at the Wilbraham Academy; and, some time before, another, William M'Kendree Bangs, had entered upon a circuit as an itinerant preacher. He records his delight at this fact; for, though no man knew better the hardships of the itinerancy, especially to a young man, no one held it in higher honor.

"This," he writes, "was the most joyful news I had ever received. I have often thought that should I live to see my children converted it would be the consummation of my happiness on earth. It has, therefore, been my constant prayer, that, above all things, they may be led to give their hearts unto God. And I thank him that two of my sons and my eldest daughter have afforded me this unspeakable happiness."

A few weeks later he was tried by a severe attack of sickness, and suffered some time under a prostrating bilious fever. "But," he says, "I had great calmness of mind, and a sweet resignation to the will of God, and felt that I could resign wife and children and all things into his hands without any anxiety. The dread of death was gone; still I was conscious of a wish to live on and work in the Church, that I might see more generally the salvation of God. The fever subsided and my health returned. On the day after the fever was broken, while sitting alone in my room, musing on the mercy of God to me, such a sense of his goodness rested upon me, and the smiles of his reconciled countenance were so manifest to me, that my eyes overflowed with tears, and I shouted his praise aloud. I felt as if I would proclaim his goodness to all men. As soon as I had opportunity I testified my gratitude. To a dear friend, whose visits had been most cheering to my spirit during my illness, I expressed the extraordinary comforts of my soul. The next Sunday I preached on Psalm cxvi, 12–14: 'What shall I render unto the Lord for all his benefits toward me? I will take the cup of salvation, and call upon the name of the Lord. I will pay my vows unto the Lord now in the presence of all his people.' It was a time of refreshing to my soul, and I believe to the souls of many of God's dear children. This season of affliction was very beneficial to me. I had enjoyed such uninterrupted health for years that I thought I could endure almost any labor; but God now showed me my real frailty, and my entire dependence upon him for all things—for strength of body as well as for peace of mind."

LITERARY LABORS.

He prosecuted his editorial labors with energy during this quadrennial period, preaching meanwhile habitually on the Sabbath, and diligently sharing in the management of almost every interest of Methodism in the city. Freed from much of the business drudgery of the Book Concern, he devoted himself, writes his friend, Dr. M'Clintock, "to the Advocate and Magazine with eminent success. The editorial columns of the Advocate during these four years show a vast amount of fresh and vigorous writing. The wonder is that, with little or no paid assistance, Dr. Bangs was able to give so great a variety of matter with such amplitude of discussion, not merely on questions of the passing hour, but also on topics of permanent theological interest. Nor was his literary labor confined to the newspaper. In 1829 he published his 'Life of the Rev. Freeborn Garrettson,' which is not only precious to the Church as a biography of one of her noblest preachers, but also valuable as a contribution to the history of Methodism. In 1832 appeared the 'Authentic History of the Missions under the care of the Methodist Episcopal Church.' This work was exceedingly opportune to the wants of the Church at the time; it was greeted with general satisfaction, and contributed in no small degree to stimulate the missionary spirit of the people."

His Life of Garrettson was written at the dying request of that veteran preacher. From the time when, a youth on his way from Canada to the New York Conference, he had found shelter under the hospitable roof of the patriarch at Rhinebeck, they had been mutually endeared friends. They were congenial spirits; their labors and trials had been somewhat similar, and no other two men had been more ardently and uniformly zealous for Methodism, which they deemed a genuine reproduction of primitive Christianity. In the year in which Dr. Bangs began his ministry, Garrettson published an account of his own travels and labors, extending over thirty-nine years. This romantic record reached the young itinerant in the wilds of Canada, and left an impression on his mind which was never erased. Garrettson loved him with the affection of a father. He knew that he could trust his manuscripts to him as an able and conscientious writer, for hitherto Dr. Bangs had ranked at the head of all American Methodists who had ventured before the public as authors. The book had immediate success. It passed through four editions in about two years and a half. It was substantially a history of American Methodism, and its composition was a prelude and a preparation for his later and greatest work, the "History of the Methodist Episcopal Church." His History of its Missions was the product of his own personal knowledge of and agency in the missionary enterprise of his denomination. It afforded information which has ever since given the Methodist Episcopal Church an important rank in the general history of modern missions, and has been the basis of all later accounts of our missionary operations. It was a labor of love, written amid his many other literary cares, and its copyright was given to the missionary treasury.

While it was not deemed proper to occupy the columns of the Magazine, or of the Advocate, with the controversy of the "Reformers," as this was yet an internal dispute of the Church itself, and could be better confided to independent or unofficial journals,* Dr. Bangs never-

* After it became, however, an external controversy, by the separate organization of the "Reformers," it was more fully treated in these periodicals.

theless defended vigorously his denomination through his editorial columns against exterior hostilities. He wielded, indeed, a battle-ax against her assailants. There seemed to be about this time a simultaneous movement of Calvinistic sects against Methodism. Its extraordinary progress created alarm; it appeared rapidly to be taking possession of the country; and was evidently destined to be, numerically, at least, the dominant faith of the nation. Its doctrines were, in some respects, so distinctive that conscientious men of other creeds, especially Calvinists, could not see this prospect without anxiety, notwithstanding the unquestionable salutary influence of the denomination on the masses. The "Christian Spectator," a quarterly review, conducted by professors of Yale College, commenced an energetic attack on the Theology and Discipline of the Church, and the Calvinistic papers generally copied its erroneous representations. The discussion, as usual, became extremely acrimonious; it lost itself in side issues; new questions displaced the old ones; new batteries were opened in unexpected quarters, and the confusion of battle raged generally. Methodism now learned the importance of its periodical press, and the vigor of the man who had charge of that mighty instrument. Every serious blow against it was ably repulsed. Whatever assaults have since been made on American Methodism have been but as the faint reverberations of these memorable years. The American religious public have since come to recognize the denomination with general respect. The Methodistic champion years afterward justly congratulated the Church on the result. "The discussion," he says, "tended to enlighten the public mind on these subjects, to make our doctrines, usages, labors, and success more generally known and more justly appreciated, and thus strengthened the hands and cheered the hearts of the members and friends of our Church. It tended likewise to convince our opponents, that if they presumed to misrepresent or to slander us, we had the means of self-defense, and an ability and disposition to use them; and that when the facts were clearly stated, our doctrines and manner of propagating them fully explained, we should not be considered such dangerous heresiarchs as we had been represented to be. We are glad to know, however, that these days of strife are past, and that a more friendly and amicable spirit prevails. We hope, therefore, that hereafter we may mutually strive only to 'provoke one another to love and good works.'"

GENERAL CONFERENCE OF 1832.

In 1832 he was again deputed by his Conference to the General Conference, which began its session on the 1st of May, in the city of Philadelphia. He was still first on the list of his delegation, which included nineteen men, among whom were Merwin, Sandford, Ostrander, Clark, Rice, Richardson, Emory, and Levings. By the great growth of the Church the General Conference had now become unwieldy; it comprised no less than two hundred and twenty-three members, representing nineteen annual Conferences. The numerical gains of the denomination in the last four years had been great, notwithstanding the schism of the "Reformers" and the rage of external controversies. Its aggregate membership was more than 513,000; its aggregate traveling ministry more than 2,000. Their increase since the last quadrennial session was more than 131,000 members and 434 preachers.

GREAT SERVICES.

The uniformity with which Dr. Bangs took a leading part at former sessions in the chief interests of the denomination remains unbroken in the Journals of the present Conference. He was chairman of the committees on its Missions, its Sunday-school, Bible, and Tract Societies; and was a member with Ostrander and Waugh of the Committee on the Revision of the Discipline. He never lost sight of the sufferings of his ministerial brethren, and with Dr. Capers procured the enactment of a law by which the "allowances" and "deficiencies" of the preachers, especially of the superannuated, and the widows and orphans of the ministry, together with the contributions and deficiencies of every circuit and station, should be annually reported in the respective Conferences and published in the Minutes. Thus originated the annual exhibit of these facts, which has ever since continued to be a chief feature of the Minutes, and which, by revealing the enormous deficiencies of the preachers' "allowance," and the liberality or parsimony of the individual circuits or stations, has effectually tended to improve our ministerial finances. He attempted, though without success, to effect a modification in the trial of preachers, by which the General Conference might be relieved of the excessive troubles of judicial appeals; a measure which that body has found it absolutely necessary to adopt in our day. With the same delegate who seconded this motion he attempted a much more momentous measure, but without present success. Such was the importance which he attached to the intellectual improvement of the ministry, that as early as the session of 1816 he reported, as chairman of the Committee on "Ways and Means," in favor of a Course of Study for ministerial candidates, making it the duty of the bishops, or a committee by them appointed, to prepare it, and of the presiding elders to enforce it among their young preachers. No candidate was to be "received into full connection" unless he could give satisfactory evidence of his attention to this requirement. This would seem to us a somewhat irrelevant matter for the Committee on "Ways and Means;" but as it was the province of that committee to report measures which might promote the support and effectiveness of the ministry, and as Dr. Bangs deemed the intellectual improvement of the ministry one of the surest guarantees of its pecuniary support, he ventured to propose this rule. It was adopted, and may be considered the foundation stone of ministerial education in the denomination; a slight one indeed, but sure and steadfast, and ample enough for the condition of the ministry at that time. All our subsequent plans of ministerial improvement have proceeded from this beginning. It has been more potent by its indirect than by its direct effects. The measure remained thus till the present session, when, in connection with Benjamin M. Drake, he proposed important modifications of it, extending the required Course of Study to four years, and requiring the appointment of examining committees for the different classes of candidates. This would have been indeed a stride forward; but the Conference was not yet prepared for it, and it was laid on the table. It would have put a great proportion of the ministry—all the deacons as well as all unordained candidates—under a sytematic literary training, subjecting them to annual examinations through a period as long as the usual time required for collegiate graduation. Though it failed at this session, its final success was certain. At the session of 1844 it became a law of the Discipline, and has ever since been steadily maintained.

At former sessions we have seen him procuring an accommodation of the disciplinary rule, which requires annual or biennial changes of the ministerial appointments in favor of the permanent appointment of chaplains and professors in the colleges and teachers in the seminaries of the denomination. He now united with Dr. Martin Ruter in a successful effort to obtain a similar accommodation for preachers who might be elected professors in colleges not belonging to the Church. In other important proceedings of the session did he also take an active part. He was especially gratified with the evidence presented at this Conference of the success of the educational measures which he had the honor of first introducing in the General Conference, after the failure of the early efforts of Coke and Asbury at Abingdon and Baltimore. The bishops, in their address, pronounced the result "a noble work," and could now say that "most of the Annual Conferences have established literary institutions. In some cases this has been done by single Conferences, in others by two or more Conferences united. Most of these institutions, though in an infant state, are flourishing and prosperous, and promise great usefulness to the community in general, and to the Methodist Church in particular. We cannot but regard this as a subject of vital interest to the connection at large."

Besides its numerous academies, (all of them boarding-schools,) the Church had now no less than five collegiate institutions: Augusta College, Ky., with Ruter for its president, and Durbin, Tomlinson, and Bascom among its professors; the Wesleyan University at Middletown, Conn., under the presidency of Fisk; Madison College, replaced by Alleghany College, Pa., under the presidency of Fielding; that of Lagrange, Ala., with Robert Paine for president; and that of Randolph Macon, Va., under Olin. He witnessed also now the almost universal extension, through the states and territories of the nation, of his other favorite cause, the Missionary Society. Hitherto it had been prosecuted as a domestic scheme, comprehending the frontier circuits, the slaves, the free colored people, and the Indian tribes; it had achieved great success in this wide field, and was now strong enough to reach abroad to other lands. It proposed, with the sanction of this Conference, to plant its standard on the coast of Africa, and send agents to Mexico and South America to ascertain the possibility of missions in those countries. Thus were begun those foreign operations of the society which have since become its most interesting labors.

DECLINES THE EPISCOPAL OFFICE.

He was urged by many of his brethren to consent to be a candidate for the episcopal office at this session. "I have no reason," he writes, "to doubt that I might have been elected by a large majority had I consented; but this I could not do consistently with my views of propriety." He believed that his domestic circumstances did not justify the long absence from home which the office required; he also believed that the position he occupied, in connection with the great enterprises of the Church—its missions, Sunday-schools, literature, and publishing house—an equally honorable, and a much more useful sphere of labor. Besides these considerations, there was throughout his noble nature—a nature robust for all useful labors, and courageous for all necessary contests—a vein of diffident modesty, which made him shrink from any promotion which, with whatever advantages of power and usefulness, imposed the conventional restraints of official dignity. Few men have ever been at once more constitutionally brave and diffident than Nathan Bangs. Official duties sat well upon him, but never official honors. His shield was bright and impenetrable, but could bear no heraldic symbols; the hilt of his sword was simply its handle, not its decoration. He venerated the episcopal office of his Church, and estimated highly the capability and utility of its functions in the Methodistic government; but he believed there were much more useful positions in the denomination, and he instinctively shrunk from the reverential attentions with which the people so justly treated the office. His associate in the Book Concern, John Emory, and James O. Andrew, were elected bishops, and he himself was appointed to a new editorial post at New York.

FIRST EDITOR OF THE QUARTERLY REVIEW.

The book agents had found it desirable, in 1830, to change the Magazine from a monthly miscellany to the more important character of a Quarterly Review. Besides the weekly "Advocate," they now issued the "Child's Magazine" and the "Youth's Instructor." "For the ordinary purposes," they remarked, "of intelligence, and for general miscellaneous articles, which for such mediums of communication must necessarily be short, these periodicals seem to be sufficient. It may be remarked, also, that many of the topics which formerly gave value to the monthly numbers of our Magazine—the religious narratives and lighter miscellanies—now find, since the introduction of a weekly religious newspaper, their appropriate place in that vehicle. Indeed, it has often happened, since the commencement of our weekly paper, that after having much of the matter for the Magazine actually in type, or even on the press, before we could get it into circulation, it has been anticipated and spread abroad through the speedier medium of the Christian Advocate and Journal." These were good reasons for the transformation of the Magazine; but the clear discernment of Emory (who doubtless wrote the prospectus) saw other and higher reasons. He could appreciate the moral and intellectual progress of the denomination and its prospective necessities and capacities. The Quarterly Review, as a commanding organ of opinion, he perceived to be its next intellectual want. "For this class of periodicals," he says, "there is certainly a greater vacancy in the department of theological journals at the present day than in any other, and particularly in our own denomination. There is danger, too, of satisfying ourselves on one hand with light and transient reading, and on the other with light and transient writing. We yet need a journal which shall draw forth the most matured efforts of our best writers, whether in the ministry or among other intelligent and literary contributors; where, also, they may have room for ampler and more exact discussion in a record which shall endure for the inspection of posterity. There are very many, also, in the wide circle of our friends who have both taste and adequate means for patronizing such a work; and one such is highly desirable, as well for their satisfaction, as to lead others to the cultivation of a similar taste."

Dr. Bangs had the honor to be appointed the first editor of this highest periodical of the Church—another of the many primary distinctions which seemed so spontaneously to devolve upon him in the rapid progress of American Methodism. He was to live to see it command a more extensive circulation than any other similar periodical of the New World, and to take literary rank among the first of religious quarterlies.

Dr. J. P. Durbin was elected his successor in the editorship of the "Advocate," but in about a year and a half resigned that office. At the request of the Book Committee, its laborious duties were again undertaken by Dr. Bangs, in addition to those of the Quarterly Review. Dr. John M'Clintock, who was himself connected with the Book Concern about this time, remarks that "in estimating the value and extent of his labors, as editor of the Quarterly, we must remember that he was not allowed to pay for contributions; the pages of the Review had to be filled by his own pen, by voluntary writers, or by selections from other journals. Looking in this light at the contents of the volumes from 1832 to 1836, we are not surprised to find them deficient in the breadth of scholarship, variety of range, and elegance of style which have characterized the later years of the Review. It is hard work to make bricks without straw. But it would be a great mistake to conclude hastily that because the Review, now in the strength of its manhood—with a large body of paid contributors, and having a body of readers of far higher education than our Church could furnish a quarter of a century ago—is so far in advance of the earlier volumes that these last are of no worth. Many of the editor's contributions, especially, are of permanent literary and historical value, especially those on 'Scholastic Divinity,' 'Robert Hall's Works,' 'Richard Baxter,' 'Stuart on Romans,' 'The Origin of Language,' 'Magee on Atonement,' 'Abraham's Guests,' and the 'Life of Adam Clarke.' During these four years, also, Dr. Bangs edited a number of books for the General Catalogue." It is a proof of the laborious energy of his mind that, while thus burdened with duties, as editor of the Quarterly, of the Advocate, and also of the General Book Catalogue, he produced, in 1834, a volume of "Letters to a Young Preacher." It was a necessity of the times, meeting with admirable appropriateness the wants of the growing ministry of Methodism. Having an extensive circulation, and discussing a great variety of topics in relation to books and study, as well as ministerial labors and decorum, it made a wide and deep impression on the younger portion of the itinerant ministry, who composed more than half its numerical strength.

CONTROVERSY WITH BISHOP EMORY.

A characteristic controversy took place between him and Bishop Emory in the Christian Advocate, in 1834—characteristic as illustrating Dr. Bangs's regard for the law of the Church and the rights of its ministry. The debate ended in a cordial reconciliation of the two disputants; and it might, therefore, well enough be ignored here had not Dr. Bangs deemed it misrepresented in the "Life and Times of Bishop Hedding," and left express directions that if any record of his own life should be published, the alleged misrepresentation should be corrected. The General Conference had provided, as we have seen, for a course of study to be prepared by the bishops, and to be obligatory on candidates for membership in the Annual Conferences. Bishop Emory, with the advice of the Mississippi Conference, had divided this "course," so as to extend it through four years, thus imposing it, in part, upon candidates for elder's orders, men who *were already members of the Conference.* The claim of these men for ordination, as elders, was made dependent upon their satisfactory examination in the prescribed studies. Dr. Bangs opposed this requisition as "above or without law." Not being nominally the editor of the Advocate, (though he had charge of it, Dr. Durbin having now resigned that office,) he addressed Dr. Emory in an anonymous communication. He esteemed this more respectful to the episcopate than would be a formal or official opposition of the organ of the Church against the bishop. He subsequently, however, communicated his name to the latter as the author of the unfavorable article, and soon after announced that fact in the paper.

Summarily the facts involved in this case are as follows:

1. Dr. Bangs's opposition to the course of the bishop was not opposition to ministerial improvement, but to what he deemed an episcopal and unjustifiable deviation from the law of the Church. In fact he was himself the father of the law for a course of study, as has been shown; he originated the first enactment of the kind in 1816, and with his friend, B. M. Drake, had actually introduced in the last General Conference the motion for the course which the bishop was now misapplying, as he believed. He will need not a word of defense, in this respect, with any reader of the preceding pages. He expressly declares, in his remonstrance against the bishop's measure, his wish to see the course extended through four years, if the law-making power of the Church, the General Conference, should authorize it.

2. But (what ought to have been conclusive of the controversy) the last General Conference had refused to extend the course to four years, thereby directly declining to subject deacons, already members of the Annual Conferences, to any such condition of ordination to the

higher office of elders. The motion of Dr. Bangs and his fellow-delegate had proposed a four years' course; but it was laid on the table. The attempt of Bishop Emory to do, with the sanction of an Annual Conference, what the preceding General Conference had expressly declined to allow, seemed, indeed, to Dr. Bangs an extraordinary and inadmissible stretch of episcopal power.

3. There was precedent, and even episcopal precedent, against the course of the bishop. A committee of the New York Conference had, years before, prepared and published a four years' course of study for its own preachers; but when it "was presented to the bishops for their sanction they refused to sanction the *third* and *fourth* years, for *want of authority*, and in this decision the committee fully concurred, and accordingly this part of the course" was never used.

4. The question of Conference authority, or "Conference rights," became complicated with the dispute. "As the whole broad power of judgment, as to fitness or qualification for the elder's office, and also of election to it, had been vested in the Annual Conferences," the biographer of Hedding supposes "the prescribing of such a course of study to be clearly within the legitimate functions of an Annual Conference." The "whole broad power of judgment" is here a very broad phrase. The Annual Conferences have, indeed, the power of judging of the qualifications of their candidates, but only of judging according to a *prescribed standard*, and have no power to subtract from or add to that standard. The Annual Conferences are executive and judicial bodies; the legislative power of the Church is exclusively in the General Conference, and the General Conference had prescribed the qualifications of candidates for eldership, and had declined to include the one in question between Drs. Emory and Bangs. An Annual Conference has no more authority to prescribe a new term of ordination than to prescribe a new term of Church membership. The

ministry of the Methodist Episcopal Church is a unit, though for territorial convenience distributed into several Conferences. But if an Annual Conference can enact a term of ordination or of Conference membership, a term which has not been enacted by the General Conference, what becomes of our ministerial unity or identity? What of the episcopal right of transferring men from one Conference to another, especially in the case of candidates? A candidate who might be proscribed in one Conference might be admissible in another; and, what would be still more preposterous, might, immediately after his admission, be transferred back from the latter to the former in full rights as an elder. One Conference might make abstinence from tobacco or from long beards a condition of elder's ordination, or of Conference membership, while an adjacent Conference might refuse to do so. Were the above "broad" principle admitted, hypothetically every Conference might adopt some peculiar term, and thus every Conference be isolated from all the others. In fine, Annual Conferences have no legislative authority; they have power to do only what the General Conference prescribes for them to do, except as a matter of mutual concession or courtesy between their members and the presiding officer, the representative of the General Conference.*

* These views are sanctioned by the highest authority of the Church. The bishops, in their message to the General Conference of 1840, explicitly avow them. "Have the Annual Conferences a constitutional right to do any other business than what is specifically prescribed, or, by fair construction, provided for in the form of Discipline? Has the president of an Annual Conference, by virtue of his office, a *right* to decline putting a motion or resolution to vote, on business other than that thus prescribed or provided for? These questions are proposed with exclusive reference to the principle of constitutional right. The principles of courtesy and expediency are very different things. The General Conference is the only legislative body recognized in our ecclesiastical system, and from it originates the authority of the entire executive administration. The exclusive power to create Annual Conferences, and to increase or diminish their number, rests with this body. No Annual Conference has authority or right to make any rule

MINISTERIAL EDUCATION.

The General Conference of 1844 ordained a four years' course of study, and thus gave it unquestionable authority, completing what Dr. Bangs had, twelve years before, proposed, and conferring inestimable advantage on the Church. Dr. Bangs was the first man to admit into the official, that is to say, the General Conference periodicals of the Church, the proposition for institutions of ministerial education, and resolutely endured a storm of editorial and other hostility for this bold measure. In reply to the attacks upon him he said: "What is the question so gravely put forth for the consideration of the Church? We answer, so far as we understand it, it is this: 'May not a voluntary as-

of discipline for the Church either within its own bounds or elsewhere. No one has the power to elect its own president, except in a special case, pointed out and provided for by the General Conference. Whatever may be the number of the Annual Conferences, they are all organized on the same plan, are all governed by the same laws, and all have identically the same rights, powers, and privileges. These powers, and rights, and privileges are not derived from themselves, but from the body which originated them. And the book of Discipline, containing the Rules of the General Conference, is the only charter of their rights, and directory of their duties, as official bodies. The general superintendents are elected by the General Conference, and responsible to it for the discharge of the duties of their office. The primary objects of their official department in the Church were, as we believe, to preserve, in the most effectual manner, an itinerant ministry; to maintain a uniformity in the administration of the government and discipline in every department, and that the unity of the whole body might be preserved. But how, we would ask, can these important ends be accomplished if each Annual Conference possesses the rights and powers set forth in the foregoing summary? [Claims of legislative authority made by certain Conferences.] Is it not greatly to be feared that, with such a system of ecclesiastical jurisprudence, what might be law in Georgia might be no law in New England? that what might be orthodoxy in one Conference might be heresy in another? Where, then, would be the identity of the law, the uniformity of its administration, or the unity and peace of the Church?" The General Conference of 1840 decided that the president of an Annual or Quarterly Meeting Conference had a right to decline putting a motion or resolution to vote, if he considered it foreign to the proper business of a Conference, or inconsistent with constitutional provisions.

sociation be formed of men friendly to the object which may provide means for the education of such young men as give evidence of a call from God to preach the Gospel, and who have been approved, according to our usages, as local preachers, who choose and desire to obtain a more thorough education before they enter upon the enlarged field of itinerancy?' This is the question. And shall we be afraid to meet it fairly and fully? Let it be remembered that it is not to be met by sarcasm, put to silence by ridicule, nor its meaning perverted by misrepresentation. Some seem to look at this question as though our Church had just now for the first time awaked up to this subject, as though we had all our days been averse to an educated ministry. But is this so? We think not. The history of Methodism will show that, although a classical education or a systematical theological training has not been considered essential to a Gospel minister, yet that sound knowledge, various reading, and particularly a thorough acquaintance with biblical truth, were always considered essential prerequisites to usefulness and continuance in the ministry. We consider it, therefore, a settled point, an established policy in Methodism, that its ministers should be well educated, that they should thoroughly understand the science which they profess to teach, and the language in which they communicate their thoughts to others. The only question then is, What is the best method to obtain this knowledge? And we think it will be admitted on all hands that the method which will lead to the attainment of the object with the greatest facility, with the least expense of time and labor, should be adopted. On this we may offer some thoughts hereafter. We conclude what we have to say at present by remarking that if the Methodist Episcopal Church has suffered ministers to graduate to office without acquiring knowledge, and without contracting a taste for it, she has so far departed from primitive Methodism. Mr. Wesley not only encouraged learning among his sons in the Gospel, but insisted, as an indispensable condition of their continuance in the ministry, that they should contract such a taste for it as to love it, to spend at least five hours of the twenty-four not in mere desultory reading, but in close application to study. And hence arose from his 'school of the prophets,' from his severe literary discipline, some of the brightest ornaments of literature, and some of the soundest divines, the ablest linguists and biblical critics. As a confirmation of the truth of this remark we might name Walsh, Morgan, Oliver, Benson, Clarke, Watson, and others both among the dead and living, 'whose praise is in all the Churches.' Had Wesley thrown cold water upon the early sparks of their literary ardor, or suffered their brethren to throw discouragements in their way by sarcasm and contemptuous ridicule, is it to be supposed that they would have ever risen to that literary eminence by which they became so justly distinguished? Well, we have seen that the Methodist Episcopal Church has held the same language to all her ministers. If, therefore, any of them have passed along in inglorious ignorance, it has not been because the Church has not appreciated the value and importance of sound theological knowledge, but because she has neglected to enforce her own rules, either from the force of circumstances she could not control, or from inattention to her own most solemn engagements. Perhaps an apology may be offered for the little progress we have hitherto made in general literature, from the extensiveness of our itinerant labors, in a country comparatively new, and the general poverty of our people; but as these impediments are removed and removing out of the way, we hope that means will be applied to surmount the difficulties which have lain in the way of our improvement, and that the Methodist Episcopal Church shall 'not be a whit behind the very chiefest' of the Churches in Christendom in the literary and theological eminence of her ministers."

CHAPTER XX.

PROSPERITY OF NEW YORK CONFERENCE.

Such had been the prosperity of the Church that, though his own Conference had been territorially reduced by successive offsets—the Canadas on the north, and the great Genesee Conference on the west—it was again necessary to divide it at its session following the General Conference of 1832.* It now reported more than forty-seven thousand members; their increase in the last year had been nearly one sixth of the whole number. It was the largest Conference in the Church, except that of Philadelphia. When Dr. Bangs was admitted as one of its candidates, in 1802, the membership of the denomination throughout the United States and the Canadas did not amount to twice the present membership of this single Conference. On his first attendance at its session, in 1804, its communicants numbered not a fourth of their present force, though the Canadas and Genesee were not set off till years later. The number of Methodists in what was the territory of the Conference at the date of his ordination had increased from 11,700 to more than 110,000; its ministry from 59 to nearly 500; and yet he was in the vigor of his life, not fifty-five years old, apparently not forty-five. Identified with all the great affairs of Methodism, he felt, perhaps more than any other man, the inspiration and invigoration of its unparalleled success. He had seen its numerical force increase from 72,874 members and 307 preachers (including the Canadas) in 1801, to 548,593 members and 2,200 preachers (exclusive of the Canadas) in 1832. It had gained 375,719 communicants and 1,893 itinerant preachers

* The Genesee Conference had itself already been divided, otherwise it would have been at this time the largest Conference in the nation.

since he joined its humble but victorious ranks in the wilds of Canada. Its membership was more than quintupled, and its ministry more than sextupled in this period. He had seen its revivals extend over all the states and settled territories of the republic like fire on the western prairies. It possessed now not only the principal publishing house of the religious world, and numerous literary periodicals, colleges, and seminaries, but its original chapels were almost universally renewed. It had dotted the country with its new churches and parsonages, and was at this moment projecting those schemes of foreign evangelization which were to extend its salutary power before his death to the remotest parts of the earth. Had he died now, it would have been amid the general triumph of his cause; and well might he have expired with the grateful exclamation of the Hebrew saint: "Lord, now lettest thou thy servant depart in peace, for mine eyes have seen thy salvation!" But he was to witness its struggles and triumphs through thirty years more, a generation, and to be recognized as one of its chief standard-bearers through the contests and victories of nearly all this remaining period.

GREAT SUCCESS.

Strong in body, in intellect, and in faith, and stimulated by the sense of this general success, he not only pursued with unabated vigor his onerous official duties, but continually appeared in the pulpit a powerful preacher. Remarkable religious interest prevailed about this time in many parts of the Church; it pervaded the societies in New York city, and he shared effectively in its promotion. He says: "The work in general throughout the bounds of the several Annual Conferences, both on the older circuits and stations and on the missions, was in a prosperous state, and the spirit of revival, and of liberality in support of our various institutions, was evidently rising and prevailing more and more. For the last two years, through the instrumentality of protracted meetings, there had been a powerful revival in the city of New York. This work commenced in the Allen-street Church, and spread more or less in the different congregations in the city; but its most powerful effects were felt and seen in the church in Allen-street, where the meetings were continued for upward of forty days, and in the evenings for nearly three months; so that the 'revival in Allen-street' became notorious all over the country, and the increase during the two past years was not less than one thousand four hundred. This extension of the work created the necessity of having an additional number of churches, which eventuated, in the course of a few years, in the erection of seven, making in the whole twelve, (in two of which the slips were rented,) and three of the old ones were rebuilt. Our preachers and people more generally began to feel the necessity of building larger and more commodious houses of worship, and of providing parsonages for the married preachers, as well as of contributing more liberally for the support of our infant colleges, missions, and Sunday-schools. Indeed, such had been the hallowed and happy influence of these institutions thus far, that opposition to them was mainly disarmed of its power, and success spoke loudly in their behalf." In 1833, also, "the work of God was generally very prosperous. The agitations which resulted from the radical controversy had generally ceased, our institutions had been successfully defended against their rude assailants, and hence all went forward with alacrity and delight in the discharge of their respective duties. In addition to the ordinary means used for the promotion of the cause of Christ, the 'protracted meetings' contributed much, for they were now very generally adopted throughout our bounds; and the circuits and stations, particularly in the older parts of our work, were brought into more compact order, so that pastoral duties could be more conveniently performed. But that which contributed still more to enlarge our borders, more especially in places before unoccupied by our ministry, and in the frontier settlements, was the energetic action of the Missionary Society." In 1834, he writes, "the enlargement of our borders on every hand, and the increase of membership in the older circuits and stations, generally created an ability in our brethren and friends to supply the means to furnish accommodations for the people and their preachers; and the necessity for these things, together with the urgent calls from the pulpit and the press, particularly in the columns of the Christian Advocate and Journal, excited them to activity in the discharge of these duties. Hence, churches more commodious and central than heretofore were erected and erecting, parsonage houses built or rebuilt, and partially furnished, by which means the difficulties and expenses of removing were very much lessened, and the congregations became more numerous and permanent. It will be seen, therefore, that our increase this year and last was unusually large, and the missionary work went on most delightfully and prosperously, the whole being aided by protracted meetings, missionary anniversaries, and prayer-meetings. These things, also, by diminishing the inducement to desist from traveling, lessened the number of locations." "It was evident, also," he adds, "that our ministry was improving in learning and general knowledge, and consequently in usefulness and respectability; while the continuance of revivals was a sure indication that they were not retrograding in piety and zeal."

FOREIGN MISSIONS BEGUN.

Practically, if not officially, the principal agent of the missionary cause of the Church, he was especially zealous in its incipient foreign plans. At the last General Conference, as we have seen, it was proposed to extend the operations of the Society to other lands—to send preachers to Africa, and a commission of inquiry to South America. Hitherto it had no foreign missions proper, though its stations among the American aborigines were classed as such. These Indian Missions had now become numerous, and some of them were remarkably prosperous; "attended," he says, "with unparalleled success." In Upper Canada they numbered in 1831 no less than ten stations and nearly two thousand Indians "under religious instruction, most of whom were members of the Church. Among the Cherokees, in Georgia, we had at the same date no less than seventeen missionary laborers, and nearly a thousand Church-members. Among the Choctaws we had about four thousand communicants, embracing all the principal men of the nation, their chiefs and captains." And more or less, along the whole frontier, Indian Missions were established. Meanwhile the destitute fields of the domestic work proper were dotted with humble but effective mission stations, from the St. Lawrence to the Gulf of Mexico, and these stations were rapidly passing from the missionary list to the Conference catalogue of Appointments as self-supporting Churches.

In 1832 Melville B. Cox sailed for Africa, the first foreign missionary of American Methodism. He organized the Liberia Mission. He fell a martyr to the climate, but laid on that benighted continent the foundations of the Church, never, it may be hoped, to be shaken. The next year a delegation from the distant Flathead Indians of Oregon arrived in the states soliciting missionaries. Their appeal was zealously urged through the Christian Advocate, and received an enthusiastic response from the Church. Dr. Bangs, who had been a leading promoter of the African Mission, now, in co-operation with Dr. Wilbur Fisk, advocated this new claim with his utmost ability. Jason and Daniel Lee and Cyrus Shepard were dispatched as missionaries in the spring of 1834. An extraordinary scheme of labors was adopted, involving great expense; but, writes Dr. Bangs, "the projection of this important mission had a most happy effect upon the missionary cause generally. As the entire funds of the Society up to this time had not exceeded eighteen thousand dollars a year, and as this mission must necessarily cost considerable, with a view to augment the pecuniary resources of the Society, a loud and urgent call was made, through the columns of the Christian Advocate and Journal, on the friends of missions to 'come up to the help of the Lord' in this emergency; and to assist in this benevolent work, the Messrs. Lee were instructed, while remaining in the civilized world, to travel as extensively as possible, hold missionary meetings, and take up collections. The 'Flathead' Mission, as it was then called, seemed to possess a charm, around which clustered the warm affections of all the friends of the missionary enterprise, and special donations for the 'Flatheads' were sent to the treasury with cheering liberality and avidity. As an evidence of the beneficial result of these movements, the amount of available funds had risen, in 1834, from $17,097 05, the sum raised in 1833, to $35,700 15. So true is it that those who aim at great things, if they do not fully realize their hopes, will yet accomplish much."

The surges of emigration have overwhelmed nearly all that grand transmontane region; the aborigines are sinking out of sight beneath them; but the Oregon Mission, after some useful labors among the Indians, became the nucleus of the Christianity and civilization of the new and mighty state which has since arisen on the North Pacific coast.

Meanwhile, Fountain C. Pitts was sent on the mission of inquiry to South America. In the autumn of 1835 he visited Rio Janeiro, Buenos Ayres, Monte Video, and other places, and the Methodist South American Mission was founded the next year by Justin Spaulding. Thus had the Church borne at last its victorious banner into the field of foreign missions. It was to be tried severely in these new contests, but to march on through triumphs and defeats till it should take foremost rank among denominations devoted to foreign evangelization.

INVIGORATION OF THE CHURCH.

No man felt, no man had a right to feel greater gratification in these important advancements than Dr. Bangs. He had been identified not only with the Missionary Society from its beginning, but particularly with these new measures; they kindled higher than ever the ardor of his earlier manhood. He had seen the Church, in whose history for nearly half a century his own personal history had been so entirely merged, extend from Canada to Mexico, from the Atlantic to the Pacific; he now saw it, as he believed, begin its march around the world. In 1835 he wrote: "The usual peace and harmony prevailing in our ranks for the five years past, and the zeal exemplified by ministers and people for the promotion of the cause of God by the ordinary means of the Gospel, as well as by institutions of learning, Sabbath-schools, and the distribution of Bibles and tracts, the building of churches and parsonages, seemed to awaken new energies, and to call forth the resources of the Church in a much more liberal manner than heretofore for the extension of the work on every hand, but more particularly by means of missionary labors. We did not know, indeed, how much could be done until the trial was made. And the several institutions alluded to, instead of weakening one another, acted reciprocally upon each other; the one tending to excite the other to more vigorous action, and all uniting to produce the most salutary and happy results. This was seen in every department of our extended work, and the truth of the inspired declaration was exemplified by every day's experience: 'He that deviseth liberal things, by liberal things shall he stand;' and 'he that watereth shall be watered again.' In the same proportion that we enlarged the sphere of our operations for the conversion of the world did the means accumulate for carrying on our work; and by inducing all to contribute something, none were oppressed, while each one felt that he had an interest in the general cause he was aiding to support. By means of these appliances the fields of missionary labor especially, both in new countries and hitherto unoccupied places in the older settlements, were constantly supplied with Gospel ordinances, the vigorous action of the heart of the Church sending out through these main arteries the life-blood to every limb and member of the spiritual body, and they in return, by a lively exercise of their functions, sending it back to the center, thus keeping up that constant circulation which is essential to the health and growth of the entire system."

DEATHS OF M'KENDREE AND EMORY.

As the close of his present quadrennial term of office drew near he shared deeply with the whole Church in the mournful loss of two of its ablest bishops, M'Kendree and Emory, who both died in 1835. He has left us reminiscences of these great and good men, as of so many others—utterances from his warm heart. Of M'Kendree he says: "From the time of his entrance upon the arduous duties of his office until his death he labored most assiduously to fulfill his high trust in such a manner as to preserve the unity, the purity, and integrity of the Church, and thereby to promote the cause of God among his fellow-men. In some of the first years of his labors as an itinerating superintendent of the Methodist Episcopal Church he was in the habit of traveling from one end of the continent to the other on horseback, frequently exposed to the hardships and privations incident to the new countries, and to the fatigues of preaching every day, besides giving attention to the numerous calls arising out of his official relation to the Church. To those unacquainted with the peculiar work of an itinerating superintendent of the Methodist Episcopal Church, it might seem strange that a man enfeebled by disease, oppressed by an accumulation of cares and labors, should nevertheless constantly move about from one part of the continent to another, cross and recross the Alleghany Mountains, descend the valleys of the western rivers, preach to a few hearers in log-cabins, to thousands under the foliage of the trees at camp-meetings, and then visit the populous cities and villages, and make the pulpits sound with the voice of mercy and glad tidings! Yet such was the mode of life of Bishop M'Kendree. Habit had, indeed, rendered it necessary to his life and comfort, so much so that the very thought of being confined to one place was painful; and whenever such an event seemed inevitable, you might see the strugglings of a soul anxious to avert what he considered a calamity. Down to the General Conference of 1832 he continued his itinerant tours, often in the midst of such debility that he had to be assisted in and out of his carriage by his faithful traveling companion, through various parts of the continent, mostly in the South and West, enlivening the hearts of his friends by his cheerful submission to the Divine will amid the pains and afflictions of life, and receiving every favor shown him with the smile of gratitude and the embrace of paternal affection. At this Conference he seemed to be tottering under the infirmities of age, and withering under the corroding influence of protracted disease; while his soul exerted its wonted energies in devising or approving of plans for the prosperity of the Church. Like a patriarch in the midst of his family, with his head silvered over by the frosts of seventy-five winters, and a countenance beaming with intelligence and good-will, he delivered his valedictory remarks, which are remembered with lively emotions. Rising from his seat to take his departure from the Conference the day before it adjourned, he halted for a moment, leaning upon his staff; with faltering lips, and eyes swimming in tears, he said, 'My brethren and children, love one another. Let all things be done without strife or vainglory, and strive to keep the unity of the Spirit in the bonds of peace.' He then spread forth his trembling hands, and lifting his eyes toward heaven, pronounced, with faltering and affectionate accents, the apostolic benediction.

"He had an understanding sufficiently strong and acute to enable him to grapple with any subject within the range of the human intellect, and equal to the acquirement of any branch of human knowledge. This was evident to all who were intimate with him and could duly appreciate his worth. His mind, indeed, was capable of the nicest distinctions, of the most critical researches, and of the widest expansion. How often did he, by a well-timed and pointed remark, unravel the sophistry of the sciolist, and confound the pedantic pretender to wisdom and science! As if by a sudden inspiration of thought, he would make a ray of light flash upon a subject, and thereby render that clear and intelligible which before was obscure and perplexed. There was great variety in the character of his sermons. Though he seldom failed to 'make out what he took in hand,' yet he sometimes sunk rather below mediocrity; while at other times he soared and expanded, and astonished you with irradiations of light, and with the power and eloquence with which he delivered the tremendous truths of God."

With Emory Dr. Bangs had maintained intimate relations in the Book Concern during eight years. "Early," he writes, "on the morning of Wednesday, December 16, 1835, he left home in a one-horse carriage, for the purpose of visiting Baltimore on business connected with his episcopal office. His horse ran away with him and he was violently thrown from the carriage, and received such a severe wound in the head that he expired about seven o'clock of the same day. His death was the more melancholy to his friends because his fall and the wound he received deprived him of his senses, so that he was unable to converse with those who stood around his dying bed, though he was heard to respond an amen to one of the many prayers which were offered up in his behalf in this hour of trial and affliction. No one doubted, however, of his preparedness to meet his fate and to enter into the joy of his Lord. He died in the forty-eighth year of his age. He possessed an acute and discriminating mind, a sound and comprehensive judgment. Having received a thorough education in his youth, and devoting some time of his more mature and vigorous days to the study of the law, his understanding had become accustomed to close thought and accurate research, and he could, therefore, quickly and easily distinguish between truth and error, between right and wrong, while his heart forsook the one and cleaved to the other. He always evinced a mind thoroughly imbued with his subject, familiar with the truth, and well trained to the exercise of its powers in weighing evidence and balancing the claims of the various subjects which might be presented for consideration. And the acuteness of his intellectual powers was in no instances more strikingly illustrated than in his capacity to distinguish the nicest shades of truth, to detect the smallest intrusions of error, and so to analyze a subject as to view it in all its parts, and then so to combine it as to grasp it in his mind as one undivided whole. He could with all the ease imaginable fix upon an antagonist the very point in which he erred, trace it in all its windings and shiftings, and then bring the whole weight of his powerful intellect to bear upon him, with a force, collected by a regular course of argument, which he could not well resist. Though he was extremely sensitive, and could quickly perceive the slightest aberrations from the rules of strict propriety, he knew equally well how to make due allowance for human frailties, and to apologize for those faults in others which seemed the unavoidable result of either ignorance or inattention. Nor could he retain a spirit of resentment toward any man after discovering the slightest emotion of repentance; and he was as ready to make atonement for an offense as he was to accept it."

BURNING OF THE BOOK CONCERN.

About three months before the end of his present term of service in the Book Concern—a period with which his long official connection with that institution was finally to close—a great calamity fell upon it, and in a few hours laid it in ashes. "It was," he says, "on a very cold night in the month of February, 1836, but a short time after the great fire in the city of New York, which destroyed about twenty million dollars' worth of property. I was awakened about four o'clock A. M. by a ringing at my door, and a voice which apprised me that the Book Room was on fire! I sprung from my bed, dressed, called my two sons, and repaired with all possible speed to the scene of conflagration. I hoped, at least, to save the library. But the smoke was already issuing from the windows of my office, and the flames from other parts of the house! Here I found the agents, who were on the spot before me. The hydrants were frozen, and the waters were thrown but feebly, though all exerted themselves to their utmost. We saw that all was gone. Suddenly, and with a tremendous crash, the roof fell in! The flames seemed to ascend in curling eddies to the heavens, carrying with them fragments of books and papers, which the winds swept over the city to the eastward, as if to carry the news of the sad disaster to our distant friends. Indeed, a leaf of a Bible was found about three miles from the place, on which the following verse was but just legible: 'Our holy and our beautiful house, where our fathers praised thee, is burned up with fire; and all our pleasant things are laid waste,' Isa. lxiv, 11. Our 'beautiful house,' and all our 'pleasant things,' our books, and printing, and binding apparatus, were, indeed, 'burned up with fire!' But the fire-proof vault had, by the skillful management of the firemen, preserved the account books, and most of the registry books for subscribers were saved by the timely exertions of the clerk of that department. The rest was gone, except about three hundred dollars' worth of books, and some of the iron work, stone, and brick about the building. 'How did this fire originate?' This question has been asked a thousand times, but never satisfactorily answered, although an inquiry was immediately instituted, and diligent search made, with a view to ascertain the fact. It still lies buried in obscurity; but my own opinion is, that it took fire by accident in the interior of the building, in the second story, where the fire was first discovered by the man who came to open the office and make the fires for the day. The reasons for this opinion, though satisfactory to myself, I cannot here detail; and as they do not involve any one connected with the establishment in blame, while it relieves us from entertaining the cruel suspicion that any one was wicked enough to set fire to the premises, it may pass for what it is worth, without injury to any individual concerned. In the deep affliction felt by the agents, and indeed all in any way connected with the establishment, it was no small consolation to be assured of the sincere and wide-spread sympathy which was both felt and expressed by our brethren and friends for us on account of this heavy loss. At a public meeting held a few days after in the city of New York, about twenty-five thousand dollars were subscribed toward relieving us in this distress; and as the news spread, similar meetings were held all over the country, and liberal donations and subscriptions were made, which mightily cheered the hearts of those more immediately interested in the Concern. The entire amount received toward making up this heavy loss was $88,346 09. This, as it came in, enabled the agents to continue their business, and they recommenced building, even while the smoke gave signs that the fire was not entirely extinguished.

"What made this fire the more disastrous was, that the much more destructive one which had preceded it only about two months in the city of New York had prostrated most of the insurance offices, and rendered them unable to pay the demands against them, and made it impossible to get insured in New York with any safety for some time. Most of the policies held by the Concern had expired about this time by their own limitation; and such were the fears entertained abroad for New York fires that it was next to impossible to get insured elsewhere on any terms. Hence but a small portion was under insurance at the time of the fire, so that only about $25,000 were realized from these sources to make up the loss."

The agents and editors, encouraged by the general demonstrations of sympathy and liberality among the people, devised a plan of new buildings and of enlarged business, and in a few weeks presented it to the General Conference, when it was promptly sanctioned, and the establishment rose, phœnix like, from its ashes to a more commanding importance than it had ever before possessed.

CHAPTER XXI.

GENERAL CONFERENCE OF 1836.

THE delegation of the New York Conference to the General Conference of 1836 was reduced to about one half of what it had been at the preceding session; but the name of Nathan Bangs was still retained as indispensable in the representation of his brethren before that supreme judicatory of the Church. It was second on the list, preceded only by that of the veteran Ostrander, and followed by Beverly Waugh, Peter P. Sandford, and six others of similar note. The session began in Cincinnati on the 2d of May, and continued twenty-six days. It comprised a hundred and fifty-four delegates. Dr. Bangs was active, as usual, in its most important business. He procured the appointment of committees on the better support of Preachers, their Widows and Orphans, the support of Bishops and their families, on Bible, Tract, and Sunday-School Societies, and on judicial business—an anticipation of a later measure by which the excessive inconvenience of appeals in the General Conference has been greatly mitigated; a favorite scheme of his, as we have seen. He gave particular attention to the interests of the Book Concern, Education, Missions, Temperance, the Chartered Fund, and the still unadjusted claims of his old friends, the Canada brethren. He was chairman of the Committees on Missions, on the Quadrennial Address of the British Conference, on the Pastoral Address, and on an Address to the British brethren in behalf of the Temperance Reform.

The late disaster to the Book Concern, and the loss of two bishops, by death, within the last year, threw over this session a shade of sadness, which was deepened by a reported decrease of between two and three thousand communicants within the same year of affliction.

PROSPERITY OF THE CHURCH.

The aggregate gains of the quadrennial period were, however, very encouraging, being no less that 139,414 communicants, and 748 traveling preachers; an average per year of more than 34,800 communicants and 187 preachers. The prominent interests of the Church had all advanced. Its colleges and seminaries had multiplied even to excess: there were now seven of the former and more than twenty of the latter. There were no less than eight weekly periodicals published within the denomination, half of them "official," at New York, Cincinnati, Charleston, and Nashville; half independent, at Boston, Portland, Auburn, and Richmond. The missionary cause had grown rapidly since the last General Conference. In the last single year its receipts surpassed those of any preceding year by about twenty-two thousand dollars; and in the various missionary stations there had been within the same time an accession to the membership of the Church of more than four thousand converts. The Liberia Mission was now organized into an Annual Conference, and the operations of the Missionary Society had assumed such importance, and involved such responsibility, as to justify, in the judgment of the Conference, the appointment of a special officer, or "Resident Corresponding Secretary," who could devote his whole attention to them. Of course the mind of the Conference, as indeed of the general Church, turned spontaneously to Dr. Bangs as the man for such an office, and he was elected by a majority which surpassed that of any of the three bishops, or any of the numerous editors and Book Agents (save one of the latter) who were elected by ballot during this session.

MISSIONARY SECRETARY—GERMAN METHODISM.

At the adjournment of the Conference he returned to New York, and entered with energy upon his new functions. The first year of his secretaryship (1836–7) was signalized by the first recognition and announcement by the Missionary Society* of one of the most remarkable events in the history of modern missions, the beginning of the German Methodist Missions. Professor Nast, a young German scholar of thorough but Rationalistic education, had been reclaimed by Methodism to the faith of the Reformation. In 1835 he was sent to labor among his countrymen in Cincinnati; in 1836 he was appointed by the Ohio Conference to a German charge on the Columbus District, comprising a circuit of three hundred miles and twenty-two appointments. Thus originated the most successful, if not the most important of Methodist missions; and in the next Annual Report of the Society the "German Mission," and the name of "William Nast," its founder and missionary, were first declared to the general Church. German Methodism rapidly extended through the nation, to Boston in the North-east, to New Orleans in the South-west. German Methodist Churches, circuits, districts, were organized. "In the brief space of fourteen years," says the historian of Methodist Missions, "the German Missions have extended all over the country, and now there are seven thousand Church-members, thirty local preachers, eighty-three regular mission circuits and stations, and one hundred and eight missionaries. One hundred churches have been built for German worship, and forty parsonages. The increase in membership during the past year (1848) was nearly one thousand. Primitive Methodism appears to have revived in the zeal and simplicity and self-sacrificing devotion of the German Methodists. May they ever retain this spirit! No agency

* Missionary Report of 1837.

has ever been employed so specifically adapted to effect the conversion of Romanists as that which is immediately connected with the German Mission enterprise. The pastoral visitations of the preachers bringing them into immediate contact with German Catholics, their distribution of Bibles and tracts, their plain, pointed, and practical mode of preaching, all combine to bring the truth to bear upon that portion of the population; and the result is the conversion of hundreds from the errors of Romanism."* The chief importance of the German Mission has, however, been developed since this date. It has not only raised up a mighty evangelical provision for the host of German emigrants to the New World, but it has intrenched itself in the German "fatherland," and is laying broad foundations for a European German Methodism. German Societies and circuits, a German Conference, a German "Book Concern" and German periodicals, with all the other customary appliances of evangelical Churches, have been established; and, in our day, this Teutonic Methodism comprises, on both sides of the Atlantic, nearly 27,000 communicants, and nearly three hundred missionaries. It early engaged the attention of the new Missionary Secretary as a chief interest of his office.

TRAVELS FOR MISSIONS.

Though, as Resident Secretary, his most responsible duties were local, he traveled extensively in promoting the cause. In 1836 he journeyed up the Hudson, preaching for it in all the principal communities on his route. He passed into Connecticut, and over much of Long Island, and as far south as Baltimore. In the summer of 1837 he again traveled over eastern New York and western Vermont, preaching almost daily, and spreading the missionary spirit among the Churches. "Methodism," he writes, "has taken deep hold of the understandings and

* Strickland, page 199.

hearts of the people; but in many places the Church suffers greatly by emigration to the West." He records some rather unfavorable reflections on the character of the ministry as he observed it in this tour. "Most of the preachers are young, and some of them ill-informed in the studies and duties of the pastoral office." He thought that he perceived an unfortunate change from "the burning yet steady zeal" of the earlier ministry, with its deeply pious temper, to "an affected refinement" in some, and a "mere ecclesiastical or controversial zeal in others." "This remark," he adds, "must not be indiscriminately applied to all, for I found some, who for their talents, gravity, and evangelical simplicity would compare advantageously with the earlier preachers. Nothing is more important for the welfare of the Church than an experienced, evangelical, and well-qualified ministry." It must, however, be borne in mind, that about this time the great antislavery controversy was sweeping over that portion of the Church, moving all minds. It was hardly a fitting time for a just estimation of the spirit of the ministry, and the secretary's own standpoint in that controversy was hardly the best for an impartial judgment.

IN CANADA AGAIN.

In the autumn of the same year he visited the west of the state, and passed again into Canada, refreshing, with deep and affecting interest, his early Christian remembrances. He found his beloved sister still living in the province, about eight miles from Niagara, "well, and deeply devoted to God." Their meeting was one of much tenderness and many tears. On Sunday he preached in a church occupied by the society which he had first joined as a Methodist about thirty-six years before. "What a change," he writes, "did I witness! Only two persons, a widow and her daughter, did I recognize as having been among my old acquaintances and classmates. The children of my old friends had grown up, and many of them had taken the places of their fathers in the Church. They remembered me, but I could not recollect them, for they had changed from childhood to manhood. The reception they gave me was peculiarly cordial and respectful, and what inexpressible memories and emotions were called up by this passing return to the place of my spiritual birth and of the commencement of my ministerial labors. How many prayers and vows did I make years ago, while bowing before the Lord in a grove which stood near the spot where stands the Church in which I now preached; and how many scenes of joy and sorrow have I passed through since those days! In the evening I preached at Thorold; the congregation was very large, and there I had the pleasure of renewing my acquaintance with George Theifer, Esq., who joined the Methodists about the same time that I did. After spending two days with my sister I left for Buffalo, taking my course along the shore on the Canada side through Chippewa. Here also I passed along the scenes of my youthful travels and labors. I lodged with a Brother M'Affee, at whose house I was refused a lodging in those days of trial by another person on a winter's night, after the piercing cold had been shaking my frame throughout the day. Now, through the religion of Christ, I was welcomed with kindness and hospitality. The next day I had the pleasure of greeting an old acquaintance, in whose house I had often preached in those early days. On Tuesday we crossed to Buffalo in a horse-boat. What a change has taken place here! At my first visit it had two or three log-huts; now it is a city of nearly twenty thousand souls, with elegant houses and costly churches, and its harbor is alive with steamers and other vessels. What a country may these United States be if they only keep together, and fear God and work righteousness!" In this excursion he traveled about a thousand miles, and preached nearly every other day for missions.

SEA ADVENTURES OF HIS BROTHER.

In November of the same year he turned southward as far as Virginia. On his route he paused in Philadelphia to see one of his brothers, the only one who remained out of the Church. "I lodged," he says, "in Philadelphia with my brother, Captain Elijah K. Bangs. This brother has been a seaman ever since he was about sixteen years of age. Indeed, before my father moved from Bridgeport, Conn., when he was but eleven years of age, Elijah went as a cabin-boy, at his own request, on a voyage to the West Indies. Though he afterward removed with us to Stamford, Delaware Co., N. Y., yet such were his predilections for a seafaring life that he never was contented until he obtained his father's consent to go to sea again. Accordingly, when about sixteen years of age he left his father's house, went to Philadelphia, embarked as a common sailor, and has continued the life of a seaman ever since. He rose, however, so rapidly that in his twenty-first year of age he took the command of a ship for the East Indies, and has made several voyages to that country. When I was stationed in New York city, in 1811, he put into that harbor, where I saw him after an absence of fifteen years. How different were our conditions! Since we had seen each other I had experienced religion, and had been for about ten years preaching the Gospel in different parts of the country; while he had been a sailor, had risen to command, had been almost to every part of the world in quest of the riches that perish with the using, and yet had not obtained that after which he had so laboriously sought. But I had forsaken the pursuit of worldly good to obtain an 'inheritance incorruptible, undefiled, and that fadeth not away,' and had so far obtained the object of my pursuit as to have, as I believed, a well-grounded hope of possessing this inheritance. There was, therefore, but little congeniality of views between us in these respects, notwithstanding we felt and loved as brothers in the flesh. In the beginning of the troubles between our country and Great Britain, which terminated in the war of 1812, he was first taken by a British cruiser under the 'Orders in Council' and carried to a British port; but the Court of Admiralty acquitted him because it was proved that he had left the American port before the 'Orders' were promulgated. The first day after leaving the English harbor he was boarded by a French cruiser, taken to Dunkirk in France, and his ship and cargo were condemned under the 'Milan Decree' because he had suffered his flag to be *denationalized*, as they called it, that is, to be taken by the English. What injustice was this! But it was the decree of a tyrant, and must be enforced. A short time before he sailed my brother had married his second wife, a Quaker lady of Philadelphia, and had her with him. They were detained as prisoners in Dunkirk for about two years. Here their eldest son was born. At the time I saw him in New York harbor he had a new ship, built as a fast sailer, with a view to elude the chase of cruisers; but I told him he would probably fall into the hands of one or the other of the belligerents. On his arrival in France he wrote me, stating that although he had been chased twice by the British he had eluded their pursuit, and had arrived safely at Bordeaux. He exchanged his freight for a cargo of French brandy, and on his return voyage, near the banks of Newfoundland, was taken by a British man-of-war, carried to Halifax, in Nova Scotia, and ship and cargo were condemned for having traded with the French. Not long after this, in another ship, he was wrecked on the coast of Holland, and in the mean time lost his estimable wife, by which four children were left motherless. After various vicissitudes of good and ill luck he was finally forced to abandon that and all other employments by an obstinate and, it seems, an incurable attack of rheumatism, by which he has been confined to his room, and much of the time to his bed, not able even to walk, for seven or eight years. In this state of decrepitude I found him. I conversed with him much on religion, but seemingly with no effect. I left him with a prayer to God in his behalf—that he may be saved. He is now living with his daughter Rebecca, an amiable woman, who has an estimable husband."

TRAVELS SOUTHWARD.

He passed on by steamboat and stage-coaches through Baltimore and Washington, arriving at the latter city in about thirteen hours, a speed which draws from him the exclamation, "Such is the velocity of steam! What a mighty power does man possess over the elements and laws of nature!" He was to live to see the time when this surprise should itself become surprising. He visited Fredericksburgh, Petersburgh, Richmond, and Norfolk, preaching for missions, and taking collections which in that day were considered extraordinary in amount. He was much pleased with the warmth of religious feeling which he found among the Churches of Virginia. A visit to the venerable Bishop Moore, at Richmond, afforded both of them no little gratification. "He is a truly venerable man, and received us with all the simple courtesy of a primitive bishop. His conversation was of a pious strain, but also enlivened by interesting anecdotes, and remarkably catholic in its allusions to other Christian communions than his own. He is by no means exclusive in his views of ordination, but holds the principles of the late Bishop White, of Pennsylvania."

On his return route he spent some time in Washington, the guest of the late eminent Dr. Sewell, "whose Christian simplicity and hospitality," he writes, "made me thankful to God for raising up such a man to stand as 'a burning and shining light' in the land." He delivered five missionary discourses in the District and returned to New York, recording some saddened reflections on Virginia. "Melancholy impressions were made upon my mind as I passed through the state. That it is fast retrograding is manifest to any observer. The blighting influence of slavery has left indelible marks of deterioration upon the whole condition of the country. Much of the land has become exhausted and sterile. It will not pay the agriculturist for his toil, and the state seems to be groaning under the curse. No one can doubt that slave labor is the most expensive of all labor, and, therefore, could it be abolished a regard for the temporal interests of the people alone would dictate the policy of emancipation. I am satisfied that it costs twice as much to rear a family in Virginia as it does in the free states, and of this fact many of the people of the state seem to be fully convinced, and they would relieve themselves of the evil if they could; at least so those expressed themselves with whom I conversed. I am also convinced that had not the injudicious measures of ultraists betrayed them into such sweeping denunciations of the South, before this day a train of measures would have been put in operation which would have eventuated in emancipation. As things now are, however, I know not how this is to be brought about. I wish here to record my conviction that slavery is a curse from which every good man ought to labor to be delivered; but I see that our northern measures are exasperating the difficulties of emancipation." These were his candid opinions; he could not yet accept the equally candid opinions of other men, that extreme measures alone could uproot this extreme social vice.

THE CONTROVERSY ON SLAVERY.

From his infancy he had been trained to abhor slavery. His Church had always considered it a legitimate subject for its remonstrating testimony; but of late years it had become a question of rife controversy, especially in the north-eastern Conferences, and it seemed to him so badly managed, and so menacing to the unity of the denomination, as to justify his persistent opposition to the anti-slavery leaders, whom he considered destructives rather than reformers. It was difficult indeed for even moderate men to maintain their equanimity under the prevalent excitement. Slavery became a party question—a test question in fine; the elections for delegates to the General Conference, and of even Conference secretaries and committees, being complicated with it. The administration of the bishops was impeached, and Bishop Hedding especially was pursued by fierce and unrelenting hostility as he passed from Conference to Conference. "Generally," says his biographer, "a cloud of lecturers (mostly Methodist preachers) hung about his path, perverting and misrepresenting his acts and character." * The bishop appealed to one of the New England Conferences for redress against the charges of two of its members, Rev. Messrs. Scott and Sunderland. The Conference sustained these men, and if it did not thereby virtually indorse, it refused at least to rebuke their reflections upon him. The bishops generally were treated with similar severity. Dr. Wilbur Fisk was formally accused by Rev. La Roy Sunderland, and would have been judicially tried before his own Conference (a majority of which were opposed to him) had it not been for a private compromise, through which the charges were withdrawn. Dr. Bangs was now (1838) cited to trial before the New York Conference by Rev. Orange Scott, under grave charges of public misconduct toward the latter in the course of the controversy. These charges related to newspaper articles of the doctor on the speeches and

* Rev. Dr. Clark's "Life and Times of Hedding," etc., chapter xvi. I must refer the reader to this book for a somewhat full and candid report of the controversy.

writings of Mr. Scott. They were referred to a committee, consisting of Rev. Drs. Holdich, Hodgson, and Kennady, and Rev. Messrs. Arnold and Seney. The accused and accuser appeared before this committee, and "the charges and specifications were successively presented and duly considered." The committee reported that "they are unanimously of the opinion that there is no cause of complaint against the defendant, and therefore respectfully submit the following resolution: That the charges against Dr. Nathan Bangs are not sustained, and that his character pass." The Conference adopted the resolution by a vote of one hundred and fifty-one for, and nine against it. In his manuscript journal Dr. Bangs says: "God enabled me to vindicate my conduct against these charges in a manner perfectly satisfactory to myself, and I think also to my friends, as well as to the confusion of my adversaries. The motive of my accuser I leave to himself and to the Judge of all, hoping he may find acceptance in that day which shall disclose the secrets of all hearts."

This great controversy, beginning about 1834, had now extended through many of the northern Conferences. It had raged in the last General Conference. It continued to shake the denomination for years. Numerous conventions were held for the discussion of the subject. It was debated in Annual Conferences and Quarterly Conferences, in individual Churches, in pamphlets, and in the periodicals of the Church. It became the absorbing theme of large portions of the denomination, the ministry and people being distributed into at least three parties, or classes, the extreme antislavery party, the extreme opposition, and an intermediate class. Both extremes, as usual, were obnoxious to animadversion. The "ultra-abolitionists" were accused of dangerous impetuosity, of illegal measures, and unjustifiable severity of language; the extreme opposition, while professing sound antislavery sentiments, was accused of too much reticence on the question, of less zeal against slavery than against the antislavery leaders, and was called "pro-slavery." Meanwhile the moderate party pronounced both extremes in error, insisting that the Church Discipline presented a good testimony against slavery, that prudent "free speech" could be maintained on the subject in the Church organs, and otherwise, without disloyalty to the denomination, and without personal wranglings; and that if by such legitimate discussions a time should come when circumstances and public opinion should justify any modification of the disciplinary rules respecting slavery it could be constitutionally made, and that all good Methodists should submissively abide the result. The extreme opposition predicted, as probable if not inevitable, from the measures of the antislavery leaders, a rupture of the denomination, and consequent danger of a rupture of the Federal Union, for Methodism was the chief religious and, in a sense, the chief social tie between the northern and southern States, its ramifications extending through every city, town, village, and almost every neighborhood of the South. The other extreme party, if not disposed to smile at these prophecies, deemed the more active opposition of the Church to slavery a duty paramount to the consideration of any such contingent perils. The moderate party, or rather class, believing that the Church could maintain a legitimate policy on the question, with due caution against such fearful hazards, asserted that the chief, if not only difficulty in the way of such a policy was the personal passions, not to say the official ambition, of the party leaders on both sides. The agitation swept at last like a hurricane over the northern and especially the eastern Conferences. Their sessions were sometimes attended with incredible excitement. The bishops while officially visiting them were usually attended by leading brethren from other Conferences, men who sympathized with the episcopal policy on the question, and whose influence and ability could, it was supposed, aid in sustaining the episcopal administration amid the storm. Dr. Bangs was active in this sort of service, as his missionary secretaryship led him to many Conferences. He loved the Church as few men then living could love it; he thought he saw in the agitation the portents of frightful disasters; he, therefore, spoke strongly; the personal severities of his opponents provoked him to severe replies, and his voice and manner in debate gave an exaggerated impression of his temper. His brotherly sympathy with his old friend, the saintly Hedding, and with the equally devoted Fisk, both chief objects of the hostility of the ultra antislavery leaders, led him to stand by them in the hardest brunt of the contest. The biographer of Hedding says the bishop "witnessed, with painful emotion, the excited state of feeling in the New England and New Hampshire Conferences. He was distressed beyond measure at the ultra measures that were adopted by many members, the harsh expressions that were used, and the consequent alienation of feeling among those who had long lived and labored together as brethren, and also at the imperious and arrogant spirit of some of the leaders, which he felt assured, unless timely checked, could end in nothing but the most radical and determined opposition to the government and salutary discipline of the Church. He had also shared largely in the personal abuse that was heaped upon those who, on account of prospective evil, sought to arrest or modify the course of the new and radical movement. The sessions of the New England and New Hampshire Conferences for 1835 had been anticipated by an 'Appeal' on the subject of slavery, addressed to the members of each by some of the prominent abolitionists, though prepared, we believe, principally by La Roy Sunderland and George Storrs. To counteract the influence of this 'Appeal,' a 'Counter Appeal,' signed by Dr. Fisk, John Lindsay, Bartholomew Otheman, Abel

Stevens, and others, was issued in the fall of the same year. It was also accompanied by a note from Bishop Hedding, in which he expressed his belief of the correctness of its statements and arguments, especially those relating to the acts of the General Conference."

This document, however unsound in some of its secondary positions, was essentially sound in its antislavery doctrines. It agreed with the general sentiment of biblical critics and the Christian world respecting the scriptural doctrine on the subject, and it was written with remarkable ability. The biographer of Hedding, after citing examples of its opinions, adds: "A document containing sentiments like the above must have been singularly incongruous to have been pro-slavery in its general character; or, had its authors designed it as a defense of slavery, they certainly shot very wide of their general design in these passages. The pen of so skillful a logician and so forcible and scholarly a writer as Professor Whedon, by whom the main labor of its preparation was performed, could hardly have been guilty of such aberrations; and yet both of these charges were laid against the 'Counter Appeal' and its authors. The conflict had now fairly commenced. That Church which had always most strongly protested against the great evil of slavery, was most fiercely denounced. Some of the more ultra and less cautious did not hesitate to declare that they would never falter till they had 'split the great Methodist prop to slavery.'"

The "Counter Appeal," and indeed every counter effort, seemed only to afford the ultra leaders new material for the spreading combustion. It raged on amid dissonant brethren, divided Churches, and contending Conferences. If any observer, praying and trembling for the Church, dared to hope that the violence of the storm in the General Conference of 1836 would be its culmination, he was speedily disappointed. It swept on for years. At last, however, wiser counsels began to be suggested, especially in the eastern Conferences. "Zion's Herald," published in Boston, had been from the beginning largely occupied by the writings of Messrs. Scott, Sunderland, and their fellow-leaders of the extreme antislavery party. Other men, equally zealous for the slave, but more considerate of the safety of the Church, began now to speak in its columns, and it became manifest that the people were losing their confidence in the ability and discretion of the old leaders of the controversy. The Herald was published by a company of laymen, who elected its editor, and many of whom had been always opposed to the extreme violence of the agitation. At the suggestion of Dr. Fisk, a young man who had been educated by himself, and who had signed with him the "Counter Appeal," and was, therefore, known to be "conservative," though decidedly antislavery, was appointed by these laymen editor of the paper. He immediately adopted and published in its columns certain restrictions on the controversy which were violently resented by the party leaders, but as promptly sanctioned by the Churches generally. The former soon revolted and organized a secession, and thus relieved the denomination of many disturbing and uncontrollable spirits. They ceased not, however, to assail the Church; they transferred from Lowell a small journal and planted it near the Herald in Boston, as an opposition organ. It was not sustained there, however, and before long was removed to New York. The schismatic Churches expired generally in the New England States, and it is doubtful whether an important trace of them still remains there. The policy of the Herald was to maintain in its columns a perfectly free interchange of opinions (for all parties) on the general question of slavery, but to exclude all personal wrangling, all local disputes on the question between Churches and their pastors or their presiding elders, (some of which had become grievous evils,) to expunge from all articles vituperative language, and to allow no disloyal reflections on the Church, its laws or its administrators. It asserted that the Discipline of the Church is evangelically antislavery, though it has always recognized the right of Christian masters to membership in its communion, and has never, from its organization, been one hour without such members; that in this respect it is conformed to the example of the primitive Church and the Pauline counsels to masters and slaves, (as had been shown in the "Counter Appeal," and taught by all accredited biblical expositors,) but that, like the apostolic Church, it places both masters and slaves under a moral regimen adapted to purify their mutual relation from its prevalent evils, and prepare the way for its extirpation; that the Church tolerated the relation, but pronounced it a "great evil," and aimed expressly at its "extirpation," interdicting meanwhile the slave traffic and other abuses; that, in fine, all its moral discipline, as prescribed in the "General Rules," applied directly or indirectly to slavery as to the other relations of its members. The schismatic leaders accused the denomination of not only tolerating but of sanctioning slavery, and defined slavery in such a manner as to include in it traffic in the bodies and souls of men, the separation of families, adultery, the lash, etc. This was especially done by a convention held at Utica, N. Y. The loyal antislavery writers spurned the monstrous misrepresentation. Much perplexed discussion prevailed on the ethics and metaphysics of the subject—on the essence of slavery as logically distinguished from its mere form, on slavery *per se*, slavery in the abstract and slavery in the concrete, and the controversy, in fine, created a vocabulary, a terminology of its own. If the Utica definition of slavery were correct, then the Methodist Episcopal Church admitted no slavery in its Discipline. Absolutely it admitted no essential slavery, but only the form of the relation, and this because of the civil laws of certain states, which prohibited emancipation, or because there were circumstances—of age or childhood, of infirmity or incapacity—in which, as Bishop Hedding argued, the "Golden Rule" itself might render the mere form of the relation a duty on some men already involved in it—in other words, on the same grounds on which the apostolic Church tolerated it. The Utica definition was admissible as a characterization of slavery in general, and as virtually defensive of the Discipline of the Church; but as an imputation against the Church it was repelled. In view of this definition and the discussions which followed, "Zion's Herald" declared that slavery has no more constitutional right in the Methodist Episcopal Church "than the devil has in heaven;" and this was said, and said justly, while the paper was declaring habitually that the form of the relation was tolerated in the Church; that Christian masters had, and (as an unquestionable historical fact) had always had a constitutional right to membership, and that no new law (that is to say, no new term of membership) could be constitutionally made against that right, except by the stringent process prescribed by the "Restrictive Rules" of the Discipline. Vindicating the Church against the impeachments of the schismatics, and yet hoping to see it more actively and generally interested for the slave than it had been, the tone of the eastern Churches on the question became healthful and loyal. If less was said on the subject than before, there was not less interest for it, but less necessity for its discussion, as the Churches had become harmonized, if not indeed unanimous. The verbal or metaphysical discriminations and hair-splitting (evasive, apologetic, or legitimate) of the discussion gave way to more intelligible and practical views, and the eastern Conferences presented a comparatively uniform and tranquil aspect. They were soundly antislavery and soundly Methodistic.

In other sections of the denomination, however—those which had more recently become the scenes of the controversy—the spirit of contention prevailed disastrously, and afforded more permanent and more fertile fields for the schism which had begun but was now expiring in New England. The "Northern Independent" became at last the organ of extreme opinions; and the organ of the seceders, formerly transferred from Boston to New York city, was removed from the latter to the interior of New York, and became the intimate and co-working neighbor of the "Independent." The interior and western Conferences of the state were shaken, if not to some extent shattered, by the collisions of parties. Dr. Bangs entered into these agitations with his usual energy, sometimes in the journals of the Church, and sometimes in speeches. The controversy continued to extend, and grave ecclesiastical questions arose in connection with it which again excited New England. The denomination was rent asunder in 1844; an event which Webster, Clay, and other senators pronounced the probable omen of national disaster if not of national disruption. Dr. Bangs was destined to live to see the latter calamity with its attendant horrors of civil war, and such a civil war as the world had never seen before within the range of recorded history. Antislavery and patriotic to the last, he shrunk not before the coming storm; he continued to write, not only for the Church, but for the slave; he published, as we shall see, a volume in behalf of the latter. He seldom paused to ask which party was to blame for the terrible issues of the long and violent contest, if indeed he supposed either party to be responsible for them, or that they could possibly have been averted after the profound degeneration of the South by slavery. He died believing that God had at last taken the problem into his own almighty hand, and thrusting aside nearly all the original party leaders, would work out its solution with such retributions, on Church and State, North and South, as should astonish all the civilized world, and rebuke alike the truculence and cowardice of men. We shall hereafter have occasion to notice his maturest views of the great question. This rapid glance at the general scope of the controversy must here suffice. The time has not yet come for the impartial judgment of history on its more personal and more painful details. Whatever that judgment, however, may finally be, it will admit that such men as Hedding, Fisk, and Bangs were sound in the antislavery sentiments of the fathers of the Church and of the republic; that if they erred in respect to practical methods of rendering those sentiments effective, their error was the result of a sincere devotion to the unity and peace of the Church and the State. History will probably show that the leaders on both sides were nearly, if not quite identical in their essential opinions on slavery, and that their mutual hostilities, resulting in such lamentable strifes and follies, were the consequences of their common infirmities.

MISSIONARY LABORS—SICKNESS.

Signally acquitted of the charges brought against him, before his own Conference, in 1838, Dr. Bangs continued his labors as Missionary Secretary. Accompanied by Rev. Mr. Seyes, who had just returned from Africa, he passed rapidly through the Eastern States, pleading for the cause before their Conferences and the congregations of their principal cities, as far as Augusta, Me. The next year he pursued his beneficent errand westward, crossing the Alleghanies, and attending the Pittsburgh Conference. In every place, where an opportunity occurred, he presented the claims of the Missionary Society. After a long absence he returned to New York, so exhausted that he was seized with a dangerous fever. "Dr. Reese," he writes, "was much alarmed, but by bleeding, calomel, and emetics he subdued the fever, and then, by the use of quinine, prevented its return. When it left me, which was on the seventh day of the attack, I was so reduced that I could scarcely speak;

but, by the blessing of God, I soon began to regain my strength, and am now (Sept. 16, 1839) able to walk the streets and attend to some business. During the severity of the attack my mind has been free from all anxiety; such a sense of the goodness of God has rested upon me as to remove all fearful apprehensions, whether for life or for death. How unspeakably precious, at such a time, is the religion of Christ! It seemed that I beheld the reflected rays of the Divine glory shining from the face of Christ, dispelling every cloud, and brightening the heavenly world as the future residence of the saints. I desire here to record my gratitude to God for such manifestations of his grace to my soul, and for blessing the means used for my recovery. Though I felt no fear, in the extremity of my sufferings, nor any anxiety respecting the future, yet when I began to improve I felt the love of life return gradually, and a grateful desire yet to live and labor for humanity with my renewed strength. How admirable is this instinct of nature, this law of Providence! Did we not naturally cling to life, who would endure its sufferings, its toils, its disappointments? This love of life is one of the wisest and most beneficent provisions of our Creator, as the means of heightening the pleasures of social and individual existence, of perpetuating the struggling race, of inducing man to make a suitable provision for his sustenance and comfort. Hence I am pained to hear Christians talk of their contempt of life—of the world and its blessings. These are all the gifts of our heavenly Father, and are to be *used*, not *abused*, in his service; and the love of life is to be cherished and employed so that we may answer the great end of our existence in the longest and best possible term of probation."

LITERARY LABORS.

He was soon again abroad for his favorite mission work, visiting the large cities, consulting with cabinet officers at Washington in behalf of the Indian tribes, and meanwhile conducting a laborious official correspondence. He could not altogether abandon his old studious habits. His pen was busily employed, during these years, in writing articles for the periodicals of the Church on missions, on the antislavery controversy, and on more general topics. Over the signature of "Ecclesia," he published a series of essays in the Christian Advocate — an elaborate discussion of the polity of the apostolic Church and the scriptural validity of the government of the Methodist Episcopal Church. Not a little patristic learning is displayed in these papers, and they are replete with that robust, practical sense which characterized all his opinions. They were afterward issued in a volume, bearing the title of "An Original Church of Christ."

In snatches of leisure, during these four years—evening hours or days of travel, or of occasional rest—he was busy, reading or meditating the materials for his "History of the Methodist Episcopal Church." He had labored upon this work about twelve years, and had brought the narrative down to the year 1810, when his manuscript was consumed in the fire which destroyed the Book Concern. No one but an author who has suffered a similar calamity can fully appreciate it. In the collection of materials, the study and collocation of books, pamphlets, periodicals, manuscripts, the clearing up of obscurities, the solution of apparent contradictions, the grouping of events, the portraiture of characters, the very labor of style, of individual phrases, there is, with much drudgery, no little pleasure. Much of the zest of original discovery attends the task. Its labor is over before it can well be estimated, and is then crowned with the joyous sense of a successful achievement. But the studious worker then also feels that, had he fully anticipated the difficulties through which he has happily wrought his way, his courage must have failed and his task never have been begun. The necessity of repeating it, with such a knowledge of its difficulties, though conquered difficulties, is perhaps the most repugnant, the most formidable trial that can depress a literary man. Dr. Bangs's courage was, however, equal to this exigency—the loss of a record extending over forty-four years, considerably more than half of the chronological range of his four volumes. His strong love of the Church, the conviction that his long personal relation to its history afforded him peculiar facilities, and imposed upon him peculiar responsibility for the task, constrained him to resume it. At the preceding General Conference he was authorized, by express vote, to use its manuscript documents, and he was now hard at work upon them, laying a much broader basis for his History than he had originally designed. It was the toil and, in no small degree, the pleasure of years. "I find," he writes, "great difficulties, but also great satisfaction, in thus tracing this widening stream of evangelical truth from its small beginning in 1766. What has God wrought by Methodism in this country since that time!" The first volume was published in 1838.

CENTENARY OF METHODISM.

In 1839 was celebrated the hundredth anniversary of Methodism. Dr. Bangs was active in promoting the plans of this great commemoration in America. The English Methodists appointed the 25th of October as a day of festive religious observance throughout their Churches in all parts of the world. Pecuniary contributions for certain great interests of the Church were called for, and the call was answered by a liberality never before equaled in any one instance in their history, if, indeed, in the history of any other Christian body. The Wesleyans gave one million and eighty thousand dollars. The American Methodists gave six hundred thousand. The latter had for years been expending extraordinary sums in providing their new states with churches, colleges, and academies. If they had more wealth, they had also vastly more expenses than their English brethren, and their centenary donations were considered liberal. "A very general pulsation," writes Dr. Bangs, "was felt throughout the entire Methodist community in favor of the celebration, and the several Annual Conferences adopted measures for its observance on the day appointed. As nearly as can be ascertained, the amount collected was divided as follows: About one half was to be devoted for the benefit of superannuated preachers, the widows, children, and orphans of preachers; two-tenths for the support of missions; and the remainder for the promotion of education. The manner in which the celebration was conducted had a hallowing influence upon the Church generally, and tended very much to increase the spirit of devotion. Sermons were preached and addresses delivered in almost every society throughout the connection, both on the 25th of October, the day on which the foundation of Methodism was laid by forming the first class, and on previous days for the purpose of taking up collections for the objects specified. It was indeed a sublime spectacle to contemplate the assemblage of more than *one million* of people, joined by perhaps three times that number of friends, uniting to offer up thanksgiving to God. It gave us an opportunity of reviewing first principles, of estimating anew the blessings bestowed upon us as a people, of praising God for the past, and of clustering together motives for future trust and diligence."

On the 25th of October Methodists throughout the earth met in their temples to thank God for his blessings upon the first great cycle of their history. Signal indeed had been those blessings. Wesley died in 1791, at the head of a host of 550 itinerant preachers, and 140,000 communicants in the United Kingdom, the British Provinces, in the United States, and the West Indies; at the centenary, less than half a century later, the denomination had grown to more than 1,171,000, including about 5,200 itinerant preachers, in the Wesleyan and Methodist Episcopal Churches; and, comprising the various bodies bearing the name of Methodists, to an army of more than 1,400,000, of whom 6,080 were itinerant preachers. Its missionaries, accredited members of different Conferences, were about three hundred and fifty, with nearly an equal number of salaried, and about three thousand unpaid assistants. They occupied about three hundred stations, each station being the head of a circuit. They were laboring in Sweden, Germany, France, Cadiz, Gibraltar, Malta, Western and Southern Africa, Ceylon, Continental India, New South Wales, Van Dieman's Land, New Zealand, Tonga, Habai Islands, Vavou Islands, Fiji Islands, the West Indies. They had under instruction in their mission schools about fifty thousand pupils, and in their mission Churches were more than seventy thousand communicants. At least two hundred thousand persons heard the Gospel regularly in their mission chapels. The Methodist missionaries were now more numerous than the whole Wesleyan ministry, as enrolled on the Minutes of Wesley's last Conference, and their missionary communicants were about equal to the whole number of Methodists in Europe at that day. Wesley presided over Methodism during its first half century and two years more; during the remainder of the century it reproduced, in its missions alone, the whole numerical force of its first half century.*

SUCCESS OF THE MISSIONARY SECRETARYSHIP.

At the conclusion of Dr. Bangs's present quadrennial appointment the Church had reason to congratulate itself on his official success. A committee of the Board

* History of the Religious Movement of the Nineteenth Century, called Methodism, vol. iii, p. 509.

of Managers of the Missionary Society reported on his services in emphatic language. "His duties," they said, "have been extensive and arduous, both at home and abroad, demonstrating the necessity of having such an officer. In addition to the preparation of Annual Reports and other documentary manuscripts, the correspondence of the Society exhibits more than five hundred official letters to missionaries, etc. During the four years, besides the duties of Corresponding Secretary in the office at home, and the preparation of multiplied reports for publication in the Advocate, he has traveled in the service of the society more than eleven thousand miles in visiting ten Annual Conferences, some of them twice and thrice, and in holding missionary meetings in ten different states in the Union. He has delivered one hundred and thirty-four missionary sermons and addresses in various parts of the country, and been directly instrumental in this way of bringing into the treasury the amount of $13,427. How far his labors and writings have been further tributary to the increase of our funds we have no data upon which to make the estimate. We invite attention, however, to the increased contributions to our treasury since his appointment, as affording evidence that the cause is improving annually under the present system of operations. During the first year of his appointment the receipts were $62,749; the second, $90,105 36; the third, 135,521 94; and this, too, notwithstanding the unprecedented prostration of the times. The amount of the fourth and last year is not yet ascertained, but will be found comparatively large, though less than the previous year, because of the special efforts made for the centenary fund, a portion of which is destined to our treasury.

"From a review of the whole subject, your committee respectfully submit the following resolutions to be communicated to the next General Conference:

"*Resolved*, That the experience of the last four years

has amply confirmed the propriety of the appointment of a Corresponding Secretary devoted to the interests of this Society, as prayed for at the last General Conference.

"*Resolved*, That this board bear their united testimony to the diligent, faithful, and successful performance of the duties of the office by the present incumbent; and in view of his long experience in the service of the board, we shall rejoice at his reappointment by the next General Conference." *

* History of the Methodist Episcopal Church, etc., vol. iv, p. 384. The following table shows the financial growth of the Society from the year preceding Dr. Bangs's appointment to the session of the General Conference of 1840.

	Amount Received.	Amount Expended.
1836	$59,517 16	$53,865 20
1837	62,749 01	66,536 85
1838	90,105 36	95,110 75
1839	135,521 94	103,664 58
1840	116,941 90	146,498 58

CHAPTER XXII.

SERVICES IN THE GENERAL CONFERENCE OF 1840.

THE name of Nathan Bangs headed the list of ten delegates from the New York Conference to the General Conference of 1840, which began its session in Baltimore on the first of May. Having been at every session from its organization as a delegated body, no member was more familiar with its functions and order of business. His authority on almost every important question was spontaneously recognized by his fellow-delegates. It is a striking proof of his parliamentary skill, that in the proceedings of a single morning he had occasion to appeal three times from the decision of the chair to the Conference on points of order, and was voted to be right in every instance—no less a disciplinarian than Bishop Hedding himself being in the chair. His name appears on the records of every day's proceedings for more than the first three weeks; and there are but eight days in the whole thirty-four of the session on which it does not occur in the Journals. This activity was not in long and obtrusive speeches; he seldom or never made speeches in the General Conference, but was ever ready to prompt or abbreviate business by pertinent suggestions or timely motions. As usual at preceding sessions, his attention was particularly given to the leading affairs of the Church, Missions, the Book Concern, Sunday-schools, Educational Institutions, Slavery, African Colonization, the revision and more methodical arrangement of the Discipline, the relations of superannuated and supernumerary preachers, and the Chartered Fund.

He initiated at this Conference the custom, ever since followed, of publishing the daily proceedings by official reporters. He was chairman of what may be considered the most important committee of the session, that on Slavery, including a delegate from every Annual Conference, and such men as Hamline, Bascom, Pierce, (afterward bishops,) George Peck, Wightman, Smith, Power, Hopkins, Spicer, Orange Scott—of a committee on an application of Bishop Hedding for Redress of Grievances suffered by him from some of his opponents in Annual Conferences, and also of the Committee on the Chartered Fund. He served as a member of the committees on Education, on African Colonization, and on a new and improved edition of the Discipline. He was appointed, with Drs. Durbin, Bascom, Tomlinson, Early, and other leading men, a Commissioner of the Church in behalf of its educational interests, and finally was re-elected General Secretary of the Missionary Society of the Methodist Episcopal Church. The great growth of the missionary enterprise induced the Conference to appoint two additional secretaries, Dr. William Capers, for the South, and Dr. E. R. Ames, for the West.

The session was much agitated by the antislavery controversy, but achieved a great amount of useful business. Rev. Robert Newton, representative from the Centenary Conference of England, added much to its interest by his extraordinary eloquence. Dr. Bangs had assisted at his reception in New York, and addressed him there, in the name of the Church, at the public services of his leave-taking for home. With prosperity in all its leading enterprises during the last four years, the statistics of the Church showed a great advance in its ministry and membership. At the preceding General Conference it reported 2,781 traveling preachers, and 650,678 communicants. In September preceding the present session they amounted to 3,296 preachers, and 740,459 communicants, showing an increase of 515 preachers, and 89,781 communicants. "We record it with thanksgiving, though we reckon not our strength by numbers," said the Conference in its letter by Dr. Newton to the Wesleyan Conference.

ELECTED PRESIDENT OF WESLEYAN UNIVERSITY.

Dr. Bangs's services in the Missionary Secretaryship continued but about one year longer. On the 20th of January, 1841, he was elected President of the Wesleyan University, Middletown, Connecticut, an appointment which he always afterward regretted, and by which he made the greatest self-sacrifice of his life. He was content, more than content, in his late position; he was thoroughly acquainted with all its duties and interests. No other man in the denomination was equally familiar with them. It identified him with a cause which was most vital and most important in his Church, and of which he has justly been called the father. For this reason he had declined a former election to a college presidency in Augusta, Ky., and two nominations to the episcopal office. He doubted his qualification for a collegiate chair; for though he had been an assiduous student, and was somewhat acquainted with the Hebrew, Greek, Latin, and French languages, and competent to teach the Moral and Intellectual Sciences, he possessed no knowledge of collegiate discipline, and was too far advanced in life for any successful preparation for his new office. But his predecessor, Dr. Olin, had failed in health, and had nominated him for the place. The Faculty of the University visited New York, and urged upon him the importance, the necessity of his acceptance. He appealed to his ministerial brethren of the city, but they voted that it was his duty to yield; and at last, by a denial of his best predilections, he did so, in deference to the general command of the Church. It is unnecessary to delay our narrative with any detailed account of his services at Middletown. He found the institution tottering under debt and declining in public patronage, through the long vacancy of its presidential chair. Its friends did not expect of him any important services as an instructor, but it was supposed that his high denominational reputation and his paternal superintendence of the government of the University would command public confidence, while a competent Faculty would maintain its rank for scholarship. He was encouraged at first by an apparent return of prosperity to the institution. In the spring of 1842 he wrote: "One thing which has operated much to the disadvantage of the University has been the diminished confidence of the public after the death of Dr. Fisk. The number of students began to decline, so that the Junior class of this year, which was the Freshman class after his death, consists only of twenty-two, not quite half the number of the Seniors who were the Freshmen of the year previous to his death, then numbering forty-six. The number of new students at the beginning of the last term was thirty-six, though the Freshman class consists of only twenty-four, the remainder having entered in advanced classes. We have also had six added to the Freshman class this term, making the whole number thirty. This, I am informed, is an unusual number for the middle of the year. These facts are encouraging, and show that the public confidence is returning."

There was discontent, however, among the students; their president was himself not a graduate; they discussed among themselves the significance of his name on their diplomas; their dissatisfaction reached him in a painful manner, and he resigned his office. The Faculty and some of the students remonstrated against this act, but he persisted. The "Joint Board" adopted resolutions expressing their regret at his resignation, and tendering him thanks for his services. The Faculty addressed him a letter of affectionate farewell. The Alumni, at their annual meeting for 1842, sent him a letter expressing "their sincere regret that circumstances have induced him to resign the Presidency of their Alma Mater!" and a number of students united in a protest against the alleged unjustifiable form of the opposition of the malcontents.

HE RETURNS TO THE PASTORATE.

Dr. Bangs retired from the University immediately after the commencement of 1842. He had suffered much in his health and spirits while at Middletown, "and now," he writes, "I was thrown out of employment and had no means of support." The Missionary Society appointed him to collect funds for its treasury, but his successor in the secretaryship "violently opposed" this appointment, and it was considered not to be authorized by the acts of the General Conference respecting the institution; he abandoned therefore these labors. It seemed hard to him, in view of his arduous, and for many years gratuitous services for the Society, that a temporary engagement like this, which could not fail to be advantageous to the treasury, should be so fastidiously criticized. As he had collected some hundreds of dollars, the Board tendered him a compensation; he declined to receive it, and retired submissively but sadly. "I was again afloat," he writes, "upon a rough sea. My God, however, soon provided for me. A vacancy occurring in the Second-street Church, New York, I was appointed to it, through the kindness of Rev. Phineas Rice, the presiding elder. He assured me that the official brethren unanimously wished me to take charge of them. I thankfully accepted. My family was still at Middletown, but I was accommodated with comfortable board at Mr. Miller's. His excellent wife soon informed me that she was one of my own spiritual children; she was indeed a daughter to me in the Lord, and treated me as a father in the Gospel. I was attacked with a dangerous illness, which disabled me for a fortnight, and left me feeble the remainder of the year. This affliction had a sanctified effect upon my soul, and tended, through the blessing of Divine grace, to lead me nearer to God and make me more diligent in preparing for another world. I endeavored to urge upon my congregation the necessity and privilege of entire sanctification, and I had the happiness of witnessing the blessed fruit of my labors in the awakening and conversion of sinners, and the 'building up of believers in their most holy faith.' A very considerable revival of religion took place, without any extraordinary effort, other than preaching plainly and pointedly, praying earnestly for the outpouring of the Holy Spirit, and urging upon all classes the necessity of holiness of heart and life. O what seasons of refreshing from the presence of the Lord did I experience while unfolding to the people the unbounded love of God to a lost world! And how eagerly did the people of God receive the word, while apparently they were made to rejoice in God their Saviour. I must say that the time I spent in Second-street was the most happy two years I had enjoyed for the last thirty years. Though I had endeavored to discharge my multifarious duties while in the Book Concern, and while Corresponding Secretary of the Missionary Society, yet such was the pressure of those duties, not to say burdens, that they were often like a heavy load upon my shoulders, and kept my mind in a continual state of anxiety, devising plans for the furtherance of these and other enterprises of benevolence in which I felt it my duty to engage. And although I can look back with gratitude upon those busy days of my life, and, bating my many imperfections, can praise God for the many tokens of his approbation, yet I would not be hired for any earthly consideration to pass through the same scenes, suffer the like anxieties, and perform the same duties. Nevertheless I cannot but rejoice at beholding the present prosperous state of the Book Concern and Missionary Society in general, which I may humbly and gratefully consider the result of my labors conjointly with my colleagues. Those who are now in that establishment know but little from their own experience of the difficulties of former days, as everything almost was prepared for their hands before they came there.

"These things, I humbly trust, are not said in a spirit of vain boasting, but simply as matters of fact. While I would ascribe honor to God alone for all the good that has been accomplished, and for giving his people patience to bear with my many weaknesses, I rejoice for the many valuable friends he has given me, and for the confidence reposed in me by the Church of my choice. For all my unfaithfulness, my numerous infirmities and failures, I ask pardon of God and man; while I claim for myself, through the abounding grace of God in Christ Jesus, purity of motive and uprightness of intention."

GENERAL CONFERENCE OF 1844.

His name was again first on the list of delegates from the New York Conference to the General Conference of 1844. They were eleven, and included Drs. Olin, G. Peck, Rice, Reed, Sandford, and other influential men. The session began in New York city on the first of May, and was the most memorable one since the organization of the body. It was to be the epoch of the division of the Church.

Dr. Bangs was now nearly sixty-six years of age; his health was broken; but he was as active as ever in the business of the Conference. In the forty days of the session there were but about ten in which his name did not appear on the record of the Journals, and, as usual, mostly in connection with the great interests of the Church. At no former session had there been abler discussions or longer speeches; but even in the absorbing controversy which now issued in the division of the denomination, he never obtruded a formal speech, or any remarks requiring ten minutes of the time of the Conference. He was chairman of the Committees on Missions, on the Sabbath, on the Memoir of Bishop M'Kendree, on the Collection of Materials for the History of the Church, (consisting of one member of each Annual Conference,) and of the Commissioners to settle the claims of the southern division of the denomination on its property. He was a member of the Committee of Nine to report on the remonstrance of the southern delegates against the proceedings of the Conference in the case of Bishop Andrew—of the Committees on Slavery, on Reporting and Publishing the Doings of the Session, on Estimating the Expenses of Editors and Book Agents, and on a Revised Edition of the Discipline.

His votes on the slavery questions, which arose in connection with the case of Bishop Andrew, were against the South, except so far as what he deemed an equitable division of the denominational property with that portion of the Church should be made in the event of a formal division of the denomination. He voted also for the repeal of the Act of the preceding session against the testimony of colored people in Church trials. It would be impossible here to narrate adequately the history of the slavery controversy as it culminated in this Conference; it belongs to the history of the Church rather than to a biographical record, like the present volume. Dr. Bangs had witnessed the organization of the first delegated General Conference; he now saw it rent asunder, the South from the North. While maintaining his habitual conservatism, and conceding every equitable claim of the South, he was equally faithful to his antislavery convictions. "I am as liable," he wrote soon after the session, "as any man to be led astray by the influence of strong prejudices; but such has been the goodness of God that his grace has kept my mind in peace amid the war of words, and I have an inward satisfaction in reflecting on the course I have pursued."

CONDITION OF THE CHURCH.

The condition of the denomination, aside from this conflict, was most gratifying to him. The bishops could say, in their Address to the Conference, that "no period of our denominational existence has been more signally distinguished by great and extensive revivals of religion and the increase of the Church than the last four years. Our missions in general are in a prosperous condition, and some of them have been distinguished by extraordinary success." The Church comprised more than 1,170,000 members, and more than 4,600 traveling preachers; it had gained, since the last General Conference, 430,897 members and 1,325 preachers, an average of 107,724 members and 331 preachers per year. Thus, in the hour of its most gigantic strength and capacity for usefulness, when its arms could be outstretched to the ends of the world with the blessings of the Gospel of peace, was the mighty Colossus broken in twain. Both North and South had shared in the guilty responsibility of slavery; all parties had grievously erred, in measures, in temper, and in language; all were destined to suffer a righteous retribution. Had the division of the Church restored its tranquillity, the disaster, though inexpressibly mournful, might have been tolerable; but it was followed with exasperation and disputes, with "confusion worse confounded." The religious, the strongest ties between the North and South being broken, (for soon the desolating fracture rent all the leading denominations of the land,) the national mind swung loose from its moorings; in a few years war broke out; hundreds of thousands of lives, hundreds of millions of money were sacrificed; the Republic bowed its head, humiliated to the dust, before the civilized world. The atrocious purpose of founding a nationality on the basis of human slavery was audaciously announced by the utterly corrupted South. Foreign nations, jealous of the greatness of the country, and wishing its overthrow, gave moral support to the rebellion in spite of their holiest traditions against slavery, and fear and trembling fell upon all the land amid the confusion of its counsels and the din of war.

In northern Methodism itself the controversy, taking new phases, chiefly of an ecclesiastical complexion, entailed further discords. Dr. Bangs, now venerable with years and hardly-paralleled services to the Church, became the victim of severe attacks. He has left in his manuscript touching reflections on the treatment he had to endure, especially from the Church paper which he had helped to found, and of which he was the first official editor, in which he says he was held up to the ridicule of his brethren. I forbear to cite these remarks; they had better, with so many other grievances of the times, be committed to oblivion, or to the historian who, at some future and more tranquil period, may be able impartially to discuss them. This passing allusion must suffice here. Mourning for the desolations which were coming, more even than for those which had already come, he retired, after some unavailing efforts of his pen, more and more from the raging storm, devoting his attention chiefly to his own spiritual culture and the moral improvement of the Church. He hoped that the time for his admission to that "rest which remaineth for the people of God" was not very far off, and during the remainder of his life we shall see him more than ever hiding himself "with Christ in God," meditating the great themes of spiritual life, which have been the comfort and strength of saints in all ages of the Church, and waiting in gracious patience for his deliverance from the agitations of his times.

CHAPTER XXIII.

MATURE CHRISTIAN LIFE.

I FIND no record, in Dr. Bangs's manuscript, from the General Conference of 1844 till May 22, 1847. His autobiographical sketch ceases, in fact, with 1844; the remainder of the manuscript being an occasional journal noting prominent facts of his inward or outward life at the times of their occurrence. He has now nearly concluded that part of his long career which, by its connection with the marvelous development of his Church, may be called historic. With the exception of one more General Conference, and one or two more publications, he confines himself hereafter to the tranquil labors of pastoral life for a few years, and then to the retirement of a "superannuated" veteran. This portion of the record appears to me, however, to be the richest, the most interesting, and the most edifying of all his manuscript. The romantic incidents and adventures of his early itinerancy, and the historic importance of his middle age, have detained our attention, with no little interest and with a growing estimation of his character and usefulness, through many years. If our narrative now becomes less historical, it becomes more personal and characteristic. Morally he seems to return to the freshness, the very bloom of youthful life. A cloud of affliction occasionally flits across the serene sky, but the prospect shines brighter and brighter unto the perfect day. We enter not upon the dreary winter of a failing and discontented life, but this concluding scene opens like the lengthening day and the increasing brightness of spring-time, grows into the radiant and blooming summer, and ends in the rich fruitfulness and beauty of the still genial autumn. Seldom has there been recorded a more consolatory example of happiness in old age—a more striking instance of ripening, mellowing Christian character amid the infirmities of declining life. The religious earnestness of his former years rises into an intense joyousness, a saintliness of faith and charity, a piety which reminds us of the holiest Mystics, but exempt from their superstitions and morbid self-consciousness; an example, in fine, of that sanctity of heart and life, that healthful and evangelical mysticism which distinguished Wesley, Fletcher, and so many of the early Methodists.

The notes of this journal are abundant, though inserted often at considerable intervals. Deeply significant as expressions of spiritual life, they would yet of course become monotonous if cited largely. I shall limit myself therefore to but occasional quotations, passing rapidly over his remaining years, and giving only such passages as record actual facts, or present marked phases of his spiritual experience.

PASTORAL LIFE AGAIN.

Under the date of May 22, 1847, he writes: "The New York Conference of 1846 appointed me to the Sands-street Church, Brooklyn. The two previous years I spent at Greene-street Church, New York, where I labored with much satisfaction to myself, and enjoyed much communion with God and his people. The affectionate manner in which I was received, and have since been treated, by the brethren in Sands-street, has both endeared them to me and rendered my stay with them delightful, and my labors in and out of the pulpit pleasant and, I trust, somewhat useful. My health was never better, and in preaching I have found great enlargement of heart and liberty of speech, though sometimes cramped from barrenness of mind and want of ready utterance. This, however, I have had to endure at times from the beginning of my ministry. It is accompanied with fear and trembling whenever I stand up to speak, which makes it exceedingly embarrassing, and often causes much mortification from the reflection of the imperfect manner in which I have performed my duty. Is this necessary to humble me, 'lest, being lifted up with pride, I fall into the condemnation of the devil?'

" *October* 15, 1848.—Some time in the month of April last I was compelled, from debility, to desist from preaching. I had attended a protracted meeting for about three months, during which time I was under continued excitement, and in one week preached four evenings successively, and the succeeding Sabbath three times, administered the Lord's supper, and held a society meeting, yet felt no weariness; but when the meeting closed a reaction took place in my system, and a throbbing in my head, accompanied with dizziness, which rendered it difficult for me to walk without help. This continued for some time, until I was quite prostrated, and was confined for most part of the time to my bed. By the blessing of God, however, on the means used, I so far recovered as to be able to attend the sessions of the New York Conference. Here an election of delegates to the General Conference took place, and I was left off for the first time since 1812, which was the first delegated General Conference ever held. I know the cause of this treatment. It was occasioned by my opposition to the course pursued by the editor of one of our papers, for which I rejoice and praise God. I look back upon what I have said and done in these agitations with gratitude. I inwardly rejoice that I have been counted worthy of suffering in such a cause. These trials have never deprived me of one moment's sleep, nor soured my spirit, nor damped my zeal in the cause of God.

"At this Conference I was reappointed to Sands-street, and my health being extremely feeble, the brethren consented that the bishop should appoint for me an assistant, so that I might labor only as my strength might permit.

This I considered a great favor, for which I felt truly thankful to God and his people."

The illness under which he suffered was attended with a throbbing of the left lobe of the brain and general prostration of his strength. "It was difficult," he says, "for me to walk in the street, and I seldom attempted it without some one to assist me. At last any noise, even of a footstep on the floor of my room, became painful to me." By careful diet he overcame these symptoms, but they were the premonitions of a constitutional tendency to cerebral congestion, which was to trouble him the remainder of his life, but which he controlled by rigorous temperance and mental tranquillity.

At the session of the New York Conference for 1848 that body was divided, in accordance with an act of the General Conference. Notwithstanding its preceding abridgments by the separation of the Canadas, the interior of New York, and the Troy Conference, its Churches and ministry had grown so much as to render their annual Conference business burdensome, if not impracticable.

Dr. Bangs was appointed to preach a sermon before the session on the present division. "I gave a succinct history of the rise and progress of the Conference from its beginning, in 1789, to the present time. This sermon was published at the unanimous request of the Conference. After its delivery the elders were ordained, and the sacrament of the Lord's supper administered."

PULPIT EMBARRASSMENT.

In referring to this sermon he makes some interesting remarks on the exercises of his mind "in the pulpit." "I was always constitutionally timid, and when I commenced preaching it was with much fear and trembling. This inconvenience, however, gradually subsided, so that I could generally command myself in the desk. But since my debility, for a long time, whenever I entered the pulpit, such a tremor came over my whole frame that I could scarcely stand, and hence I generally had a chair near me, on which I would take hold, and I frequently stood in the altar in preference to the pulpit, as in that position my nerves were not so much affected. At the commencement of this discourse before the Conference I felt such a trembling in my whole frame that I could hardly stand, and as I had the sermon written, I sat down and read it; but before I got through the tremor left me, and I felt at perfect liberty. My soul was like a 'well-watered garden,' and I could rejoice in God my Saviour.

PRESIDING ELDER—SANCTIFICATION.

"I was now appointed presiding elder of the New York East District, in the eastern division of the Conference, for which appointment I felt unfeignedly thankful, as it gave me an opportunity of traveling considerably in the country, and in some measure relieved me from the pressure of pastoral duties, though it imposed others of a higher order. My health was still feeble, and in standing up to preach my nervous debility was such that it was with difficulty that I could command myself; but the Lord blessed me in an unusual degree, and gave me great enlargement of soul, and much peace and joy in the Holy Ghost. At times I felt such a Divine power rest upon me that I was almost overwhelmed. O the goodness of God my heavenly Father!

"When I went on the district I felt it my duty to urge upon all, both preachers and people, the necessity of entire sanctification of soul and body. In explaining and enforcing this doctrine I enjoyed great enlargement of heart and much divine consolation, and God has raised up a number of witnesses of the doctrine.

"What added much to my comfort was the cordial manner in which I was received, and the respect with which I was treated, both by preachers and people. They treated me as a father in the Gospel, and sought in every possible way to make my visits agreeable. God has, indeed, abundantly blessed me in soul and body, so much so that my health has been so far restored that I now read, write, preach with as much facility as ever. I rejoice in all the great things the Lord has done for me.

"I believe the Lord sanctified my soul about six months after he justified me; but I did not always retain an evidence of it, nor live in its enjoyment, though whenever I recurred to it, either in conversation, prayer, or preaching, my heart was inflamed with divine love. About ten years since the Lord pressed upon my heart the necessity of regaining this inestimable blessing, and inspired me with an ardent desire and determination to seek after it until I could say, O Lord thou knowest all things; thou knowest that I love thee with all my heart. He heard my prayer, though the restoration of the blessing was not in the manner in which I first received it; it was more gradual, less perceptible, yet equally strong and permanent. When I compare my present enjoyment, the inward tranquillity which pervades my soul, with what had been my experience for some years, I see the difference. I cannot, indeed, describe the peace, the love, the uninterrupted communion with God, and the fellowship with all God's people which I now daily enjoy.

"I would not say that I have such a happiness as excludes all temptations, trials, and afflictions. By no means. If Christ, who was 'holy, harmless, separate from sin,' was 'tempted on all points, like as we are,' surely we cannot expect to be exempt from temptations, much less from those afflictions which are inseparable from humanity. In addition to these, we have to contend with the infirmities which arise from the imperfection of our judgment and our inability always to distinguish between truth and error. All these things are sources of trial. But 'all things,' *all* things—good and bad, little and great, blessings from God or curses from men—'shall work together for good to them that love God.'

"The firm belief of this truth has been a never-failing source of consolation to my soul even in seasons of severe trial and in times of heavy affliction, whether of body or mind, and sometimes when both together have pressed upon me. In such seasons that gracious promise has been presented so vividly to my faith, that instantly the clouds have dispersed, and the sun of righteousness has shone upon me with such brightness as to dispel all doubt and fear. At other times, though the load has not been immediately removed, yet hope has sustained me; I have been enabled to hold fast until God appeared for my deliverance. 'I will never leave thee, nor forsake thee,' is a promise which every faithful soul may claim for himself, under every trial through which he may be called to pass, however severe it may be.

"*April* 18, 1850.—I humbly adore the God of love for his goodness to me. My health has been so fully restored that I am able to preach with earlier strength, and my soul is strong in the 'Lord of hosts, and in the power of his might.' In the latter part of the past winter I attended a protracted meeting at Mamaroneck for two weeks, during which I preached thirteen sermons, and attended three general class-meetings, besides the prayer-meetings after the sermons. These were seasons of much spiritual comfort."

By a happy coincidence he found his old fellow-laborer in Canada, his own father in the Gospel, Joseph Sawyer, living in extreme age and comfortable retirement in this beautiful town, and very touching and consoling were their interviews. They worshiped together, as of old, in the temple of God, and recalled, in the converse of the social circles of the place, the battles and victories of their old frontier fields.

While in this village he was entertained at the hospitable home of Mr. Halsted. At the breakfast table on Sunday morning each of the company repeated a passage from the Holy Scriptures, after which, at Dr. Bangs's instance, they cited each a stanza from the Church Hymn Book. When it was his turn to quote one he repeated the words,

"Jesus, thy boundless love to me
No thought can reach, no tongue declare;
O knit my thankful heart to thee,
And reign without a rival there:
Thine wholly, thine alone, I am;
Be thou alone my constant flame."

His face became radiant, his utterance broken with emotion; "a halo of Divine glory" seemed to surround the circle, as he afterward said; he "could neither speak nor eat," but retired from the table rehearsing the words of the poet:

"A solemn reverence checks our songs,
And praise sits silent on our tongues."

A love-feast and the Lord's supper were held that day in the village Church. In giving out the first hymn at the former "I was so overwhelmed with a sense of the presence of God," he says, "that it was with the utmost difficulty I could read, and when we kneeled in prayer I could utter but a word or two. I called on my old friend, Mr. Sawyer, to pray, which he did. I then endeavored to relate my experience of the goodness of God; a powerful emotion ran over the assembly, and we had a time of 'refreshing from the presence of the Lord.' We had, indeed, one of the most joyful seasons I have seen and felt for a long time. O what a sweet and indescribable union I felt with God's own people, and more especially with those who enjoyed the sanctifying influence of the Holy Spirit! The world may call this foolishness or enthusiasm; but I call it the holy communion of saints, the 'fellowship of kindred spirits.'

"I often wonder, in view of my past unfaithfulness and present unworthiness, how it is that God condescends to bless me so abundantly! The explanation is found in the language of St. John, 'God is love,' otherwise expressed by the psalmist, 'For he is good; for his mercy endureth forever;' therefore we are called upon to 'give thanks unto his name.' And surely, of all beings upon the earth, I have the greatest reason to praise him, and give thanks to his name. The methods he has taken to save me by leading me in a way I had not known, by subduing my will, by disappointing me in my early expectations, mortifying my natural ambition, and by sending his Holy Spirit to seek me in the wilderness, and finally by shedding abroad his love in my heart, saving me from sin, delivering me in the hour of temptation, and giving me favor in the eyes of his people, are all instances of his loving-kindness. He keeps me in perfect peace. To God be all the glory for every blessing I enjoy!"

It was about this time that he wrote for the Christian Advocate the articles which afterward composed his volume on "The Present State, Prospects, etc., of the Methodist Episcopal Church." They glowed with the freshness and hopefulness of his present fervent spirit of piety. Tracing the extraordinary progress of the Church, not only in its numerical growth, but in its practical schemes of charity and evangelization, and the extending revivals of pure religion in many parts of the world, he concludes that Christianity never had better prospects. In his journal he refers to doubts expressed by some of his friends respecting his sanguine views. He says, "I know that some of my brethren differ from me in respect to the present state of pure and undefiled religion; but I am fully convinced, from as impartial a survey as I have been able to take, that there never has been since primitive times, nor was there even then, so much pure religion in the world as there is at the present time; and surely the world was never in such a favorable condition for the spread of the Gospel. This, I think, I have abundantly proved in the articles to which I have referred.

"*May* 2.—This is my birthday. I have lived seventy-two years a monument of God's mercy. I desire to record my gratitude to him for all the way in which he has led me, for lifting up my head in the hour of affliction, for strengthening my heart in the time of weakness, for supplying my wants in the time of need, and for permitting me to live so many years. O that the remainder of my days may be exclusively devoted to him! I think I can adopt the language of the poet:

'Now, my God, thine own I am;
Now I give thee back thine own;
Freedom, friends, and health, and fame,
I consecrate to thee alone!
Thine I live, thrice happy I!
Happier still if thine I die.'

MRS. PALMER.

"*May* 3.—I have just returned from Carbondale, Pa., where I was invited to dedicate a church to the service of Almighty God. I was accompanied by Mrs. Palmer, who was also invited by the brethren, with whom she had some time last year formed an acquaintance, and had been made instrumental of promoting the work of God among them. And here I feel it a duty to record my belief in the deep devotion and the intrinsic usefulness of this Christian woman. The prejudices which have existed against her have arisen chiefly from misapprehension of her opinions. I have known her from her childhood, for she was a member of my catechetical class in 1817, when she was only eight or nine years of age. She was made a partaker of pardoning mercy at an early age, married soon after, and lived a pious and blameless life for several years, when (about thirteen years since) she was enabled to rejoice in God's sanctifying grace. She felt it her duty, as every devoted Christian ought and, I cannot doubt, does feel it to be, to strive in every scriptural way to promote this unspeakable blessing among her fellow-Christians, and she has been remarkably successful. Many have been raised up under her teachings and prayers as witnesses of the saving efficacy of Christ's blood and righteousness to save them from all sin. And why should any one oppose another, even though a female, so eminently owned by the Head of the Church in the conversion of sinners and in the sanctification of believers? For my part I dare not. I cannot but rejoice in whatever instrumentality God shall use for the salvation of souls. And I have abundant reason to believe that this devoted woman has been thus used of God as an instrument of good to others. She possesses the happy art of winning their confidence, and of pointing them directly to the Lord Jesus for life and salvation.

"Some object to her phraseology. I do not pledge myself to the correctness of every word she may utter any more than I can expect every other person to agree with me in all my words and phrases. But why should I dispute about words so long as the substance is retained? I care not by what name this great blessing be designated, whether holiness, sanctification, perfect love, Christian perfection, so long as is meant by it an entire consecration of soul and body to God, accompanied with faith that he accepts the sacrifice through the merits of Christ alone."

The singular usefulness of this "elect lady," in both America and Europe, by both her writings and her personal communications to the Churches, Dr. Bangs deemed it his duty to recognize; he pronounced her teachings substantially orthodox and Wesleyan, and in this opinion he had the concurrence of many of our best minds; he esteemed her as a commendable follower of the "holy women"—Mary Fletcher, Hester Ann Rogers, Ann Cutler, Ladies Maxwell and Fitzgerald—who gathered about Wesley as his correspondents and helpers in the Gospel; and with St. Paul did he say to the Churches, "I commend unto you Phebe our sister, which is a servant of the Church: . . . that ye receive her in the Lord, as becometh saints, and that ye assist her in whatsoever business she hath need of you: for she hath been a succorer of many, and of myself also." Providentially placed in circumstances, pecuniary and domestic, which have allowed of the devotion of her time to religious labors, she has served the Church with a diligence and success which should be imitated rather than criticised. Her house in New York has been for years a sanctuary, where not only such men as Olin, Hamline, and Bangs have found hospitable shelter and taken sweet counsel together in the deep things of God, but where thousands of earnest minds from all parts of the land have sought and found guidance and consolation. It may indeed be doubted whether any one occasion of social devotion in the great city has, in the last twenty years, had a more profound and wider influence in favor of the special doctrines of Christian experience, as taught by Methodism, than the crowded weekly assemblies at her home. At no place have those doctrines been more thoroughly and devoutly discussed; and in these discussions representatives, clerical and lay, of nearly all evangelical Churches, have delighted to share. For years Dr. Bangs acted as the virtual president of these meetings, communicating to them the matured wisdom and receiving through them the richest consolations of his Christian experience. He incessantly recurs to them with delight in his journals. The abuse which fanatical or indiscreet minds have occasionally made of the doctrine of sanctification; their perverted or cantish phraseology, or monomaniacal absorption in the theme, no man regretted more than he; but he saw that such perversions are made of the doctrine of justification itself, of all important doctrines; and he deeply mourned that intelligent Christians and pastors should find in the infirmities of their neighbors apologies for their neglect of, if not opposition to, a truth so profoundly important; a truth which, according to the earliest and best lights of their Church, is fundamental in Methodism, and expressly enjoined in the ordination vows of its ministry.

CHAPTER XXIV.

HE REVISITS CANADA.

DR. BANGS was not elected to the General Conference of 1848, as we have seen. But that body honored him with an appointment, as its representative to the Wesleyan Canada Conference. He was again to enter the scene of his early itinerant struggles and triumphs. The interest of the visit was greatly enhanced by the fact that his early fellow-laborer in that distant field, Joseph Sawyer, now about eighty years old, accompanied him. A half a century had passed since Sawyer received him into the Church and called him out to the itinerancy. The two veterans, who had traveled the frontier wilderness in the vigor of their youth, now returned leaning upon their staves, their "hoary heads" wearing that "crown of glory" with which old age circles the brows of those who are "found in the ways of righteousness."

They set out from the city of New York on the 2d of June, 1850. "What a contrast," wrote Dr. Bangs, "in the mode of traveling since Fulton introduced the use of steam to propel boats through the water! In 1804 I was four days in sailing from Rhinebeck to New York, eighty miles. Now we sailed from New York to Albany, twice the distance, in about ten hours! And then the accommodations! Formerly we were pent up in a small cabin, in which there was scarcely room to stand erect, and so closely confined at night that one almost suffocated with heat and the confined foul atmosphere. Now we can sit in the sumptuously furnished saloon, or promenade the upper deck, sheltered from the scorching sun by a tight roof with open ends and sides which permit a free circulation of the air, and we can, at the same time, enjoy a view of the beautiful, and sometimes magnificent scenery, particularly while passing through the high-lands of the banks of the Hudson River. The day was clear and bright, the atmosphere soft and bland, the company polite and agreeable, and my heart expanded while my eyes beheld God's magnificent work, and glowed with gratitude to him for the rich displays of his power, wisdom, and goodness, which were exhibited all around us; and more especially for the wonders of redeeming love in the gift of Jesus Christ, through whose death and continual intercession we are made partakers of all these blessings. I could not refrain, indeed, from adoring him. Thanks be to the 'Author of every good and perfect gift,' for steamboats, the telegraph, and for railroads, as well as for every other improvement of the age in which we have the happiness to live!

"Finally we landed safely at Brockville, and were met on the quay by several of the preachers, who were expecting us, and were conducted to our lodgings in the hospitable mansion of Mr. Flint, a wealthy brother in the Church in that place, of whose hospitality we partook while we remained at the seat of the Conference. We were soon visited by others, and among them was my beloved brother, the Rev. William Case, formerly, when traveling in Canada, my colleague and companion in labor and suffering in the cause of God. Our meeting, after years of separation, was mutually gratifying, and we passed a few moments in recounting the goodness of God in days gone by, and expressions of gratitude to him for permitting us to see each other once more in the land of the living.

GREAT CHANGES.

"When I first visited Canada, in 1799, we lay five nights in the woods in traveling through the country to Buffalo; and when we arrived at that place there were only two or three miserable log-huts, in which some very poor people lived, or rather burrowed, for they seemed to live almost under ground. Now, in traveling from New York to Brockville, a distance of not less than five hundred miles, we performed the tour in about thirty-one hours, traveling time; or in three days, including two nights, one at Albany, and another at Oswego, and the five hours we were detained at Syracuse.

"Since that time cities, villages, and cultivated farms, canals and railroads, have come into existence in those parts of the country which were then covered with a dense forest. Even in Brockville, when I traveled in this country in 1805, there was not a single house, and it was an entire wilderness. Now there is a village of between three and four thousand inhabitants, built up with large substantial stone houses and stores, and everything appears in a flourishing state. Religion, pure and undefiled, has kept pace with the progress of the settlements on both sides of the line which divides Canada from the United States."

SCENES IN THE CONFERENCE.

On Thursday they were conducted by Mr. Case to the Conference. As they entered the church the whole assembly rose, greeting them while they passed up the aisle. Their aged conductor presented them with much emotion to the president, Dr. Richey, who, taking the hand of Dr. Bangs, introduced them to the Conference with an address of welcome. Dr. Bangs followed with a speech, which produced a profound impression. It was some time before he could command his own feelings enough to proceed with it, and when he sat down, "overwhelmed," he says, "with a sense of the goodness of God and the love of the brethren," the Conference responded with universal cheers.

"After taking my seat," he writes, "I looked around to see how many I could recognize as known by me in former days. I could see but five or six, namely, William Case, Anson Green, William, John, and Egerton Ryerson—all brothers—and Robert Corson; all the rest had been raised up since my Canadian days. Death had thinned the ranks of these veterans of the cross. I was reminded more forcibly than ever of the mutability of all terrestrial things, and that my own earthly race must soon end. Be it so, I thought; when my heavenly Father shall have served himself with me, according to his own good pleasure, he will sign my release, and discharge me from service, so that I may 'enter into the joy of my Lord.'"

His address contained some striking allusions to his early life in Canada. He said:

"You will excuse me, sir, if I advert to a few items in my personal history in relation to the commencement and progress of Methodism in this country. This was my spiritual birthplace. It was here that I commenced my ministry a little over forty-nine years since, under the fostering care of my venerable father in the Gospel, the Rev. Joseph Sawyer, who is now present with us, and who lives in a green old age to adorn that Gospel which he has preached for upward of fifty-three years. I remember well the time and the circumstances under which I commenced my feeble labors, and the trials through which I passed in those days of my childhood, when the woodman's ax and the preacher's voice were heard almost simultaneously; when the hardy pioneer of Methodism followed the immigrant; carried provender on his horse, tied him to a sapling in the night, because there was neither a barn to shelter him nor a pasture to feed him; when we used to eat, preach, and sleep in the same room in the log-hut of the settler; when at other times we held our meetings in the groves, in barns, or log school-houses, and slept under the foliage of the trees when night overtook us in our travels through the wilderness.

"At that time the Methodists did not amount to much over 200,000, all told, in Europe and America. Now they number, including those who have seceded from us, but still hold fast our cardinal doctrines, nearly 2,000,000, besides the millions who have already gone to glory. At that time there were only about 1,200 in Canada. Now there are about 25,000 belonging to your body, exclusive of those who have seceded from you. And all this has been accomplished in about fifty years. Have we not abundant cause of gratitude to God for his abounding grace toward us as a people?

"When I commenced my ministry I was in my twenty-fourth year. I have now just entered my seventy-third year. It will, therefore, be forty-nine years next September since I entered the itinerancy, under the presiding eldership of the Rev. Joseph Jewell, and as a colleague with my esteemed father in the Gospel, Rev. Joseph Sawyer, on the Niagara Circuit; and in the month of December of the same year I was sent to form a new circuit on what was then called Long Point, including Burford, Oxford, and several other neighboring towns and settlements. Here God gave me manifest tokens of his approbation by the conversion of a number of sinners as seals to my ministry.

"How has God enlarged our borders since that time! There were then only about 73,000 in the United States. Now, including the North and the South—I am mortified to be compelled to make this distinction, as indicating two separate branches of the same Church—there are upward of 1,000,000; and, as before said, throughout the world there are nearly 2,000,000.

"And what more shall I say? Will you allow me, sir, to add a few words of admonition and advice? If we would secure the continuance of God's blessing—the blessing which he bestowed upon our fathers in the Gospel—we must imitate their spirit and practice. What was that spirit? They were deeply imbued with the spirit of Christ. They commenced with the spirit of revival. Methodism was begotten, fostered, and grew up under the influence of the spirit of revival. If, therefore, we would perpetuate its prosperity, we must cultivate this same spirit, aiming to promote it by every possible means, urging ourselves on, and pressing our people forward after entire sanctification of soul and body to God. This doctrine of entire sanctification was that which, above all others, distinguished Wesley among his compeers in the ministry, and has been the distinguishing characteristic of Methodism from his to our day. If we would, therefore, have the mantles of Wesley, of Asbury, and of the many other fathers in our Israel, who have been carried in chariots of fire to heaven, fall on us, we must make their motto ours, namely, HOLINESS TO THE LORD."

By request of the president of the Conference he addressed its candidates in a public assembly, giving chiefly a narrative of his early struggles and successes in their now flourishing fields of labor. Of course the dream of the shivered rock was not omitted. He concluded by saying: "Now, my young brethren, all you have to do is to smite the rock. It is God's work to split it. All you have to do is to preach the word, and attend to the other duties of your office. It is God's work to bless the labor of your hearts and hands, and to give effect to your well-meant efforts. Go on, then, in the name of your Divine Master, and he will be with you 'always, even to the end of the world.'"

An afternoon session was devoted to "conversation on the best method of promoting the work of God, and in relating religious experience. This was truly a spiritual festival, a 'feast of marrow and fat things, of wine on the lees.' Mr. Sawyer and myself took part in this exercise, in which several of the preachers participated with apparent delight. I cannot but think that this mingling of spirits in the interchange of the knowledge of experimental religion, with the regular routine of Conference business, by breaking in upon the dull monotony of dry discussions and formal voting—such discussions and voting as necessarily arise out of the questions which must be disposed of in the course of things—has a tendency to relieve the mind of some of its burdens, to soften those little asperities which are sometimes excited in the conflict of opinions, and, finally, to promote brotherly love and Christian harmony."

Sunday was a great day with the community as well as the Conference. There were four sermons preached, besides the love-feast, the sacrament of the Eucharist, and the ordination of preachers. Dr. Bangs preached at the latter service a discourse of remarkable power and effect, on Rom. x, 14, 15. At the conclusion of the sermon fifteen candidates were ordained to the "office and work of the ministry."

The next day he visited the town where he had married his wife, and was received by the remnants of the household. He preached in the village. "Here, again," he writes, "I was forcibly reminded of the ravages which death makes in the ranks of the living. Most of the old people whom I knew in former days were dead, but their children had grown to manhood and womanhood, and some of them came to me, took me by the hand, and reminded me that they knew me when I was at their father's house, or they had heard me preach in the neighborhood."

HIS RETURN.

He assisted at the missionary anniversary of the Conference, and departed June 12, refreshed by the interview, and leaving a grateful impression upon the minds of the ministerial brethren who were now the prosperous successors of the little band of pioneers which, with his co-operation, had opened the way for them in these thriving regions. On his return he paused at

Toronto, and wrote: "We put up with Dr. Ryerson, whose excellent lady received us with Christian courtesy. Here, also, I met with an old acquaintance, the mother of Mrs. Ryerson, whom I knew before she was married, in 1802, and her excellent husband, with whom I formed an acquaintance in 1824, and we were mutually refreshed in each other's society. What a change has been effected in this place! I believe I was the first Methodist preacher that ever attempted to preach in Little York—as Toronto was then called—and I preached in a miserable half-finished house, on a week evening, to a few people, for there were not over a dozen houses in the place, and slept on the floor under a blanket. This was in 1801. I was then attempting to form a circuit on Yonge-street, a settlement west of Toronto, and I was induced to make a trial in this new little village, the settlers of which were as thoughtless and wicked as the Canaanites of old. Now there is a city of between 25,000 and 30,000 inhabitants, and it is the seat of government, of a university, and of several houses of worship, and the Methodists have their full share of religious influence, having their Book Concern established here, and likewise the 'Christian Guardian,' a weekly paper which is exerting a hallowed influence on the community throughout the province. In this city there are four stationed preachers, who have the charge, according to the Minutes for 1849, of 703 Church-members, and I suppose they minister to more than twice that number of hearers. In addition to these ministers, the Book Steward, the editor of the Christian Guardian, and the Rev. Dr. Ryerson, the superintendent of schools, a government officer, reside here, and preach as often as their other engagements will permit, and of course exert a favorable influence on the interests of religion. Indeed, Methodism in this country exerts a preponderating power on the population generally, as it is the most numerous sect in the province."

He reached New York on the 28th, "praising God for all the manifestations of his loving-kindness toward us and our friends. I humbly trust this visit has had its use, if to no one else, to myself, in calling forth my gratitude to him for all the good that he has done and is still doing for the people in Canada."

THE FEAR OF DEATH CONQUERED.

He resumed his labors as presiding elder, but not without admonitions of the decay of his constitution. "I have been," he writes, "three or four times, within about a month of each other, suddenly deprived of recollection and almost of consciousness, the attacks lasting, I am told, from five to ten minutes. The last came upon me while preaching on Saturday at the Quarterly Meeting at Roxbury, by which the sermon was suspended; and when I came to myself I found a brother speaking to the people. At first I did not know who he was, nor where I was; but my recollection returned, and I was able to transact the business of the Quarterly Meeting Conference without difficulty, and likewise on Sunday morning to attend the love-feast, preach with my usual liberty, and administer the sacrament of the Lord's supper. During these times I feel no pain, and if God should take me away in one of these paroxysms, I should, I think, glide easily and swiftly into eternity, and be forever at rest. I thank God they give me no trouble or anxiety.

"*Sept.* 16.—I can now look upon death with pleasure, though I have been habitually in bondage to it most of my life, from, I suppose, a constitutional cause in part. I was told in early life that some time before my birth my mother went to visit a sick friend, but on entering the room found the person dead. The unexpected sight struck her with terror, so that she nearly swooned away. When I was born I was as white as a corpse, my hair was as white as snow, and remained so until after I grew to manhood, and my countenance presented a blanched appearance also even until I was over twenty years of age. I was moreover always afraid of death, could not bear to look upon a dead body, and this fear continued with me even after I experienced religion, a fact which sometimes gave me much trouble, though whenever I thought of its cause I could account for it without attributing it to a lack of faith; for when I looked beyond the grave I could rejoice in hope of the glory of God. It was simply in the contemplation of death, viewed as a mortal dissolution, that it appeared so appalling. I have often prayed to be delivered from this slavish fear, and I thank God that he has heard my prayer."

HIS CATHOLICITY.

With his maturing piety a catholic sentiment of fellowship with other Christian denominations than his own became more habitual and ardent with him. At a meeting of the Council of the Christian Alliance, while the city pastors were responding to the inquiry how far they had promoted the objects of the society in their pulpits, he replied: "I have preached on the subject of love and union among Christians with great satisfaction, as this is a theme upon which I delight to dwell. I have indeed been a man of war all my days—have fought the Calvinists, the Protestant Episcopalians, and others, or rather have defended the Methodists when they have been assailed by those denominations, and I cannot repent of what I have thus done, as I have acted in the fear of God, and have not willfully defended an error, however much I may have erred in judgment unconsciously. I have, however, long since laid aside my polemical armor, and now delight chiefly in proclaiming brotherly love." When he sat down a member of the council arose and said: "Glad am I to hear my brother Bangs speak as he has. I too have been a man of war. I have fought him and he has fought me, but now I feel like giving him my hand," and reaching out his hand

Dr. Bangs grasped it heartily. "We had," he writes, "a time of rejoicing together."

This sympathetic communion with saints grew into an inexpressibly tender affectionateness toward all who love the Lord Jesus Christ in sincerity. "I find uniformly that in the same proportion as the love of God increases in my heart my love to the brethren increases, and I feel such a union of spirit with them as I cannot describe. This sacred union is known by communing with them in conversation, in prayer, and in interchange of friendly association, by which my spirit is drawn toward them in an irresistible manner; and I cannot but think that among holy souls there is an intuitive, a mystical reunion of spirit with spirit which binds them together in kindred feelings far surpassing all the fellowship founded in worldly ties, or even in natural relationship. I feel this now in an unusual degree toward my Christian friends, though not one of them is present with me; many, of whom I think, are hundreds of miles absent, yet my spirit communes with them, and joyfully anticipates the day when we shall unitedly and with joyful hearts bow around the throne of God together, and in a sacred harmony celebrate the praise of Him who hath 'washed us in his blood and made us kings and priests unto God forever!' O my most merciful God, may it be so!" He was at times apprehensive that he was "guilty of a species of idolatry in loving some of his friends too much." "They cling about my heart and, perhaps, usurp too much the place in my affections which belongs only to God. Our God is a jealous God."

HIS LOVE OF NATURE.

With these ardent affections, apparently freshened rather than abated in his old age, his enjoyment of natural scenery seemed also to be renewed. His journals abound in picturesque descriptions of the finer landscapes that adorn portions of his District, especially along the coast of Long Island Sound. In the spring of this year he writes that, "returning from a quarterly meeting at East Chester, I could not but be delighted with the beautiful landscapes along a portion of my route. Some of the fruit-trees are in blossom, the forest trees are bursting into foliage, the meadows are carpeted with green and decked with the earliest flowers, the streams sing along their courses, and the rays of the sun stream through a transparent atmosphere; all presents a scene of surpassing beauty on which my eye gazed with exquisite delight, and I exclaimed, 'These are thy glorious works, Parent of good!' 'Thou hast stretched out the north over the empty place, and hung the earth upon nothing! Thou hast not only made all things for the use of man, but hast adorned the works of thy hands with beauty for the gratification of his senses, that he may be filled with delight before thee.'" He draws an inference which once might have seemed questionable to some of his stricter Methodist brethren. "While observing the flowers and blossoms I asked myself, Why is it that the Almighty Maker has expended so much skill in merely beautifying things, and things so evanescent as the flowers, which spring up in the morning and perish at evening? Surely beauty cannot be displeasing to him; and hence I infer that it cannot be wrong to adorn and beautify our persons and homes." But he gives the legitimate inference its necessary qualification. "Nature herself is a safe example; everything is befitting, all rightly proportioned, all simple and yet perfect. How different the fashionable displays of men and women! Simplicity and modesty in dress are its best beauty."

PHYSICAL HEALTH AND HABITS.

By adopting a vegetable diet he found his health greatly improved. Notwithstanding his advancing age, his attacks of faintness or unconsciousness became much less frequent, and his mental animation much greater.

"I can," he writes, "think, read, pray, and preach with much more freedom than formerly. O the goodness of God to me!" He was also careful in all his other physical habits. "I find it essential to my health," he says, "as well as beneficial to my spirits, to take as much exercise in the open air, in walking and riding, as I possibly can. Hence, whenever I find my spirits flagging I lay down my pen or book and take a walk, by which my mind becomes buoyant, and I can then apply myself to mental labor with renewed vigor and satisfaction. I have also been in the habit, for thirty years, of bathing myself, whenever convenient, every morning, summer and winter, in cold water, which I do, when I have no bath, by rubbing my body from head to foot with a wet towel and then with a dry one till I am warm, after which I usually expose myself to the open air. I find these means exceedingly refreshing to both body and mind. But while they tend to invigorate the physical and mental man, the love of God filling the heart gives me a tranquillity and comfort far surpassing human language to express. Glory be to God!"

CHAPTER XXV.

THE GARRETTSON HOMESTEAD.

WHILE prosecuting his duties as presiding elder he made occasional excursions for his health and the renewal of old Christian ties. In June, 1851, he revisited the Garrettson homestead at Rhinebeck, the scene of early and endeared reminiscences. "My old friend Freeborn Garrettson has been dead," he writes, "about twenty-four years, and his sainted widow took her departure to the world of bliss about two years ago, in her ninety-sixth year. I found their only daughter maintaining the original Christian hospitality of the house, surrounded by pious domestics and every comfort, and having everything in the exactest order within and without the dwelling. Here was the identical old arm-chair in which my venerated friend used to sit while conversing with us; the same table, around which we used to talk and eat, still stands in its old place in the middle of the room; and the same old settee remains in its place at one end of the veranda, where we used to sit and gaze, with delighted eyes, over the lawn, and down upon the scenery of the Hudson. With these mementos I could but recall to mind the memories of other days, in which I spent so many happy hours with that patriarchal man, his sainted wife, and their intelligent, pious, and animated daughter. But alas for the inroads of death! Yet I thought their spirits still linger about the place. From twenty to forty years ago I was on terms of closest intimacy with this family;* how precious are yet the recollections of my frequent

* His own family resided in Rhinebeck when he had charge of the "old Rhinebeck District."

visits, our converse on the veranda, our walks on the lawn or in the gardens, our pleasant hours on the benches under the trees, commanding the prospects of the river! My old friends are gone, but the beautiful scenery remains, and their spirit still lives in the daughter, who kindly cheered my heart with her Christian fellowship and the old hospitality of the house. The mansion is unaltered, except the addition of a library room and some other small improvements; the old garden in front of the house is gone, changed into a beautiful lawn, gently sloping toward the river. I thanked God for permitting me once more to visit this place, endeared by so many pleasing recollections.

SUNSHINE ON THE DECLINE OF LIFE.

"*June* 24.—I attended the meeting at Mrs. Palmer's. I have attended it for some years, and find it to be among my best means of grace. It is sad that these useful assemblies, doing so much for the promotion of holiness, should be opposed by some of our people. The experiences which I have heard there are generally sound and scriptural, well suited to promote experimental and practical godliness."

"*August* 4.—Last Saturday and Sabbath I attended a Quarterly Meeting at East Chester. O how powerfully present was the Lord, both in the love-feast and in preaching, particularly on the Sabbath! In the love-feast I endeavored to explain how, from the omnipresence of God, he is with us in every place, and therefore must be among his people always, to sustain and comfort them. While speaking the Lord filled my heart with his love, and put words and arguments into my mouth of which I had not thought before, and they appeared to go like fire through the assembly. It was a time of refreshing from the presence of God. While preaching my heart expanded with enlarged views of the goodness of God, and my tongue was unloosed to speak,

I cannot but believe, 'in the Holy Ghost with much assurance.' O how good is the Lord to me! When I look back upon my life and see how very little I have done for him I wonder at his mercy in sparing me, and so abundantly blessing me; and such a view have I of his goodness that I feel sometimes a wish that I was young again that I might devote myself more ardently to his service in proclaiming his loving-kindness unto the children of men. A vain wish! I must be content to hobble along under my infirmities, and fill up my few remaining days as I may, allowing no moments to run to waste; and I do praise God most sincerely for the many, *very many*, tokens of his mercy toward me in my declining life. He gives me friends everywhere, who treat me with love and great respect; and I meet with one and another who tell me how often they have been blessed under my ministry, for which I praise God from my inmost heart. May I meet them in another world, a world of unending bliss!"

PRESIDENT OLIN.

"*August* 20.—Yesterday I returned from attending the funeral of Dr. Olin, President of the Wesleyan University, at Middletown, Conn. He died on Saturday about six o'clock A. M., in the fifty-fifth year of his age. Surely a great and good man has fallen in our Israel! He had a collegiate education, was soundly converted to God when about twenty years of age, soon entered the ministry, and gave evidence of a warm heart, and of a powerful and comprehensive mind. I have been intimately acquainted with him for upward of twenty years, and in all my intercourse with him have I ever found him a warm and affectionate friend, and though possessing a giant intellect, he manifested the simplicity of a child and the humility of a true disciple of Jesus Christ. His spirit was tender and affectionate in an eminent degree. I loved him as a Christian brother, venerated him as a

Christian minister, and admired him as a powerful writer. In preaching he laid hold on the grandest truths, and was exceedingly powerful. We have not his fellow remaining. How mysterious the providence of God, that such a man should be taken away in the very zenith of his usefulness, while so many of us are left so long with our inferior powers! I returned in time to attend the meeting at Mrs. Palmer's, and there, beneath the roof where he was so often sheltered, related the scenes of his death and funeral. Sensations of the love of God pervaded my heart as I spoke of his goodness to his servant and to me. O my soul, praise the Lord for his redeeming love! I cannot describe what I then felt, and still feel, of the love of God. It is indeed 'unspeakable and full of glory.'

"'Our brother the haven hath gained,
Outflying the tempest and wind;
His rest he hath sooner obtained,
And left his companions behind,
Still toss'd on a sea of distress,
Hard toiling to make the blest shore,
Where all is assurance and peace,
And sorrow and sin are no more.'

"I know not what God may have in store for me in this world, whether I may be spared for some few years, or whether I am to die shortly; nor does it give me any trouble, for I feel as if I were fully prepared either to live or to die. Such is the amazing mercy of God in Christ Jesus toward me, a sinner saved by grace!"

Such rapturous expressions have now become the habitual language of his journal. He has got high up the acclivities of the mount of vision and sees all things below, even in "the valley and shadow of death," by the reflected light of its glory. But he is still in his probation and needs its occasional tests.

"*Sept.* 5.—Though my confidence in God is unshaken, and my peace uninterrupted, yet my heart has been burdened with a load that I cannot easily shake off. No one but he who has experience of it can comprehend the otherwise deep mystery of how the mind, while staid on God and kept in perfect peace, can nevertheless be harassed with cruel temptations, the heart torn and lacerated with sorrow of an indescribable character. Yet so it is with me at present. All this God sees necessary for my good or he would not permit it to come upon me, and I have no doubt that he will bring me through the fire without hurt.

"*Sept.* 6.—After writing the above, yesterday morning, I went in the evening to hear a sermon. It was on the peace of God, and while listening the clouds gradually dispersed from my mind, my heart was lightened of its burden, and I could praise God for his consolation. I came home, committed myself to him in prayer and faith, lay down in my bed and slept most sweetly, and when I awoke toward morning I was praising God aloud. O how sweetly and delightfully my soul rests in the Lord this morning, in him who orders all things well! So true it is that they who trust in the Lord shall never be confounded."

"*Sept.* 23.—Last Saturday and Sunday I attended a Quarterly Meeting at Stamford. I had a blessed time in preaching, Sabbath morning, on the influence of the Holy Spirit. It seemed as if the fire of His inspiration came down upon me while speaking and upon the assembly while listening, so that we were abundantly refreshed and strengthened, and felt as if we could go on our way rejoicing. I am deeply humbled under a consciousness of my utter unworthiness before God, and often wonder how it is that he condescends so abundantly to bless and comfort me. It is not surely for my sake, but for Christ's sake, and for the sake of his people whom he loves, and to whom he sends me to minister, that he pours the riches of his grace into my poor heart."

ADDRESS TO KOSSUTH.

"*Dec.* 11.—On attending the preachers' meeting on Monday I was requested to introduce them with an address to Louis Kossuth, the Hungarian hero and exile. More than a hundred Methodist preachers accompanied me on the appointed day." Dr. Bangs alluded in his address to the religious character of Kossuth, and said: "We wish especially to address you as Christian ministers, prompted, as we humbly trust, by that religion which has its seat in the heart, and that moves and sanctifies the affections, to congratulate you on your adherence to that stern religious principle which led you indignantly to reject the tempting offer of the Mussulman. He offered you liberty and protection upon condition that you should renounce your Christianity and embrace the Mohammedan faith. While some of your fellow-exiles accepted the boon on such terms, you, sir, nobly replied that you would prefer death to the abjuration of your faith. This firm adherence to Christian principle, even in the sight of a prison, as the alternative of the acceptance of the tempting bait, has endeared you to our hearts, and won for you a glory almost equal to that which surrounds the memory of the martyrs."

Kossuth, in his reply, said: "In relation to the circumstance that happened at Kutahia, there is no need to speak of it. There is no merit in it. Every honest man must be obedient to his religion, and—"

Dr. Bangs (interposing.) "But begging your pardon for interrupting you, will you please tell us whether that is a fact or not? We heard of such an offer being made."

M. Kossuth. "It is a fact. I take no merit for what I did. Every honest man would do the same. That is not worthy of being mentioned. If man be not truly faithful to his God and to his religion, would he be faithful to his country? [Applause.] I have regarded, and will always regard my unshaken confidence in the justice of God as the richest source of consolation, and the solid basis of my hopes for the future of my life, because I am intimately convinced of the justice of the cause of my unhappy land, and that it is not possible that the blessing of the Almighty God should not be allotted to its future. Very often Divine Providence takes courses which apparently cannot be understood by weak human minds, but by and by circumstances prove that even in misfortune we shall find realized at last the great truth that what God blesses is well done. Even misfortune is often only the means to come to that end and to that aim which God in his Divine providence has assigned us to pursue."

DEATH OF SUSAN O. BANGS.

"*March* 25, 1852.—Yesterday I attended the funeral of Susan O. Bangs, wife of my son Nathan. What a loss has he sustained in the death of such a wife! She was one of the best of mothers in training her children, as well as the best of wives. She professed religion and joined the Church about three years since, and though she enjoyed peace with God, yet her faith was feeble, and she often trembled in view of death. She lingered some time with consumption, and shortly before her death the great desire of her heart was granted. Some of her Christian friends were singing the hymn beginning,

"'O thou God of my salvation,
My redeemer from all sin.'

When they came to the words,

"'Angels now are hov'ring round us,
Unperceived amid the throng;
Wond'ring at the love that crowns us,
Glad to join our holy song:
Halleluiah,
Love and praise to Christ belong!'

though she had been scarcely able to articulate a word intelligibly, her countenance suddenly lit up with a heavenly radiance, she waved her emaciated hand, and broke forth in a song of holy triumph, shouting 'Victory, victory, victory, in the blood of the Lamb!' After she calmed down a little she called her two eldest children (boys, the only ones able to understand her) and gave them her dying charge, then addressed her weeping husband and all the friends present, and gave directions respecting her funeral. In this peaceful frame of mind she remained until she died, once giving intimation that she saw the spirit of her little child who had died about a year since, and she sunk sweetly into the arms of death without a struggle or a groan. I praise God for giving me this testimony among so many others of the power of religion."

CHAPTER XXVI.

THE GENERAL CONFERENCE OF 1852.

At the New York East Conference of 1851 Dr. Bangs was again elected delegate to the General Conference. "Four years ago," he writes, "a strong current of prejudice was set in motion against me in one of our papers, because of my views on subjects connected with the late division of the Church, and with the editorial course of that paper. I was, therefore, left out of the delegation to the General Conference at that time. This, however, never gave me a moment's uneasiness. I knew that, having acted in the fear of God, he would take care of the consequences. My brethren have now elected me by a large majority on the first ballot. I thank God that I have not lost their confidence, for they have given me sufficient evidence of their respect and love in this and in a thousand other instances during my ministerial life." His name was preceded on the list by that of his old friend, Dr. Laban Clark, and followed by that of his brother, Heman Bangs. Both his name and kindred were represented by three delegates at this session.

The General Conference assembled in Boston, May 1, 1852. Dr. Bangs rejoiced to stand again among the representatives of the Church in a comparatively tranquil session of its supreme body, for the great controversy which had agitated its deliberations during so many years had passed away, for the present at least. His extreme age exempted him from any onerous services in the Conference; he was chairman of no committee, and member of but one or two. His voice was seldom heard in the proceedings, and then chiefly in suggestions of parliamentary order, which his long familiarity with the body enabled him to make.

THE METHODIST PRESS.

He attempted a reform which he deemed of urgent importance in the conduct of the journals of the Church, by moving the resolution, "That all the editors and correspondents of periodicals under the patronage of this General Conference be instructed to avoid, as far as practicable, all personalities in controversies which may arise, and in no case to admit an anonymous writer to assail any man's character, either in or out of the Church." Allusion has already been made to his difficulties with one of the Church papers, and the alleged management of its editor against his election as a delegate to the preceding General Conference. He deemed himself traduced in its columns. The paper became noted for both the frequency and the ability of its sarcasm, especially for its attacks on Methodist preachers who differed from it on public questions. Dr. Bangs deplored the moral influence of its example, and considered it the more perilous for the unquestionable skill of its satires. He feared that, from its supreme position among the Church organs, its example would be copied, and the denominational press be thus generally perverted. It was in reference to these facts and fears that he introduced the present resolution. He had been one of the founders, and the first official editor of this very paper, and it seemed hard that he should, in his old age, be caricatured by it before the whole Church, which he had so long and faithfully served. But his own sufferings were past, and it was not to resent them that he now wished this moral restriction to be imposed upon the dangerous power of the incumbents of the Church press; it was for the protection of the Church and its individual preachers in the future. There were, indeed, peculiar perils besetting the organization of the Methodist press, and requiring peculiar guards. As that press, and the whole "Book Concern," are the property of the

General Conference, and the General Conference is exclusively a clerical body, the clergy exclusively own and control the vast apparatus of the literary instruction of the denomination—its books, tracts, Sunday-school publications, its powerful periodical organs stationed in all sections of the country. The election of publishers and editors being solely with the clergy in the General Conference, except the filling of vacancies in the interim of its sessions, any public question, respecting which there may be a division of opinion in this body, may become a test question in these elections. The majority may appoint representatives of its own side, and the minority, of both clergy and people, however large, be thus dependent upon their opponents for the habitual reading of their families, their habitual reading, it may be, on the very questions in controversy. Obviously such an anomalous fact requires peculiar moral guards, at least. Free discussion, however emphatically avowed, can readily be overpowered by the dominant editorial influence; it can be made even perilous to the writer who dares to avail himself of it by the indiscretion, the sarcasm of the controlling pen of the paper. Dr. Bangs believed that this had been the case in the instance alluded to. He hesitated not to express his conviction that few calamities equal to this editorial example had ever befallen the denomination, for he believed that it would infect its journalism generally with the demoralizing spirit and style of the political press of the times. This was his honest conviction and frequent assertion; whether rightly or wrongly, need not here be discussed. He did not, however, believe that such evils were inevitable, much less would he impeach the ministry with any selfish design or usurpation in this peculiar organization of its great publishing institution. The anomalous fact had been historically an accidental fact. The early Methodist ministry had begun, in a very humble way, the publication of works for the benefit of its people. It had no anticipation of the future power of this scheme. Its publishing plans came, properly enough, under the direction of the annual ministerial assemblies, and, at last, under that of the delegated quadrennial assembly. The preachers provided its first small capital; they were the real, if not indeed the only salesmen of its publications on their extended circuits. The profits of their sales augmented its capital, until at last they found under their control the largest religious publishing establishment in the world, with important subsidiary institutions, as Sunday-School and Tract Societies, and the most extensive and powerful periodical press of Protestant Christendom. The success of the enterprise was, indeed, a most honorable fact, and no one man had done more for it than Dr. Bangs. But perceiving now, as he believed, these liabilities of the abuse of so stupendous a power—a power which, belonging to a purely clerical body, might be controlled by a simple majority of that body, might be manned by representatives of a dominant party of that body, might, in all its tremendous agencies, stationed in all parts of the land, be directed in concert for or against any particular public question, or, possibly, for or against any particular man—he saw the necessity of some special moral restraints upon it, some special guards, enforced by the supreme power of the Church. Otherwise he feared that this, one of its most potent agencies for good, might, in times of public agitation and confusion, and especially in the hands of injudicious men, become one of the most potent agencies of evil. He saw but two means of safety for it: either the moral restrictions that he now proposed, or an effective unofficial press, outside of but, on all common interests of the Church, co-operative with the official press. I am not disposed to obtrude here any discussion of the expediency or inexpediency of his views on this question further than is necessary for their intelligible statement. Many of his brethren differed from him upon the subject.

It was at least a delicate and an extremely difficult one to legislate upon; it came suddenly before the General Conference, and that body saw at a glance that it could not be safely determined in the midst of its many other important questions. His resolution was, therefore, laid upon the table.

SUPERANNUATED LIFE—REVIEW.

Dr. Bangs had sat in the first delegated General Conference; he was now sitting in the last of which he was to be a member. On the first of June he made its last public prayer, and retired with the veneration of all his colleagues. But one member, besides himself, of the first General Conference which he had attended, was a delegate to the present session, his life-long friend, Laban Clark. All the bishops, all the leading officers of the Church in his early days, had now gone to the grave. He was moving among a new generation, and felt that it was time to retire and rest a little before he also should depart hence and be no more. He returned to his own Conference and took a "superannuated relation," thus concluding his active official career in the seventy-fifth year of his age. Asking the reader now to glance back in his own mind over the outlines of that long, energetic, devoted career, as narrated in these pages, I am sure I do not risk much in pronouncing that the lives of few, if indeed of any other men in the history of American Methodism surpass it in fidelity, in steadfast devotion to the Church, in successful labors for its substantial and enduring interests, or in exemplary personal piety. He had received from the authorities of the Church fifty consecutive annual appointments, and including his first year in the itinerancy, when he was employed by his presiding elder, he performed fifty-one years of ministerial service. Twenty-nine of these were spent in the pastoral office, eight in the book agency, eight in Church editorship, nearly five in the missionary secretaryship, and between one or two in the presidency of the Wesleyan University. He sat in all the General Conferences, save one, from 1808 to 1852; and he was, as we have seen, a chief actor, if not indeed the chief actor, in the most important measures of these quadrennial sessions. His personal history has thus far been, more perhaps than that of any other man, a history of his denomination. Of his services in founding or promoting the leading interests of the Church, those which have most contributed to its development and permanence, I need here add nothing; they have appeared throughout this narrative. A bishop of the denomination says that "his pulpit and pastoral labors in this city and in his other appointments were highly useful to the Churches. His sermons were sound in doctrine, sententious in style, affectionate in spirit, and direct and pungent in application. In his advanced age they were less energetic in manner, but equally edifying. In the pastoral work and the administration of discipline he had few equals in the days of his strength. In the office of presiding elder he was pre-eminently useful. When without a pastoral relation, and filling other highly responsible and very laborious departments of service, he was accustomed to preach regularly. His sermons on special occasions were very able and useful. Since he has held a superannuated relation to his Conference he has preached frequently most of the time. Dr. Bangs loved to preach, and in his later years was accustomed to discourse on the deep things of God with great delight to himself and great profit to the Church."*

He was now to enjoy an enviable evening of life, comfortably sheltered in the home of his eldest son Lemuel, blessed with the kindest ministrations of affection and veneration from innumerable friends, preaching as his declining strength would allow from church to church, using his pen occasionally in the public papers, attending, with notable punctuality, the "Board Meet-

* His funeral sermon by Bishop Janes.

ings" of the philanthropic institutions of the denomination, especially of the Missionary Society, where his seat was, by courtesy, invariably on the platform of the president; and attending social meetings of devotion, especially that which was held for the "promotion of holiness" at the house of his former catechetical disciple, Mrs. Palmer, of which he had become the virtual president, and where it was his habit and one of his choicest pleasures to remain after the public services to join the family and numerous guests in religious sociability at the tea-table.

DEATH OF A SON.

Serene and beautiful were these declining years; but the tranquil and radiant picture had also its shades. On Sept. 7, 1852, he writes: "Yesterday, at about four o'clock A.M., my son, William M'Kendree, died in great peace of mind, in the forty-second year of his age and the twenty-second of his itinerant ministry. I felt the stroke most sensibly, but was comforted in the belief that he had gone to his rest. Such 'saint-like patience' he exhibited through all his sickness, such meekness and humility as I scarcely ever witnessed, and he truly 'fell asleep in Jesus;' for so peaceful was his death, not a struggle or groan escaping him, that the bystanders did not perceive the moment when the spirit fled.

"It does not become me to say much of his excellencies or of his defects; but thus much I may say, that, in the judgment of all who knew him, he was a man of undoubted piety, a close student, of an acute, comprehensive mind, always retiring in his manners, and unobtrusive in his conduct.

"*Sept.* 9.—Yesterday his obsequies were attended in a very solemn and appropriate manner, his friends and mine manifesting the most tender sympathy. O how consoling it is to have such friends at such a time! After his corpse was deposited in the earth I felt in a great measure relieved, and could say, 'The Lord gave, and the Lord hath taken away; blessed be the name of the Lord.'"

Rev. Dr. Sprague has devoted several pages of his "Annals of the American Pulpit" to the memory of William M'Kendree Bangs. Rev. Dr. M'Clintock says in that sketch: "He possessed rare powers of investigation, of analysis, and of reasoning. He had a remarkable command of the English language, and selected his words with great taste and judgment. Whether conversing familiarly with his friends, discussing some difficult abstract question, preaching to a congregation, or addressing a throne of grace, his style was remarkably adapted to the subject and the occasion. His sermons were clear, systematic, easy to be understood, neither encumbered with extraneous matter, nor disfigured by learned pedantry. They were characterized by a beautiful simplicity, and bore the impress altogether of a great mind. His manner in the pulpit was solemn and dignified, expressive of a deep sense of his responsibility to God for the souls committed to his charge. Among his friends he was social and communicative, but among strangers he was reserved, and not inclined to make new acquaintances. He was kind and affectionate, very conscientious, and a devout and sincere Christian.

"His talents, learning, and piety would have placed him in eminent positions in the Church had his health been equal to the efforts necessary to sustain them. No critical mind can examine his articles in the Methodist Quarterly Review for 1836 and 1837 without becoming convinced that the Methodist Church lost, in the death of William M'Kendree Bangs, one of the noblest intellects ever committed to its care. His criticisms on Richard Watson's 'Institutes' show an acuteness and comprehensiveness of the highest order. He was eminently fitted to be a theologian, and, with good health and longer life, he would probably have become a standard authority in Divinity among his brethren. Bishop

Hedding's opinion of his capacity, formed upon these writings, was most flattering. The bishop pronounced him the ablest theological thinker in the denomination."

HAPPY OLD AGE.

"*Oct.* 26.—Yesterday I attended a meeting at Mrs. Palmer's. There were many testimonies given in favor of 'perfect love,' and among others, a brother preacher remarked that a devoted Christian, when on his dying bed, said that Satan appeared as his accuser, reminding him of this sin, and then of another, and finally the dying saint asked him if that was all? The tempter seemed to answer 'No; such and such a one you have committed.' 'Is that all?' 'Yes, but it is enough.' 'Well, then,' said the dying saint, 'write underneath, "The blood of Jesus Christ cleanseth from ALL sin,"' and the tempter flew, and left him triumphing in God his salvation! This, with other testimonies equally pointed, thrilled through my soul like electricity, and I at last rose, as I believed, under the influence of the Holy Spirit, and said, 'I did not know that I should have anything to communicate, but while musing upon what I have heard the fire has burned in my heart, and I must speak and declare the loving-kindness of the Lord.' God sent the word to the hearts of his people, and they seemed melted down into tenderness before him. I concluded by remarking that, this salvation of which we had heard was of God most emphatically. That neither our repentance, prayers, faith, nor anything else we had done or could do saved us from our sins, but that God, by the operation of the Holy Spirit, wrought the whole of it. This doctrine humbles us in the dust, strips the soul of all self-dependence, and leads it to ascribe the glory of our salvation to the grace of God in Christ Jesus. The work is wrought in the heart by the Holy Spirit. This, and this alone, destroys sin, and fills the soul with peace and joy in believing. I believe God blessed these remarks to the good of all present. I felt my own heart warmed with Divine fire, and my understanding illuminated. After my return home, in secret prayer I enjoyed such an access to the throne of grace as I have not felt for a long time, and my soul exulted in the beams of the Sun of righteousness. Glory and honor be to God for his unbounded love!"

"*Jan.* 1853.—Another year has rolled around, and yet I am permitted to live, a monument of God's mercy! I desire here to record my sense of his goodness. When I took a superannuated relation at the last Conference I was fearful that my health and spirits would run down, and I dreaded the thought of giving up all responsibility or charge of any particular branch of the Church; but the effect of the change has been directly the reverse, my health has gradually gained, and my spirits have been more buoyant than usual, for all which I praise God most sincerely. It is true, I have endeavored to keep myself busy in reading, writing, preaching, and attending various meetings for the promotion of the cause of God, and more especially the cause of holiness, in doing which I have been abundantly strengthened and comforted, and I look forward with an increasingly bright anticipation of everlasting happiness.

"What abundant cause have I to praise God for the manner in which he has dealt with me all the days of my life! I am now in my seventy-fifth year, surrounded with all the blessings of life, so that I want for no good thing to make it agreeable, and, above all, enjoy peace of mind, and a firm hope of eternal life. Surely I ought to be thankful to my heavenly Father for his unbounded love to me, a sinner, a sinner saved by grace.

"My children are grown up around me, all blessed with temporal prosperity; some of them are religious, all steady and moral, and all show a tender regard for my welfare. How thankful I am that I have not had a profligate in my family, though two of my children, a daughter and son, have suffered aberration of mind. This, to be sure, was a keen affliction, known only to a father who is called upon to experience it."

On his birthday he resumes this grateful strain, now almost continually recurring in his manuscript.

"*May* 2.—This day I am seventy-five years of age. What a miracle of the divine goodness am I! The last year has been one of much mercy. My health has much improved, so that I have gained ten pounds in weight, am able to move about nearly as well as ever I could, to preach once every Sabbath, sometimes twice, and attend other meetings for the promotion of the cause of Christ. After rising from bed I endeavored anew to consecrate myself to God, praising him for all his past blessings, and praying him to accept the offering I thus make to him, whose I am, and whom I endeavor to serve in the spirit. I do feel indeed that he accepts me, unworthy as I am; that he lifts up the light of his countenance upon my soul and gives me peace. O that my heart, as well as my lips, may praise him.

"'God of my life, to thee
My cheerful soul I give!
Thy goodness bade me be,
And still prolongs my days:
I see my natal hour return,
And bless the day that I was born.'"

He was able to attend several camp-meetings this summer, preaching at them all, and enjoying their social and Christian privileges with the zest of earlier years. He was reminded occasionally, however, of his advancing age by the return of his former symptoms of cerebral congestion, sometimes suffering brief periods of unconsciousness. "In all things," however, he "gives thanks." "Indeed," he writes, "often when I kneel before the Lord in secret my prayer is turned into praise, so that I cannot but thank God with a full and overflowing heart for his numerous acts of loving-kindness manifested to me and mine. Glory! glory be to God most high!"

Thus pass slowly and tranquilly his declining years; they are seldom marked now by any very salient events, and their peaceful tenor, full of quiet enjoyment and moral beauty, is sufficiently indicated by the occasional citations already given. Pages could be filled with similar passages; they would, however, not only be superfluous, but monotonous, notwithstanding their devout spirit. Let us then pass rapidly along his remaining course, pausing only at its most marked incidents.

OLD REMINISCENCES.

In the spring of 1855 he received the following letter —full of grateful reminiscences—from his early colaborer in Canada, the veteran William Case:

"ALNWICK, *March* 16, 1855.

"REVEREND AND DEAR BROTHER: What scenes and changes have passed since we commenced our ministry! Most of our early associates in the ministry in this country have passed triumphantly to the great reward; yet the Church is supplied abundantly and ably. The membership, too, have increased from scores to hundreds and thousands. Once we addressed the few in private dwellings; larger assemblies were congregated in barns, for churches were 'few and far between.' We now preach to thousands; churches have arisen, large and numerous, in our cities, towns, and circuits! Brother, after more than half a century of toil, you, perhaps, are scarcely able to visit the scenes of your former labors. Would it not be delightful to do so? Your appearance among the descendants of your early Christian friends would fill them with delight; and could you not do more for God and the Church by traveling at large than by tracing a thousand times the streets of a city? Your experience in the things of God, your counsel in the interests of the Church, would have its influence favorably in the *closing scene* of so lengthened a ministerial course. Could you not again visit Canada, the land of your youth, of your conversion to God, your early ministry, and of the mission field you have aided to cultivate? The railroad would bring you to Kingston or to Hamilton in a few hours. Once we toiled on horseback through wild forests, from two and a half to four miles an hour; now forty miles is the speed we move! Brother, try it before leaving for the 'fairer climes.' Sickness prevented last season your meeting your appointment in Toronto. Perhaps you may be with us at our Conference in London the first Wednesday in June. The two or three hundreds of Canada preachers would be happy to meet you there.

"During the winter just passing I have enjoyed the unspeakable pleasure of visiting the scenes of our early labors, yours and mine. I passed through Hallowell, Belleville, Kingston, Elizabethtown, Brockville, Augusta, Matilda, and thence to Bytown, (Ottawa City;) thence to Perth and Wolford, on the Rideau; then home, through a portion of the northern new settlements. In this route I found some, though few, of our former religious friends now living. Arthur Youmans, Rufus Shorey, Mrs. M'Lean, (formerly Widow Coatt,) and William Brown, are yet living, at the ages of from eighty to ninety-one. Youmans (at the latter age) was one of the members of the first class formed in Hallowell, January, 1793, by Darius Dunham. A class paper of the same class was written by Elijah Wolsey in 1795. But the parents of the Johnsons, Congers, Van Deusens, Robbins, Germans, Huffs, Emburys, Detlors, Clarkes, Parrots, Maddens, Keders, Colemans, Hecks, Coons, Brouses, Aults, Dulmages, Laurences, are all gone; yet they live in their examples of piety, integrity, hospitality, and Christian benevolence. These virtues are prominent, to a great extent, in their numerous descendants. The progeny bears a striking impress of their worthy patriarchal fathers.

"You will remember the names of Samuel and Jacob Heck, of Augusta, and the Emburys, of Bay of Quinte—the former the sons of Paul Heck and his worthy companion, the parents of Methodism in the city of New York and in America. The parents are gone, and the sons have followed them in the way of holiness to glory; but a numerous train of grandchildren are pursuing the Christian course 'their fathers trod'—intelligent, pious, and wealthy. '*Blessed are the meek: for they shall inherit the earth.*' A few years since I visited John Embury and his worthy companion. He was then ninety-eight years old. The scenes of early Methodism in New York were vivid in his recollection, and he referred to them as readily as if they had recently occurred. He said: 'My uncle, Philip Embury, was a great man—a powerful preacher—a very powerful preacher. I had heard many ministers before, but nothing reached my heart till I heard my Uncle Philip preach. I was then about sixteen. The Lord has since been my trust and portion. I am now ninety-eight. Yes, my Uncle Philip was a great preacher.' After this interview he lived about a year, and died suddenly, as he rose from prayer in his family, at the age of ninety-nine. The Emburys, Detlors, Millers, Maddens, Switzers, of Bay of Quinte, are numerous and pious, and some of them ministers of the Gospel, all firmly grounded in Methodism. Their Palatine origin is prominent in their health, integrity, and industry; and their steadfast piety by Irish training on Mr. Wesley's knee. Old Mrs. Detlor, forty years ago, told me, 'When a child, in Ireland, Mr. Wesley took me on his knee, when I sang for him

"'Children of the heavenly King,
As we journey let us sing.'

"You will remember Rev. William Brown, of Wolford, River Rideau. He was once, as you know, one of our most efficient and talented traveling ministers. He is now eighty-six. A few weeks since I spent a Sabbath at his house. He is yet vigorous in mind, his voice pretty clear and full. He took part in the exercises of the Quarterly Meeting, opened the love-feast, and addressed the congregation at the close of the sermon. He spoke of the early ministers, and the piety of our steadfast saints, who had gone to glory, and seemed animated with the prospect of soon joining them in the song of redemption."

HIS GOLDEN WEDDING.

April 23, 1856, he writes, "was the fiftieth anniversary of my wedding-day. A large number of my friends attended at my son's house." The following account, from the Christian Advocate, will show how it was observed: "A private social entertainment of a rare but most agreeable character took place at the residence of Mr. Lemuel Bangs on Wednesday evening of last week. The occasion was the fiftieth anniversary of the wedding of Dr. Nathan and Mrs. Mary Bangs. There was a large assemblage of Dr. Bangs's personal and social friends, who came to felicitate the venerable couple at their entrance upon the second half century of their married life. The doctor's descendants were also present to the second generation, the *infantry* of the family only being absent. There were none of those who were witnesses of the event which was commemorated, but there were none upon whom the occasion did not exert a genial and happy influence. The pervading spirit was happily represented by the Rev. Dr. Foster, to whom an opportunity was given in the course of the evening, and on behalf of those assembled, to make a congratulatory address to the doctor and his lady, in which he briefly, but most touchingly expressed the feelings suggested by the occasion, and pictured the contrast between the wedding fifty years ago and its anniversary at that hour. From 1856 to 1806: what a retrospect in the lives of those to whom he conveyed the greetings and the kind wishes of their assembled friends. To this congratulatory address the doctor made an appropriate and happy reply. Dr. Reese and Mrs. Palmer also contributed to the festivity by two appropriate hymns, which were sung by the company, and an elegant supper concluded this memorable reunion."

An elegant little *brochure*, entitled "Memorial of the Golden Wedding of the Rev. Nathan and Mrs. Mary Bangs, April 23, 1856," was published, giving a full account of the ceremonies of the occasion, and finely executed portraits of the aged couple. There were present one hundred and eleven persons, including many of the most familiarly known preachers and laymen of New York Methodism, and no less than twenty-eight bearing the name of Bangs. After Rev. Dr. Foster had addressed to Dr. Bangs the congratulations of the assembly the doctor replied, sketching somewhat his long career. "We have of course," he said, "passed through some afflictions, and had our share of toil and trials, as well as seasons of prosperity and times of rejoicing; but in them all the Lord has been with us, to sustain and comfort us, and his people have treated us kindly, and been ever ready to supply our wants. The first year of our marriage we went to Quebec, where Methodism was known only as a term of reproach: there we labored hard, and suffered a little without seeing much fruit of our labors, only so far as to open the way for our successors. The next year we were stationed in Montreal, where, in the midst of many privations, God was with us and blessed our labors, and comforted our own souls. The next year, 1808, we moved to the United States, and were stationed on the Delaware Circuit, in the midst of our relations, where we enjoyed many consolations, though the labor was great. Thence we went the next year on to the Durham Circuit, where I held a public controversy with a Hopkinsian minister, and wrote the first book I ever published, a small pamphlet against the "Christians," so called. Those were then comparatively new countries, the rides long, and the fare not the best; but the people were kind, and the Lord was with us and blessed our labors. The next year, 1810, we were stationed in the city of New York, where there were only three churches and five preaching places; there was only one parsonage, that in John-street, consequently we had to occupy parts of houses, but were received and treated with great kindness. All our wants were supplied, and God owned and blessed our labors abundantly.

"From that time to this, with the exception of about eight years, we have resided in this city, filling various stations, as preacher, book agent, editor, corresponding secretary of the Missionary Society, and presiding elder; and O, what has God wrought for the Church since that time!

"In 1806, the year we were married, the Methodist Episcopal Church numbered 130,570; it now numbers, including the North and South, 1,320,566. And what abundant cause have we, personally, for gratitude! During all this time God has been with us in adversity and prosperity, supplying our wants in the time of need, blessing us temporally and spiritually, lengthening out our years—my own to seventy-eight, and my wife's to sixty-eight—bearing with our infirmities; and though we have had our share of afflictions of body and mind, our consolations have been great, and we have found that all things have worked together for our good.

"My beloved wife has been a fruitful vine. We have had eleven children, six sons and five daughters, and we have fifteen grandchildren. Seven of our children are now living, five sons and two daughters; and four of our sons are married, and live near by us. In the house of the oldest of these we are now assembled, surrounded by the rest of my children and grandchildren, all who are able to be here; and with this assemblage of affectionate and Christian friends we are permitted to celebrate the fiftieth anniversary of our wedding-day! I must say that this, if not the happiest, yet is one of the happiest days of my life."

The "Memorial" adds: "The meeting of early friends, whom circumstances and the varied interests of life had separated for many years, was most cordial and sincere; the friendly grasp of hands, and the hearty recognition of faces long unseen, led to many exclamations of happy surprise, and presented altogether a scene rarely to be met with. From every part of the city were observed those who were early engaged in the service of the Church, well known to each other, but not often meeting around the social board. The old, the middle-aged, the young, were alike represented, and all alike were enthusiastically alive to the interest of the occasion. In the midst of this friendly enthusiasm supper was announced, when the company partook of the rich repast and soon after separated for home. Thus ended this rare festive occasion, owing much of its interest to the eldest beloved daughter-in-law of the aged couple. At her suggestion it was commenced, and through her perseverance and happy management it was gracefully accomplished."

DEATH OF ANOTHER SON.

The next domestic event noticed in his journals is one of the shades of the serene picture. "My dear son Nathan died on the 17th of December, 1856. I was with him much of the time during his sickness, and of course witnessed his sufferings, and could but sympathize with his sorrowing wife. He was, indeed, a remarkable child in some respects, for I do not remember of his ever having given me a cross word, but until he set up business for himself my word was his law." The following obituary, written by Rev. Dr. Foster, gives a true account of his character, conversion, and death.

"He was born October 21, 1813, in Sharon, Connecticut, and died of erysipelas on the 17th of December, in the city of New York. Though naturally of a most amiable and lovely character, and scrupulously careful in the observance of all the requirements of an elevated standard of morality—one of the best of sons, kindest of husbands, and most upright of citizens—it was not until August, 1855, in the forty-second year of his age, that he made a profession of religion. Always gentle and quiet in his disposition, regular in his habits, and punctual in attendance upon the public worship of God, his religious life was scarcely, in its external manifestations, attended with any observable change. The marked change was in his interior experience. His soul was brought into living, conscious communion with God, and he was enabled to feel that he was a child of God and an heir of heaven. A short time before his death he remarked to his father, 'I have been under a gloom for three or four days, but now all is peace and tranquillity, and I am perfectly resigned to the will of God.' This was his dying testimony, as he shortly afterward became incapable of communicating with those who watched mournfully about his dying bed. The large class of intelligent gentlemen connected with the book trade in its various departments throughout the country will long cherish his memory as a most worthy member of their fraternity, and as an ornament of the great business firm of which he was a prominent member, that of Bangs, Brother, & Co. His funeral was numerously attended by a thoughtful and sorrowing public."

The death of this son was a severe blow to the father. He bore the father's name and honored it in the business world in the highest department of mercantile life, the book trade. At the sixty-fifth Annual Trade Sale ex-Mayor James Harper, of the house of Harper & Brothers, addressed the assemblage respecting the deceased. "We all," he said, "knew him, and not only respected him in our business relations, but we cherished the highest esteem for him personally as a true-hearted man. I knew him intimately for many years; my associations with him are now hallowed by his death. The recollection of them saddens me, especially on an occasion like the present, when I see so many old friends and familiar faces. Most of us now present were also here in September last, a little more than six months ago. Our deceased friend was here among us. Successive trade sales have made us long familiar with his tall, active form—his straightforward, manly look—his energetic business capacities—his courteous and amiable demeanor. At each sale we had been welcomed by the hearty, frank grasp of a true hand, always acting from a warm, true heart. That hand now lies cold in death. He was in the prime of vigorous manhood, dearly beloved by his family and friends, endeared to them by many domestic virtues. Possessed of rare tact, energy, and perseverance, and of a high sense of justice and honor, he was an ornament to our trade. God, in his all-wise providence, has seen fit to suddenly remove him from among us. Let us fondly cherish the memory of our deceased friend. Let us also cherish it worthily, by resolving that our intercourse with one another shall be kindly and amicable, so that if before we meet again death should remove another from among us, our remembrance of the departed one may be as kindly and pleasant as our remembrance now is of our late esteemed friend and brother, Nathan Bangs, Jr."

Resolutions of respect for his memory were also passed on this occasion.

CHAPTER XXVII.

PEACE IN SUFFERING.

On the 18th of February, 1857, Dr. Bangs records in his journal: "I have been very sick. About six weeks ago I was suddenly seized with chills and fever, shook all over like an aspen leaf, and soon seemed consuming with a hot fever. A homeopathic physician, Dr. Palmer, was sent for, and in about three hours, by the blessing of God, he succeeded in subduing the fever by inducing a profuse perspiration, so that I was measurably relieved. When I came to myself, for I was delirious, I found my children standing around my bed watching me with great anxiety, for they thought me in danger. In the midst of my bodily distress my soul was wonderfully borne up with the consolations of the Holy Spirit, and I could joyfully exclaim, in the strong language of John Wesley:

"'O Love, thou bottomless abyss!
My sins are swallowed up in thee;
Cover'd is my unrighteousness,
Nor spot of guilt remains on me:
While Jesus' blood, through earth and skies,
Mercy, free, boundless mercy, cries.'

"I had three attacks, one every second day, of this dreadful fever, though the last was comparatively slight. When it left me my strength was much prostrated; but I was free from pain, my mind buoyant, and my heart filled with love to God and man. Every night when I laid me down to rest these words came sweetly to my mind,

"'Jesus protects; my fears, begone:
What can the Rock of Ages move?
Safe in thy arms I lay me down,—
Thine everlasting arms of love,'

and I could calmly resign myself to the care of the Divine love, and rest without any fear. Nay, I could look upon death with pleasure, having not only no fears, but a joyful anticipation of future bliss, and the pleasure of meeting the friends of Jesus who had gone before me into the land of rest."

RELATIONS OF FAITH AND SANCTIFICATION.

"*March* 15.—On the 10th inst. I attended a meeting for the promotion of holiness at Mrs. Palmer's. This I did in the spirit of self-sacrifice, as I felt it my duty to speak against certain theories which have sometimes been broached there and elsewhere. I prayed most earnestly to God that he would be pleased to direct my thoughts and words, so that I might speak forth the words of 'truth and soberness' in love and meekness. I rose under a trembling sense of my responsibility, and remarked that I had been a minister of the Gospel for about fifty-six years; that I was converted or justified about fifty-seven years ago, and in about six months afterward received the blessing of sanctification; that both blessings were so clear, and the evidence of them so distinct, that I have never had any doubt of them from that day to this, though I must confess, to my shame, that I have not lived in the enjoyment of sanctification at all times since; yet whenever I recurred to it, either in conversation or preaching, it always set my soul on fire.

"I did not make up my judgment on this subject hastily. In addition to reading the sacred Scriptures with diligence and prayer, and conversing with God's people in reference to it, I read Mr. Wesley's 'Plain Account of Christian Perfection,' some portions of Mr. Fletcher's writings on the subject, and was fully convinced of its necessity, nature, and fruits, so that I sought it understandingly, and found it, to the joy of my heart. From that day to this I have read most that has been written by various authors, in our own and other communions, on the subject of holiness, and I am not conscious of having deviated during the fifty-six years of my ministry from the theory marked out by Mr. Wesley, which I first embraced. On the contrary, everything I have heard or read, whether written by enemies or friends, has only confirmed me in the correctness of Mr. Wesley's views.

"I fully believe that we are both justified and sanctified by grace, through faith in the Lord Jesus Christ, and that when so justified or sanctified the Holy Spirit sets his seal upon our hearts, and gives us an evidence that the work is done. All those Scriptures, therefore, which speak of the necessity of having faith in God, of believing in the Lord Jesus Christ, etc., I need hardly say I fully embrace, and urge upon others as necessary conditions of justification and sanctification. But what is this faith by which the believer is sanctified? Though the holy Scriptures frequently speak of faith, and urge its necessity, saying that 'without faith it is impossible to please Him,' yet I recollect but one place in which a definition of faith is given, and that is Heb. xi, 1, where it is said 'Now faith is the substance of things hoped for, and the evidence of things not seen.'

"The *substance* of things hoped for! What are the things hoped for? They are everything future to the Christian; that is, heaven with all its glories, embracing every intermediate blessing necessary to fit us for that holy and happy place. Now, it seems hardly proper to say that faith is now the *substance* of all these divine realities, as though we had them already in possession. This could not have been the meaning of the apostle. I think, therefore, with many good critics, that the Greek word there rendered *substance* should have been translated *confidence*, as it is so translated in a number of other places in the sacred Scriptures. Thus rendered the sense will be clear and complete: 'Now faith is the *confidence* of things hoped for, and the *evidence* of things not seen;' that is to say, all the veterans whom the apostle enumerates in the subsequent parts of that chapter, as well as all others, have had the fullest *confidence* in the truth of God's promises which relate to future glory, and, of course, have had an *evidence* through the same medium; that is, a firm *confidence* in the truth of God respecting these things.

"In exact conformity with this inspired definition of faith, Mr. Wesley gives the following definition of the faith which instrumentally sanctifies the soul: 'But what is that faith whereby we are sanctified, saved from sin, and perfected in love? 1. It is a divine evidence and conviction that *God hath promised it in the holy Scriptures.* Till we are thoroughly convinced of this, there is no moving one step further. 2. It is a divine evidence and conviction that what *God has promised he is able to perform.* 3. It is a divine evidence and conviction *that he is able and willing to do it now.* To this confidence, that God is both able and willing to sanctify us now, there needs to be added one thing more, a divine evidence and conviction *that he doth it.*'

"This definition is quoted by Mr. Fletcher with approbation, and therefore he sets his seal to its correctness. Now, it is most manifest that Mr. Wesley considered that the faith by which we are sanctified is inseparably connected with a *divine evidence and conviction that the work is done;* and hence the theory which teaches that we are *to lay all upon the altar or surrender up our hearts to God by faith in Christ, and then believe that God has accepted, or does accept the offering, without our having any evidence of the Holy Spirit that it is accepted, or having any change in our disposition, or any emotion of joy and peace, more than we had before,* is not sound, is unscriptural, and anti-Wesleyan; for the Scriptures assert that 'he that believeth on the Son of God hath the witness in himself;' and Mr. Wesley says in the above definition that 'faith is a *divine evidence and conviction* that God hath promised to sanctify all those that come unto him; that he is both able and willing to *do it*, to *do it now*, and lastly that he *doth it*.' All this is accompanied with a *divine evidence and conviction* that the *work is done;* and hence, according to him, if we believe it is done *before* we have this *divine evidence and conviction*, we believe *without evidence*, and are therefore every moment liable to deception.

"But in opposition to this view it is asserted that we have the Holy Scriptures as an evidence of the work, and Abraham is cited, who 'believed God, and it was counted to him for righteousness.' But Abraham did not derive his faith from the Holy Scriptures, for they were not written until more than four hundred years after his time. It is stated in Gen. xv that the word of the Lord came unto Abram in a vision, and during the interview with this 'word of the Lord'—probably the Lord Jesus himself—the promise was made to Abram that he should have an heir in his old age. This he firmly believed, and this faith was reckoned unto him for righteousness. Let God appear to us, and speak to our hearts through whatever medium, and bear witness to our spirits that we are justified or sanctified, and then, and not till then, are we authorized to believe it. In the very nature of things a fact, and its evidence must precede the belief in it and its evidence, otherwise we make the existence of the fact depend upon our faith, which is simply absurd. We must, therefore, be sanctified, and have an evidence of it before we have any scriptural authority to believe it; so it appears to me, for the existence of the fact and its evidence must precede our belief in their reality, otherwise we may believe as whim or fancy may dictate, having no foundation for our faith.

"To the assertion that the Holy Scriptures are our evidence I answer that the Holy Scriptures, though true and infallible, are not in themselves any evidence to *me* that I am either justified or sanctified; they simply declare who are sanctified, and give marks or evidences of the work. For instance, St. Paul says: 'Being justified by faith, we have peace with God through our Lord Jesus Christ.' Here peace with God is the evidence of my justification. Where shall I look for this peace? Not in the Scriptures, but in my own heart, and if I find it there I have a scriptural evidence that I am justified. So St. John says: 'Perfect love casteth out fear' that hath torment. This also I must find, if anywhere, in my own heart. Do I then, by careful examination, find that I am delivered from the slavish fear of death and hell, of men and devils, and of the judgment? If so I have reason, on scriptural ground, to conclude myself sanctified, more especially if I bring forth the fruits of the Spirit in my tempers and dispositions, and keep the commandments of God. These and such like evidences of sanctification were enlarged upon, and pressed home upon all present.

"But it is possible that I am deceived. How shall I detect deception? I answer, The Holy Scripture has furnished me with a test. Do I bring forth the fruits of the Spirit—'love, joy, peace, long-suffering, gentleness, goodness, faith, meekness, temperance?' If these fruits 'be in me, and abound,' then I have a right to believe that I have that Holy Spirit that produces them, for such is their excellence that the apostle says, 'Against such there is no law,' either of God or man. This test is given both to prove the truth of our sanctification, and also to detect deception should there be any, for 'the tree is known by its fruits.'

"I have referred to Abraham. After the messengers left him he offered a sacrifice to God. This sacrifice, as well as all the sacrifices under the Mosaic law, was typical of the sacrifice of Christ, and they had their complete fulfillment when he died upon the cross, so that 'he is the end of the law to every one that believeth,' that is, the law of sacrifices had its end completely accomplished by the sacrifice of Christ upon the cross; and hence, all we have to do in order to salvation, including justification and sanctification, is to receive him by faith, and when we thus receive him we are so saved, and have an evidence of it by the internal testimony of the Spirit.

"But this faith is always accompanied by works. Even the penitent sinner, seeking the pardon of his sins, must repent and 'do works meet for repentance;' he must 'cease to do evil, and learn to do well,' according to his light and opportunity. And the penitent believer must 'walk in the light, as God is in the light;' that is, he must go forward in every good word and work, 'grow in grace and in the knowledge of the Lord Jesus,' in order to exercise that faith in Jesus Christ by which he obtains the sanctifying love of God, and this is according to the scriptural representation of the faith of Abraham. 'Seest thou how faith wrought together with his works, and by works was faith made perfect.' This was the substance of what I said, as nearly as I can recollect it, and I believe my memory does not fail me, for it was deeply impressed upon my heart, and I had deliberated for some days on the subject and thoroughly digested it in my mind; had prayed over it, most earnestly had prayed God to direct my thoughts and words, that I might speak according to his will and word. I arose under a trembling sense of my responsibility, and spoke, I fully believe, in the fear and love of God with all the deliberation I could command, knowing that I must give an account in the great day for my words. I felt, indeed, the vows of God upon me, and spoke as a minister of the Lord Jesus, even in his name, who had accounted me worthy to be put in trust with the Gospel. I therefore solemnly warned those who professed to believe that merely because they had laid all upon the altar, or had surrendered up their hearts to God, he had adopted them, without any evidence of the Holy Spirit that they were adopted, or any change in their disposition, or any emotion of love and joy, to beware that they did not deceive themselves, as I greatly feared some had done; for if this be all that is required of us, namely, to believe that we are accepted before we have a witness that we are, it is to believe without evidence, and hence I fully believe that many have been deceived and are deceiving themselves daily. I therefore exhorted them to examine themselves carefully and prayerfully, and not to rest satisfied with anything short of the witness and fruits of the Holy Spirit.

"I ought, perhaps, to add that I do not think, nor did I intend to insinuate, that all who thus speak are deceived. Their hearts are better than their heads, and how far God may make allowance for merely mental errors is not for me to say; but this I know, that he bears much and long with such infirmities, or he would never have borne with me as he has. Hence we are commanded to 'bear each other's infirmities, and so fulfill the law of Christ.'

"But the error at which I aim is not a mere incidental error. It is, in my judgment, a fundamental one, as it strikes at the root of experimental religion, for if I may believe myself sanctified without any evidence of the Holy Spirit that the work has been wrought, I may believe anything else before I have any evidence of it, and this tends to destroy all rational and scriptural belief, as it supersedes the necessity of evidence in faith; I may believe or not, as whim or fancy dictate." *

DEATH OF A DAUGHTER.

On the 21st of October he lost by death his daughter, Mary Eliza Bangs—one of the dearest of his children. One of her intimate friends † writes: "She was born at Rhinebeck, N.Y., October 31, 1815, and from her infancy

* Dr. Bangs left a written charge that if any public use should be made of his manuscript journal this important passage should not be omitted.

† Mrs. C. R. Deuel Wright.

may be said to have been a child of God, for at her baptism such a heavenly influence rested upon those assembled that the Rev. Freeborn Garrettson, who baptized her, remarked, 'I had such nearness to God while praying for that infant that I believe the Lord regenerated her soul in the baptismal rite.' During her early childhood she evinced great seriousness of thought, ofttimes surprising her parents with the depth of her remarks on religious subjects, causing them to feel that their little daughter was indeed a child of rare excellence and acquirements. When she was in her thirteenth year she felt the need of a direct witness of the Spirit that she was indeed born again. She sought the Lord with all her heart, and was most powerfully blessed with the assurance of her adoption. To use her own expression, 'I felt that all within and without praised the Lord the most high; even the trees of the grove seemed to break forth in rejoicing.' From that time until her death she never lost the witness that she was a child of God. A short time after her conversion her mother's health became feeble, and, young as she was, she manifested so much stability of character, united with mature judgment, that her parents felt no hesitancy in confiding to her the culture and training, to a great degree, of the younger children, and thus early she was taught the lesson of self-sacrifice, which so eminently characterized her through life. Added to this charge, the wife of a beloved brother died, leaving an infant son, who was placed under her care, and upon whom she bestowed all the affection and attentions of a mother. A few years elapsed when a second brother met with the same bereavement, and two more motherless children were added to her cherishing care, at her own request. Hers was indeed a love which knew no burdens, for at the death of the wife of her third brother the dying mother gave her infant to Mary, thus proving the strong confidence her whole family had in her capacity and affection. Thus was the life of our beloved friend spent in doing good. In the Sabbath-school, the Bible class, and the Class and prayer-meeting, she was always listened to with the deepest interest. She was collected, serious, yet cheerful. Her surprising gift in addressing the throne of grace often led her father to call upon her to conduct the religious devotions of family worship. Her paternal uncle remarked on the day of her death that he had never known her to speak ill of a human being. She had been so long taught in the school of self-sacrifice, that she seemed to have an abiding resignation to the will of her heavenly Father, and when called to part by death with one after another of her brothers and sisters, she would say, 'I must resign them; I must not murmur; He who loves me knows what is best, and we ought, as Christians, under every circumstance of life, to learn to say, 'Good is the will of the Lord.' For several years her health seemed to decline, but she continued to administer to the comfort and happiness of all around her, in entire forgetfulness of self, and when urged to take less care of others and more of herself, would reply, 'I shall soon be better; it is only temporary.' On the morning of her death we found she was fast sinking. She remarked, 'How weak and helpless we are when sickness takes hold of us.' We repeated the words, 'But Jesus does make a dying bed feel soft as downy pillows are.' She turned to the friend addressing her, and asked, 'Do you think I am dying?' She replied, 'Dear Mary, you will soon be in the celestial city; you are going home to die no more.' 'Do you think so?' was the calm and significant reply. 'I am willing, for the Lord always knows what is best for me, and his will, not mine, be done.' A little while after another friend came to her bedside, and commenced repeating, 'Though I walk through the valley and shadow of death,' etc. Mary took up the words of the verse, and repeated them several times, laying great stress on the words, 'his rod and his staff, they comfort me.' An hour or two after she said she had such a view of her future home that she felt she would soon be with her Lord and Saviour. To her afflicted mother she said, 'Don't weep for me; it won't be long; you will soon come.' She asked for her sister, and putting her arm around her neck, as if to leave some parting wish, said, 'Dear Rebecca, live only for heaven. I know you are striving, but go on.' About one hour before her death her uncle, Rev. Heman Bangs, approached the bed, and taking her hand, said, 'My dear child, if Jesus is precious to you now, press my hand.' She made an effort to speak, and, her lips being moistened, replied distinctly, 'O yes, yes; unspeakably so.' She then sank into a sweet repose, and seemed conversing with some invisible friend, and would answer, 'Yes, O yes.' We scarcely knew when the spirit left the body; it did not seem like death, but a transition from 'God on earth to God in heaven.'"

"I do not know," writes the afflicted father, "that I ever had a greater struggle of soul than I had during her sickness, it seeming impossible to resign her up to death. Indeed, she was so entwined around my heart that it seemed like cutting its strings asunder to surrender her to the grave. I accordingly now pleaded earnestly with God in prayer that he would, if possible consistently with his will, spare her valuable life, and I sometimes persuaded myself to believe she would recover; but when I saw that all hope of this was fled, I cheerfully resigned her up to God; and when her breath was gone, I shouted out, Glory to God in the highest! I could hardly refrain from so doing, for I felt that I had another jewel in the Saviour's crown. We all miss her indeed, but there is nothing gloomy about her departure, as her whole life, and more especially her sickness and death, were surrounded with a halo of glory, so that the recollections of her life and death are all pleasant, grateful, and delightful."

Thus did the veteran linger, while his children and

early associates were departing. On his next birthday he writes: "On the second day of this month, May, 1858, I completed my eightieth year. I record my gratitude to God for his boundless mercy to me. My old companions are dying off. P. P. Sandford, W. Jewett, A. Hunt, E. Washburn, and George Coles, all old preachers, ranging from seventy to ninety-one years, have recently departed in peace, and I must soon follow them. But I thank God for permitting me to live to see this day; such a day as I never saw before; a day of general revivals in America and Europe!"

REVIVALS.

He took a lively interest in the revivals which prevailed about this period; and in the autumn of this year he shared in the celebration of the "Religious Jubilee" at the Fulton-street Church, which was addressed by Rev. Drs. De Witt, Krebs, Gillette, Van Pelt, Adams, and Spring, besides himself. The temple was crowded, and the assembly was largely composed of clergymen. Dr. Bangs said, among many other remarks: "The recent revival of religion among us, and throughout the country, I have considered as a very remarkable manifestation of the goodness of God. I have been in the ministry now for about fifty-seven years, a little over fifty-seven years, and I have seen a great many powerful revivals during that time in various parts of the country, and in Canada. Many sinners have been awakened and converted, and believers sanctified; but those revivals of religion were of a local character; they were confined to one or two denominations, and they were opposed, in fact, by a great many professors of religion as fanaticism. But what is the character of the present revival? It is not confined to time nor to place. It has spread through all the different denominations of Protestant Christians—pretty much all, I believe; some, perhaps, have not shared so largely in it as others. Still, what has been the effect of it? Why, sir, we see the effect of it here to-day. It brings the different denominations together, and makes them for a moment forget their denominational peculiarities; it tears down their sectarian prejudices, and makes them feel all as one. So I feel, and so, I trust, you feel also. I feel as though it was my duty to preach principally upon experimental and practical religion, and I am ready to give the right hand of fellowship to every man that will join me upon that theme."

AN INTERESTING SCENE.

On January 24, 1859, an emphatic testimony of respect was made to him by his New York friends, which was reported as follows in the public journals: "Last Saturday evening for a long time will live in the memories of the leading Methodists of the commercial emporium. Some three hundred of the friends of the venerable Dr. Bangs, now near eighty-one years old, assembled at the house of Dr. M'Clintock, in Irving Place, and led by Bishop Janes and his amiable lady, in a body proceeded to the residence of L. Bangs, Esq., where Dr. Bangs now lives, and soon crowded the rooms of the large domicil.

"The assembly was immediately called to order, and Bishop Janes made a most impressive address to the veteran of the cross, sitting in the front parlor, surprised at the unexpected call of such a host of friends. The bishop touched on the leading points in the career of this eminent servant of the Church—his early labors in Canada, his ministerial work in bygone days in the East, his long-to-be-remembered contests with Calvinism. The bishop well remembered the text of a sermon delivered by the doctor, to which the speaker listened when young in his native town. The doctor's services as Book Agent, editor of the Christian Advocate, and as an author were felicitously dwelt upon, the bishop remarking that in his episcopal visitations from Maine to

Texas he found Dr. Bangs's books in nearly every Methodist library. The speaker alluded to the great age attained by the worthy subject of the evening's gathering, its serenity, and the many blessings with which Providence surrounded it. Dr. Bangs was an exception to a peculiar characteristic of old men; they frequently were the fault-finders with progress, dwelling on the good days that were gone. Not so with the addressed; he favored progress. A head white with the snows of many winters, but a young heart, were his.

"After Bishop Janes ended his remarks, the Rev. Thomas Carlton, the main-spring of this delightful movement, took the chair—he stood in one—and added his testimony to that of Bishop Janes as to the moral worth, ministerial usefulness, and purity of Dr. Bangs; spoke of his instructions from the pulpit, and from his pen. He said that his numerous friends had determined to present him with a (what the speaker called trifling, but some may deem considerable, to wit, two thousand dollars) testimonial of their respect; that he thought a staff or cane would be very comfortable for him in his declining years; when the doctor was young he could get along without one, but now his old age called for a staff; that this (which Mr. Carlton held up) was a very expensive one—it cost two thousand dollars.

"The venerable recipient of the gift was well nigh overcome by his feelings, and his tears at first prevented a response. However, he soon recovered from his emotions, and in a very distinct and audible voice said he truly felt he deserved not the praises bestowed on him, and he was thankful they did not puff him up. He knew his weaknesses and infirmities; was thankful to his friends for thus having remembered him, and he received the gift as further proof of God's goodness to him. He stated that he had been fifty-eight years an active minister of the Cross, and for that long period the Great Disposer of events had signally blessed him, and he still found his heavenly Father was remembering and encircling him with many loving friends.

"Dr. M'Clintock then lined the following verses:

"'Blest are the sons of peace,
Whose hearts and hopes are one;
Whose kind designs to serve and please
Through all their actions run.

"'Thus on the heavenly hills
The saints are blessed above,
Where joy like morning dew distills,
And all the air is love.'

"This was sung in a familiar tune with good will and sonorously. Dr. M'Clintock then made a prayer exactly fit for the occasion. During the services many faces were bedewed with tears, and hearty amens resounded through the rooms.

"The rest of the evening was pleasantly spent in talk and mutual salutations among old friends, meeting each other after, in some cases, years of separation. It must not be omitted that a bountiful supply of ice-cream and other delicacies were furnished to the guests. The cane spoken of is of ebony, quite large, and hollow, and contained four hundred five dollar gold pieces. Thus passed one of the pleasantest incidents of my life's journey. With the best of poets, (changing one word,) when my eyes rested on the placid features of Dr. Bangs I exclaimed:

"'Let me embrace thee, good old chronicle,
That hast so long walked hand and hand with time;
Most reverend preacher, I am glad to clasp thee.'

"Although there were so many contributors, each being limited to ten dollars, it is worthy of particular notice that the surprise was a real one to the doctor's household."

The last entry but one in his journal is on his birthday. He writes in a scarcely legible hand: "*May* 2, 1860.—This day I am eighty-two years of age. My health and strength have much improved within two or three years past, for which I desire to praise God. My peace flows like a river, and I feel contented with my lot in the world." Such was the genuine Christian "philosophy" of the patriarch as the evening shades closed quietly around him.

CHAPTER XXVIII.

LAST DAYS.

"MARK the perfect man, and behold the upright: for the end of that man is peace." The current of life which we have thus traced—beginning in the turbulent if not turbid restlessness of youth; sweeping with widening and majestic course and bearing many a precious freight through middle age; declining with still broader and profounder, though more tranquil stream, toward its end—is about to glide out peacefully and radiantly into the limitless ocean.

"The years of Dr. Bangs's superannuation, since 1852," writes Dr. M'Clintock, "have been anything but idle. Besides numerous contributions to the various periodicals of the Church, he has published several books during that time—among them the 'Condition, Prospects, and Responsibilities of the Methodist Episcopal Church,' 18mo.;* 'Letters on Sanctification,' 18mo.;

* There is a slight error of date here. I find the following list of his publications among Dr. Bangs's manuscripts: "1809, A small pamphlet against the Christians, so-called, a copy of which is not to be found; 1815, The Errors of Hopkinsianism; 1817, Predestination Examined; 1818, Reformer Reformed; 1820, Vindication of Methodist Episcopacy—this year I was elected editor and Book Agent; 1829, Life of the Rev. Freeborn Garrettson; 1832, History of Missions; 1835, Letters to a Young Preacher; 1836, The Original Church of Christ; 1839, The first volume of the History of the Methodist Episcopal Church; 1841, The fourth and last volume of the History of the Methodist Episcopal Church; 1848, Emancipation; 1850, The State and Responsibility of the Methodist Episcopal Church; 1851, Letters on Sanctification; A Life of Arminius. In addition to these, several sermons, one on the Dedication of the John-street Church, 1817; Funeral Sermon of Dr. Adam Clarke, 1832; Funeral Sermon of Dr. Fisk, 1839; Centenary of Methodism, 1839; On the Division of the New York Conference, 1843."

and an 'Essay on Emancipation,' 8vo. This last named work treats briefly of the history of slavery, and of its introduction into this country, and proposes a plan for its removal; the substance of which is, that 'Congress make a proposition to the several slave states that so much per head shall be allowed for every slave that shall be emancipated, leaving it to the state legislatures respectively to adopt their own measures for effecting the object.' The objections to this plan are next considered; and then follows an array of motives to emancipation, strong enough, one would think, to rouse all but the dead to the importance of the task. The book is written in a most earnest spirit, but in language singularly calm and moderate, furnishing an excellent model, in this respect, for all who write on either side of this exciting question. In these later writings of Dr. Bangs there is no diminution of vigor in style or of independence in thought." With the exception of his brief residence at Middletown, Conn., he lived about forty-five years in New York city and Brooklyn. "No figure has been," adds Dr. M'Clintock, "better known in the streets of the great city than his; no name stands in higher repute. His unspotted life, his simplicity of character, his earnest devotion to goodness and truth, and his no less earnest hatred of wrong, have gained him the love and esteem of all denominations of Christians in New York; while his intellectual force and energy have left their mark upon the moral condition of the city."

"His old age," says Bishop Janes, "was beautiful. Exempt from official cares, surrounded by warm and sympathizing friends, in the society of his dutiful and affectionate children, who delighted to minister to his comfort and pleasure, his declining years passed serenely and sweetly away. Like the descending sun in the western sky, disrobed of his meridian splendors and deprived of his noontide fervor, unclouded, full-orbed, with mellow radiance we see him slowly and serenely descending to the horizon of life. Most enchanting was the moral beauty with which his cheerful, holy old age was invested."

Unlike most old men, he was, to the last, progressive in his views. He sympathized with all well-considered measures for the improvement of his Church. To him its history was all providential, and the very necessity of changes was the gracious summons of providence for it to arise and shine still brighter. He was especially zealous to promote the powers and activity of the laity in the affairs of his own denomination. His hearty, resolute love of his friends and his cause was one of the strongest, noblest traits of the venerable and war-worn hero. It made him as lovable as he was loving. His old age seemed to mellow rather than wither his generous dispositions. He was always deeply devout, but with advanced years he seemed to attain advanced heights of Christian experience and consolation. The Pauline doctrine of sanctification, as defined by Wesley, became, as we have seen, his habitual theme of interest and conversation. He seemed to take increasingly cheerful views of life, and of the prospects of the kingdom of God in the world, as he approached the end of his career. His last sermon was on the certain triumph of the Gospel. There was no querulousness in his temper, no repining in his conversation at the changes which were displacing him from public view, no invidious comparison of the present with former times.

LAST ILLNESS—HIS DEPARTURE.

"His last illness was of six weeks and three days' duration. The greater part of the time his sufferings were acute. But his resignation and fortitude and patience never failed him. He was favored with the full possession of his mental faculties to the last. If there was any exception to this it was simply from lethargy, which sometimes overcame him, but from which he was easily roused.

"His religious consolations during his illness were abundant, and at times his joys ecstatic. He remarked to a brother minister that he felt that his work was all done; he was only waiting for his Lord, and could rest till he came. To another minister he said:

"'The promised land, from Pisgah's top,
I now exult to see;
My hope is full (O glorious hope!)
Of immortality.'

Then with emphasis repeated, 'I *now* exult to see.' Then again, 'I now *exult* to see.'

"One afternoon a friend, who spent much time with him and ministered to him in his sickness, entered his room. He exclaimed: 'O sister! what a manifestation I had yesterday afternoon. It was glorious. The presence of Jesus was in this room, and it was all light and luminous.' The next time this friend called he referred to the circumstance again. Raising both hands, he exclaimed: 'It has lighted up the entire way to heaven.' At another time, speaking to the same person, he said: 'That glorious manifestation was unlike anything I ever expected to witness in heaven above or earth beneath.' She asked, 'Tell me, doctor, what it was like.' 'Don't ask me,' he replied, 'for I could not find language to tell you; but it has brightened up everything. My way is clear into heaven. What infinite condescension! Boundless mercy! Jesus is very precious, unspeakably precious!'

"He spoke to many others of this special revelation of the glory of God to him, and always seemed, when referring to it, to be filled with unutterable joy.

"On the 9th of April his Conference held its annual session in Waterbury, Conn. I think it was the only time of his absence for sixty years. As soon as organized, it sent him by telegram their affectionate greetings in the Lord.

"The next day the Conference received from Lemuel Bangs, Esq., the following telegram:

"'My father received the greeting of the Conference very gratefully, and dictated the following answer: "The Lord is good. I have received such an overwhelming sense of his goodness as I cannot express, and it remains with me yet."'

"During all this blessed experience he was careful to ascribe his salvation to Christ. To one friend he quoted with tears of joy this verse:

"'O Love! thou bottomless abyss,
  My sins are swallowed up in thee;
Covered is my unrighteousness,
  Nor spot of guilt remains on me,
While Jesus' blood, through earth and skies,
Mercy, free, boundless mercy, cries.'

"A friend who watched by him one night heard him say: 'Blessed Jesus, how good thou art! It is all of mercy. O yes! with Wesley I can say, "I am damned; but Jesus died and lives again. Because he lives, I shall live also."'

"These are a few of his utterances during his last illness, showing how he gloried in the cross of Christ, and how ecstatic was his religious joy.

"During the night preceding his death his daughter said to him, 'Father, God is love.' Utterance had failed him. With most expressive signs he showed that he understood her, and that he was enraptured with the truth. This was his last intelligible communication to us while in the body."

On Saturday morning Bishop Janes called and found him too lethargic for conversation. He stepped into an adjacent apartment to see the aged consort of the doctor, who herself has long been a sufferer by chronic illness. On his return he observed a change in the countenance of the venerable patient, which indicated the commencement of the final struggle. The struggle extended over a half hour, and then, at a quarter before ten o'clock in the morning, and in the midst of the assembled family, he expired without pain, without a groan, without convulsive motion, and probably without consciousness—literally fell asleep—the normal death of good old age, and a Christian exit—one day after his eighty-fourth birthday.

FUNERAL.

"The funeral took place," says the New York "Methodist," "on Tuesday afternoon at two o'clock, in St. Paul's Methodist Episcopal Church. It was crowded. Rev. Drs. Tyng, (Protestant Episcopal,) De Witt, (Dutch Reformed,) Spring, (Presbyterian,) Reicher, (Moravian,) Rev. Messrs. Clark, (New York East Conference,) Richardson, (New York Conference,) Porter, (Newark Conference,) President Cummings, (New England Conference,) Cook and Kenny, (deputed from the Philadelphia Preachers' Meeting,) were the pall-bearers, and a large number of his brethren in the ministry were in attendance. The services at the church were a voluntary by the choir; reading of Scripture lessons by Rev. Dr. Stevens; prayer by Rev. Dr. Osbon; hymn read by Rev. Dr. Carlton; sermon by Rev. Bishop Janes."

Hundreds gazed for the last time on the beloved face in the coffin before the altar. He was then conveyed, followed by a numerous procession of carriages, to Greenwood Cemetery, where he rests in the family inclosure. At the latter place the funeral service was read by Rev. Dr. Hagany. This part of the solemnities was peculiarly impressive. The grave is on the summit of a hillock, amid some of the finest scenery in the cemetery. The hour was that of sunset; the slant rays flooded the surrounding foliage with softened hues; quiet was falling on all things, while the solemn utterance of the impressive ritual seemed to pass with peculiar distinctness through the neighboring glens, already reposing in the twilight. As the assembly retired the sun sank below the horizon, and the heavens, to the very zenith, glowed with the most magnificent variegations of light. Never has it been our privilege to record a more blessed death, or more beautifully impressive obsequies than those of this "Prince and great man fallen in Israel."

Many aged heads of lay as well as clerical Methodists could be seen in the assembly at St. Paul's. Among them was that of the venerable Laban Clark, who had come from Middletown, Conn., to follow his old friend to the grave. "Precisely fifty years ago this month," remarked this veteran, "the first Delegated General Conference of the Methodist Episcopal Church was held in this city; Dr. Bangs and myself were delegates; I am now the only New York Conference delegate who remains. Daniel Webb is the only New England delegate alive, and the New England Conference then included all New England, except its western margin, which belonged to New York Conference. I do not know of one surviving delegate from the Philadelphia Conference, which then comprehended New Jersey; of the delegates of the large Baltimore Conference, Henry Smith, of 'Pilgrims' Rest,' alone lives. The only other survivors, so far as I know, are Bishops Soule and Early and Dr. Lovick Pierce, of the Methodist Episcopal Church, South." Dr. Laban Clark is but a few months younger than Dr. Bangs; he preceded Dr. Bangs in the ministry about one year; he is enjoying a green old age, and may remain some years yet—one of the last remnants of that primitive Methodist ministry which has been called its *legio tonans.*

HIS CHARACTER.

The pulpits and papers of the Methodist Church, and the press of the country generally, noticed the departure of the aged citizen and Christian, with emphatic eulogies on his long and effective life. The Missionary Board published a grateful testimony of his services as one of its founders and most assiduous colaborers; and its periodical organ said: "From the time he entered the ministry of the Methodist Episcopal Church in 1802, 'he was clad with zeal as a cloak.' Our melancholy province this day is to make a record of his relation to the Missionary Society, as the author of the Constitution under which it was organized on the 5th of April, 1819, as the author of the first Address and Circular which it issued to the Church, and as its steadfast friend and laborer until called to enter his Master's joy.

"At the time of its organization he was elected the third Vice-president, Bishops George and Roberts being the first and second. In the course of a year or two he succeeded Joshua Soule as the Treasurer of the Society. In April, 1836, he was elected the fourth Vice-president and Corresponding Secretary; in 1838 the resident Corresponding Secretary. In 1840 he was one of three corresponding secretaries, Rev. Dr. Capers and Rev. E. R. Ames being associated with him, one for the South, the other for the West. In 1841, removing temporarily from the city, his active connection was suspended. Up to this time it is probable he had written every one of the Annual Reports. In 1848 we find him again taking an active part in the doings of the Society, which he continued to do down to the monthly meeting in February last. It is supposed that he never missed a meeting, when in the city, from the very first, except on account of sickness.

"The receipts of the treasurer for the first year were $823 04; the amount for the year 1861 was $250,374 93; the total amount of receipts from the beginning to the day of his death was $4,569,094 95.

"In 1819 we had no missions to those of a foreign tongue, but now our general summary shows under that head 316 missionaries and 28,458 Church-members. He commenced his course as a missionary himself to Canada, and was sent to the Bay of Quinte, when there were but 1,500 members and nine ministers besides himself in that country, all of whom preceded him in the passage over Jordan. Now the Canada Wesleyans alone number 53,564 members and 476 ministers, and there are also 18,250 members and ministers of the Methodist Episcopal Church in Canada. The total number of members in the Methodist Episcopal Church in America when he entered the ministry was 72,874, and of ministers 358. The total number of members at his death is, including the probationers, (without any reference to those Churches which have gone out from us,) 988,523, and of ministers, effective and superannuated, 6,984. 'What hath God wrought!' This prince and great man in our Israel not only started with our Society, being one of its principal founders, but has ever been our missionary standard-bearer. No mission has been started but has either been originated by him or had his hearty approval and zealous support. No man could more properly say, though no one would be less likely, to say it of himself, 'The zeal of thy house hath eaten me up.'"

"I have known him for upward of half a century," writes Francis Hall, Esq., "and my recollections of him are of the most pleasing character. He was perhaps as well known among other denominations as any of our preachers since the days of Asbury. He was a man of prayer, and full of faith in the promises of God. I remember he made me a visit during a sickness in which many believed I should not recover. I had been visited by several old friends of the John-street congregation, and as they were leaving my chamber Dr. Bangs entered. He conversed with me, closing with prayer. Leaving the room, he said to Mrs. Hall: 'Mr. Hall will recover.' I heard the remark, and my conviction was immediately, the prayer will be answered. It was so:

from that moment I recovered. He was a model of punctuality, whether he had to fill the pulpit or attend any of the societies. No weather prevented his presence, and a meeting did not wait for a quorum in consequence of his absence."

It would be superfluous to extend this volume with any particular summary of his life and character. Both have been sufficiently delineated in the course of our narrative. The institutions he founded, or helped to found, and the productions of his pen, are his monuments. If most of his literary works may not take permanent rank, it will be because they were written for immediate utility, to meet cotemporary wants, and are therefore, by their very adaptations to their purpose, less adapted to the demands of the future. His robust mind was always practical, and direct in its aims. He did the work of the hour for the wants of the hour, and to have done otherwise, by an anticipation of the future, would have rendered his work less effective, though it might have rendered it more durable.

In literature his name will be chiefly recognized for his History of the Methodist Episcopal Church, in four volumes, completed in 1841. It was a book for the times, if not for all time. Methodism had now reached numerical supremacy as a form of Protestantism in the nation. Its schemes, domestic and foreign—ecclesiastical, educational, and literary—had become gigantic; but though now the predominant religious fact and interest of the country, its history was unwritten. The publicist, the scholar, the churchman, concerned to know its real character, had no adequate historical resource for such information. Lee's history was an early production; it could claim no historic rank whatever; it could only afford assistance, and that very limited, to a more capable hand. With but this very imperfect example, Dr. Bangs undertook the task of preparing a full history of his Church, from the introduction of Methodism into the new world down to the year which preceded the publication of his last volume. None but he who has attempted a similar task can conceive of its difficulties—its perplexing, wearisome research in manuscript documents, in periodical publications, in scattered, meager books of biography, journals of ministerial travel, controversial pamphlets, in Minutes of Annual Conferences for sixty-seven years, proceedings of General Conferences for forty-four years, in personal or local manuscript data, procured by correspondence from all parts of the country. And then the study, the collocation, the harmonization of these often conflicting materials, the delicate care requisite for the personal feelings and reputations of living actors in the long and varied scene, or of the sympathies of surviving families of its deceased actors—such are some of the difficulties we must bear in mind in estimating this important service. As it was to be really the first "history" of the Church, it must of necessity be largely a documentary compilation, for the most important documents upon which it was to be founded had not yet been published. This fact has given character to the work. It includes in its text whole "reports" of public bodies, rolls of names, large extracts of "Minutes." It could hardly have been satisfactorily prepared otherwise. It is thus an invaluable repertory of historical materials. Documentary histories of the kind must necessarily precede any artistic or philosophic historical literature, whether of States or Churches. He prepared it, as he did all his other writings, for the actual necessity of his Church. He accomplished his purpose, and accomplished it better by far than he could have done by attempting a more artistic work. As a historian of the Church he will be immortal; he must forever be acknowledged as the principal authority of all future historical writers on American Methodism, and if his volumes ever cease to be the popular manual of our history, his name must nevertheless incessantly recur as an authority in the marginal acknowledgments of writers who may supersede him.

Bishop Janes, who knew him most intimately for many years, says: "His mind was comprehensive, vigorous, versatile, and eminently practical. Mental honesty was his crowning glory. In all his discussions he employed no metaphysical subtleties, no sophistries, but candidly looked every question in the face, and met it in a direct, frank, ingenuous manner.

"His moral characteristics were beautiful. He was ardent, affectionate, sympathetic, and constant; an earnest, honest, public-spirited man; a true, abiding friend; a loving, devoted husband, and an affectionate and faithful parent.

"His Christian excellences were many and great. His experience was deep and positive. He enjoyed an abiding consciousness of the favor of God. His devotement to God was full and joyous. He counted everything but loss for the excellency of the knowledge of Christ Jesus the Lord. It was his constant aim to magnify Christ, and evidently his spiritual life was hid with Christ in God. He seemed always to be forgetting the things which were behind, and pressing toward the mark of his high calling of God in Christ Jesus. Practically he was an 'example of the believers in word, in conversation, in charity, in spirit, in faith, in purity.'

"He was a Methodist from conviction and preference. He honestly and heartily embraced the doctrines, and cordially approved the ecclesiastical economy of the Methodist Episcopal Church. These profound convictions of the scriptural character of her doctrines and polity made him a staunch defender of the Church of his choice. This zeal for the Methodistic form of Christianity sometimes involved him in earnest controversies with persons of other Churches. He said to me during his last illness: 'I have had many sharp controversies. I have sometimes used strong and, perhaps, harsh language, but I never had a bitter spirit.' Dr. Bangs, with all his attachment to Methodism, was one of the most catholic Christian men in spirit and sympathies I ever knew. He was always ready to say from the heart, Grace be with all them that love our Lord Jesus Christ in sincerity."

Down to his last sickness very little decay of his mental faculties was discernible. His conversations, his addresses in social religious meetings, his occasional writings for periodicals, continued to show much of his old vigorous judgment, his manly sense, his direct, honest utterance. If less attention to style, than in his earlier years, might sometimes be apparent, the old sound head and sound heart remained. His last sermon was preached at Seventeenth-street Methodist Episcopal Church; he sat at a table in the altar while delivering it. It was heard by nearly all the congregation; it required considerable effort of memory in the citation of statistical facts, but there was no faltering of even that faculty. The whole discourse was characterized by the warm, strong, demonstrative qualities of his earlier preaching.

In person Dr. Bangs was tall, robust, but not corpulent; with a high indented brow, crowned for many years with silvered locks. His eyes were small, and somewhat deeply set; his complexion fresh, and often flushed by a determination of blood to the head; his voice was peculiar—a sort of double voice, which he attributed, as we have seen, to an injury of his lungs by his early preaching and exposure, after a serious illness. In its finer notes it had a silvery melody, but in its stronger tones there was a hoarse roughness which, with his robust attitude and flushed aspect, sometimes gave to the hearer, especially in controversial discussions, a false impression that he was irritable in temper. There was, doubtless, temper, mettle in his manly and vigorous nature; no man could show a nobler indignation against anything unrighteous or mean; no man could speak more unflinchingly or directly to the very face and teeth of a pretentious, an evasive, or disingenuous disputant, but no man ever had a more genial heart, a more instinctive sympathy with whatever is generous, heroic, or tender. His friendships were as steadfast as adamant. His whole nature was vigorous; he was robust in intellect, in soul, and in body. He had his faults, and, like everything else in his strong nature, they were strongly marked. But if he was abrupt sometimes in his replies, or emphatic in his rebukes, no man was ever more ready to retract an undeserved severity, or acknowledge a mistake. This excellence was as habitual with him as it is rare with most men.

For some years the late Dr. Francis, his friend and "the last of the Knickerbockers;" Dr. Spring, his still surviving friend, and himself, have been the three most notable representatives among us of the elder New York. No form has been more familiar, more venerated in our assemblies, or on our streets, than that of Nathan Bangs. The early Methodists, remnants of whom are still scattered, with gray heads and tottering frames, among our numerous Churches, felt that he continued to be, in an endearing sense, their old pastor, the pastor of their fathers and of their childhood. Their decayed eyes glistened whenever he appeared in their pulpits, and their trembling hands grasped his, with the ardor of earlier years, when he passed down their aisles. He fell among them, almost the last primitive pillar of the structure of Methodism; to them, then, more than ever, "old things had passed away; behold! all things had become new;" and more than ever did they then feel that they too must go hence, that their "company had gone before," and they themselves "desired to depart."

The final estimate of such a man is not difficult. If we cannot award to him the greatness of what is called genius, we cannot deny him the greatness of an effective life—a life of inestimable effectiveness. Nor can we attribute his effectiveness merely to what are called circumstances. Circumstances are, perhaps, as requisite for the success of genius as for that of any other ability. Genius, so-called, has usually peculiar infirmities, requiring peculiar incentives and supports. It is not the lack of available circumstances that subjects so much of human life to inferiority or mediocrity, but the lack of moral dispositions to use rightly actual circumstances. There are few public positions, especially such as the Christian teacher or preacher occupies, which might not be rendered superior or distinguished if sustained by proper moral dispositions, aside from any extraordinary intellectual powers. The circumstances necessary for success are seldom if ever wanting to the man of earnest conscience and resolute purpose. He is the great man who, though of ordinary talents, energetically avails himself of his circumstances; he the yet greater man who, in lack of favorable circumstances, creates them, and then avails himself of them. Nathan Bangs did both. A profoundly religious conscience, tireless industry, unwavering perseverance, the ready acceptance of the duty of the day or the hour, whatever it might be—these, inspirited by a fervent religious zeal, rather than by what is vaguely called the inspiration of genius, characterized his life. And they made that life genuinely great—great in goodness, the supreme greatness; but great also in what is conventionally, but fallaciously, considered still superior greatness—great in practical success. It was not, therefore, by convenient accident or "good fortune" that he became prominently connected with so many Christian achievements of our century, achievements which promise to shed ever-increasing luster upon his grave. Doubtless there were many men in the ministry of his Church during his day who had intellectual powers or genius superior to his own; but who among them has had a superior life, a life more pregnant with salutary results? The legitimate answer to the question is obvious, and its legitimate lesson is too obvious to need a further word of comment.

Singularly effective, definitive, and symmetrical in his life—in the struggles and self-discipline of his youth, the activity and success of his manhood, the sanctity and peace of his old age—we take our leave of him at the grave, assured that it has been good for the world that he lived, and good for us that we have traced the lessons of his life.

THE END.

Stevens's History of Methodism.

The History of the Religious Movement of the Eighteenth Century, called Methodism, considered in its Different Denominational Forms, and its Relations to British and American Protestantism. By ABEL STEVENS, LL. D. 3 volumes.

Large 12mo.

A charming work—full of thrilling facts, combined and stated in the most interesting manner. The work has been read and highly indorsed by the most distinguished authors. One says, "It is wonderfully readable;" and another, "I have been interested beyond measure." It will be a standard for all Methodists for all time to come, and will be read by thousands of Christians of other denominations.

It contains a new steel engraving of Rev. JOHN WESLEY, the best ever seen in this country.

The volumes which are to follow will be put up in the same style, so that those who get the whole will have uniform sets, though they buy bu one volume at a time.

Hymns and Tunes.

Hymns for the Use of the Methodist Episcopal Church. With Tunes for Congregational Worship.

8vo., pp. 368.

This work embraces all the hymns in our standard Hymn Book, and no more. It contains also more than three hundred of the most popular old and new tunes in print, and is offered at a very low price for a book of its cost, in the hope that it may be generally adopted.

Autobiography of Peter Cartwright.

Edited by W. P. STRICKLAND.

12mo., pp. 525.

This is one of the most interesting autobiographies of the age. The sale of this remarkable book has averaged two thousand copies per month since its appearance. Thirty-two thousand have been printed, and still the orders come. It is useless to add anything by way of commendation. The people *will* have it, and we are prepared to supply the continued demand.

What must I do to be Saved?

By JESSE T. PECK, D.D.

18mo., pp. 192.

A new revival book, written by request, designed to awaken the sinner, guide the penitent to Christ, and establish the young convert.

BOOKS PUBLISHED BY CARLTON & PORTER,

200 Mulberry-street, New York.

Elements of Logic.

Adapted to the Capacity of younger Students, and designed for Academies and the Higher Classes of Common Schools. Revised edition. By Rev. C. K. TRUE, D.D.

We are glad to see that this excellent hand-book is being introduced into many schools and seminaries. If our friends connected with school committees through the country wil take a little pains they may introduce it into thousands of schools with advantage to all concerned.

We believe that, with a treatise as simple as Dr. True's, all college students might understand logic, and the higher classes of our academies and grammar schools be emboldened to study it; while the study of the treatises in ordinary use is now almost wholly confined to colleges, and the *understanding* of them to a small percentage of each class. We give the book, therefore, our cordial commendation. It is short and simple, not because it is shallow and superficial, but because the author has the mastery of his science, knows how it ought to be taught, perceives the utility of its study to all persons of intelligence and culture, and has adapted his presentation of it to this so desirable end.—*North American Review.*

This is a thorough popular treatise on the Elements of Logic, the best undoubtedly in the market for schools and colleges. Those who have not had the advantages of schools would do well to give it a thorough study.—*Zion's Herald.*

Clergyman's Pocket Diary and Visiting Book.

Arranged by JAMES PORTER, D.D.

Here we have an admirable memorandum book, the want of which has been felt, we venture to say, very generally by our ministerial brethren. It contains the following departments: Funerals attended, sermons preached, alphabetical list of members, alphabetical list of probationers, alphabetical list of friends not members, record of baptisms, record of marriages, subscribers for periodicals, cash accounts, general accounts, general memorandum, etc.—*Canada Christian Advocate.*

Parkerism:

Three Discourses delivered on the occasion of the Death of THEODORE PARKER. By W. F. WARREN, FALES H. NEWHALL, and GILBERT HAVEN.

12mo.

The discourses before us are worthy of being preserved in a permanent form. They were elicited in consequence of the death of a man who had acquired a world-wide reputation. In this volume we have truthful delineations, clear conceptions, and weighty arguments, and throughout there is a remarkable exemplification of Mr. Parker's own words, namely, "I am no flatterer nor public liar general; when such a one is wanted he is easily found, and may be had cheap; and I cannot treat great men like great babies. So, when I preached on Mr. Adams, who had done the cause of freedom such great service, on General Taylor and Mr. Webster, I aimed to paint them exactly as they were, that their virtues might teach us and their vices warn" —*Canada Christian Advocate.*

www.ingramcontent.com/pod-product-compliance
Lightning Source LLC
LaVergne TN
LVHW021144110826
845150LV00005B/1118

* 9 7 8 1 4 2 5 5 4 8 1 1 7 *